Gulf Research Center

Knowledge for All

Gulf Yearbook
2004

Gulf Research Center
187 Oud Metha Tower, 11th Floor,
303 Sheikh Rashid Road,
P. O. Box 80758,
Dubai, United Arab Emirates.
Tel.: +971 4 324 7770
Fax: +971 4 324 7771
E-mail: sales@grc.ae
Website: www.grc.ae

First published in 2005
Gulf Research Center
United Arab Emirates

ISBN 9948 400 93 3

The opinions expressed in this publication are those of the author(s) alone and do not necessarily state or reflect the opinions or position of the Gulf Research Center.

By publishing the Gulf Yearbook 2004, the Gulf Research Center (GRC) seeks to contribute to the enrichment of the reader's knowledge out of the Center's strong conviction that "knowledge is for all."

Abdulaziz O. Sager
Chairman
Gulf Research Center

Chairman and Editor in-Chief
Mr. Abdulaziz O. Sager

Editorial Team
Dr. Christian Koch
Prof. Hasanain Tawfiq Ibrahim

Translation Supervisor
Dr. Sulayman Awad Ibrahim

Table of Contents

List of Abbreviations

AMS	(Sunni) Association of Muslim Scholars
AMRAAM	Advanced Medium-Range, Air-to-Air Missile
AFP	Agence France-Presse
AWACS	Airborne Warning and Control System
AEOGC	Arab Education Office of the Gulf Countries
AED	Arab Emirates Dirhams
AP	Associated Press
ASEAN	Association of Southeast Asian Nations
BFH	Bahrain Financial Harbor
b/d	Barrels per Day
bpd	Barrels per Day
BP	British Petroleum
CSO	Civil Society Organization
CEDAW	Committee for the Elimination of All Forms of Discrimination Against Women
CG	Council of Guardians (Iran)
EIU	Economist Intelligence Unit
EADS	European Aeronautic Defence and Space Company
EU	European Union
FBI	Federal Bureau of Investigation
FNC	Federal National Council (UAE)
FDI	Foreign Direct Investment
FSU	Former Soviet Union
FTA	Free Trade Agreement
FTZ	Free Trade Zone
GMEI	Greater Middle East Initiative
GDP	Gross Domestic Product
GSDF	Ground Self-Defence Forces (Japan)
GCC	Gulf Cooperation Council
HRH	His Royal Highness
ISRO	Indian Space Research Organization
IT	Information Technology
IAEA	International Atomic Energy Agency
ICJ	International Court of Justice
IISS	International Institute for Strategic Studies
ILO	International Labour Organization
IMF	International Monetary Fund
IOC	International Oil Companies

IRI	International Republican Institute
KUNA	Kuwait News Agency
LNG	Liquefied Natural Gas
MP	Member of Parliament
MoU	Memorandum of Understanding
MEPI	Middle East Partnership Initiative
NCES	National Center for Education Statistics
NDIIR	National Democratic Institute for International Relations
NOC	National Oil Companies
NGO	Non-Governmental Organization
NPT	Non-Proliferation Treaty
NATO	North Atlantic Treaty Organization
ODA	Official Development Assistance
OPEC	Organization of Petroleum Exporting Countries
OIC	Organization of the Islamic Conference
PNA	Palestinian National Authority
QNA	Qatar News Agency
QR	Qatari Riyal
SFD	Saudi Fund for Development
SR	Saudi Riyals
SRI	Stanford Research Institute
SCIRI	Supreme Council of Islamic Revolution in Iraq
SCS	System of Collective Security
UEA	Unified Economic Agreement
UAE	United Arab Emirates
UN	United Nations
UNICTAD	United Nations Conference on Trade and Development
UNESCO	United Nations Educational, Scientific, and Cultural Organization
US	United States (of America)
WMD	Weapons of Mass Destruction
WB	World Bank
WTO	World Trade Organization
YR	Yemeni Riyal

Foreword

Abdulaziz Sager

Chairman, Gulf Research Center

In presenting the Gulf Yearbook 2004 in both Arabic and English, the Gulf Research Center (GRC) acknowledges the wide recognition that the first Yearbook in 2003 received from scholars, experts and research centers in the Arab region and beyond. Many political and media organizations expressed their deep interest in the publication. Their appreciation and encouragement motivated us to sustain our efforts to improve the content and format of the latest Yearbook in order to make it a reliable reference for all those interested in the affairs of the Gulf region.

The Gulf Yearbook 2004 is a well-documented and analytical review of the most salient developments and interactions across the Gulf Cooperation Council (GCC) States and those of Iraq, Iran and Yemen during 2004. Its content not only encompasses the political, economic and security developments on the domestic scene of all the nine countries, but also explores the dynamics and scale of relations at the regional and international levels. In parallel, the Yearbook investigates the positions held by some key international powers towards the Gulf region and analyses possible future scenarios in the region.

The Yearbook also devotes much of its content to explore security, economic and social developments. Keeping in mind that education driven by excellence is the key to sustaining regional development, this edition examines the current conditions and the future prospects of the education sector in the GCC countries. In light of the momentous challenges this field faces, it is imperative for the GCC States to modernize and develop their education policies and institutions. This publication also investigates the status of the media in the GCC and the various media policies pursued by the governments. In view of the developments that have occurred in terms of the regional media scene and the intense pressure, both external and internal, on the media organizations this is certainly a timely topic.

The idea of the Yearbook is that it serves as an important contribution to the field of specialized Gulf studies and as a key channel of communication among Arab scholars specialized in regional affairs and their peer non-Arab experts. In this respect, the Yearbook includes contributions by Arab as well as non-Arab specialists drawn notably from the United States, European countries, India, China, Japan, Turkey, and Iran.

Let me emphasize that a great deal of preparation went into ensuring all contributions reflect a high degree of academic excellence. I extend my sincere thanks and gratitude to the distinguished pool of contributors, both in-house and those working from outside as part of the Center's extensive network of scholars. This Yearbook could not have been successfully completed without their valuable contribution.

Appreciation is also due to the translators and those involved in the process of editing and proof-reading the publication. Each of them, without exception, conducted their tasks in professionally and with dedication and committment to the task. It is their concerted efforts that helped GRC publish the Gulf Yearbook 2004 on schedule.

I should also thank the various governmental and non-governmental departments and organizations that never failed to offer, and indeed continue to offer, their encouragement to the GRC. I express my special gratitude to the GCC Secretary-General and to all the specialist and non-specialist readers who commented on the Gulf Yearbook 2003 and who through their contributions have allowed us to improve the publication.

The Gulf Yearbook is one of GRC's premier publications. It complements a series of other publications that already includes the Iraq Studies series, Yemen Studies, Iran Studies, Gulf Translations, Research Papers, Gulf Papers, the Gulf Studies Journal published periodically, Araa magazine published monthly since January 2005, and the series of specialized books released by the Center. All these publications are available in Arabic and English, and all of them are published in print and in electronic versions. The latter is available at the Center's website - www.grc.ae.

GRC welcomes all outstanding academic contributions to be published as part of the Center's diverse publications in order to enrich academic research on the Gulf region.

Out of GRC's mission statement - "Knowledge for all" - and out of its strong conviction that constructive dialogue and critical awareness are central components of any efforts to boost academic endeavors in the GCC countries, the center welcomes comments and critiques on the Gulf Yearbook 2004. Our progress as a Center

dedicated to excellence in academic research rests on such committment by our readers.

Introduction

Because of its complexities, interrelated issues, and variety of concerned parties, the issue of Iraq remains at the forefront of regional and international developments. The steady deterioration of security conditions and continuous challenges within the US-led project shroud the future of Iraq in ambiguity.

As such, developments in Iraq reverberate throughout many of the issues and topics explored within the Gulf Yearbook 2004. Concerns grow both over the domestic possibility of civil strife as well as the broader implications on stability and security in the region as a whole. Indeed, developments in Iraq have been among the key determinants of the relations between the GCC States and Iraq on the one hand, and between the GCC and the US on the other. The phenomenal surge in oil prices at some intermittent periods during 2004 was due in part to events unfolding in Iraq, especially as acts of sabotage against pipelines and oil facilities continued unabated. Washington's relations with the UN, the EU and NATO, too, were palpably, albeit partially, affected by the ramifications of developments in Iraq.

Besides the myriad developments that unraveled in Iraq and their reverberations across the Gulf region, the Arab world and the international scene, there were a number of other salient developments in the Gulf region in 2004.

o The continued process of implementing political reforms in the GCC States in light of the rising political polarization between the ruling elites and the various forces representing political opposition, particularly as far as Bahrain and Kuwait were concerned.

o The terrorist attacks conducted by extremist and terrorist groups in Saudi Arabia, together with periodic confrontations between security forces and terrorist groups, constituted a prominent aspect of the political scene in Saudi Arabia during 2004. While Saudi security forces were able to deal a serious blow to terrorist groups operating within the kingdom, the real mission of extinguishing the phenomena of extremism coupled with drying up the sources of their funding in Saudi Arabia and other Arab and Muslim countries, means effectively treating the root causes of the climate that allows for the emergence and growth of extremist groups. Such a goal cannot be achieved unless and until a comprehensive and well-integrated strategy is adequately articulated and implemented - one which takes into account the wide palette of political, economic, social, cultural, educational and religious aspects.

o The death of Shaikh Zayid bin Sultan Al Nahyan on November 2, 2004, which sounded the end of an era and the beginning of a new one in the history of the UAE. Power was transferred smoothly and swiftly through the consentuel election by the rulers of the seven emirates and members of the Supreme Council of the UAE Federation of Sheikh Khalifa bin Zayid Al Nahyan to the post of Ruler of Abu Dhabi and President of the UAE.

o The decline of the role of reformists in Iran and the rise in dominance of the conservative political forces as evidenced by the legislative elections held in February 2004. This development is likely to have deep implications for Iranian politics, both domestically and internationally. In addition, developments related to Iran's nuclear file and its implications for the region have been a key issue, particularly in light of the possible heightened tensions between the US and Iran.

o The unprecedented rise (it has been described as 'a second boom') in oil prices during 2004. GCC governments, as a result of the huge revenues that have been flowing into their public treasuries, have been and will be able to better confront economic difficulties, namely public deficit and public debt issues.

o The re-election of George W. Bush as President of the United States for a second term. Raising many questions as to the nature of future US policies towards the Gulf region in particular, and the Arab world in general, the key issues revolve around US policies towards Iraq and Iran, the US stance toward political, economic and educational reform in the region and the US role in any future security arrangements in the Gulf region.

Themes of the Gulf Yearbook 2004

The GRC Gulf Yearbook 2004 addresses the most relevant issues and critical developments that have impacted the GCC states, as well as Iran, Iraq and Yemen, in 2004 at the domestic, regional and international levels of analysis. In this context, the main issues explored in the Gulf Yearbook 2004 are as follows:

1. Domestic Political Developments in the GCC States

This particular theme focuses on tracing, analyzing and evaluating the key domestic political developments in the GCC States during 2004. Special attention is devoted to developments in the field of political liberalization at the constitutional, legal and/or institutional level or the patterns of the relations and interactions among the ruling regimes and the forces of political opposition.

It is worth noting that the relations linking the ruling regimes and some of the legitimate political opposition groups in some of the GCC States generally evolved around issues related to political reform, like the constitutional amendment in the Kingdom of Bahrain, the amendment to the electoral law in Kuwait, and the demand for speeding up the process of political and constitutional reform in Saudi Arabia. Women's issues and women's political rights constituted another pivot around which the views between the regimes and opposition groups in some of the GCC States diverged.

Given the importance of legislative bodies in the development of political systems, the GRC Gulf Yearbook 2004 offers an assessment of the institutional performance of legislatures in the GCC States in light of the corresponding powers both in the legislative and oversight fields. With the notable exception of Kuwait's National Assembly, and to a limited extent the Bahraini parliament, legislative institutions in the other GCC States continue to play a largely restricted role in the political process due mainly to their limited scope of powers.

In that context, the Gulf Yearbook 2004 emphasizes the importance of pursuing efforts to boost political reform movements in the GCC States both at a reasonable pace and on the basis of a national accord between ruling elites, groups representing the political opposition, and existing as well as emerging civil society organizations. If political reform is a sine qua non requirement that needs to be enacted gradually and peacefully, it is also important that reform be implemented in a manner that generates momentum so that the reform process as a whole does not stagnate at any time. What truly gives reason for optimism is that the great majority of the forces and groups demanding reform in the GCC States recognize the legitimacy of the ruling regimes, therefore placing their demands and calls for reform within the context of the existing governments. By building a social contract founded on the principles of citizenship, an institutionalized state structure, the rule of law, and on guarantees for the respect of human rights, the implementation of reform is added.

2. The Economies of the GCC States

As economic reform is an issue of paramount importance for all the GCC countries, the GRC Gulf Yearbook 2004 places particular emphasis on the numerous factors that make economic reform a pressing imperative. These include the increasing rate of population growth in the GCC States, the large percentage of youth as part of the population as compared to other age groups, and the rise of unemployment rates as a result of the failure of both the private and the public sectors to absorb the increasing numbers of entrants into the labor market.

In light of this reality, the main aspect of economic reform in the GCC countries centers around the need to carry out and accelerate the process of economic diversification away from the current over-reliance on oil revenues as the key engine driving economic activity. To achieve this end, nationals ought to be more entrepreneurial and cease relying on the state, the imbalance in the labor market should be efficiently corrected, the process of privatization should be enhanced and private sector operators further encouraged, and, of course,

economic integration among the GCC countries should be accelerated.

Although the GCC governments have enacted a slew of measures slated to buttress the process of economic reform, the process still faces a number of hurdles that obstruct its effective implementation. First, despite the surge in oil prices throughout 2004 GCC governments remain hesitant to implement necessary economic reforms in fear of possible negative social and political repercussions such as a large part of the population becoming dependent on state financed welfare schemes. Second, external factors, both regional and international, together with security considerations, represent direct and indirect impediments to economic reform in the GCC countries.

Broadly speaking, the Gulf Yearbook 2004 emphasizes that economic reform in the GCC countries is both an inevitable reality and a national imperative. It is high time for the GCC governments to turn the much-touted slogan of economic diversification into palpable reality. By fostering economies driven by diversified production, GCC states will be better able to create job opportunities while remaining less affected by the fluctuations that characterize oil prices and oil revenues. In doing so, GCC economies will build greater self-sufficiency and sustainability in a post-oil era.

The Gulf Yearbook 2004 positions economic reform as a primarily political decision. It is understandable, therefore, that governments formulate programs and policies whereby the negative consequences that might accompany reforms are accommodated. This does not mean, however, that reform efforts in the GCC economies should be delayed as they remain the essential means by which sustainable development can be attained both in the medium and the long term.

The Gulf Yearbook 2004 provides an in-depth analysis of the dramatic rise in oil prices in 2004, assessing the underlying causes while at the same time analyzing the probable and actual implications of soaring oil prices for the GCC economies. In essence, the high oil price environment appears to be grounded in a fundamental shift in the structure of market supply and demand. While demand for oil increased in many regions of the world, especially in China, oil supply was negatively affected by a number of factors, notably the decrease of reserve production capacities across the world and the fact that production and refining operations had reached their maximum capacity. Meanwhile, major oil producing countries such as Iraq, faced enormous difficulties sustaining any level of oil production. Markets were thus deficient in supply in turn causing prices to move upwards. These developments in the international oil markets yielded higher revenues for the GCC countries, thereby creating an environment where these countries can rebalance their public budgets, feed their currency reserves and reduce their debts. It also provides an opportunity for the GCC governments to accelerate their reform efforts alongside invigorating the capacities of national oil companies so that they could properly adjust to the new fundamentals that govern the international oil markets.

3. Defense and Security Issues in the GCC States

In terms of the defense and security environment in the GCC States, the Gulf Yearbook 2004 takes an in-depth look at developments within defense budgets - reported to have reached $30 billion - manpower issues, the availability and use of various arms systems and combat equipment, the status of command, control and communication systems, and the efforts of coordination undertaken, particularly the operations conducted by the Peninsula [Al-Jazeera] Shield forces. On another level, the Yearbook analyzes the issues impacting the security

and stability of the Gulf region, especially in connection with the absence of a stable regional security architecture and the explosive conditions in Iraq. Particular attention is granted to the assault operations staged by Iraqi insurgents against oil pipelines and oil facilities. The ramifications of Iran's nuclear program, too, are explored in light of Washington's threat to resort to any means necessary in order to prevent Iran from developing nuclear weapons. Here, the Yearbook underlines the need for all parties concerned to formulate a set of measures can ensure the security and stability of the strategic region of the Gulf.

The GRC believes that no security measures could ever be sustainable unless and until they include Iraq, Iran and Yemen, bearing in mind that such an inclusive approach would entail a number of commitments and guarantees. With this as background, the GRC devotes special attention to promoting cooperative and collective security arrangements in the Gulf region. In April 2004, the Center held a workshop on ongoing developments in Iraq and the probable ramifications for the security and stability of the Gulf region. Within the framework of a possible European role in a future Gulf security architecture, and in light of the widespread feelings that the US tends to monopolize the issue, the GRC organized in November 2004 a workshop on the role of the EU in Gulf security. Finally, in a determined bid to focus on the issue of weapons of mass destruction (WMD), a workshop in December 2004 under the title "Voices from the Region: The Gulf as a WMD Free Zone" established a permanent research program with the objective of expanding research endeavors in the field of WMD disarmament. In conjunction with the workshop, the GRC released a non-official initiative on declaring the Gulf region a WMD-free zone to promote the idea in the region.

The re-election of President George W. Bush raised

many questions about the nature and objectives of future US policies in the Gulf region in particular and the Arab world in general, the GRC has placed this specific issue high on its agenda for 2005. The Center will devote a great part of its research activities to probing and analyzing the ongoing developments and future prospects of US policies towards the Gulf region in the next four years. The GRC will likewise explore the ramifications, both current and probable, that Washington's policies might yield and the way they might impact not just the security and stability of the Gulf region, but also the process of political reform and the development of the energy markets. No doubt, the quagmire in which the US is caught in Iraq and the worsening complications of US-Iran relations infuse this issue with importance.

4. Women and Civil Society in the GCC States

In hindsight, the issue of women seems to have been among the key issues that have divided the ruling elites and the opposition forces in some of the GCC States. Within this context, the Gulf Yearbook 2004 traces and analyzes the various developments in 2004 in connection with the issue of women, particularly in light of the increased interest evinced in both the Gulf region and the Western world towards the status of women in Gulf societies. Overall, there were numerous conferences, symposia and workshops held throughout the year focusing of how to better empower women to assume a greater role in political life.

Several decisions passed in 2004 have allowed women to become more active in political life. In fact, the year could appropriately be called the 'ministerization year' of Gulf women with a number taking up ministerial appointments. Similarly, women involved in business have managed to take on a more visible role in terms of the scope of their activities and in terms of the governmental decisions

issued to enhance their economic opportunities. At the level of civil society, the year witnessed many activities focused on the demand of women's political and legal rights. Even in Saudi Arabia, women are playing a more central role within the various civil society organizations.

Within this background, the Gulf Yearbook 2004 places strong emphasis on the need to bolster women's participation in political life in the GCC countries as an essential ingredient in the process of overall political reform. The GRC Yearbook also calls for GCC women to be granted a larger role in the Gulf labor market in order to remedy the existing imbalances.

The Gulf Yearbook 2004 devotes one of its chapters to the exploration and analysis of civil society organizations (CSO)s in the GCC countries in terms of the legal regulations that govern the various fields of their activities. The Yearbook puts forth an assessment of the performance and role of CSOs in the GCC and probes the patterns that define the relationship these organizations and the ruling elites. The problems and obstacles impeding the role of CSOs are also discussed at length including the need for governments to provide greater space for the development of CSOs and that CSOs improve their organizational structures and implement their programs in more efficient ways. CSOs should not be confined to circles of elitism, but rather should expand membership and interact openly with the larger society. It is in that light that CSOs in the GCC countries need to display a greater movement towards internal democratic development.

5. The GCC States' Policies in Education

A particular focus of the GRC Gulf Yearbook 2004 is on developments in the field of education. This includes at the outset the major issues and problems related to pre-university education, especially educational curricula and the quality of the educational system. Some well-thought solutions are offered in this respect. As for higher education, the Yearbook investigates key indicators such as the number of public and private higher education institutions in the GCC countries, the number of students registered in universities and the distribution of education according to gender and specialization of these institutions. Other aspects of higher education in the Gulf States, too, are probed in sufficient depth, notably the low number of institutions for arts and technical studies, as well as the low number of registered students in these institutions and the preponderance of theoretical over scientific and engineering specializations. Emphasis is placed on the higher rates of registration among female students compared with those among male students.

What is equally clear in addition to the available statistics is that the higher education system in the Gulf is confronted with a number of challenges. At the top stands the inability of existing universities to cater to the educational needs of a growing population and the deepening awareness among the GCC societies of the importance of education, a trend that requires raising the number of public universities and higher education institutes, encouraging the establishment of private universities, diversifying the sources of funding for higher education institutions and promoting non-traditional patterns of education, notably distance education and the establishment of open universities. In a similar vein, there is the need to improve the quality of the education curricula, the performance of teaching faculties, teaching techniques, the style of managing higher education establishments and the systems adopted in educational assessment and certification. The perennial problem of the mismatch between the quality of university graduates and the requirements

of the GCC labor markets and socio-economic development is also highlighted. This dilemma seems today to be more critical than ever in light of the presence of large expatriate communities in the GCC countries and the rise in unemployment rates among local graduates.

The Yearbook thus highlights the need for reform in education in the GCC countries with importance being placed on the need for reform to develop in conjunction with national priorities and agendas, while simultaneously retaining a realistic view of the problems and objectives. What is clear is that without well-developed systems of education based on the principle of a balanced match between quantity and quality, the educational enterprise would fail to bring into existence a well-trained labor force capable of remedying the existing disequilibrium in the GCC labor markets.

6. Intra-GCC Relations

Moving beyond the domestic issues that define Gulf development, the Gulf Yearbook 2004 broadens its scope to the external environment and begins by looking at the relational patterns shaping the cooperative interactions among the GCC States, both at the bilateral level and within the context of the Gulf Cooperation Council. The overall performance of the Council during 2004 is assessed, particularly in light of the 25th summit of GCC leaders held under the title of the 'Zayid Summit.' The absence of Saudi Crown Prince Abdullah bin Abdulaziz from the summit revealed a number of structural problems that continue to beset joint Gulf cooperation. These existing problems call for urgent remedies so that Gulf integration and better coordination among the member states of the Gulf Council can be fully enacted. As the Yearbook underlines, there is a new set of formidable challenges arising at the domestic, region and international level. This includes:

o The dispute between Saudi Arabia and Bahrain (which threatened to abort the GCC summit) on the issue of the bi-lateral free trade agreement signed by Manama with the US thereby indicating that Washington was once again, albeit indirectly, acting as a divisive force among the GCC countries. The incident illustrated the fact that the GCC States continue to lack a common policy through which to manage their relations as a regional bloc with the US. It also stressed the need for GCC States to make better efforts to keep bilateral relations with other countries from negatively affecting their relations at the intra-GCC level.

o The fact that precedence to national interests continues to dominate over the collective interests of the member states as evidenced by the fact that some GCC States tend to prioritize commitments signed with extra-GCC parties over intra-GCC commitments ratified by the Gulf Council. This trend must be reversed in order for the GCC States to strengthen their integration.

o In spite of the achievements realized by the GCC Council, its performance in some specific areas remains rather modest. Many political analysts attribute this condition to the weak commitment by the member states to the resolutions and decisions of the Council and the subsequent slow pace of execution, rather than the lack of actual collective agreements. While this is a dilemma faced by the Arab states in general, it is a situation that has severely inhibited the qualitative integration of the GCC member states.

o In the Saudi-Bahraini case, the kingdom argues that such agreements run counter to the customs union agreement signed by the GCC member States. Bahrain, for its part, contends that the GCC customs union agreement does grant member states

the right to sign bilateral agreements with external parties. Regardless of which of the two arguments is tenable, the whole issue proves that intra-GCC agreements either remain far from being sufficiently clear, or the texts of collective agreements are overly clear-cut in their stipulations, leaving no room for multiple interpretations by the member states.

o It is apparent that the issue of transparency in managing intra-GCC relations is critical since only through such transparency can the GCC States build mutual trust, dissipate suspicions and be able to preempt situation before they develop into full-force crises. For example, Manama signed and committed itself to the agreement forcing Saudi Arabia to vociferously and publicly oppose it. As a result, the issue is no longer simple to resolve. At the same time, if the dispute is not settled soon, it could not only cripple all aspects of economic integration among the GCC countries, but also threaten the future of the GCC Council as such as Saudi Foreign Minister Prince Saud Al Faisal made clear in his statement from December 12, 2004. It is worth pointing out here that besides causing the dispute with Riyadh, Bahrain's move could constitute a further element of discord between Saudi Arabia and the US, however indirectly. Washington could view Riyadh's position as an obstruction to its desire to develop relations with the other GCC States.

o If the latest GCC summit revealed some structural problems at the level of GCC joint action, such problems reinforce the need to enhance the role of the GCC Council in order to boost its credibility in the eyes of the people of all the six member states. In this respect, there are many points that have to be articulated and debated.

In light of the above, and out of its belief in the central importance of the GCC Council, the GRC decided (on the anniversary marking a quarter century of the Council's existence) to launch a comprehensive research program to study and assess this unique experience in the Arab world. The research program will seek to identify the strengths and weaknesses of the entire experience. It will also analyze the obstacles that have impeded the evolution of the Council while articulating suggestions to adequately deal with present hurdles. Additionally, the GRC research program will examine the views and expectations of the GCC populations both in terms of the past experience and the future outlook. In that context, the GRC program takes a closer look at the conditions and ramifications likely to arise from the membership of Yemen (Sana'a is already a member in some of the Council's organizations) and Iraq. The experience of the Gulf Council is set in comparative perspective with other experiments in regional cooperation in order to make the best use of their positive aspects and boost the role and continuation of the Council.

7. The GCC-Arab and Regional Relations

Going beyond the immediate GCC region, the Gulf Yearbook 2004 analyzes the policies of the GCC states towards the regional environment including a number of core issues, primarily the Palestinian issue, which lies at the heart of the Arab-Israeli conflict, and the Iraqi issue, particularly in light of the epoch-making developments and shifts that have unfolded in Iraq throughout 2004. Outside of this parameter, developments such as the crisis between Libya and Saudi Arabia in the aftermath of the accusations against Libya for being implicated in an assassination attempt against Saudi Crown Prince Abdullah bin Abdulaziz are examined as are the relations linking the GCC States to Iran, Turkey, India, Pakistan, and the Red Sea states.

As far as Iran is concerned, the impact of the parliamentary elections of February 2004 on regional relations and the concerns over Iran's nuclear program are dominant themes in the GCC relationship with the Islamic Republic. Furthermore, factors like Iraq and the US are important as both have an influence on the regional policies of the Iranian state. The Yearbook also analyzes the myriad developments in the economic and trade relations between the GCC states and Iran as well as the political relations, again particularly in light of developments in Iraq. Finally, the Yearbook discerns the possible political dimensions of the incident that involved Iran on the one hand and Qatar and the UAE on the other over the issue of fishing vessels trespassing territorial waters.

In relation to the GCC states' relations with both India and Pakistan, the Yearbook traces and analyzes developments at the level of trade and economic relations between the two sides. Here, it is clear that the Indian and Pakistani expatriates working in the GCC states will remain a key component of the relations between the two parties.

As far as GCC-Turkey relations are concerned, the Yearbook investigates developments that have unfolded during 2004 within the framework of such issues as Iraqi, the Greater Middle East Initiative, Ankara's attempt to join the EU, and developments regarding trade and economic relations.

When it comes to the GCC states' relations with the Red Sea states, the Gulf Yearbook 2004 places particular focus on the various developments that have unraveled in the relations with Yemen and Sudan.

8. The GCC States' International Relations

In terms of the broader international environment, the GCC has established a variety of relationships that has a distinct impact on the region. As can be expected, the US plays the most central role in this regard but countries such as the EU, China, Japan and Russia are in fact also rising considerations.

As a sub-theme on the subject of GCC-US relations, the Yearbook contends that although relations between Riyadh and Washington have moved markedly towards normalization during 2004, they have not yet reverted to the traditional coziness that defined their bilateral relations prior to the events of September 11. For the other GCC states, relations with Washington continue in much the same way as before. In other words, these relations continued to be based on close bilateral cooperation, even though public opinion in some of the GCC States tended to express mounting disaffection with US policies towards the Arab and Muslim worlds. In general, there are four major fields to consider: security and the war against terrorism; oil and economic issues; domestic political reform in the GCC states; and the Iraqi crisis.

As far as the GCC states' relations with the EU, China, Russia, and Japan are concerned, the Yearbook examines the key developments that characterized the relationship over the twelve months of 2004. Naturally, oil stands at the core of the GCC states' relations with all of these countries, particularly in light of the late developments on the international oil market in 2004. As is the case with the other relations, developments in Iraq represented a major common concern for both sides as well.

9. Developments in Iraq, Iran and Yemen

The Gulf Yearbook 2004 devotes special attention to tracing the various events in Iraq, Iran and Yemen throughout 2004, both at the level of their respective domestic scenes and at the level of their regional and international relations. Clearly, developments in these three countries have a direct impact, whether positively or negatively, on the security and stability of the entire Gulf region. As such, Iraq, Iran and Yemen ought to be actively engaged in any future regional security project if it is to prove successful and sustainable.

On the Iraqi crisis, the Yearbook sheds light on a few core issues, namely the relentless deterioration of security conditions and the sharpened polarization over the political process between political groups maintaining opposite positions towards the electoral project. The Yearbook also puts forth a global assessment of the project for the post-war reconstruction of Iraq, tracks the landmark events and developments that unraveled on the Iraqi scene during 2004, notably the battle in Fallujah, the scandal in Abu Ghuraib prison, the phenomenon of kidnapping, and the attacks that targeted oil facilities. As for the probable scenarios likely to evolve in Iraq in the foreseeable future, the Yearbook presents the following:

First: A Civil War Breaks Out and Security Conditions Deteriorate Dramatically

The majority of Iraqis refute the likelihood of such a scenario given their long-standing experience and social traditions. However, there is much evidence on the ground that suggests that Iraq might slide into more serious domestic strife. Ethnic and sectarian polarization is at a very high level and organized and tit-for-tat assassinations are widespread. While some Iraqi sects are filled with a sense of euphoria, others are deeply frustrated about ongoing developments. External parties are constantly and effectively interfering to support certain Iraqi groups. Up to this point, the Iraqi political forces have managed to prevent a further deterioration into civil strife, but an end to violence and resistance is unlikely for the foreseeable future. The wave of violence sweeping across Iraq is poised to expand in the form of retaliatory acts out of nationalist and religious sentiments.

Second: Stabilization of Political Conditions and the Containment of Violence

This specific scenario rests on the extent to which

the Iraqi government succeeds in carrying out the political process without triggering any domestic political conflicts. In the event the Iraqi government manages to conduct a process of national reconciliation, set up an Iraqi government on the basis of a general consensus by all the major Iraqi political forces, improves the living conditions and the public services provided to Iraqis, and ensures the secularization of the country, then the government would have succeeded in its mission. The foreign military presence, too, would need to make itself less visible in a bid to enhance the performance of Iraqi military security services both quantitatively and qualitatively. Certain neighboring countries need to refrain from interfering in the internal affairs of Iraq. This set of interlocked and complex conditions makes this scenario quite unlikely.

Third: Setting into Motion the Political Process while violence continues

As long as conditions contributing to the rise of violence remain, so too will violence and resistance. Further, as domestic policies and international interests are not expected to change dramatically over the next year, the scenario most likely to unravel in Iraq is a combination of the two previous scenarios. In other words, the political process will continue while violence will gradually be confined to particular regions across Iraq.

As for developments in Iran in 2004, the Yearbook analyzes and evaluates the outcome of the legislative elections held in Iran in February 2004 where the conservative camp has increased its influence at the expense of the reformist camp. As can be expected, this development in Iranian domestic politics will undoubtedly have, as mentioned earlier, some ramifications on the domestic and international levels.

On another level, the Yearbook discusses Iran-Iraq relations especially in light of the public accusations directed on many occasions by a number of prominent Iraqi officials against Tehran, lashing out at Iran's interference in Iraq's internal affairs and helping some groups sustain violence. For its part, Tehran has sought to manipulate the Iraqi issue as part of managing its relations with Washington. In fact, Iranian officials have on numerous occasions declared that Tehran could help Washington wade its way out of the Iraqi quagmire.

Throughout 2004 Iran's nuclear program stood out as one of the most central issues on the Gulf regional stage. Although Iran and the EU have reached an understanding, Iran's nuclear file is not yet closed. All probabilities are still open, as Washington has reiterated threats to resort to any means necessary in order to stop Iran from acquiring weapons of mass destruction.

As for Yemen, the Gulf Yearbook 2004 sheds light on the main political developments, marked particularly by Yemen's sustained democratization policies in spite of the wide political polarization and periodic tensions that have strained the relations between the ruling regime and the political opposition. At the level of security developments in Yemen, the Yearbook explores the efforts deployed by the government of Sana'a to fight terrorism. The armed standoff between the security forces and the members of the group known as 'the believing youth' under the leadership of the clergyman Hussein Bader-eddine Al-Houthi was a milestone development on the Yemeni domestic scene in 2004. The confrontations erupted in June and continued until September, when the authorities announced the death of Al-Houthi. The Yearbook also examines the salient aspects of the economic developments in Yemen, particularly the reform program implemented by the government in coordination with, or rather under the pressures exerted by, the International Monetary Fund (IMF) and the World Bank (WB).

Finally, relations between Yemen and Saudi Arabia in particular and the GCC countries in general on the one hand and between Yemen and both Eritrea and the US on the other are investigated.

Future Conditions in the Gulf Region in the Foreseeable Future

Under this final theme the Gulf Yearbook 2004 seeks to provide an outlook for the developments likely to occur in the Gulf region in the short to medium term. Among the key factors that are bound to impact the direction of the region are the demographic imbalance in the GCC States and its probable ramifications; the external and domestic demands for across the board reform; the likelihood of a continued high oil price environment and its related consequences; the deteriorating situation in Iraq and its implications on the region and the world; the internal developments inside the Islamic Republic of Iran and associated with this the escalating tensions over Tehran's nuclear program; and the role and policies of a second Bush administration including the increasing role of neo-conservatives in both the policy-making and policy-design process in Washington.

Within the context of a broader outlook for the Gulf, there are a number of scenarios that can be envisioned as far as the region is concerned:

o Political liberalization is poised to continue in the countries of the region although for the moment increased polarization appears to be the hallmark in terms of the relations between the ruling regimes and the various opposition forces in one or more of the GCC States.

o Efforts to implement economic reform will continue although palpable results at the level of diversifying the sources of income are unlikely.

o Iraq will continue to be plagued by political instability and insecurity even post-election. The reasons are multiple and involve the continued US military presence in the country, the deterioration of general socio-economic conditions, the tottering project to build an Iraqi police force and a national army capable of securing and stabilizing the country, as well as the absence of a genuine consensus among the diverse Iraqi political forces over the future of the state and the nature of the political system to be put in place in post-Saddam Iraq. It appears unlikely that Iraq will turn into a viable and stable democracy in the foreseeable future. Iraq is, in fact, one of, if not the thorniest candidates for any democratization project in the Arab world.

o Relations between Washington and Tehran will remain highly contentious in particular as conservative forces in Iran and neo-conservatives in the US maintain their hold on a large part of the policy-making process.

o Predictably, the US role in the Gulf region will continue unchallenged, except perhaps for the challenge of finding a suitable exit out of the Iraqi quagmire. In fact, Iraq has become a litmus test for America's much-touted strategy based on military superiority and pre-emptive strikes.

It is essential that the region avoid a further deterioration in its stability. As such, the Gulf Yearbook 2004 sets forth a few points that need to be seriously taken into account:

o Political reform in the countries of the Gulf region has become a national imperative and reform is a sine qua non condition in order to boost reform in all other fields. Hence, it is important that the Gulf states sustain the gradual and accumulative process of political reform while granting more freedom to civil society organizations and allowing Gulf women to take on a more substantial role.

o The recent rise in oil revenues has to be a factor for accelerating, not delaying, the process of economic reform. Due to the large revenues accruing to their coffers, the GCC governments have the opportunity to balance out the negative impact of the required reform adjustments.

o Close attention needs to be paid towards remedying the imbalance and deficiencies in the labor market. The prevailing conditions in the GCC labor markets call for urgent action without delay. In the meantime, attending to the problems besetting the labor markets will help reduce unemployment, particularly among the youth. As experience in many countries testifies, unemployment generally produces a suitable atmosphere for violence, extremism and organized crime.

o Without competent managers and without excellent education and an enlightened and credible media, the countries in the Gulf region will be caught in a vicious cycle of problems that is only likely to worsen over time. In this regard, the Gulf states have to speed up reforming their administrative processes and review their educational and media policies to ensure that these are in conformity with national agendas and founded on well-defined priorities.

o A quarter of a century after the establishment of the Gulf Cooperation Council, the GCC states need today to further develop the Council's role in order to reinforce its credibility in the eyes of the people of the member states. No doubt, greater transparency would be a great asset to better manage intra-GCC relations. Yet, there also has to be a stricter

commitment to implement resolutions ratified by the Council and the development of a common approach to managing relations with the US. The role of the Secretariat-General of the Council must also be boosted.

o The goal of reviving security and stability in Iraq rests on several main factors: articulating the terms of comprehensive national reconciliation; setting a timetable for the withdrawal of foreign troops from Iraq; giving a push to the political and economic reconstruction process and allowing the UN to assume a greater role in the execution of the process; reviving the concept of the national state in the minds of Iraqis; and fostering the efforts to re-build the Iraqi security forces while disbanding all armed militias across the country.

o No future regional security arrangements can ever be sustained if they fail to involve Yemen, Iraq and Iran.

o A focused effort needs to be put forward to secure the right conditions and requirements likely to lead to the total elimination of weapons of mass destruction from the Gulf region. This includes settling all pending disputes among the regional states, enhancing confidence-building measures among concerned parties, and re-formulating relations between Tehran and Washington.

o It is in the interest of the GCC states to enhance and improve relations with a number of international powers, notably the EU, China, Japan, and Russia. Such an orientation would help create greater balance in international relations and help boost the security and stability in the region.

It is with all of these issues in mind that the Gulf Yearbook 2004 was formulated and put together. As is clearly evident, there exists a plethora of outstanding issues that require urgent attention and immediate policy action. This report is an attempt to focus on the most urgent issues and to provide a comprehensive understanding of the forces at work in order to pave the way ahead for the region.

Section One

Domestic Political Developments in the GCC States

Internal Political Developments: A General Overview

Dr. Ghanim Al Najjar

Professor of Political Science, Kuwait University

The year 2004 was characterized by a number of internal political changes and developments in the GCC domain. These developments varied in their nature and degree from one country to another, with Saudi Arabia, Bahrain, and Kuwait witnessing the majority of events; Oman, the UAE and Qatar proved to be less affected by the changing political scene.

At the outset, it must be pointed out that there exists a stereotype within many Western academic and media circles whereby the GCC countries are considered as one political entity whose political changes share the same features and characteristics. Similarly, the prospects and mechanisms of change in the GCC countries are seen as being the same, as if there exists no difference between their respective political systems. It would be erroneous, however, to treat the political environment in the GCC as being one homogenous unit. In fact, each of the six GCC countries has a distinct political development program under which it accommodates political change and adapts to shifting circumstances.

The cycle and mode of developments were influenced to a great degree by events over the past three years, starting in particular with the September 11 attacks and the manner in which both the international community and the GCC states reacted to the new environment. Moreover, the US invasion of Iraq and the continued instability in the country in the aftermath influenced the way the GCC states constructed their responses internally, regionally and internationally, resulting in different views and positions in regards to demands for change. With such continued external pressure for reform, the internal debate occurring within Gulf societies has also heated up. This discussion basically revolves around accepting the concept of reform in principle while taking into account the differences in its details, identity and pace. What one can clearly state is that external factors are only a handful of the many elements in the region's reaction to the demands for political reform. The fact that the Gulf regimes are all traditional hereditary systems means that these states will construct individual processes that balance the need to maintain the hold on power with the demands for increased openness and public liberties. As such, some reform plans suggested in recent years fall short of the Kuwaiti model which has been in place since 1962.

There are a number of internal factors affecting the degree and nature of political reform in the GCC countries: first, the orientation and the scope of the openness adopted by the ruling family, the nature of inter-relations within that family, and the status of its relations with its subjects, which varies from one country to another; second, the nature and efficiency of the political elite and the extent of the maturity and efficacy of the civil society; third, the Western stance and the international and regional changes that affect the governments' orientation to reform; fourth, the extent to which the regime feels it is under threat, particularly if that threat is internal; finally, oil, which plays an important part, depending on the rise and fall of its revenue, in the tendency towards reform in the Gulf. When examining these five factors, it becomes clear that there are obvious differences between the Gulf countries, thus explaining why a particular Gulf country is more open than another or why one particular country adopts reforms more quickly than others. Therefore, a state-by-state survey of the more important events in this respect is appropriate.

The State of Qatar

In 2004, Qatar witnessed many internal events which indicated the willingness on the part of the political leadership to comply with international pressures for political reform. In this context, it was the Qatari Foreign Minister Sheikh Hamad Bin Jassem Al Thani who stated in both March and April 2004 that the American initiatives for political reform must be taken into account.

In June 2004, the Qatari Permanent Constitution was published in the Official Gazette meaning that the constitution will come into effect one year later, i.e. in June 2005. A large majority of people had approved the document in a referendum held in April 2003. Although the constitution provides for separation between executive, legislative and judiciary powers, it leaves far-reaching powers in the hands of the Emir. The Constitution also provides for a 45-member parliament with 30 members to be directly elected by the people and the remaining 15 to be appointed by the Emir. However, no date was set for those elections.

Willingness on the part of the political leadership to comply with international pressures for political reform.

The month of June witnessed a number of functions in Qatar. A Christian-Muslim dialogue conference was held under the auspices of the Emir, who brought up the possibility of widening the dialogue so that Jews can also take part. In the same month, in a conference on democratic reform, the Emir stressed in a speech read on his behalf, the necessity to carry out political, social, and economic reforms in order to avoid internal problems and that Arabs should stop using the Arab-Israeli conflict as a pretext to delay such reforms.

Also in June, a Qatari court sentenced two Russian security men to life imprisonment for assassinating the former Chechen president Zelim Khan Yanderbyev in a car bombing. In the wake of that incident, Qatar issued an anti-terror act which allows for the detention of terror suspects without charge depending on the confidential evidence available. The act also allows capital punishment. Qatari officials denied that the timing had anything to do with that incident or that it was in reaction to it.

In an unprecedented step, the ex-Emir of Qatar, Sheikh Khalifa Bin Hamad Al-Thani visited the country for the first time since his son (the incumbent ruler) overthrew him in 1995. Although the reason given for this visit was the attendance of his wife's funeral, it certainly had political dimensions, since the incumbent Emir had called upon his father many times at his residence in Europe since he overthrew him. The power structure in Qatar has also witnessed an important development, as the incumbent Emir named his younger son, Tameem as crown prince instead of his brother, Jassim.

In a speech at the opening of the 33rd session of the Qatari Consultative Council in November, the

Emir again stressed the need to proceed with democratic reform and announced a reshuffling of the council. At the same time, the new term for the council was extended for only one year, a step that seems to be meant to pave the way for parliamentary elections when the permanent constitution comes into effect. In the same context, Qatar announced that it intends to legalize trade unions as of the year 2005 under Act 14/2004. This new law, which came into effect on January 6, 2005, grants any Qatari citizen the right to set up a union under the Qatari Trade Union Congress. It also allows the establishment of labor bodies at various levels: labor committees at the corporate level, general committees at the professional level, and finally at the level of the Qatari Trade Union Congress. Furthermore, this law guarantees the independence of the said bodies and allows them to negotiate for rights of workers whether they are Qatari or foreign.

The Kingdom of Bahrain

In 2004, the Kingdom of Bahrain witnessed various events throughout the year, with tension and political conflict persisting on many fronts and at many levels. This includes the rift between the government and the political groupings which refused to take part in the elections as well as the clash between the executive power and a number of civil society activists which led to the arrest of the director of the Bahrain Human Rights Centre for 45 days in September.

The month of January witnessed a heated dispute between the executive and legislative powers in which parliament accused three ministers of "serious mismanagement" of the Pension Fund and the Social Security Public Corporation. As a result of the severe criticism and the subsequent recommendations by the House of Representatives - which were supported by the King and the Cabinet - the boards of both bodies were reorganized. Yet, the political debate remained tense with issues such as municipal elections and naturalization issues pointing towards different perception between the two sides. Throughout all of the discussions, it should also be noted that the Bahraini Crown Prince began to pay an increasingly prominent political role.

Elections for the Secretariat-General of the Bahrain Trade Union were held on January 14 in the presence of 40 union representatives. All 13 seats of the Secretariat were won by the bloc widely believed to be favored by the Islamic National Accord and the National Democratic Action Society, both of which had boycotted the parliamentary elections held in October 2002. Furthermore, there was an election for the board of the National Accordance Society, which was mainly won by former members. Controversy also continued between political groupings over the convening of a constitutional conference to discuss the Bahraini constitution issued in February 2002 and whose deficiencies deprived the House of Representatives of its legislative powers. In addition, the Head of the Al-Islah Society, Shaikh Issa Bin Mohammad Al-Khalifa declared his intention to issue an act regulating party activity independent of government authority, further demanding a reshuffle of the powers-that-be unless they accept political reform. It has also been noticed that the economic elites have assumed an emerging political role. This was manifested in the statement by the Bahrain Chamber of Commerce and Industry in which it

Dispute between the executive and legislative powers

objected to the increase of holidays for religious reasons, as was demanded by the Islamic blocs.

On February 14, four political societies which had boycotted the parliamentary elections in 2002, namely the Islamic National Accord, the National Democratic Action Society, the Nationalist Democratic Rally and the Islamic Action Society declared their intention to hold a constitutional conference to discuss the shortcomings of the Bahraini constitution and ways to rectify it. This call led to a severe crisis between the said societies and the government, as it appeared that the government exerted pressure on the management of the hotel designated as the conference venue and forced it to renege on its obligations. As a result, the conference was held at the Al-Uruba Club. It was also reported that the Bahraini government contacted the Egyptian and Kuwaiti embassies to express its dissatisfaction with the conference, for invitations to attend went out to Egyptian and Kuwaiti politicians. The Egyptian parliament turned down the invitation to attend while a Kuwaiti group confirmed that it intended to attend, prompting Bahraini authorities to prevent a number of Kuwaiti and other politicians - including Kuwaiti politicians Ahmed Al-Saadoun, Adnan Abdulsamad, and Abdulmuhsin Jamal, the Qatari politician Ali Al-Qawari, and the Jordanian politician Saleh Al-Armooti as well as others from Europe - from entering the country. The Bahraini government justified the action by stressing that the people concerned came to attend a conference whose organizers had not completed the legal procedures required for it to be convened. Despite the setbacks, the conference was held on March 18 at the Al-Uruba Club, where its organizers reconfirmed their reserved stance on the constitutional reform process and their demands for fundamental amendments. It is worth noting that the King had called upon those who boycotted the conference to take part in the elections due to be held in 2006.

In a move that reflected a desire on the part of the four societies which boycotted the elections to escalate their political protest against what they saw as a great deficiency in the Bahraini constitution, a massive campaign was launched on April 21 to collect signatures in support of amendments to the constitution. In reply, Shaikh Ahmad Bin Khalid Al-Khalifa warned the collectors that they were, in fact, in breach of law as amending the constitution can only be carried out by the King or the Shura (Consultative) Council, in accordance with the constitution itself. The Minister of Labor and Social Affairs, Majid Al-Alawi, threatened to disband the four societies if they collected signatures from people other than their own members. On the first of May, the authorities subsequently arrested 16 people who were collecting signatures as well as six people who were suspected of planning sabotage acts. The security forces then dispersed a demonstration that took place on May 21 to condemn US attacks on Najaf in Iraq. This caused the Bahraini king to react to the unprecedented oppressive action by dismissing the Minister of Interior, Shaikh Mohammad Bin Khalifa Al-Khalifa, who had been in that position since 1974, replacing him with Shaikh Rashid Bin Abdullah Al-Khalifa.

The activities of the non-governmental organizations continued to act as a thorn in the side of the Bahraini authorities. At the end of September, the government closed the Al-Uruba Club - which was later reopened - and arrested Abdulhadi Al-Khawajah, the director of the Bahrain Centre for Human Rights. A regional and international campaign was later launched to set Al-Khawajah free. On October 2, the head of the centre, Nabil Rajab, met with the Attorney-General Shaikh Abdulrahman Jaber Al-Khalifa and asked for access to Al-Khawajah, which he was denied. A defense committee for Al-Khawajah held various protest functions and activities including demonstrations and sit-ins that led to a member of arrests; Al-Khawajah and a number of detainees went so far as to go on a hunger strike. The next day, the Bahraini Al-Wasat newspaper quoted Majid Al-Alawi as saying the Bahraini Centre for Human Rights would not be closed because of the lecture delivered by Al-Khawajah at the Al-Uruba Club on the issue of poverty in Bahrain, but because of "insulting" statements by the president of the center after the symposium. On November 22, Manama magistrates convicted Al-Khawajah of incitement against the government and sentenced him in absentia to one year imprisonment. The defense lawyers had boycotted the trial, dismissing it as unconstitutional while the judge, Sayed Mohammed Al-Kafrawi, did not provide any basis of his judgment. In a remarkable development that took place hours following the sentence, the King issued a decree pardoning Al-Khawajah and dropping the remainder of his sentence. The King also instructed the Attorney-General to release those arrested for taking part in the protest against the arrest of Al-Khawajah.

The release of Al-Khawajah, however, was but a minor glimmer in an otherwise dismal year in Bahrain's reform process. Al-Wasat reported on October 3 a warning issued by the Minister of Labor and Social Affairs that he would close 80 non-governmental organizations if they did not abide by the government request that each of them specify a headquarters and an address. Within the same context, the government tabled a bill for rallies which requested that all existing societies reapply for registration. If the bill passes, it will require all societies to abide by the 2002 constitution thereby effectively terminating the political societies that oppose the constitution. It will further prevent officials from the Ministry of Interior, the diplomatic corps, the judiciary, and the army from joining such societies and will ban societies from establishing relations with foreign organizations. Any breach of the law would carry a maximum penalty of life imprisonment.

The Kingdom of Saudi Arabia

Saudi Arabia's internal political situation has remained dependant on a number of factors since the September 11 attacks. The kingdom continues to be subjected to intense American pressure - more so from the American media than by the US administration - to cooperate in the fight against terrorism; at the same time, the Saudi government continues to face pressure from within for increased political reforms. Adding to these pressures is the kingdom's deteriorating internal security situation. In 2004, Saudi Arabia was the target of a string of terrorist attacks and clashes between security forces and armed men suspected of being linked to Al-Qaeda in which more than 100 people were killed. The effects of these occurrences are only exacerbated in the context of the security situations in Iraq and the Palestinian Occupied Territories.

Establishment of the first non-governmental human rights society

In response to the international pressure on Saudi Arabia to cooperate in the fight against international terrorism and the accusation that the Saudi charities abroad are among the main financiers of terror, the Saudi government established an official body to monitor and control donations to charities abroad in March 2004. The body would not only regulate the activities of a number of charities, but some them were closed altogether. Among these was the Al-Haramain charity whose activities were gradually phased out until its closure in the beginning of October.

To reduce political tension and respond to calls for openness, a national dialogue was initiated by the government. The second session of this dialogue in January 2004, was held in Mecca and attended by 60 people, 15 of whom were women. A third session was held for three days in Medina on June 15 in the presence of men and women. Whether or not this initiative will promote political reform, however, remains to be seen. To this end, the Crown Prince Abdullah Bin Abdulaziz announced in a televised speech that the Kingdom is in favor of gradual reforms and that he would not let anyone thwart the process.

On March 16, Saudi authorities arrested six advocates of reform, including Mohammed Sa'id Al-Tayyeb, Tawfiq Al-Qaseer, Shaikh Sulaiman Al-Rushudi, Dr. Matrook Al-Faleh, Ali Al-Dumeini, and Abdullah Al-Hamed. The individuals were among 116 activists who signed a petition in December 2003 calling for the establishment of a constitutional monarchy in the kingdom. Al-Qaseer and Al-Rushudi were released two weeks later, followed by Al-Tayyeb. The other three - Al-Faleh, Al-Dumeini and Al-Hamed - however, remained under arrest and were put on trial. Although the judge had filed a request for the trial to be held behind closed doors, the defendants refused to speak until the motion was dismissed and the trial was held in public. To this end, 32 Saudi activists signed a statement in which they expressed solidarity with the detained reformists.

In an unprecedented step, the government approved on March 15 the establishment of the first non-governmental human rights society, which was to be chaired by Abdullah Bin Salih, a member of the Shura (Consultative) Council. The next day, Turki Bin Muhammed, the Deputy Minister of Political Affairs, declared the establishment of a governmental body of a similar nature. In his statement, the deputy minister noted that the body had been in planning for a number of years and that it would have the authority to directly address the King and his Crown Prince.

In other developments, Prince Sultan Bin Abdulaziz held a press conference on March 23 in which he confirmed that elections to the Shura Council would be possible if popular opinion so declared, adding that currently, experts in the fields of science, culture, and economics are selected every four years to serve on the Council. On April 2, the Shura Council called for greater freedoms of expression in the kingdom; Abdulrahman Al-Inad, a member of the Council's Culture and Media Committee, said that there was a need to establish a forum for dialogue between conservatives and liberals.

On June 9, 317 Saudi journalists elected for the first time a nine-member board to the Saudi Journalists Association. Successful candidates included five former editors-in-chief and two women, both of whom worked for the Al-Riyadh daily newspaper. Although the association's incorporation act stresses its independence, one of its articles allows the Ministry of Information to reject any decision made by the association "if it clashes with the national interests."

When looked at in broad terms, it appears that Saudi authorities are trying to push forward a number of actions, albeit limited, on the path to reform. King Fahad Bin Abdulaziz commenced the meeting of the Shura Council on June 21 with references to the establishment of the King Abdulaziz Center for National Dialogue and the National Society for Human Rights as well as the holding of municipal

In broad terms, it appears that Saudi authorities are trying to push forward a number of actions, albeit limited, on the path to reform.

elections. According to the Saudi news agency, King Fahad also referred to an amendment in articles 17 and 23 of the Shura Council's statute that allows the council to table bills and amendments thereto. The municipal elections - in which the Saudi electorate will elect half of the members to 178 municipal councils all over the country - were to be organized in stages, the first of which took place in the metropolitan boroughs on February 10, 2005, and yielded a high number of seats to conservative candidates. Elections in the Eastern and South-western regions will take place on March 3 while elections in the northern and central regions, including Mecca and Medina, will be held on April 21. After a heated debate, it was finally decided that women would not be allowed to run in the elections. Electoral officials ascribed that decision to practical considerations such as the unavailability of enough female electoral workers to supervise females-only registration and polling stations as well as the fact that only a few Saudi women carry photo identity cards.

It is worth mentioning here that the powers granted to municipal councils are limited. Councils are not financially independent as their budgets come within that of the municipality, which the Councils share power with. In addition to this, decisions made by the Council must be approved by the Minister of Municipal and Rural Affairs. The Councils, which serve for four-year terms, periodically select their heads and deputy heads from among their members for a two-year renewable term. When there is a hung vote, a ministerial decision will tip the balance. In a striking development that goes against the current of reform and political openness, the cabinet announced on September 13 that the government was going to implement laws that would ban public officials, whether civilian or military, from challenging the government policies by taking part directly or indirectly in the drafting of any document

or letter, the engagement of any dialogue with domestic or foreign media, or the attendance of meetings of a critical nature.

These trends in political development, however, were largely overshadowed by the sharp increase in terrorist attacks within the kingdom, particularly during the months of April, May, and June. A chronology of the events is thus warranted:

On April 14, two time bombs were defused and five security men were killed in clashes with armed individuals, one of whom was killed; three more armed individuals were killed in similar clashes nine days later. A group by the name of 'Al-Haramein' claimed responsibility for the suicide bombing of a police station in Riyadh on April 23. The next day, two more armed individuals were killed in clashes with security men. On May 3, an armed group of extremists killed five Americans, one British and an Australian at a petrochemical complex in Yanbu run jointly by the Saudi company Sabec and the American company Exxon Mobil. On May 21, four extremists were killed in Buraida while a German citizen was shot dead in Riyadh three days later.

On June 1, a group of gunmen took a large number of people hostage at a luxury residential complex in the city of Al-Khobar. Although Saudi forces succeeded in freeing the hostages, a number of them were killed by their captors in the process. In response to the wave of attacks, Saudi authorities offered amnesty to armed fundamentalists. The plan, however, fell short of its objective, as only a small number of individuals chose to respond to the offer. The authorities even went so far as to solicit the support of six prominent Saudi sheikhs in the condemnation of the attacks. The fruitlessness of the effort, however, was accentuated with the events that took place in the subsequent days. On June 4, a wanted extremist was shot dead by security officials in the Al-Rawdah quarter of Riyadh during an armed clash. On June 19, it was reported that the headless body of Paul Marshal Johnson, an American employee of the Lockheed Martin Corporation who had been kidnapped several days earlier, was found near Riyadh. On the same day, it was announced that Abdulaziz Al- Muqrin, the Al-Qaida leader in Saudi Arabia had been killed in clashes with Saudi security forces. In response to the escalating violence, the US warned its citizens against travelling to Saudi Arabia. At the same time, the Saudi authorities took the unprecedented step of allowing foreigners to carry arms.

The State of Kuwait

In 2004, Kuwait witnessed heated events centered mostly on disputes between legislative and executive powers, particularly in regards to the adjustment of the constituency boundaries. Kuwait also saw a number of Iraq-related controversies, including but not limited to the arrest of a number of Kuwaiti Islamists accused of participating in Iraq-related violence. Of similar importance was the rising debate concerning succession given the deteriorating health of the Emir and Crown Prince. In terms of civil society, the official establishment of the Kuwaiti Human Rights Society and the setting up of the first private satellite television channel should be mentioned.

The subject of reducing the number of constituencies is not a new development as the topic has been one of heated discussion since the government unilaterally increased the number from 10 to 25 in 1981 in what analysts called a bid to create a more favorable National Assembly. Parliamentary and popular pressure in that direction

In 2004, Kuwait witnessed heated events centered mostly on disputes between legislative and executive powers.

have since increased and as soon as the government indicated that it may yield, a number of proposals were presented to reduce the number. The seriousness of the government on this matter was called into question, however, when it submitted two contradictory proposals on the issue. This struggle ended in the rejection of the reform proposals at the parliamentary session held on June 19 when the government (14 ministers) voted with 21 MPs against the amendment while 25 MPs voted for it. Following the vote, seven political groups of both an Islamic and liberal nature issued a statement accusing the government of preventing the constituency reform and of opposing reform in general. The dispute does not appear to have been completely settled, as a number of MPs voiced their intention to propose fundamental reforms in the election act. It is thus likely that the electoral code reform will continue to be a source of polarization in the political arena.

Another prominent issue was that of the supplying the US army with fuel and the use of a Kuwaiti company as a mediator for Halliburton, an American company, as well as reports on the inflated prices at which fuel was sold to the US army. The incident spurred a parliamentary and media movement to pressure the government into explaining the situation, particularly when regulations governing the sale of state oil ban the use of intermediaries. Accusations of corruption were aired, prompting the State Audit Bureau to ask the Kuwait Petroleum Corporation for an explanation to the situation and regarding the basis for dealing with the mediating company. In response to the accusations, the Minister of Oil, Shaikh Ahmad Al-Fahad stated that Kuwait was not involved in supplying the American army with fuel and maintained that Kuwait had not breached the sale terms as dictated by the world market prices.

This controversy was accompanied by a fierce campaign by the National Assembly and the media. The parliamentarian Ahmed Al Saadoun, for instance, bitterly criticized what he called the triangle of corruption in the municipality and the bodies in charge of the state property as well as the ministers responsible for those bodies. Consequently, he submitted a request to reopen the debate on the Halliburton incident. In an attempt by the government to prevent any escalation of the matter, the Minister of Oil referred the Petroleum Corporation's supply contract to the Attorney-General for investigation. However, Mishari Al-'Anjari, the deputy speaker of parliament, stressed that this referral was not sufficient. On February 12, 23 MPs demanded the establishment of a parliamentary inquiry commission to investigate the matter. In what was an obvious response to parliamentary pressure, Prime Minister Shaikh Sabah Al-Ahmad stressed at the parliament session held on February 17 the government's commitment to transparency. He also confirmed the government's acquiescence to the demand for the establishment of an inquiry commission and declared that the government would not take part in the vote - as was stipulated by MPs - as to not influence the commission's membership. Following the voting process, a five-man parliamentary commission was formed and included: Ali Al Rashed, Adel Al-Sar'awi, Waleed Al-Jari, Badr Shaikhan Al-Farsi, and Dr. Faisal Al-Musallam.

The tension kept escalating as MPs often threatened to use the questioning mechanism against cabinet ministers. MP Dr. Dhaifallah Buramiah, for example, relentlessly threatened that

he would question the minister of health. In a public statement made on August 30, he said that "I will not go back on questioning the minister of health, come what may. What I am waiting for is the right time." The MP Ahmad Al Saadoun also threatened on June 30 to question both the Minister of State for Cabinet Affairs and the Minister of Energy. Moreover, MPs Ali Al Rashid and Ahmed Al-Mulaifi voiced their intention to question the Minister of State for Cabinet and Parliamentary Affairs, there were threats by the MP Jamal Al 'Umar to question the Minister of Justice, and suggestions by a number of other MPs to question the Minister of Information. In 2004, the Minister of Finance, Mahmoud Al Nouri was questioned by the MP Musallam Al-Barrak. As usual, the questioning was accompanied by media and legislative campaigns to polarize public opinion and pressure hesitant ministers and MPs to take a clear stance vis-à-vis the questioning matter. After the March 8 questioning session, 10 MPs tabled a vote of no confidence motion against the minister to be voted on in two weeks time without the presence of ministers, as was provided for in the motion. During the no confidence session, which was eventually held on March 23, 25 MPs voted against the motion while twenty one voted for it; many MPs, however, continued to call for the minister's resignation.

In a long-awaited move, the government confirmed the Kuwaiti Human Rights Society after it had been working illegally for 11 years.

The government tried various methods in dealing with the continuing parliamentary pressure, including resorting to the constitutional court to restructure Article 99 of the Constitution, which deals with parliamentary questioning. The court postponed action from May 23 to November after MP Abdullah Al Roumi stated that there had been attempts to reconcile the House with the government, prompting the government to withdraw its explanatory request from the court. At the same time, the government announced that it intended to table a bill to amend Article 1 of the Election Act in order to allow women full political participation. Reactions to the political and parliamentary powers to this varied. The Islamic Constitutional Movement expressed its preparedness to reconsider its standpoint on the political rights of women. In contrast, the Salafi Movement declared its outright opposition. The Democratic Forum and the Democratic National Rally expressed support. Although some MPs opposed the bill, the new element was the semi-supportive stance of the Islamic Constitutional Forum.

One should note that the political tug of war has always led to talk of a government reshuffle, an outcome that the Prime Minister continually dismisses as he did on February 12. It seems that government reshuffle is connected one way or another with the expected merger between the positions of Crown Prince and Prime Minister, something which will be dictated by the actual situation on the ground but will open the door for other reshuffles in the political hierarchy.

Other developments in Kuwait bode well for political development. In a long-awaited move, the government confirmed the Kuwaiti Human Rights Society after it had been working illegally for 11 years. Reactions to this proclamation varied - some Islamic powers had reservations due to the fact that the society is liberally orientated - though the proclamation was largely welcomed. In the realm of freedom of expression, there appeared to be a state of marked annoyance on the part of the government over some journalists with regard to particular articles. It was said that Abdulateef Al Du'aij, a prominent reporter, stopped writing in the Al-Qabas

newspaper because of an article he had published on June 4 which criticized the Prime Minister after an advisor to the Prime Minister had already contacted the paper and expressed his reservations. A similar situation was also reported by the Commission for the Defense of Freedom of Expression and involved another journalist, Ahmed Diyeen, and a piece he wrote for the Al-Rai Al-Am newspaper. Despite the pressure, the management of both papers insisted that both writers carried on with their jobs. As a result of the fiasco, the Commission for Defense of Freedom of Expression held a symposium on July 6 to discuss the issue. At the symposium, which was covered by a number of newspapers, Ahmed Diyeen publicly criticized the government for intrusion. The Prime Minister reiterated his attack on the two writers, mentioning them by name at a press conference on September 22. The journalists, however, continue to write for their respective papers and have not altered their stance against the government.

The most prominent event that took place on the political arena in the UAE was the passing of Shaikh Zayid Bin Sultan Al-Nahyan

The United Arab Emirates

The most prominent event that took place on the political arena in the UAE was the passing of Shaikh Zayid Bin Sultan Al-Nahyan, the President of UAE on November 2 at the age of 86. The country was stricken with grief, as the late sheikh was immensely popular both domestically and internationally. His death also brought forth a recurring issue, namely the question of political succession in the country. What happened put an end to any speculations, however, as the transfer of power passed with utmost smoothness both in Abu Dhabi and at the Union level. The Supreme Council of the Union - made up of the rulers of the seven emirates - met and decided unanimously to choose Shaikh Khalifa Bin Zayid, the eldest son of the deceased, to be the next president of the federation.

It is worth mentioning that the government reshuffle that took place on November 1 was only the sixth since the establishment of the UAE in 1971. Among the most prominent features of it were: the mergers of some ministries, the appointment of the first female minister, Shaikha Lubna Al-Qasimi, who became the Minister of Planning and Economy; the appointment of Shaikh Saif Bin Zayid as Minister of Interior; the creation of a Ministry for Cabinet Affairs to be headed by Shaikh Mansoor Bin Zayid; and other minor ministerial changes.

During 2004, government officials were predominantly interested in contributing to the fight against terrorism. A number of statements were made and functions were held - the latest of which was the meeting on November 1 held under the auspices of the Ministry of Interior and attended by representatives of various departments of the federation - in order to coordinate the fight against terrorism. It was stressed at the meeting that the UAE had signed many international agreements in this respect. Although US President George W. Bush had indicated that B.S. Taher, President of the Dubai-based computer company S.M.B., had helped both Libya and Iran develop their nuclear programs, the Governor of the UAE Central Bank, Sultan Bin Nasser Al Suwaidi, denied there was any evidence to criminalize Taher. He also stressed that if there was any flaw, necessary actions would be taken. In the last week of March, the US embassy was closed in anticipation of possible terrorist attacks; it reopened only days later.

In other noteworthy developments, a group of citizens, including 29 lawyers, academics, and media and public personalities, asked the Ministry of Labor and Social Affairs on June 19 to set up a human rights society for the first time in the history of the UAE. These petitioners had elected an interim body headed jointly by Dr. Aminah Boushihab, a columnist in the Al-Khaleej newspaper, and Mohammed Al Roken, a professor of law at the UAE University. The signatories were the lawyers Sameerah Qirqash, Nasser Al-Jaroodi, Khaled Bou-Jessem, Ayman Abdul Raheem, and Mohammed Rashed Al Suwaidi, in addition to Dr. Abdallah Mohamed Al Shamsi, Ali Al Deebani, Mohamed Al-Mansoori, Yusof Saleh Al- Hosni, and Mansoor Abdul Rahman Asserkal.

On September 8, the US opened a permanent office at its embassy in the UAE to deal with the Middle East Partnership Initiative, which advocates education and development for women together with political and economic reform. The office covers the GCC countries as well as Yemen and Jordan.

The Sultanate of Oman

Oman did not witness many internal political developments, with the exception of some government reshuffles, the most important of which was the introduction of female appointments in the cabinet. It is worth mentioning that the Shura Council - which witnessed the election

Oman was prepared to interact with reform that is compatible with development

of 83 members in October out of 506 candidates, with only two winners out of the 15 female candidates - enjoys no real legislative powers and cannot discuss matters of defense, security, or foreign policy. However, its head, Shaikh Abdullah Bin Ali stressed in March the importance of the Council as a link between the government and the citizens. He also stressed the importance of complete cooperation and coordination with the government. In March, Rawyah Bin Saud Al-Bousaidi became the first female minister, receiving the post of Minister of Higher Education. On 15th May, Sultan Qaboos Bin Said ordered a limited government reshuffle, appointing Khamis Bin Mubarak as Minister of Housing and Minister of Electricity and Water, Abdullah Bin Salem Al Rawas as Minister of Municipalities and the Minister Environment and Water Resources, and appointing the former Minister of Housing, Suhail Bin Shammas, to the State Council. In June, Rajiha Bin Abd Al- Ameer was appointed in the newly-created position of Minister of Tourism. A third woman, Dr. Sharifah Bin Khalfan, was appointed as Minister of Social Development. In an apparently reserved stance towards political reform, the Deputy Prime Minister, Fahd Bin Mahmoud stressed that Oman was prepared to interact with reform that is compatible with development in Oman over the last three decades, stressing that there was a difference between what the state ought to achieve in the way of social justice and citizens' rights on the one hand, and external demands for modernization in the Arab societies on the other.

Conclusion

Some GCC countries have taken varying steps on the path to political reform in 2004, while the political tug of war continued between governments and their opposition, as the case has been in both Kuwait and Bahrain. Acts of terrorism in Saudi Arabia and their repercussions were among the most prominent developments in the internal political arena in the Kingdom of Saudi Arabia. By the end of the year, the passing away of Shaikh Zayid Bin Sultan Al-Nahyan, President of the UAE, marked an end of an era and the beginning of another in the history of the Emirates. The new era was launched with a smooth and fast transfer of power, with the selection of Shaikh Khalifa Bin Zayid by the Supreme Council of the Union as the new President. What is most clear, however, is that political reform will remain one as of the main issues in the GCC countries in the coming years.

Constitutional and Legal Developments

Dr. Mohamed Abdullah Al-Roken

Associate Professor of Public Law, UAE University

The development of the constitutional and legal system of a given country is an accumulative process that takes many years to crystallize in the form of a new legislation or constitutional or legal amendments. Although the young state could sometimes be excused for hastily issuing particular laws that are replaced or amended a few years afterwards, once the constitutional and legal structure of that state is established, such developments take on a slower pattern and become less urgent than before.

Legislating acts that are related to the political life of a country, such as the laws that regulate elections, the legislative process, ministerial responsibility, or the succession of rulers, normally happen after the political entity of a nation has been established due to the use of such legislation in regulating citizenship, citizen's political rights or the fact that international and regional developments necessitate issuing them.

Annual constitutional and legal developments in the GCC countries are almost unnoticeable. This could be partly due to the fact political rights are still a new issue, whether in the sense of guaranteeing them, regulating them through a book of statutes or in allowing them to be practiced freely and extensively. Yet, it can also be ascribed to the nature of the systems themselves which are characterized by stability and continuity over long periods of time. Whatever the reason, the fact is that in the GCC States only one single constitutional amendment in 2004 was proposed and that was in the UAE. Meanwhile, Qatar issued its permanent constitution more than a year after putting it to the Qatari people in a national referendum. On the legislative side, the most prominent event was the issuing of regulations for the municipal elections in Saudi Arabia, the first

written legislation that gives Saudi citizens such a political right.

Another feature to be mentioned is the development of anti-terror legislation in all the GCC States. Terrorism, the unlawful use of violence and the arbitrary killings by groups and individuals in some Gulf or neighboring countries has escalated to such degree in recent years that it became imperative for the governments to react broadly, both domestically and multi-laterally. As a result, a series of legislations, agreements and resolutions have been adopted in order to confront such excesses in some of the GCC countries.

Constitutional developments

As mentioned, the year 2004 witnessed only one constitutional amendment in relation to the UAE constitution. Article 121 was amended to include the sentence on "regulation and setting up of financial free zones and the scope of their exemption from federal legislation" in order to reflect the fact that the establishment of free zones falls under the joint jurisdiction of the federal state and its constituent members, i.e. the federation enacts a financial free zone law allowing the creation of the zone by a local emirate government.[1] To apply the rules of this constitutional amendment, Federal law No. 8 of 2004 was issued in March 2004 entitled "Regarding the Financial Free Zones." This law allows all emirates to establish financial free zones where financial and other supporting activities can be carried out in accordance with existing federal decrees The law also exempts the free zones from being subject to federal civil and commercial laws although other federal laws in areas such as penalty, civil and criminal procedures, employment, and laws related to entry into the country and residence therein by aliens still take precedence.[2] This constitutional amendment reflects the growing role played by individual member emirates as political units and grants them wider powers in the financial and economic field.

In another instance, the provisions of the constitution were applied. Upon the death of UAE President Shaikh Zayid Bin Sultan Al Nahyan on November 2, 2004, Shaikh Maktoum, in his capacity as the federation's Vice-President took over power temporarily until a new president was elected. Subsequently, article 51 of the constitution was enacted with the unanimous consent by the rulers of the emirates on November 3, electing Shaikh Khalifah Bin Zayid Al-Nahyan, the Ruler of Abu Dhabi, as president for a five year term.[3] Although Article 53 of the constitution grants a one month period for

consultation before a new president must be elected, the consultations over this matter were taken care of in one day. This can be attributed to the consensus among the seven rulers and to the constitutional custom established over the previous 33 years that presidency is reserved for the ruler of Abu Dhabi as the emirate with the largest area and economy. It is a reflection of the keen interest in the stability of the country and the importance of a smooth transition to this constitutionally important position.

Qatar in 2004 formally promulgated its first ever permanent constitution. After Shaikh Hamad Bin Khalifah Al Thani, the Emir of Qatar had issued his July 1999 Emiri decree No 11 to form a 32-member committee to draft a permanent constitution within a 3 year period, the committee presented the constitution in July 2002 consisting of five sections divided into 150 articles. The document covered public rights and liberties, as well as the establishment of a Shura Council, where two-thirds of the forty-five members would be directly elected with the rest being appointed by the Emir. It also stated that the Government system in Qatar is hereditary in the family of Al-Thani, literally the male descendents of Hamad Bin Khalifah. Thus, the ruler will name his crown prince after consulting the ruling family through 'the ruling family council' and the powers-that-be in the country.[4]

A referendum held on the constitution on April 29, 2003 won the support of 96.6 % of the Qatari people. As a result, on June 8, 2004, the Emir of Qatar issued the permanent constitution in implementation of article

---

[1] Constitutional amendment no. 1 of 2004 dated January 10, 2004. The new article now reads: "without prejudice to provisions of the pre-ceding Article, the Union shall have exclusive legislative jurisdiction in the following matters: Labor relations and social social security; real estate and expropriation in the public interest; extradition of criminals; banks; insurance of all kinds; protection of agriculture and animal wealth; major legislations relating to penal law, civil and commercial transactions and company law, procedures before the civil ans and criminal courts; protection of cultural, technical and industrial property

and copyright; printing and publishing; import of arms and ammunition except for the use by the armed forces or security forces belonging to any Emirate, other aviation affairs which are not within the executive jurisdiction of the Union, delimitation of territorial waters and regulation of navigation on the high seas, and regulation of financial free zones and the scope of their exemption from the federal legislations."

[2] Article 3 of the Federal law, no.8, of 2004, regarding financial free zones.
[3] Al-Bayan Newspaper, November 4, 2004.
[4] For more details see www.mofa.gov.qa.

(141) thereof. With the issuance of this constitution, the provisional constitution of the state which was issued on April 19, 1972 became null and void.

The Qatari constitution is noted for its inclusion of many provisions that regulate the fundamental human rights of individuals such as the right to vote and be nominated for election, the right to establish associations, the right to address the public authorities, the sanctity of private life, personal freedom, and equality before the law. The constitution also stressed the importance of universal basic principles such as the separation between legislative, executive and judicial authorities at the same time as preserving cooperation between them and asserting that people are the source of authority.

The Qatari Shura Council was granted the power to legislate although it remains restricted in a number of ways. For example, while it has the right to present bills and shares that right with the cabinet, such initiatives have to be presented as proposals to the government to be considered.[5] This is deemed as guardianship by the executive authority over the legislature in relations to the performance of tasks. Furthermore, no legislation can be passed without the approval of the Emir. The council does have the right to insist on issuing a law by a two-thir ds majority of its members.[6] What this means in practice, however, is that if the one-third of members appointed by the Emir vote alongside the executive authority, it is necessary for the rest of the council to vote unanimously in order to overrule an

The Qatari constitution is noted for its inclusion of many provisions that regulate the fundamental human rights of individuals

Emir's decision, a situation that is difficult to come by. Even if it were to come about, the Emir still has the power to suspend, for a period of his choice, the law in question, even if that law has the unanimous consent of all members, whether elected or appointed.

On another front, the Shura legislature has been granted the power to question ministers, provided such a request is made by fifteen members, a comparably high number in relations to the constitutional provisions in other Gulf countries.[7] A motion of no confidence in a minister requires a two-thirds majority, i.e. again the unanimity of all elected members.[8] It should be mentioned that, according to the constitution, a minister is politically responsible to both the legislature and the Emir in his capacity as the executive authority in the state.

One item that stands out in the Qatari constitution is that the document is more rigid than others when it comes to amending its articles. Article 144 provides for certain procedures to be followed with the responsibility for amendment lying primarily with the Emir although two-thirds of Shura members can also pass a relevant amendment. Yet, there are two constitutional prohibitions. First, the constitution prohibits any amendments related to the system of government or the succession of rulers. This, in turn, can be viewed as a contradiction to Article 95 as it deprives the people from being able to amend the constitution despite the fact that it is the people that are identified as the source of authority.[9] Second, the constitution prohibits

---

[5] Article 105 of Qatar's constitution
[6] Article 106 of Qatar's constitution
[7] Article 110 of Qatar's constitution
[8] Article 111 of Qatar's constitution
[9] This was supported by Dr. Ohtman Abdulmalek Al-Saleh in his book Constitutional System and Political Institutions in Kuwait - Part 1 (Kuwait

University, 1989), p. 192-194. He states that articles of the Kuwaiti constitution which prohibit amending rules of the Emiri system have the same legal effects as other articles of the constitution in that they can be amended but only in compliance with the strict procedures. To him, the article dealing with the permanent prohibition can first be amended followed by another amendment to the article that deals with the government system.

amending articles related to public rights and liberties in such a way that diminishes them. What is instead allowed is to propose an amendment that will enhance such rights and liberties. Moreover, amendments can only be made following a time period of ten years from the time that the constitution has come into force. Finally, the constitution can have its articles suspended in an emergency, the exception being the convening of the Shura Council. Here it needs to be mentioned that the declaration of martial law is the sole privilege of the Emir, while the Shura Council's role is confined to merely taking notice of such a decision.[10]

2 Legal developments

A- Developments related to political life legislation

The most prominent legal event took place in Saudi Arabia with the issuance by the cabinet on October 13, 2003 of a decree to enlarge the role played by the public in running local affairs through the election of municipal councils. This was followed in August 2004 by the announcement of electoral regulations by the Minister of Municipal and Rural Affairs stipulating the instructions for the election campaigns and the guidelines in terms of the legal contestation and grievance situations. Such administrative regulations were first issued in 1397 H (1979), Law No. 5/77 through the municipal and the rural law, which emphatically provides for the selection of half the members through the ballot box.[11] As one analyst noted, these regulations are "a first step that confirms an intention on the rulers' part

to embark on the introduction of reform, albeit of less significance many observers and citizens had expected."[12]

One key problem area is the fact that the role of issuing the regulations was given to the Ministry of Municipal and Rural Affairs, an arm of the executive branch. Regulations issued in this manner are easier to amend than, for example, if they had been formulated through the shura process where they would have taken on the function of standard laws. This, in turn, would have allowed one also to detail the different stage procedures as well as the conditions of holding municipal elections as a form of popular participation in the decision-making process and therefore replacing the existing municipal and rural system.

As a result, a number of observations about the election regulations and administrative guidelines issued under the municipal and rural law can be made:

o The regulations do not set a date for starting the elections but left this issue to the minister concerned. This gives an impression of instability and lack of continuity, with the possibility of postponement and delay;

o The regulations do not directly deprive women of casting their vote or running for elections as they use the term 'citizen' without restricting it to one sex. However, it has since been made clear that such participation will not be permitted.

o The voting age is 21 years while the universal trend has been one of lowering it to 18 years.

o The regulations have turned the legal situation upside down by putting the registration of electors before the designation of constituencies.

---

[10] Article 69

[11] There thus exists a 24 year time lag in the formulations of the regula-tions. The kingdom of Saudi Arabia previously held elections in the year 1343 H when citizen councils were elected in Makkah, Madinah, Jeddah, Yunbu'a and Ta'if. Prince Salman Bin Abdel Aziz, Governor of

Riyadh District, told Al-Jazeerah newspaper on June 30, 1964 that members of the municipal council would be directly elected by citizens. For more details visit www.elections.gov.sa

[12] Abdulaziz bin Othman Bin Saqr, "Elections of Municipal Councils in Saudi,' Al-Khaleej newspaper, November 7, 2004.

Furthermore, the process of defining the constituencies was awarded to the minister and not to an independent committee that takes into consideration the density of population in the cities.

o The regulations include a peculiar rule which allows physically disabled people to authorize others to vote on their behalf. There is another rule which settles the problem of a tie vote by drawing lots between candidates instead of having a re-run.

o Contestations and grievances are to be considered by quasi-judicial commission appointed by the minister although the norm is that the judiciary considers such disputes.

The regulations thus raise a number of concerns that remain to be resolved.

As for Kuwait, municipal elections were postponed for one year (law no. 83 of 2003, approved by the parliament on May 17, 2004) despite the fact that the outlines for a new Kuwait City municipal bill had been agreed to by the government.[13] As part of that bill, women would not only be allowed to vote but also run as candidates for the municipal council. The revision to the existing municipal law (no. 15 of 1972) had been forwarded to the parliament in July 2003, where it continues to be debated due to number of objections, mainly with regard to the redrawing of constituent districts. A further law (no. 55 of 2004) issued by the Emir and stipulating a further postponement of the elections for an additional year, or one year from the date of the new municipal law

has not received any parliamentary approval.[14]

B- Developments related to anti-terror legislation

All six GCC member states have ratified the 'Arab Convention to the Suppression of Terrorism' concluded by the council of Arab Ministers of Interior and Justice in Cairo in April 1998, which came into effect on May 7, 1999. Furthermore, the GCC Ministers of Interior signed a joint 'anti-terror convention' in Kuwait on May 4, 2004.[15]

On an individual state level, there were two additional anti-terror laws promulgated in 2004: Law No. 3 of 2004 by the Emir of Qatar on February 16, 2004 and the 2004 decree no.1 of 2004 (Combating Terror Crimes) issued by the UAE President on July 28, 2004. Qatar and the UAE are the only GCC countries to put legislation in effect against a crime previously undefined, a move that formally implements their obligations towards the world community in terms of UN Security Council Resolution 1373.

These laws were issued despite the fact that neither state faced any direct terrorist actions on its territory, except for one minor incident in Qatar. This is not to argue that states should not take precautions against any breaches of security.

All six GCC member states have ratified the 'Arab Convention to the Suppression of Terrorism' concluded by the council of Arab Ministers of Interior and Justice in Cairo in April 1998.

Nevertheless, a close reading of the provisions of both laws also reveals that numerous violations are now classified as being acts of terrorism that previously were not designated as such. Being more detailed than the Qatari law, the UAE law comprises

---

[13] www.alommah.gov.kw

[14] This inability to move forward off this issue continued through the sessions held by November 23, 2004. See www.kuna.net.kw

[15] This convention was signed in response to the resolution passed by the

GCC Supreme Council at its twenty fourth session held in Kuwait on December 22, 2003. It is awaiting ratification by the legislatures in each of the states for it to come into effect.

45 detailed articles covering a host of crimes that are now classified as terrorism.[16] The Qatari law consists of only 22 articles. It should also be mentioned that while in the case of the Qatari law advice was sought from the Shura Council, the UAE draft law was approved and enacted in the first week of April 2004 by the legislative technical committee headed by the Deputy Minister of Justice for Legislation and was subsequently issued by decree in July 2004 without any debate or consultation taking place in the Federal National Council.

Whereas the US and the UK define a terrorist crime as one which aims to "realize a political or social objective," the laws issued by Qatar and the UAE do not explicitly define what constitutes a terrorist crime thereby allowing the concept to be interpreted in the broad sense. In fact, the UAE law classifies "refraining from a certain act" as a terrorist crime, something which neither the Arab convention nor even the FBI have referred to, although the law is qualified in the sense that terrorizing people should be the intention of those who refrain from such acts. The two laws do not list names of groups and organizations that are deemed as terrorist either. Having such lists is, however, necessary so that people are aware of such groups' activities and can disassociate themselves completely from them.

There are other additional shortcomings to consider. For example, the right to appeal is confined to cases involving the freezing of assets. Furthermore, it does not apply to measures such as detention without charge, which at the moment is allowed for a period of six months despite the fact that the period for maximum detention defined in the penal code for ordinary offences is 21 days and can only be renewed by a separate order of the court.[17] Restricting the freedom of a person even if he/she were a suspect for up to six months by way of detention exceeds the period provided for in the penal codes as well as in the Arab anti-terrorism convention, which authorizes detention for a maximum of sixty days starting from the date of arrest.[18] Amnesty International and the UN Human Rights Commission already have expressed reservations about the length of detention provided for in the Arab Convention for the Suppression of Terrorism. In fact, some countries considered this to be arbitrary arrest and in contravention of the International Convention for Civilian and Political Rights.[19]

In terms of the issue of capital punishment, both the Qatar and the UAE appear to expand on the concept, referring to it five and 12 times respectively. On the one hand, there is no doubt that a deterrent is provided in the form of severe penalties that commensurate with the gravity of terrorist crimes. On the other hand, however, the emphasis in these two cases stands in contrast towards the general legal trends elsewhere with the move towards restricting the use of the death penalty and the number of crimes covered by it. The result is a negative impression of the law. It would have been more appropriate to clearly state that the death sentence would only be handed down in cases where a criminal act results in the death of the victim, something which is compatible with Shari'ah law.

The UAE law goes even further by criminalizing terrorist acts whether propagated verbally or in writing. Likewise, it makes the possession or acquisition of publications or recordings related to terrorist acts a criminal offense provided that these items are meant to be distributed or used as a recruiting toll for others. One further item to be

---

[16] For more details, see Mohamed Abdullah Al-Roken, "Anti-terror law,' Ar-Ra'a Magazine, Gulf Research Center (September/October 2004): 9.
[17] This is longer than the detention period set in the British Anti-terror Act at a maximum of 28 days.

[18] Article 26/1 of the convention for countering terrorism.
[19] See "Arab Anti-terror Agreement is a great danger to Human Rights," Amnesty International, No. 1/001/2002, December 2002.

considered is the use of terminology. Thus, while terms such as 'possess,' 'acquire' and 'promote' are all precise legal terms in criminology, others like 'favor' terrorist acts are not, thereby leading to unnecessary confusion.

On the positive side, both require that perpetrators stand trial before civil court instead of state security, terrorism, or military courts as is the case in some Arab countries. The UAE law guarantees defendants the right to appeal decisions. Both laws also prohibit the financing of terror in

The Qatari and the UAE laws were the most prominent examples of anti-terror legislation. In the other GCC states, such legislation remained very limited in focus.

any shape or form, whether through passage, payment, transfer, deposition, boarding, or misrepresentation of money, provided that the perpetrator is aware of the terrorist intention of these acts. This is a necessary component in order to dry up sources of financial support underpinning terrorist activities. Finally, the two laws provide suitable ways for people to admit to their crimes and for rehabilitation. For example, they provide for exemption from punishment to those members of terrorist groups who provide information that prevent attacks or for clemency if the perpetrator cooperates with authorities in the aftermath, leading to appropriate arrests.

The Qatari and the UAE laws were the most prominent examples of anti-terror legislation. In the other GCC states, such legislation remained very limited in focus. Saudi Arabia saw the issuing of a royal decree providing for 'anti-terror allowance' to be paid to security men, general intelligence officials, and special branch forces charged with such missions.[20] In Bahrain, three laws were issued.

The first concerned the kingdom's decision to sign the UN Convention against Transnational Organized Crime and its two protocols that deal with fighting the smuggling of immigrants and trafficking in people, especially women and children.[21] The second related to Bahrain's decision to sign the International Convention for the Suppression of the Financing of Terrorism.[22] This conforms to international efforts to curb the finances of terrorist individuals and organizations, be they direct or indirect.[23]

Bahrain also agreed to sign the International Convention for the Suppression of Terrorist Bombings. Kuwait meanwhile confined its efforts to issuing the law no. 27 of 2004 to sign the latter international agreement.

C- Other legislation

In addition to the above, a number of other laws and amendments were made throughout 2004 in the GCC countries. Among the most prominent were those to the Kuwait citizenship law, those related to property issues and in the UAE case the move toward the establishment of trade unions.

Another new Kuwaiti law deals with the ownership of property by other GCC nationals. Here, the concept of reciprocity was introduced. A similar decree was issued by the Sultan of Oman which allows nationals of GCC countries to rent and buy real estate either for personal use or for investment.[25] These two laws were closely tied to a resolution passed by the GCC Supreme Council at its 23rd session held in Qatar from December 21-22, 2002

[20] Royal decree No. 90 dated 7/3/1425 H
[21] Law no. 4 of 2004, Official Gazette no. 2628, March 31, 2004.[22] Law no. 8 of 2004, Official Gazette no. 2638, March 31, 2004.
[23] Law no. 9 of 2004, Official Gazette no. 2628, June 9, 2004.

[24] Kuwait Today, No. 672. This amendment affected article (7a) of the law.
[25] Sultan Decree No. 21/2004, regulating ownership by GCC nationals of property in member states, issued November 11, 2004.

in conjunction with the GCC economic agreement. In fact, such legislation reflects the extent to which economic cooperation within the GCC countries has progressed over recent years.

In the UAE, press reports in May 2004 indicated that the Ministry of Labor and Social Affairs was drawing up a bill providing for the establishment of labor unions for the first time in the history of the country, including the idea of elected labor bodies[26]. The ministry made it clear in its statement that the main purpose of the bill was to set up labor organizations to defend the interests of workers and members of such bodies while allowing them to take up various activities. The bill would also extend the right of membership to expatriates in fixed proportions. While the ministry declared that its bill would be presented to the International Labor Organization (ILO) at its annual meeting in Geneva, the terms were never divulged. Nor has the proposal been referred to the Federal National Council for debate and opinion.

Similar to the Kuwaiti and Bahraini constitutions, the UAE constitution does not touch on the issue of labor unions. None of its articles mention such a right in clear terms, only in the indirect sense of freedom to form associations. A decision to establish labor unions needs to take into account the current realities affecting the UAE, notably the obvious demographic imbalance, the almost complete dominance of foreigners in the private sector, and the lack of efficient trade and industry policies to involve UAE nationals in this sector. The majority of nationals work in the federal public sector (ministries, public institutions, security and armed forces) and local government (official departments, municipalities) and avoid private business, professions, and crafts. There is also a general lack of trade unionist legacy in the country in addition to the fact that many expatriates come from countries where free trade unionism is either non-existent or controlled by the government. In closing, this means that the trade unionist experience as well as its awareness are completely absent.

Conclusion

The year 2004 witnessed a remarkable constitutional development in Qatar embodied by the endorsement of a permanent national constitution. It is expected that Qatar will in the near future hold free and democratic legislative elections open to all political groups. It is hoped that the stipulations embedded in the constitution will be implemented, particularly as far as the principles of human rights, ministerial accountability and transparency are concerned.

A stark contradiction is dominant in many developing countries, including the GCC States. It lies in the gap between the dispensations of optimistic constitutional texts, on the one hand, and the harsh daily reality. As a consequence, many people in most of the developing countries have lost confidence in the power of their constitutions and the promises floated by politicians.

In terms of legislation, the GCC countries saw the unfolding of two key and qualitative developments. The first one has to do with the implementation of the right of Saudi citizens to participate in municipal elections. Though some reservations have been voiced about the limited scope of participation in those elections, the very fact that elections are planned in the Kingdom is in itself a promising sign, indicating that the authorities in Saudi Arabia have responded positively to some domestic demands and to the changes unravelling across the region.

---

[26] *Al Bayan*, May 27, 2004.

The second development relates to issuing of two anti-terrorism laws during 2004. It is important to note in this context that there should be a balance between the right of the state to safeguard its own national security and face any threats by enacting swift and efficient means on the one hand, and the citizens' right to protect their public freedoms and fundamental rights on the other. This, to be sure, is not an easy task, as has been amply manifested by the experience of many countries with a long history in democratic practices and respect for human rights.

Legislative Institutions in the GCC States: Analysis and Assessment

Muhammad Salem Al-Mazroo'i

Secretary-General, Federal National Council, UAE

Legislative institutions are acquiring increasing importance within political systems, particularly within the context of the process of democratization, part of which is based on the holding of regular elections to set up such institutions. Thus, it is important to analyze and assess the performance of parliaments at the legislative and supervisory levels, as this is considered an indication of the degree to which democracy exists within the political system. Specifically, this should reflect the application of the basic democratic principle of the separation of powers as this also indicates the ability of the political system to adapt to new developments in a world characterized by rapid change.

This report seeks to monitor, analyze and assess the performance of legislative institutions in the GCC states in the year 2004, with respect to the nature and extent of the efficacy of the exercise of the authorities and powers vested in them pursuant to the institutions, basic regulations and bylaws. It will also address the manner in which these institutions have exercised their function in the field of legislation and supervision. Because matters pertaining to the legislative institutions in some GCC states are still classified, the analysis will be limited in terms of the information available.

There are a number of quantitative and qualitative criteria that have been used in specialized political studies regarding the performance of legislative institutions that cannot be addressed in detail in this context. Of greater importance is that the assessment of the performance of any legislative institution should focus on the powers and authority it possesses in conformity with the constitution, laws and bylaws that regulate its action. Judgment of its performance, then, should be carried out within this frame of reference and pursuant to the degree of its efficiency in exercising its powers. For reference, tables (1) and (2) attached hereto detail the legislative powers and the supervisory capacities of legislative institutions in the GCC states.

During the year 2004, legislative institutions in all of the GCC states were in session, although according to different schedules and timings. During this year, some councils also began to exercise new powers that had been vested in them and apply new methods that had been approved, as exemplified by the Shura Council in both the Kingdom of Saudi Arabia and the Sultanate of Oman. In the following, an overview of each of the respective GCC States is provided.

The United Arab Emirates

In the year 2004, the Federal National Council (FNC) completed its second term of the thirteenth legislative session. The first term had commenced on

February 18, 2003. In terms of its composition and extended powers, there occurred no changes during either the first or the second terms.

The Legislative Function

As the National Council has no jurisdiction regarding the proposal of laws, draft laws are referred to it by the government for consideration. While the Council is empowered to discuss and amend such draft laws by deletion from, addition to or rejection of the laws, this is not final decision as it is the Supreme Council of the Federation that has such jurisdiction and is the final authority in this respect. With regard to laws passed by decree, as well as the decrees that cover international agreements and treaties, the Council can only express its observations. The same applies also to financial matters. While the constitutional provisions provide that the final accounts and the general budget of the Federation should be brought before the Council while in session, its right does not go beyond being able to provide commentary.

Draft Laws: Eight draft laws were brought before the Council in 2004 including five pertaining to the amendment of laws and three related to new laws. In addition, nine financial draft laws pertaining to final accounts were referred to the FNC, as well as one draft law referring to the general budget of the Federation. Moreover, 29 decrees, including two legislative and 27 decrees pertaining to agreements and treaties were forwarded to the Council. In all these cases, the amendments presented were only partial and did not cover substantive changes. The Maritime Law, for example, contained 433 articles and was discussed in just one session, during which the Council introduced only some minor amendments. Also,

during a closed session, the National Council raised the question of "constitutional reforms."[1] When observing the manner in which the Council dealt with the legislation in accordance with its powers, one can see that several sessions are required to study draft laws. Of particular note is the fact that while the Council recognized the draft laws brought before it, it did not comment on any of them.

The Supervisory Function

The Council is entitled to exercise its supervisory powers through a number of options, including questioning, general discussion, and the issuing of recommendations and complaints. The Council exercised these options during its present term with members putting forth 22 questions, adopting 18 subjects for discussion and issuing 11 recommendations. In view of the confidentiality of the committee meetings, the number of complaints made is unknown.

In terms of the supervisory role and the way it exercises its powers, the Council is still discussing the same issues as in the previous terms, albeit under different titles. There were, however, some items pertaining to developments, such as the bolstering of the federal budget resources after the Council realized, based on responses by ministers, that there was a financial problem that restricted the ability to execute federal projects required by the ministries. Another matter related to the creation of job opportunities for citizens in the private sector as the problem of unemployment has become rampant in the community. In this regard, the council raised three issues, all focused in the direction of finding solutions to the problem. Finally, there was the complaint about the low standard of services in the remote areas of the UAE which prompted the

---

[1] *Al-Sharq Al-Awsat*, June 6, 2004.

Council to set up a committee to visit these areas and report on the conditions.

The State of Qatar

Since the inception of the state and the establishment of the Shura Council in Qatar in the early 1970s, there have been no major changes in the manner of the formation of the Council and its powers. The new constitution, however, approved in a referendum in 2003, promulgated by the Emir on June 8, and to become official one year after its publication in the Official Gazette, (i.e. in 2005)[2] states that a new council will replace the current one. As a result, the performance of the Shura Council during the period in question has to be seen in light of the uncertainty of its continuation, as there were rumors of the impending issuance of a decree ending its activities and initiating the application of the new constitution.

The Legislative Function

As the Council is not empowered to propose laws, all the draft laws which it considers are referred to it by the government. Among the most important ones in 2004 were: an anti-terrorist law, a draft law on commercial cover-up, a draft law on regulating the acquisition of and benefiting from property and residential units by non-Qataris, a draft law on the transformation of consumer cooperative societies into Qatari joint stock companies and a draft law on the establishment of the Qatari charity board. The anti-terrorist draft law and the draft law on the Qatari charity board most likely emanate from similar policies enacted by other GCC and Arab states following the events of September 11, 2001.

There are several observations on the performance of the Council that can be made in this respect:

o The consideration by the Council of more than one draft law in one session and the short period allocated to the study of these draft laws by the relevant committees. This was clearly manifested in the last session held on June 28, 2004 during which the Council discussed four draft laws only one week after referring them to the relevant committees. These draft laws included one on an amendment to the existing advocacy law, one on regulating the auditing profession, one on establishing a general board concerned with minor affairs and one on the custody of the property of minors.

o Failure by the Council to introduce substantial amendments to the decrees and draft laws referred to it as they were often approved in the same form in which they were submitted by the government.

The Supervisory Function

The Council's supervisory activity has been limited and was restricted to general matters and proposals. On general matters, the Council discussed citizen complaints against obstruction procedures applied by the Car Technical Testing Company and issued recommendations aimed at easing such procedures. As far as proposals are concerned, council members filed three in total. The first referred to the subsidiary streets of the Doha City's districts and other Qatari cities; the second concerned Doha's Securities market; and the third dealt with the industrial zone, whereby the Council demanded the allocation and distribution of lands in the zone among the citizens, particularly orphans, widows and people with a limited income. The Council's recommendations in that respect were to instruct the competent authorities to reconsider the zones of industrial lands that had

---

[2] Al-Raya Newsletter, May 25, 2004.

not been used and the re-planning and distribution of the same at symbolic prices. This was to be taken into account when establishing new industrial zones, markets or commercial centers owned by the state in order to complement the income of the aforementioned citizens, raise their standard of living and provide them with a decent life.

Although the Council is empowered to use such supervisory methods as questioning and complaints, it did not exercise the former during the recent period. It is not known whether a complaint was issued as doing so in committee is handled confidentially according to the applicable bylaw.

In general, the Council's activity was limited and inefficient whether at the legislative or at the supervisory level. Its legislative function, however, was more effective than the corresponding supervisory function, a fact that can be attributed to the number of the governmental decrees and draft laws being referred to the Council.

The Kingdom of Bahrain

Although Article 51 of the Constitution has vested the legislative power in the Shura Council and the Council (Chamber) of Deputies under the name of the "National Council," this report has chosen the Council of Deputies as a unit of analysis, as it is the elected council that enjoys the most efficient powers. The second term of the first legislative session commenced in October 2003.

Within the Council of Deputies, there are ordinary sessions and extra-ordinary sessions. In terms of the latter, the focus was on such matters as the discussion of the report of the parliamentary investigation committee pertaining to the pensions and social security funds, as well as discussion of the Council's statutes. Overall, the Council has held 29 ordinary sessions and six extra-ordinary sessions in this term.

The Legislative Function

Within the frame of the powers vested in the Council, its activities focused on constitutional amendments, draft laws and law proposals. Since the approval and application of the Constitution, a number of constitutional articles relating to the council have been debated by the political blocs in the country. The Council's committee on constitutional amendments has received numerous proposals for amendment that have dealt with the following: increasing the legislative powers of the council; restructuring the National Council (i.e. both the Shura and council of deputies) by reducing the number of the members of the former; the chairing of the joint sessions of the two Councils by the speaker; and making the Financial Supervisory Board subject to the supervision of the legislative authority. The majority of the parliamentary blocks agree on the importance of enacting these amendments despite the reservations expressed by the Shura Council and its refusal to relinquish its legislative role.

It should be mentioned that after the Council had exercised its functions during its first term, it became apparent that there was a tangible need to carry out amendments on the statutes in order to correct aspects that had negatively affected its method of operation. While the government had submitted proposals in the form of draft laws to the Council, many members considered this to be an attempt by the government to constrain the Council and limit its work. The Council did negotiate the bylaw, the most important amendments of which were the articles concerning the process of questioning. Up to that point, the bylaw provided for the process to be conducted in committees rather than the entire parliament.

With regard to draft laws, the government referred to the Council's numerous laws and decrees of both an ordinary nature and pertaining to agreements and treaties. These included the draft law on civil service and another one with reference to the regulation of the press, printing and publishing. Finally, as far as law proposals are concerned, members submitted several ones, some of which were later approved by the government. This included the Council's draft bylaw, the Workers Trade Union Law, the setting up of a disbursement fund, and the allocation of lands for endowments and political societies. Council members also pushed forward a draft law on political parties, which failed to win approval due the lack of a majority vote. Currently, the law is once again being debated by the various political blocs. Overall, in terms of their legislative function, there existed significant variation between what the Council submitted and what the government approved indicating two distinct visions.

The Supervisory Function

The Council exercised its supervisory functions as stipulated in the articles of the Constitution and, when compared to the first term, was certainly more active. The Council members submitted more than 90 questions to various ministers although none were directed at the President of the Council of Ministers. Most of the questions concerned service issues including some regarding expatriate labor and the employment of Bahraini citizens in the government and private sectors and others on economic issues including privatization. With regard to the issue of the pensions and social security fund, three separate questions were addressed to the Minister of Finance, the Minister of Labor and Social Affairs and the Minister of State respectively. Yet while the first minister was questioned by a committee - in accordance with the Council's bylaw

- the round with the Minister of Labor and Social Affairs was cancelled on the grounds of lack of jurisdiction and the one with the Minister of State not pursued due to an inconsistency in the by-laws. Even in the first session, the Minister was able to reply to all matters thus leading to no further results.

In addition to questioning, Council members submitted 145 proposals mostly concerned with matters pertaining to affairs of the Council itself; of these, the government responded to only seven. There were also demands for investigations, again primarily concerning the issue of the financial conditions of the General Boards of the Pension Fund and Social Security. An investigation committee was set up during the first term, ultimately issuing a report that highlighted statements identifying encroachments that had been made by the two boards over several years and exposing the shortcomings of those in charge. Following several extraordinary sessions, the council submitted recommendations for administrative and financial reforms. It was only until after the investigation that the questions were addressed to ministers responsible for the activity of the two boards. Other investigation committees included one concerned with the question of naturalization and one on residential matters. In the case of the former, no evidence of wrongdoing was uncovered although different opinions were expressed.

In short, the Council exercised both its legislative and supervisory powers to a good extent despite the novelty of the experiment. Nevertheless, some members remained disappointed about the overall performance.

The Sultanate of Oman

The fifth legislative term of the Omani Shura

Council started with changes affecting not only the elected members of the Council but also certain amendments to the regulations and bylaws that regulate Council activity. Among the most important amendments were:

1. Increasing the term of membership from three to four Gregorian years renewable for similar periods.

2. Operating on the basis of scheduled terms of assembly and not according to the previous system of isolated periods; as a result, the Council now has a legislative term of no less than eight months beginning in October of every year.

3. Amendment of Article 29, paragraphs A and C of the Council bylaw to read as follows: "The Council shall have the right to review the draft laws before proceeding with the adoption thereof, with the exception of the laws which public interest requires that they be referred to the Sultan." Thus, the Article's former restrictions exempting administrative and procedural laws from Council activity were abolished.

4. Authorizing the Council to submit recommendations to the Council of Ministers in connection with the draft development plans and public budgets that are referred to the council by the government before proceeding with the adoption thereof.

In assessing the council's performance, it should be pointed out much of the internal proceedings remain subject to confidentiality clauses. Overall, there were five council meetings during the last term which ended in June compared to two meetings during the same term in 2003. The first three meetings were devoted to procedural matters, such as the constitutional oath, election of the two deputy speakers and the setting up of committees. Another session was devoted to the discussion of the procedural matters in connection to the regulatory amendments; it was made clear in this session that rules and procedures had to be proposed to regulate the work of the council sessions in a manner consistent with the recent amendments. These rules and procedures were submitted to the Council at its session of January 19, 2004.

The Legislative Function

Although the Council enjoys many legislative powers, it has yet to discuss any draft law, whether referred to it by the government or on its own initiative. This aspect thus remains entirely absent from the Council's activity.

The Supervisory Function

The five Council committees submitted their plans and programs, identified the matters they would study in the two sessions, and obtained Council approval of the proposed matters. As the Council possesses a number of supervisory functions, it exercised its role through questioning, proposals and discussion requests. With regard to questions, a number were addressed to various ministers, but the replies have not yet arrived[3]. Members submitted a large and variegated number of proposals regarding the ways and means of developing and improving services and public amenities as well as ones pertaining to the constraints on economic activity; these were referred to the government for clarification. The Council also has agreed to two discussion requests, the first of which was discussed at the last session of the first term on June 22, 2004 and related to the rising prices of consumer commodities and building materials. The other matter involved the issue of social security.

The past assembly term reveals the council's limited activity whether in regard to the number of

---

[3] Based on reports published at the end of the Council's last term of assembly (the number and nature of the questions is not known).

the sessions held (not more than one per month) or in the number and nature of the subjects it discussed. Despite the Council's powers, it has refrained from exercising its legislative function. As for its supervisory function, although the five committees submitted plans concerning matters in their field of competence, the committees adopted only a few decisions and the council approved even fewer. The report of the Education and Culture Committee on the question of educational qualification and of the recognition of university degrees, for example, was referred to the Council. The Council, in turn, agreed to entrust to the committee concerned with services and local community development the study of a company that collects the accumulated financial dues owed by the citizens, and has also approved the establishment of an ad hoc committee to follow up the programs connected with the employment of national labor, a vital local subject. The results arrived at by the Council, however, are far less than convincing.

In short, the recent assembly term has to deal with the implementation of a new system of work based on the amendments introduced to the bylaws. For the council members, this means a transition process in order to ensure that new procedures are implemented and followed. Much of the delay in the council's work in the period under study here can be explained by this transitory period, particularly in view of the few sessions that were held. Moreover, the cumbersome procedures adopted by the Council and the central role of the Board of the Council's Bureau in the field of legislation and supervision have had a negative effect on the performance of the former; this is because the Bureau's approval being required in case of a study of the laws in force and its presence in the framework of general discussion is both tangible and substantial.

The State of Kuwait

The Kuwaiti National Assembly is older, more experienced and perhaps has more powers than the other Gulf councils. In 2004, the parliament held the second term of its tenth legislative session. During this period, many of the issues raised during the previous election campaign were considered.

The Legislative Function

The Kuwaiti National Assembly has numerous legislative powers including the right to propose laws, although such laws are subject to the ratification of the Emir. In total, there were 27 draft laws referred to the assembly by the executive authority while 123 draft laws remained on the legislative agenda from the first term. The various committees dealt with 94 draft laws with a further 107 draft laws pending consideration. Among the laws, this included:

o A draft law on the manner in which the state can buy and collect debts.

o A draft law on the amendment of the Kuwaiti state treasury.

o A draft law on welfare.

o A draft law on compulsory education.

o A draft law on the conversion of Kuwaiti Airlines into a joint stock company.

In terms of law proposals, a total of 222 were submitted during the second term, which started at the end of October 2003. There were also 27 proposed laws pending from the previous term. Overall, the assembly decided on 88 cases and referred them back to the government. 160 proposals laws are still under consideration including:

o An amendment to the law on electoral constituencies.

o Establishing rules for the preparation of the state's public budget and supervision of the implementation thereof, together with a section on the state's general reserve and reserve fund for future generations.

o Establishment of the constitutional court to unilaterally rule on controversies connected with the constitutionality of laws, legislative decrees and bylaws and to decide on controversies over jurisdiction among the courts.

o Establishment of an administrative supervisory board for following up administrative breaches and the criminal offences of citizens.

o Naturalization of children of naturalized individuals.

o Financial liability of ministers, deputies and agents. The government has already expressed its reservations in this regard.

o Establishment of a Kuwaiti human rights board.

o Amendment of some articles of the printed materials and publication law.

The government did approve a draft law granting Kuwaiti women suffrage and the right to stand for election to the National Assembly. This law is expected to be brought before the Assembly during 2005.

Among the most important proposals mentioned above is the amendment of the law of electoral constituencies. In 1981, the number of constituencies in Kuwait was extended from previously 10 to 25 with each constituency electing two members to the Assembly instead of the previous five. In recent years, however, it has become increasingly apparent that this system did not prevent the practices of vote-buying, transfer of votes, gross inequalities in the size of constituencies etc. In response, assembly members submitted a number of proposals ranging from a single constituency to six (commensurate with the number of current governorates), reverting back to the original number

of ten and maintaining the status quo. Out of these, the idea of re-instituting ten constituencies received the majority backing.

This has not ended the controversy with some members being accused of trying to position themselves into a favorable electoral position despite the fact that a redrawing of the electoral districts is not necessarily seen as an urgent requirement. In addition, questions remain as to whether even an amendment to the electoral law will put an end to the shortcomings of the current system. The government has tried to postpone deciding on the subject, pointing out that the amendment requires thoughtful consideration to realize its objectives and to avoid the negative outcomes generated by the previous stage. Although the government had previously approved the ten constituency idea, it later retracted its support, thereby blocking the legal quorum necessary for the discussion of the subject. The draft was then returned to the committee on internal affairs and defense for further study.

The Supervisory Function

As the assembly has numerous supervisory functions, which it regularly exercises, this consumes a large period of time for assembly members.

In terms of formal questions, members regularly file requests encompassing all fields. As ministers are members of the Assembly according to the existing bylaw, as soon as a member files his question with the office of the speaker, the latter refers it to the competent minister and the question is raised in the next session. At this point, the minister must either reply or request postponement for a period of time. In either case, the Assembly designates a certain period in each session for the responses to the filed questions. This, in turn, explains the difference between the number of questions filed by members, the time allocated at some sessions, and the number of the sessions themselves. Not all questions addressed to the ministers are answered in front of the Assembly, the reply at times merely conveyed to the requesting member if the question can be handled that way.

The constitutional articles and bylaws also specify the jurisdiction of the Assembly to conduct open questioning session of government ministers. Throughout its history, the Assembly has exercised this jurisdiction as a constitutional right, a practice that has often led to tensions between the Assembly and the government even to the point of contemplating the dissolution of the Assembly, the resignation of the ministers or the reshuffling of ministers. During the period under consideration here, the Assembly conducted three sessions: one with the Minister of Health; a second with the minister of finance; and the third with the Deputy Prime Minister and Minister of State for Cabinet Affairs and Minister of State for National Assembly Affairs.

In the session with the Minister of Health, the questioning focused on such matters as favoritism, illegal benefits, violation of human rights in the health field, breach of legal provisions, deliberate refraining by the minister from responding to questions addressed to him by the Assembly, and opposing and obstructing the investigative efforts of the competent national agencies. The session with the Minister of Finance related to the disbursement of public funds, the status of Kuwaiti investments abroad and the overall management of the ministry. In case of the Deputy Prime Minister, the focus was on administrative reforms and the combating of corruption in government institutions. In each of the cases, the session did not lead to a vote of no confidence. In the first instance no recommendations were given by the Assembly, in the second a motion of no-confidence failed to gain the necessary number of votes, and in the third case, the subject

was referred to the Audit Bureau. All of the sessions, however, revealed some shortcomings and they forced the ministers to concede to taking the Assembly's reservation into consideration. For its part, the government was unified in the questioning and was able to rally support for its position, specifically in terms of defeating the motion of no-confidence as far as the Minister of Finance was concerned. It should be noted, however, that the frequent hint by Assembly members of their intention to take minister to account also increases the tensions between the Assembly and the government.

There were also a number of subjects which Assembly members brought up for discussion. This encompassed the fields of education, health, settlement, unemployment, residence, sports; the high price of building materials; residential lands not commensurate with civil servant salaries; the role of institutions in protecting the new generation and the safeguarding of morality; Islamic values; and entertainment. Unemployment was among the most important subjects discussed, with rising rates of unemployment attributed to poor planning. Members accused the government of not being serious in effectively promoting the integration of Kuwaitis into the labor force, of failing to put forward a concrete implementation schedule and suggesting applicable mechanisms. Moreover, the question of how to fight and eliminate corruption was repeatedly raised in various sessions.

Finally, in terms of the supervisory function, Assembly members filed some 729 proposals. Under the bylaws, a proposal is to be referred to the ad hoc committee for study; the committee is then expected to submit a report on its findings to the Assembly. While the committees rejected seven proposals submitted to them, the government approved 169 proposals with the remainder still under consideration.

Regarding the performance of the Assembly, the

following observations can be made:

o Both Assembly members and the government were unanimous in their opinion that the performance was not up to expectations. A great deal of time was wasted in debates that in most cases did not lead to worthwhile results.

o The failure of assembly members to attend sessions or committee meetings has resulted in a repeated lack of a quorum when voting takes place. Thus, out of 35 sessions, which were supposed to be held from the beginning of the year until the end of the Assembly term on June 3, 2004, 22 sessions were delayed and nine were postponed; only four sessions of the Assembly were held on time. This prompted some Assembly members to file a draft law giving the assembly the authority to deal with any deputy who fails to attend five consecutive or ten intermittent sessions by publishing his name in two daily newspapers at his own expense and to deduct a portion of his remuneration. The first procedure was perhaps an activation of the provisions of the Assembly's bylaw, while the second proposal was rejected by the Assembly members.

o The supervisory function of Assembly activity has exceeded the legislative function, which in turn has obstructed the completion of many projects, proposals and draft laws that were submitted to the Assembly. Instead, the majority of the time was spent on submitting questions, preparing for questioning sessions which consumed a great deal of the assembly's time at the expense of its legislative function.

o The fact that question sessions were often preceded by public statements about possible charges and hints at measures of no-confidence meant that these sessions primarily strained the relationship with the government instead of actually resolving a particular situation. In any case, ministers were able to respond to the matters raised against them and explained their views in respect thereto.

o Although Assembly members filed a large number of parliamentary questions and proposals with the government, the responses were often not acceptable to the Assembly. This is explained in part by the tense relations between the two sides and again indicates a diversion of attention away from more pertinent matters.

o Some issues repeatedly surfaced during Assembly sessions including those related to government performance, corruption and favoritism, as well as issues that are of interest to the Kuwaiti community. The solutions proposed for such issues, however, did not lead to concrete results, for example in terms of recruitment practices, the preservation of public funds, etc.

o Many of the issues associated with election campaigns have also been the subject of debate within the respective districts of members. This is reflective of the role of the parliamentary blocs and the spirit of coordination and competition between them. The government has managed to establish itself as a strong party in the Assembly and has exercised its power to take initiatives on a number of occasions. This is particularly visible in its preparation of the draft law on the political rights of women. Pro-government elements that follow the liberal current blame the delay of the law's passage on a lack of seriousness by the government. They argue that had the government wished to see the draft law adopted, this would have been easily possible given the distribution of seats in the Assembly, on the one hand, and the noticeable shift in the attitude towards this issue since 1999 on the other.

The Kingdom of Saudi Arabia

The present session of the Shura Council, the third

to be held since its inception, was characterized by numerous developments including amendments of Articles 17 and 33 of the Council bylaws. Article 17 now reads: "the resolutions of the Shura Council shall be referred to the King for deciding on which of them are to be referred to the Council of Ministers, so that if the points of view of both the Council of Ministers and the Shura Council coincide, then the resolutions will be passed after approval by the King. In case of difference of opinion, the matter shall be returned to the Shura Council to decide as it deems appropriate and to refer its decision to the King to take whatever steps he deems fit." In accordance with this amendment, the final exchange is confined between the King and the Shura Council; the final decision, however, rests with the King alone, thereby relegating the Council to an advisory role. The amendment to article 33 has given the Shura Council the right to propose new draft laws or to propose and study a law that is in force and referring it to the King for the appropriate decisions. Although this amendment has given the Council the right to propose laws, such laws are eventually referred to the King, thereby diluting the powers given to the Council.

The current session also witnessed the appointment of a Minister of State for Shura Council Affairs within the Council of Ministers, in addition to the decision to telecast council sessions. In monitoring and assessing the performance of the Council, the confidentiality of council activity makes it somewhat difficult to gain access to information.

The Legislative Function

A large number of draft laws were referred to the council, the most important being: the draft law on combating encroachment on public funds; the draft law on the amendment of an income tax; the draft law on commercial competition; the draft law on amendments to the Saudi nationality law; the draft

law on the Credit Bank; and the draft law on imposing a highway toll system. In respect to the law pertaining to combating encroachment on public funds, the Council discussed a strategy for combating corruption and abuse of authority, including the establishment of internal supervision units within government agencies, activating citizen complaint and proposal boxes, and boosting the role of the Shura Council in the sphere of financial and administrative supervision. As far as commercial competition is concerned - a draft law which had previously been approved by the Council but was returned by the Council of Ministers following some objections - the Shura Council did not approve the suggested amendments, arguing that these would weaken the overall law and link competition policy more to the Minister of Trade rather than the Council of Ministers. The Council did approve the amendments by the Council of Ministers regarding the issue of an Income Tax Law, whereby the Council had previously approved a tax rate ranging between 20 and 25 percent. It rejected amendments concerning constraints to investment and requiring the exemption of foreign investors from taxation in the rural areas for a period of ten years as an incentive for them to move away from urban areas. The Council also approved the amendment of some articles to the Saudi Nationality Law including those pertaining to the conditions for granting and withdrawing of Saudi nationality, the consequences associated with the granting of nationality and the granting of nationality to women and their children. The Council rejected a draft law submitted by the government that provided for the imposition of fees on motorways with double lanes, instead requiring the Ministry of Transport - which was to secure the required funds from its own budget - to improve its services before considering the imposition of fees. Here it should be noted that highway fees had previously been imposed but were later cancelled.

The Council also discussed numerous agreements and treaties concluded by the government.

The Supervisory Function

In terms of its supervisory capacity, the activities of the Council were focused on reviewing the annual performance reports of the ministries, boards and institutions and on expressing its opinion. Among the reports being considered were those of the General Investment Authority, Saudi Airlines, the Saudi Credit Bank, and the Committee on the Promotion of Virtue and Prevention of Vice. The Council also discussed a number of annual performance reports pertaining to the ministries, including ones pertaining to the Ministry of Finance and National Economy. In this respect, the Council urged the adoption of a plan for eliminating the budget deficit, curtailing the public debt and bringing the debt back in line to acceptable limits. In addition, the Council studied issues such as the high costs of marriage and associated high dowries, the educational process in the kingdom, privatization, the role of the foreign media in waging a public relations campaign against the Kingdom, and the phenomenon of terrorism within the Saudi community. The Council expressed a number of views when studying these matters which were referred to the government. In terms of the high dowries and cost of marriage, the Council urged the government to provide better employment opportunities to youths, asked the Ministry of Labor and Social Affairs to coordinate its activities with those of the other ministries, and stressed the need for a state financial grant to those wishing to get married. In relation to the phenomenon of terrorism, members pointed out that the condemnation of terrorist criminal actions is not enough but that the phenomenon must be considered from all of its intellectual, economic and security facets.

Overall, the Council was unable to exercise its legislative function due to the fact that government did not submit any draft laws for consideration. The Council did study the annual performance reports of the government agencies and submitted its views in that respect. However, it has not participated in the overall discussions about the need for political reform in the Kingdom.

Factors affecting the performance of the legislative institutions in the GCC states

Many factors restrict the performance of the legislative institutions in the GCC states. Some are internal while others are of an external nature. Some of the more predominant factors include:

A- The manner in which the institution is set up:

Since there does not exist one blueprint for the establishment of legislative institutions or in the manner members are selected (appointment, partial appointment and election), the nature of the institution's inception is bound to affect its performance. This is exemplified by the manner in which the institutional members perform their legislative and supervisory functions including their procedure on the proposal of draft laws, the filing of questions and requests and the exercise of other supervisory functions. Moreover, the activity of a member is substantially influenced by the party that selected him for membership. An appointed member, for example, will take into account the policies of the executive authority and works within its framework while an elected member will focus more on his constituency, in turn, enjoying a degree of freedom in his decision-making. The elected member tends to be more active in respect to issues characterized by political sensitivity. This can certainly be noticed in the quantity and quality of the performance of the members of both the Bahraini Council of Deputies and the Kuwaiti National Assembly as opposed to the performance of the Omani Shura Council.

B- Legislative and supervisory jurisdictions:

It is obvious that the wider the jurisdictions of an institution, the more its members will exercise such rights. In those instance where constitutions and bylaws have vested the institutions with wider jurisdictions, the exercise of those right are more widespread. This is made apparent when comparing what the members of these institutions have produced in exercising their roles compared to those legislative institutions with limited jurisdictions - the latter often display a limited performance. It should, however, be noted that even those institutions with proper jurisdictions failed to live up to their expectations, a development that can be attributed to other internal factors. The respective roles of the speaker, the council office and the committees each affect performance depending on the powers vested in each entity. In some institutions, the extensive powers of the staff of the council office have an influential role inasmuch as they determine the orientation of the council when dealing with such matters as outlining the debates or referring matters for approval to the committees. This, again, is the case with regard to the Omani Shura Council.

The institution's relationship with the political system and the nature of the prevailing political culture: Legislative institutions are one part of the overall political system and they work in conjunction with other governmental bodies. The process of interaction and the nature of the roles vary from one system to another depending on the degree of openness of the system and its democratic character. In this context, many factors - both internal and external - have a bearing on determining the margin of freedom permitted by the system. For example,

the existence of an effective civil society and the role by the media can influence public opinion, thereby contributing to the legislative institution playing its normal legislative role. Moreover, external interventions may create positive or negative effects depending on their nature. In addition, the prevailing political culture in a given society, be it in terms of political consciousness, the accumulation of political experience, and the existence of social and political organizations are all factors that impact on the performance of legislative institutions. This is particularly the case in view of the fact that political and social forces have an impact whether they are represented in institutions or not. This is illustrated in the Kuwaiti National Assembly, in which various forces and blocs are able to participate in the deliberations of the assembly and determine its orientation. The same thing applies in the case of the Bahraini Council of Deputies, where the participating forces, the political organizations and non-participatory entities remain very influential in determining council performance.

Conclusion

In the near-term, it is unlikely that the role of legislative institutions in the GCC States will change significantly due to the similarity of the issues currently being discussed and the inability of the existing political systems to manage the political process in their own favor. In February 2005, the thirteenth legislative session of the Federal National Council will come to an end, the same applies to the Shura Council in the Kingdom of Saudi Arabia while the Shura Council in the Qatar will wind up its activities only to see an elected Shura Council take over in accordance with the new constitution.

The Kuwaiti National Assembly and the Bahraini

Council of Deputies will each witness discussions on constitutional and bylaw amendments, including such items as the electoral constituencies in Kuwait, the draft law on political rights of women, and the law pertaining to political societies in Bahrain. The Kuwaiti

Assembly is also expected to continue to make use of the questioning prerogative as well as other means of parliamentary supervision. This is particularly true in the context of current events inside the country and its associated developments.

Table (1) Legislative Jurisdictions

Legislative Powers	The United Arab Emirates	The Kingdom of Bahrain	The Kingdom of Saudi Arabia	The Sultanate of Oman	The State of Qatar	The State of Kuweit
Draft laws	Discusses only what is referred to it by the executive authority and is entitled to make amendments by addition, deletion and rejection but the final say rests with the Supreme Council of the Federation	Discusses what is referred to it and has the right to amend by addition, deletion and rejection	Discusses what is referred to it by the government (Council of Ministers) and has the right to make amendments by addition, deletion and rejection. The final say rests with the King	Discusses what is referred to it by the Council of Ministers and has the right to make amendments by addition, deletion, except for the laws which the Sultan deems it necessary to pass	They are referred to the Council by the government. It has the right to make amendments by addition, deletion and rejection	They are referred to it after being prepared by the government and has the right to make amendments by addition, deletion and rejection. They are passed only when approved by it
Draft laws	Does not have the right to propose	Has the right to propose	Has the right but the King decides	Can consider laws in force and propose amendment thereof	Has no right to propose	Has the right to propose
Legislative decrees	may be issued by the head of state and the Council of Ministers without referral to the Council	They are referred to the Council and treated as laws	Not mentioned in the law and bylaw	The Sultan has jurisdiction and are not referred to him	The Emir has jurisdiction in issuing them and the Council discusses them	Although issued by the Emir, they are referred to the Council for final say
Agreements and Treaties	The Council makes observations thereon only	Referred to it by the government and requires its approval	Studied by the Council who can approve, postpone or makes reservations on some items	Not mentioned in the constitution	Referred to the Council after being referred to the Emir	There are two kinds of treaties but they are issued by laws. Hence the Council's approval is required

Table (2) Supervisory Jurisdictions

Supervision Powers	The United Arab Emirates	The Kingdom of Bahrain	The Kingdom of Saudi Arabia	The Sultanate of Oman	The State of Qatar	The State of Kuweit
Questions	has	has	Has not	has but lies with the ministers of services	Has	has
Discussion Demands	has the right but with the approval of the council of ministers	has the right to submit them within its jurisdiction	has no right to submit them	has the right to submit them within its jurisdiction	has the right	has the right
Desires	has not	has the right	has not	has the right within its jurisdiction	has the right	has the right
Complaints and Petitions	has the right to accept and discuss them	has the right to accept and discuss them	has no right	has no right	has no right	has the right to accept and discuss them
Questionings	has no right	has the right to carry out same	has no right	has no right	has no right	has the right to carry out same
Investigation Committees	has no right	has the right to form them	has no right	has no right	has no right	has the right to form them

Section Two

The Economies of the GCC States

Economic Performance and the Challenges of Non-Oil Economic Growth

Dr. Fatima Al-Shamsi

Assistant Professor of Economics, UAE University

Since the early 1970s, GCC economies have known unprecedented socio-economic transformations embodied chiefly in an increasingly fast-paced economic growth. The result has been a structural transition from primitive to well-developed economies. Oil revenues have been at the heart these transformations also indirectly rolling the wheel of development of the various economic sectors, creating job opportunities and improving the overall socio-economic indicators.

However, in the wake of repeated oil crises and the subsequent fluctuations of oil revenues, calls were issued for the GCC countries to overhaul their economic systems by reducing their reliance on oil-generated income and encouraging instead privatization and offering incentives to attract foreign direct investments (FDIs). Global changes in the contemporary world economic order have added a new dimension, making it an imperative for the GCC countries to review their economic policies and legislative frameworks. At the same time, the GCC countries need to assess their unification experience in order to move forward from tenuous cooperation to genuine integration. In fact over the past decade, the need to build sustainable economic integration in the region has become more pressing for numerous reasons, mainly the fact that member states of the GCC are faced with the same problems and domestic economic challenges represented by such issues as expatriate labor, rising unemployment among nationals, the deficit prone public budgets, the need to diversify the sources of income, and the necessity of building an economic platform capable of undermining the risks associated with the fluctuations of oil revenues.

This paper seeks to shed light on the major factors that impact the policies slated to diversify the sources of national income in the GCC countries by tracing and analyzing their economic performance during 2004. The paper also examines key indicators of growth in tandem with a slew of determinants that affect economic developments, trying to link ongoing transformations with efforts deployed to boost better economic coordination and integration among the six GCC countries.

Factors affecting the economic performance of the GCC countries

The surge of oil prices in world markets during 2004 had wide implications for the GCC economies whose GDP is made up of 35 to 45% of oil revenues while oil and oil products account for 60 percent of GCC exports. Throughout 2003 and 2004, GCC economies witnessed a period of economic boom, as rates of GDP growth increased, deficits in public budgets were reduced, economic activities were boosted by expanding the size of public spending, upgrading infrastructures and conducting scores of development projects while performance levels jumped and profits posted by financial and banking organizations picked up.

Rising oil prices along with increased productivity and accumulated oil revenues led to higher GDP and GDP per capita rates. The data included in Table 1 indicates that the annual growth rates hit 4% while GDP per capita climbed to US$ 11,142 in 2004. Rising oil prices also contributed to a substantial growth of exports by 21% whereas the size of imports picked up by 0.4% in 2004. External debt totaled US$ 92.5 billion as shown on Table 2.

Even though the GCC countries share roughly the same cultural, social and political attributes, their economic performance varies as is indicated by Table 2. In 2004, individual income in proportion to GDP averaged 3% in the Sultanate of Oman and 8% in Qatar.

Chart (1) Size of public debt in proportion to GDP of the GCC countries in 2003

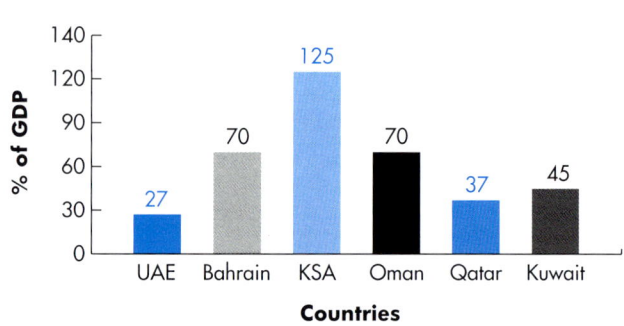

Source: Emirates Industrial Bank, Issue No. 7, July 2004.

Fluctuations of GDP growth rates closely reflect the interconnection between levels of GDP and oil prices. As

Table (1) Key economic indicators in the GCC countries*

Year	2001	2002	2003	2004**
GDP (billion dollar)	333.5	341.5	366	381.9
Rates of real domestic product (%)	4.7	2.4	7.1	4.3
Population (in million)	30.62	31.76	32.91	33.1
Per Capita Income (in US$)	10892	10573	10662	11142
Total exports (in billion dollar)	163.4	157.1	172.7	209.3
Total imports (in billion dollar)	79.9	87.6	102.6	103
Trade balance (in billion dollar)	83.5	69.5	70.1	106.3
Oil ex[ports (in billion dollar)	100.7	96.0	101.5	130.3
Oil in proportion to total exports	61.6	61.1	59.7	62.2
Gross oil revenues (in billion dollar)	112	120	140	
Gross external debt (in billion dollar)	89.4	93.3	98.5	92.5

* Source: The figures incuded in the table are based on data collected from official documents together witrh reports published by the Economic Intelligence Unit (EIU)
** As per economic forecasts

prices of crude oil rise, so do rates of annual GDP growth and as oil prices dip, so do the rates of GDP.

Similarly, the structures of the economies of the GCC countries and economic policies slated to diversify the sources of income vary. While the sector of transformative industries grows rapidly in Saudi Arabia, trade and tourism come at the forefront of economic activities in the UAE. In Bahrain, it is the banking sector that rules the day while in the Sultanate of Oman and Qatar energy and natural gas sectors dominate the economic scene. There are also notable variations among the GCC countries in terms of the size of public debt in proportion to GDP. Data included in Chart 1

indicate that the size of debt in proportion to GDP during 2003 ranged between 27 and 125%.

Economic challenges facing the GCC countries

The concern here in terms of the challenges faced by GCC States is those imposed by the ongoing economic transformation. In recent years, there has been much buzz about the role of structural economic transformations in correcting existing economic disfigurements and

Table (2) Key economic indicators of the GCC countries (per individual country)*

	Year	UAE	Bahrain	KSA	Oman	Qatar	Kuwait
GDP (in billion dollar)	2002	71.1	7.7	188.2	19.5	19.7	35.3
	2003	76.1	8.2	201.8	19.9	21.2	38.8
	2004*	80.3	8.7	208.5	20.5	23	40.9
GDP growth	2002	1.9	5.1	1	1.8	3	-0.4
	2003	7	6.8	7.2	2.2	7.8	9.9
	2004*	5.5	5.6	3.3	2.8	8.5	5.5
GDP per capita (in US$)	2002	18971	12252	8021	12250	27990	14140
	2003	24244	15776	9327	12150	32945	17942
Inflation	2002	2.9	0.5	-0.6	-0.7	1	1.4
	2003	3.1	1.6	0.6	0.3	2.3	1.2
	2004	3.2	2	0.8	0.5	3.5	2.3
Deficit/surplus (% of GDP)	2002	-11.2	-1.3	-4	3.8	8	26.7
	2003	-4.6	0.5	5.6	3.7	6.6	23.8
	2004	-2	6.3	3.5		11.6	33.5
Trade balance (% of GDP)	2002	5	-1.6	6.3	11.2	0.3	11.7
	2003	8.5	-3.4	13.8	7.1	21.3	18.2
	2004	14.9	-15	16.3	-3.8	24.6	24.8
External debt (in billion dollar)	2002	20.2	3.8	37.3	5.7	15.4	13.1
	2003	21.5	4.7	32.5	5.7	17.5	14.1
	2004	22.9	6.2	34.3	5.8	18.6	15

* Sources: Calculated on the basis of information included in The Economist Intelligence Unit (EIU), Country reports, IMF (2004) World Economic Outlook, 193.

creating a balance and diversification at the level of the economic production platform in a bid to step into the international economic order.

Declining oil prices over the past few years have concretely contributed to accelerating economic reforms and strengthening efforts seeking to enact appropriate economic remedies as the most sustainable choice capable of putting an end to structural economic imbalances emanating from fluctuating oil prices. This also applies to the public budget deficits and preparations for joining the World Trade Organization (WTO). In that context, it is necessary to look into the most critical economic transformations that have unfolded in the GCC countries and analyze their overall implications on the performances of the economies.

A- Diversifying sources of national income

In order to diversify sources of national income and embrace economic policies able to create a durable and sustainable platform away from over-relying on oil, many economic analysts in the GCC have called for the implementation of economic policy-making reforms to speed up the growth process in the non-oil sectors. Over the last few years, the non-oil sectors have gradually contributed in greater measure to the GDP. Their contribution in 2004 accounted for an aggregated 63 percent of the GDP of all GCC countries. As the share of goods production in the GDP represents some 57 percent, the oil industry appears to stand tall on the economic stage. As for the service sector, production services contribute some 24% of the GDP. The wholesale and retail trade sectors take up some 8.3%, followed by real estate with 5.7%, transports by 5.6%, and the financing and insurance sectors representing about 4%. Social services, including public services, housing and other services,

Chart (2) Gross Domestic Product according to economic sectors

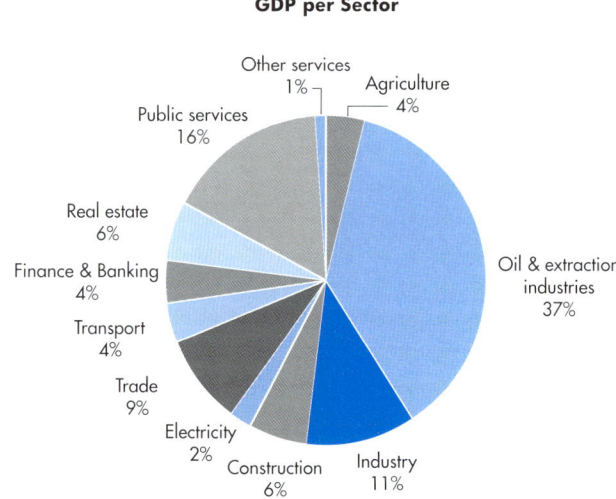

GDP per Sector

Other services 1%
Agriculture 4%
Public services 16%
Real estate 6%
Finance & Banking 4%
Transport 4%
Trade 9%
Electricity 2%
Construction 6%
Industry 11%
Oil & extraction industries 37%

Sources: Arab Monetary Fund, *Unified Arab Economic Report* (Abu Dhabi: 2003), Global Investment House, *Economic & Strategic Outlook*, different issues.

contributed around 16% of the GDP in 2004, as illustrated in Table 3 and Chart 2. At the level of the components of the goods production, transformative industries dominate all other industrial activities, contributing some 10% of the non-oil GDP followed by the construction and agricultural sector.

Based on the above, it is clear that the GCC governments have made serious efforts to diversify their economic production platforms, however, there are still marked variations at the level of the performance of the non-oil sector. It is of utmost importance to emphasize the need for the GCC countries to formulate policies of economic diversification suitable for the GCC existing economic structures within a regional framework. In fact, economic policies need to be designed in such a way as to ensure that recent developments in the international oil markets do not yield a negative impact on the performance of the non-oil sectors over the next coming years. That could lead to a retreat of the role of non-oil industries in sustaining the GDP as a result of the undermined feeling among economic policy-makers about the need to diversify sources of national income.

B- Budgets and increasing public debts

Over the past years, and as a consequence of the deficits that beset public budgets due to declining oil prices, the governments of the GCC countries resorted to belt-tightening financial policies embodied particularly in substantially reducing the size of public spending by putting off or canceling altogether capital investments without at the same time affecting current spending which stands in excess of 40% of GDP. However, the momentous rise

in oil prices in tandem with the surge of the size of oil production during the second half of 2003 and the first half of 2004 helped the GCC governments overcome their public deficits. As a result, all the GCC countries have posted a budget surplus during 2004, as Table 4 shows.

No doubt, declining deficit rates and a better balance between revenues and public spending could be regarded as indicators of positive economic performance in 2004 although huge public debt and the continued disparity among the individual GDPs of the GCC countries might impede the smooth implementation of the fundamental principles on which the project for the GCC monetary union, scheduled to go into effect by 2010, rests. Figures included in Chart 1 indicate that

Table (3) GCC States GDP by economic sectors (in million $) current rates of 2004

Sector	UAE	Bahrain	KSA	Oman	Qatar	Kuwait	Total	% GDP
Agriculture	2498	56	10425	421	70	205	13675	3.6
Oil & Extraction	25136	2574	71890	8540	13800	18405	140345	36.8
Industry	10708	972	20850	1568	1380	2863	38341	10.1
Construction	5018	329	13510	513	1610	918	21898	5.7
Electrical power	1472	194	2185	212	230	818	5111	1.3
Gross goods production	44832	4125	118860	11254	17090	23209	219370	57.5
Trade	8576	733	15595	2562	1150	2863	31479	8.3
Transports	6309	643	10425	1390	690	2045	21502	5.6
Banking & Financing	4912	553	8380	186	920	2454	17405	4.6
Real estate	5662	712	12540	863	NA	2120	21897	5.7
Gross production services	25459	2641	46940	5001	2760	9482	92283	24.2
Public services	7816	1348	38530	2016	2860	8589	61159	16
Other services	1774	434	4170	1889	NA	205	8472	2.2
Gross social services	9590	1782	42700	3905	2860	8794	69631	18.3

* Sources: Calculated from Global Investment House, Economic & Strategic Outlook, different issues and the Economist Intelligence Unit EIU Country Reports

the size of public debt in proportion to the GDP ranges between 27% in the UAE and 125% in Saudi Arabia. As the situation stands today, there is certainly a pressing need to formulate well-thought plans to appropriately invest increased oil revenues and adopt financial reform policies in order to reduce public debt so that it does not exceed 60% in proportion to GDP.

C- Privatization and boosting the role of the private sector

Privatization and an expanded role of the private sector in the national economy are among the best recognized instruments to enact economic reforms. Unsurprisingly, privatization and the efficient role of the private sector finds wide support among international organizations, particularly the World Bank (WB) and the International Monetary Fund (IMF).

Fluctuating oil prices and continued public budget deficits in the GCC countries over the last few years have led many economic analysts and international financial organizations to call for a reduction of the role of the state in managing economic activities by moving to put on sale many public enterprises to private sector operators and handing over public administrations for private management. In fact, all the GCC countries have enacted a slew of positive measures in a bid to engage the private sector in managing the process of economic growth by making production and service investments. Some GCC countries have decided to privatize the power and water sectors along with those of transports and communications. In July 2004, the UAE announced the establishment of Abu Dhabi Holding Company that will be entrusted with the task of managing all the companies belonging to the General Industrial Company in addition to the Dar Real Estate Company as part of the privatization process. In the meantime, the UAE authorities seem to be moving steadily towards privatizing the federal electricity companies while reducing the role of the government in other economic activities to the benefit of the private sector (including private foreign companies).

In Saudi Arabia, the government announced in October 2003 a privatization program covering international and domestic aviation services, apart from security services. Five agreements were linked with Saudi companies with a total value of SR638

Table (4) Total imports and spending in the GCC countries in 2003 (in million$)*

	UAE	Bahrain	Saudi Arabia	Oman	Qatar	Kuwait
Total revenues	20106.8	2119.7	78771.7	6753.2	8009.6	23475.9
Oil	15113.5	1303.2	65956	4768.8		20847.1
%	75	61	83.7	70.6		88.8
Other	4993.3	816.5	12815.7	1984.4		2628.8
%	25	39	16.3	29.4		11.2
Total spending	23711.6	3079.8	66755.7	7792.2	6404.4	15924.1
Investments	4165.6	877.7	8651.5	1755.8		1105.5
%	18	28.5		22.5		6.9
Current	19546	2202.1	58104.1	6036.4		14818.6
%	82	71.5		77.5		93.1
Deficit/Surplus	-3604.8	-960.1	12016	-1039	1605.2	7551.8

* Source: Secretariat-General of the Gulf Cooperation Council, Economic Newsletter, Riyadh, 2003.
  Investment House, Economic & Strategic Outlook, different issues.

million for the management of regional and domestic airports, according to a report by Global Research published in 2004. In January 2004, the Saudi government granted a lease contract to a private company to take charge of managing the production and distribution of electrical power and water.

In Kuwait, the government announced a plan for the creation of three joint-stock companies with the government holding a 20% share and with a capital investment amounting to KD60 million for each share-holding company. All three companies should own at least twenty benzene stations owned by Kuwait Petroleum Company. In March 2004, a preliminary agreement was sealed to transform Kuwait Aviation Company into a joint-stock company and sell it off to the private sector.

In Bahrain, thirty private companies came forward in 2003 with a proposal to establish a mobile telephony company while internet service supply was also privatized. In 2004, the first private power company was set up in Bahrain. In Qatar, the public telecommunications company was partially privatized and the electricity and water company was transformed into a joint-stock company. A company for transporting gas was established with a capital investment amounting to QR4.6 billion while 50% of the new company was put up for public subscriptions. In the Sultanate of Oman, the energy sector was privatized and eighteen companies submitted a bid in 2003 to win a contract for developing the industrial infrastructure of Sahar seaport.

In spite of all the above-mentioned measures, things do not seem to be moving as swiftly as expected. Indeed, the process of privatization is still lagging behind, probably because the process of transferring public-owned companies to private ownership entails myriad economic, financial and legal procedures. Privatization also requires the availability of administrative departments capable of planning and organizing the process in highly efficient ways.

Thus even though financial markets have evolved in all the GCC countries in the past two years, the fact remains that these countries still lack the requisite legal frameworks capable of upholding the process of transferring public companies to the private sector. Similarly, economic restructuring has not unfolded in accordance with the required changes in financial and monetary policies. Financial instruments have failed to stimulate domestic saving or attract foreign investments.

D- Labor markets: Unemployment and the development of human resources

The GCC labor markets are characterized by the excessive reliance on expatriate labor, a fact that reflects the limited size of the local labor force and the dearth of domestic labor supply. In fact, expatriate workers in most GCC countries account for about 75% of the total size of the labor force. Growth rates of the national labor force in the GCC countries ranges between 3.7% as in Oman and 1.9% in Qatar. Women represent about 19% of the GCC total labor force. Kuwait posts the highest rate of women's participation with 24% whereas the UAE registers the lowest rate at 13%.

In recent years, the GCC countries have been faced with the formidable challenge posed by the unemployment phenomenon and the need to secure jobs for nationals, particularly among university graduates. However, there is no updated data on rates of unemployment in the GCC countries. Available statistics indicate that unemployment rates range between 6% in Bahrain and 15% in the UAE as shown in Table 5.

To be sure, increasing rates of visible unemployment in countries with limited populations and rising rates of expatriate entrants in the local labor markets in excess of normal growth rates, adds a new dimension to the challenges associated with development in the GCC countries. The current situation also represents a blatant squandering of human and financial resources. It runs counter to appropriately benefiting from human capital thanks to education and training. These conditions call for a serious review of educational and training policies together with the need to articulate labor policies that could be deployed and sustained over the long run.

On another level, emphasis ought to be placed on the fact that the GCC countries do have a large platform of human resources that possess competitive capabilities and are driven by the ambition to take up a positive role in the development process of their nations. Obviously, GCC human resources are in need of being rehabilitated to become employable and move out of 'disguised' unemployment by being crammed in governmental departments without any productive contribution.

Perhaps the increasing difficulties encountered by the government sector to create jobs for GCC nationals may be a positive indicator that would induce educated nationals to step outside the circle of 'disguised' or visible unemployment and take up truly productive jobs by searching for real job offers on the labor market, i.e. the type of jobs that link efforts with merited return and rely on heavy capitalization and advanced technologies.

Although many GCC countries have sought to devise national strategies to employ job-seekers, including offering subventions to train nationals in private sector organizations, restructuring the national labor force, raising the levels of professional habilitation, and updating data on the local labor markets and job vacancies, efforts remain modest and the problem of unemployment as a result continues to be as persistent as ever, if not actually on a steady rise.

The regime of nationalization quotas and the mandatory regulations obliging private sector organizations to employ GCC nationals might prove to be successful in the short term, but in the longer term the GCC governments ought to work out employment policies that cater to the real needs and requirements of the labor market, policies that link performance and efficiency with productivity and reflect the real costs of worker employment. The GCC governments need to enact policies built on the principle of encouraging the private sector to move beyond its current negative attitudes towards

Table (5) GCC labor market indicator 2003 (in million people and in %)

	Total labor force	Labor force % to population	Growth rate	%	National labor force	Expatriate labor force	%	Share of women	Unemployment rate
UAE	2.006	42.1	2	10	0.203	1.803	90	13.3	15
Bahrain	0.319	43	2.7	40	0.127	0.192	60	20.8	5.5*
Saudi Arabia	7.708	27.9	3.4	31	2.098	5.61	69	18.8	9.6
Oman	1.18	30.2	3.7	40	0.472	0.708	60	19.9	15
Qatar	0.32	55.2	1.9	17	0.053	0.267	83	17	11.6*
Kuwait	0.937	37.7	2.8	18	0.165	0.772	84	23.7	9
Total	12.47	39.5	2.8	25	3.118	9.352	75	18.9	11

Notes: * for 2001
Sources: Arab Monetary Fund, Unified Arab Economic Report (Abu Dhabi: 2003), Gulf Center for Studies: Al-Khaleej Newspaper, Gulf Economic Report (2004)

employing the national labor force. The private sector, indeed, ought to take on its national role by striving to create jobs for nationals and help groom their practical and management skills.

E- Integrating and coordinating GCC policies

The Unified Economic Agreement (UEA) sealed in 1981 offered a detailed theoretical framework built on the principle of gradualism in adopting diverse paradigms for economic cooperation and coordination among the six member states of the GCC starting with trade liberalization and culminating in economic unification. However, real implementation of the stipulations of the UEA did not go into effect before January 2003 with the GCC counties imposing unified tariff duties as a preliminary step towards boosting intra-GCC trade through a custom union. This has indeed facilitated the movement of nationally produced goods and contributed to an increase of the volume of trade exchange as the size of exports and re-export jumped by 23% in 2003 (as reported Emirates Industrial Bank Newsletter, February 2004).

In January 2003, the GCC countries officially pegged their national currencies to the US dollar after Kuwait came on board and in line with the customs union agreement. Additionally, some GCC governments granted all GCC nationals the right to own real estate properties and take on professions previously reserved exclusively for their own nationals. Still, the volume of intra-GCC trade exchange remains limited and does not exceed 6% out of the total external trade, as Table 6 demonstrates. This is attributable in large part to what is commonly referred to as 'dormant effects of economic integration.' In spite of existing trade exchange among the GCC countries, its volume does not match the dominating economic conditions in the GCC countries, for their economic structures are, broadly speaking, similar in terms of resources and as such do not possess a competitive economic production platform.

Moreover, all the GCC markets are open in terms of the movement of imports and exports with GCC tariffs being rather low by world standards. However, the fact remains that economies benefit handsomely when they are both competitive and complementary enough at the same time. There are also a number of inhibiting custom and administrative regulations that are still in force, such as the regulations imposed on the date of entry of foreign goods into the GCC markets, in addition to the multiplicity of specifications and technical standards imposed on some goods.

In terms of the 25th GCC Summit held in 2004, its

Table (6) Intra-GCC trade in 2002 (in million dollar)*

Country	Intra-GCC exports	Total intra-GCC trade	%	Total imports	Intra-GCC imports	%	Total exports	External trade	%
Bahrain	493	894.6	9.1	4409	401.6	8.9	5544.7	9953.7	10
Kuwait	313.2	1198.4	11.4	7734.4	885.2	2	16174	23908.4	9.7
Sultanate of Oman	1145.8	2930.8	33	5399	1785	10.3	11160	16559	17.7
Saudi Arabia	4887.6	6172.7	4	32082.3	1285.1	6.7	72837.7	104920	5.9
Qatar	578.7	1119.3	19.6	2747.5	540.6	5.9	9796.2	12543.7	8.9
UAE	1083.6	2387.3	3.7	35550	1303.7	2.3	45621	81171	2.9
Total	8501.9	14703.1	7.1	87922.2	6201.2	5.3	161133.6	249055.8	5.9

* Source: Arab Monetary Fund, Unified Arab Economic Report (Abu Dhabi: 2002)

results fell mostly short of expectations. Apart from discussions on building a causeway linking Qatar and Bahrain, and Qatar and the UAE, and discussing a proposed feasibility study about a project for constructing a railway network linking all six GCC States, the final communiqué issued failed to point to the critical importance of implementing the unified currency or the GCC common market, all of which were landmark resolutions announced at the conclusion of the GCC Summit held in Kuwait in 2003. Admittedly, the intra-GCC dispute over the free trade agreement signed unilaterally by the Kingdom of Bahrain with the US and the problematic character of other bilateral agreements cast a long and heavy shadow over the proceedings of the summit. Many economic observers believe that such bilateral agreements might impede efforts deployed to set up a common Gulf market.

What is certainly required in the near future is to devote efforts to boost the dynamic effects of economic integration. In other words, the GCC governments need to draw on the benefits accruing in the long term from the expansion of their common market by creating and multiplying investment opportunities, fostering the dynamics of economic transformation which will pave the way for production specialization, cashing in on the expanded size of various projects, diversifying industrial production in order to boost intra-GCC trade exchange, inducing greater competitiveness for better economic productivity, rationalizing investment by reducing the risk and uncertainty factors, encouraging specialization, building negotiation powers by opting for collective

negotiations on importing technological know-how and foreign expertise, allocating investments for academic research and innovation centers, stressing the importance of merging economic projects, including service and production projects, particularly in the financial, banking and trade sectors, and encouraging common investments in infrastructural projects such as developing communications and transport networks linking all the GCC countries to facilitate the movement of persons, goods and capital. Also, the GCC economic decision-makers need to coordinate industrial policies in order to expand local markets, produce at lower costs, and achieve desired levels of performance in the field of industrial production by rationalizing production resources.

It is worth recalling that implementing the resolutions ratified by the Gulf Cooperation Council needs to be buttressed by an executive and follow-up department, along with enhancing the role of the institutions affiliated with the Council by unifying rules and legislative texts and making rules binding on all parties while identifying the frameworks best suited for proper implementation. The surplus posted this year by the GCC public budgets, too, ought to be allocated for implementing long-awaited financial reforms likely to drive the process of currency unification and the currency union due to take effect by 2010.

the GCC economic decision-makers need to coordinate industrial policies in order to expand local markets, produce at lower costs, and achieve desired levels of performance in the field of industrial production by rationalizing production resources

F- Attracting foreign investments

Usually, foreign investments play a key role to invigorate the economies of the host countries, especially when these countries opt for the right projects and for the right type of foreign investors. As a matter of fact, foreign investments can fill any existing gap in resources and capabilities in host countries, just as they can expand the overall investment platform. Additionally, foreign investments help achieve a host of goals, notably the easy transfer of technological savvy and concomitant skills, bringing in modern management styles, training the national labor force, contributing to the rationalization and better exploitation of available natural resources of the host country, enlisting the services of expert foreign marketers in order to acquire a share in international markets, encouraging the creation of productive and service-related projects, and diversifying sources of national income.

Recently, the GCC countries have realized the importance of attracting foreign investments. All GCC countries are offering today new incentives for foreign investors. They have also made tremendous efforts to improve the domestic investment environment by working to create better conditions for the flow of private investments. Among the most remarkable measures taken by the GCC governments one could cite in particular the initiation of new investment laws and regulations, establishing governmental departments that handle foreign investments, setting up free trade zones, launching special programs for the promotion of investment opportunities, and mobilizing local foreign financial resources for the establishment of national and joint investment companies. For instance, and for the first time ever, Saudi Arabia allowed in October 2003 ABN Bank (the second biggest European bank) to open a branch in the Kingdom. In January 2004, Riyadh announced a tax reduction on foreign investments from the earlier 45% to just 20%. Within the same spirit of attracting foreign investors, Saudi authorities signed in March 2004 a SR3 billion contract with four foreign

companies from China, Italy and Spain in the field of natural gas production. Kuwaiti authorities, for their part, signed in February 2004 an investment and trade agreement with the US. Kuwait also took a decision to cancel entry visas for 34 nationalities. The Kuwaiti National Assembly ratified a law allowing foreign banks to open branches in the country while a decision to reduce taxes on foreign companies by 25% is still pending. In Qatar, the government issued a law allowing foreigners to own residential properties and a bilateral investment and trade agreement was signed with the US.

As for the UAE, the government announced in September 2003 that it would re-open the door for foreign banks to set up branches in the country, while Dubai, in June 2004, announced the establishment of an outsourcing zone as part of the existing free trade zone. The UAE, following the suit of Kuwait and Qatar, signed in March 2004 an investment and trade agreement with the US. In Bahrain, authorities created the Bahrain Investment Center, which had attracted by December 2004 some US$ 670 million of foreign investments. In 2003, Kuwait, the UAE and Qatar topped the list of Arab countries in terms of investment security, as reported by the Financial Times.

In spite of all their efforts, the GCC countries have not yet achieved high performance in the field of attracting foreign investments. Perhaps, incidents disrupting domestic and external security in the region have led to concerns amid foreign investors. According to performance indicators on attracting foreign investments adopted by UNICTAD, Bahrain ranks in 50th place, Qatar 67, the UAE in 101, Oman at 126, Kuwait at 137 and Saudi Arabia comes in at 137 out of a total of 140 countries. This despite the fact that in 2003, the GCC countries posted an increase in the volume of capital inflow as compared with 2002, with the notable exceptions of the UAE and Qatar where capital inflow decreased by 3.4% and 2.3% respectively. Total inflow capitalization for all the GCC countries revolved around US$ 42.373 million in 2003, registering a growth rate of 4% from 2002 as compared with outflow capitalization which reached US $ 11.235 million as shown in Table 7.

Likewise, the year 2004 witnessed a contraction of economic freedoms in all the GCC countries, save for Bahrain, which maintained the twentieth rank while performance indicators moved Saudi Arabia down to the rank of 72 according to the Wall Street Journal. The UAE went down to the 48th rank, Kuwait to 54, Oman to 60 and Qatar stood at the 81st rank.

It needs to be pointed out in this context that Saudi Arabia continues to strive hard to join the World Trade Organization (WTO). In April 2004, Riyadh signed a bilateral agreement with Beijing as part of the preliminary conditions for Saudi Arabia's accession to WTO membership. As such, the number of agreements signed by Riyadh rises to 31. However, Saudi Arabia still needs to sign other agreements with the US, Indonesia, Panama, and the Philippines. Some pending disagreements, such

as the dispute over the issue of support, copyright protection, and allowing foreign insurance companies to enter the Saudi market also need to be resolved in preparation.

Economic prospects and proposed policies

Primary estimates indicate that economic performance in the GCC states is poised to post positive growth rates even tough analysts predict a decline in oil prices and a dip in production rates in the coming years. Available data indicate that all the GCC countries will post growth rates ranging from 3% to 8% while inflation rates are expected to fall below 2.4% across the GCC. The trade balance is expected to register a surplus in all GCC States, except for Bahrain and Oman. The surplus in Qatar is predicted to hover around 22% in proportion to the GDP as shown in Table 8. However, the repercussions would probably not have any wide negative impact on public budgets in the short term.

To be sure, most GCC countries do make serious

Table (7) Size of incoming and outgoing flow of foreign capital and accumulation and its proportion to gross investment accumulation in the GCC countries (in million dollar and in percentage terms) for 2003

Country	Year	Inflow	%	Outflow	%	Inflow capitalization	%	Outflow capitalization	%
UAE	2002	834	3.4	442	6.5	3080	4.3	3136	4.4
	2003	480	7.6	992	3.7	3560	4.4	4129	5.1
Bahrain	2002	217	20.1	190	23	6203	73.7	2158	25.6
	2003	517	72.2	741	50.4	6720	72.4	2899	31.3
Saudi Arabia	2002	-615	0.2	50	-1.9	25368	13.5	2126	1.1
	2003	208	0.2	54	0.6	25576	12.1	2180	1
Oman	2002	23	-	-	0.9	2597	12.9	22	0.1
	2003	138	-	-1	5.5	2735	12.6	21	0.1
Qatar	2002	631	1.9	61	19.7	2847	16.3	353	2
	2003	400	2	71	11.4	3247	16	424	2.1
Kuwait	2002	7	-4.8	-155	0.2	468	1.3	1635	4.6
	2003	67	-1.66	4989	2.2	535	1.2	1603	3.7

Source: United Nations Conference on Trade and Development (UNCTAD), World Investment Report 2004.

efforts to diversify their economies, however, the absence of a comprehensive approach to developing the non-oil sector compounded by a lack of political will to concretely implement necessary economic reforms pose some hurdles on the way to diversifying the production base and enacting the needed structural changes. The GCC countries, in actual fact, need to embrace better management policies of their financial affairs within a long-term perspective, especially when it comes to managing their natural resources for the prosperity of their own people. Appropriate policies should take into account the need to work out the ways and means capable of containing the impact of fluctuating oil prices along with striving as hard as ever to implement reforms during boom periods. On the longer-run, a number of economic analysts like Abde and Dawoodi believe that any reform policies ought to take into consideration the issue of securing equality among successive generations upon articulating the strategies of public spending and investments. Just as significantly, reducing the GCC countries' reliance on oil entails the creation of modern structures subsuming taxation policies and well-developed taxation administrations by applying wide-ranging taxation regimes while keeping taxation level as low as possible.

The GCC countries ought also to review their heavy reliance on cheap expatriate labor and adopt instead policies capable of correcting the existent demographic imbalance by formulating a set of comprehensive labor policies likely to mobilize the national labor force and empowering national employees to confront and handle the changes and developments unraveling across the world. Educational systems ought to be overhauled, employee skills upgraded, production levels boosted and emphasis placed on tapping employee skills equipped with top notch technological know-how.

The GCC countries also need to stress the importance of enacting economic reforms slated to enhance competitiveness in order to improve productivity levels, encouraging private sector operators by re-directing the contribution of private companies towards more productive and performing sectors likely to prove highly lucrative in the long term. In parallel, the GCC countries ought to sustain the privatization drive. What is happening at present is that most GCC governments support economic projects, the majority of which are economically unprofitable. Most projects rally the support of governments for the sake of ostentation or out of purely political motivations.

At the same time, the GCC governments need to encourage the creation of joint investments by inviting foreign investors, which requires that the governments endeavor to create an attractive environment for private capital, an option that calls

Table (8) Forecast: Real GDP growth, inflation rates and payment balance in real price terms

	Year	UAE	Bahrain	Saudi Arabia	Oman	Qatar	Kuwait
GDP growth	2004	5.5	5.6	3.3	2.8	8.5	5.5
	2005	4.6	5	3.2	4.8	8.3	2.7
Inflation (%)	2004	3.2	2	0.8	0.5	3.5	2.3
	2005	2.4	1.2	0.9	1.1	1.2	2
Trade balance (% in proportion to GDP)	2004	14.9	-15	16.3	-3.8	24.6	24.8
	2005	7	-3.5	5.5	-1.1	21.7	12.2

Sources: Investment House, Economic & Strategic Outlook, different issues, The Economist Intelligence Unit (EIU), Country reports, IMF (2004), World Economic Outlook.

for the aggregation of myriad political, economic, legislative, legal and administrative conditions, together with establishing appropriate oversight bodies, building comprehensive databases, and applying the principle of transparency as it facilitates the flow of foreign investments towards the GCC markets. Naturally enough, this would entail implementing anti-graft and anti-corruption laws as well as minutely studying the causes that repulse investors, such as favoritism, administrative corruption, convoluted and heavy-handed bureaucracy, the excessive number of regulations deployed to protect the local private sector in addition to the great number of departments taking charge organizing foreign investments. Even worse, some departments entrusted to deal with foreign investors often issue conflicting decisions.

Admittedly, to grant the private sector a primal role in managing national development would require that priorities of development be first determined and long-term development objectives well-defined. A suitable political, economic and social environment ought to be secured, too.

On another level, mobilizing and investing private saving in development projects would entail a number of governmental measures to ensure that private capital is protected while capital ought to be injected into projects yielding long-term benefits for the national economy.

Efforts made by the GCC governments should not be exclusively restricted to enhancing the role of the private sector at the national level; rather, efforts should be made to expand its contribution to bolstering economic integration at the level of the Gulf region. In this sense, regulations framing the activities of the private sector should be articulated through close collective discussions among all the GCC countries. Investment laws and regulations should provide incentives for the creation of joint projects and the merger of national individual projects. Private sector operators, too, should be involved in negotiations and the drafting of agreements among the GCC countries on the one hand as well as agreements with countries outside the Gulf Cooperation Council on the other hand.

The challenges facing the GCC countries are daunting and quite formidable. Governments need to move towards boosting closer coordination and cooperation through the custom union, pushing forwards the project of establishing a common regional market, avoiding similarity of national development projects, improving ways of managing and investing human resources, and strengthening the GCC collective negotiating position. Last but not least, the Gulf people should play a prominent role in formulating and deciding the changes that ought to be enacted within a free and democratic socio-political environment, for it is the interest of the Gulf people, first and foremost, to make any reform experience a success.

Conclusion

The GCC countries have moved, since the 1960s to the twentieth century, through a critical period of socio-economic transformations by re-investing oil revenues. However, with the decline in oil prices and the permanent fluctuations of oil revenues, there is a pressing need today for the GCC States to diversify the sources of national income, creating a sustainable and durable production base by moving to enact changes in the existing economic systems through a reduction of the reliance on oil-related revenues. The GCC countries ought to sustain privatization while seeking to attract wider foreign direct investments. Global changes in the contemporary world economic order have added a new dimension, making it an imperative for the GCC countries to move from fragile and unsustainable cooperation to embrace a policy of firmer economic integration in order to face up to the momentous economic challenges confronting them. In fact, over the past decade the need to build sustainable economic integration in the region has become more pressing for many reasons, mainly the fact that the member states of the GCC face nearly the same problems and the same domestic economic challenges. The next few years will represent a real litmus test for the GCC countries to achieve these necessary tasks.

References

Al Abed George & Hamid Reza Dawoodi, *The Challenges of Economic Growth and Globalization in the Middle East and North Africa Region* (The International Monetary Fund: Washington, DC, 2003).

Bright Okugo, *The Middle East and North Africa in a Changing Oil market,* (The International Monetary Fund, Washington, DC, 2003).

Emirates Industrial Bank, *"Trade Exchange among the GCC Countries in light of the Custom Union,"* Newsletter Issue No. 2, February 2004.

Kuwaidar, Ibrahim, *Developing Arab Human Resources and Policies for Creating New Jobs* (The League of Arab States, the Gulf Center for Studies, the Gulf Economic Report 2004 - 2005: Dar Al-Khaleej Press, Publishing and Distribution, 2004).

Arab Monetary Fund, *Unified Arab Economic Report* (Abu Dhabi, 2002).

Gulf Investment Corporation, *GCC Economic Statistics* (January, 2001).

IMF *International Financial Statistics* CD-ROM

(Washington, DC, 2002).

Kuwait Investment House, *Economic & Strategic Outlook*, different issues.

International Monetary Fund, "Monetary Union Among Member Countries of the Gulf Cooperation Council," Washington, DC, 2003.

OPEC Annual Statistical Bulletin, various issues.

Economist Intelligence Unit, Country Report: Bahrain, October 2004.

Economist Intelligence Unit, Country Report: Kuwait, November 2004.

Economist Intelligence Unit, Country Report: Oman, July 2003.

Economist Intelligence Unit, Country Report: Qatar, October 2004.

Economist Intelligence Unit, Country Report: Saudi Arabia, November 2004.

Economist Intelligence Unit, Country Report: United Arab Emirates, September 2004.

World Bank, *World Development Indicators* CD-ROM 2003.

UAE Central Bank, *Annual Report*, various issues.

United Nations Conference on Trade and Development (UNCTAD), *World Investment Report 2004*.

Ugo Fasano and Zubair Iqbal, "GCC Countries: from Oil Dependence to Diversification," Washington, D.C: International Monetry Fund, 2003.

The Oil and Gas Sector:
Global Trends and their Implications for the GCC

Vahan Zanoyan

President and Chief Executive Officer, PFC Energy

2004 was a year of unprecedented strength in crude oil markets. Crude oil prices soared to record highs, and the strength in global crude oil markets was unrelenting. This was not a year of temporary price spikes caused by temporary disruptions. It was a year of new market fundamentals that exposed structural shifts in both supply and demand patterns. It will be some time before the implications are fully absorbed by the market, and thus some volatility will be apparent in the short term. It remains clear, however, that there have been fundamental changes to the underlying factors driving both supply and demand, and that the world has entered a new, significantly higher price range for oil.

Oil Prices in 2004: Factors and Trends

A combination of long-term changes to the fundamentals of supply and demand and temporary but substantial disruptions drove crude oil prices into a higher price band in 2004. A surge in demand, especially from China, faster-than-expected declines in mature producing basins, minimal growth in new exploration/production activity and capacity constraints in both production and refining all contributed to the high prices.

These long-term shifts provided a fertile environment for a very bullish market psychology, establishing the right conditions for short-term disruptions in supplies to have a sustained impact on prices. These temporary stoppages do not fully explain the run-up in prices however, and one has to look at longer-term factors to understand the new price environment into which world oil markets have entered.

Foremost among these is the lack of global spare production capacity. For the first time in decades, the world's oil production and refining systems began to approach their maximum limits. The incremental production required to meet increased demand and to make up the various supply disruptions led OPEC members to produce at levels very close to their peak capacity. Saudi Arabia was the only noteworthy exception. The result was that by late 2004, OPEC had barely 1.2 million barrels/day of spare capacity.

In 2004, growth in oil production in areas outside of OPEC and the Former Soviet Union (FSU), which was generally expected to grow, was stagnant at best, and declining in many cases. The fact that non-OPEC non-FSU production growth remained relatively stagnant despite a sustained high price environment does not bode well for these areas to make substantial contributions towards meeting future demand requirements.

In addition to crude oil production capacity, other parts of the global supply chain were also stretched in 2004. Specifically, freight rates increased rapidly as it became apparent that there was a dearth of available crude oil tankers. Freight costs have risen consistently since 2002 at rates of 100-200% depending on the area, thus squeezing margins. This is especially true for shipping from West Africa, which supplies much of the world's light sweet crude used for producing gasoline and other high-grade, high demand petroleum products.

The specter of future shortages in refining capacity has also emerged as a looming problem. The problems refineries faced this year initially appeared to be more one-time disruptions rather than long-term trends, such as when US refineries were forced to retool facilities to meet stricter specifications or were shut down as a result of the hurricane season. While the impact of these events was absorbed by the market, they highlighted the fact that refining capacity, especially more complex refineries, will need to be expanded in the future to keep up with world demand growth. Investments in the refining sector are long-term propositions and the increase in capacity has been lagging behind demand growth, tightening utilization rates worldwide.

Strong demand growth was the other major contributor to high prices, and served to expose and underscore the capacity constraints of energy sector. The growth in oil demand in a number of areas, specifically China, outstripped all but the most bullish expectations. Chinese growth has been in the double digits for the past two years, and does not appear as though it might abate any time soon. While this overall trend had been apparent for some time, China's economic growth spiked in the latter half of 2003 and continued into 2004, driving

China's need for commodities, mainly oil, to unprecedented levels. This somewhat abrupt change in the demand profile of what is now the world's second largest consumer of energy was the most pronounced feature of the 2004 demand story.

A recovering global economy helped drive up demand in other areas of the world as well. Increased consumer spending and final demand in the US led to an acceleration in demand growth of approximately 50,000 barrels per day over the growth of demand in 2003, and an increase of 300,000 barrels per day over the growth in 2002. Japan was buoyed by China's rapid expansion, and saw real growth for the first time in years which in turn drove up energy demand. India was the beneficiary of a good monsoon season, which helped growth in the agricultural sector and consumer spending.

Another noteworthy aspect of the 2004 price run was the unprecedented involvement of hedge funds and "non-commercial traders". These investors wield considerable purchasing power and look for arbitrage opportunities between commodities. The oil price volatility, healthy demand growth and persistent supply security concerns led the "non-com" funds to view oil very favorably, and added a new dimension to the strength in oil prices.

Upstream Investment: Where is the Industry?

With oil prices at record highs and no strong reason to foresee an imminent decline, the

> **Increased consumer spending and final demand in the US led to an acceleration in demand growth of approximately 50,000 barrels per day over the growth of demand in 2003, and an increase of 300,000 barrels per day over the growth in 2002.**

customary cyclical behavior of the industry would have led one to expect the international oil companies (IOC) to be actively increasing their investments in exploration and production (E&P). Following the spike in oil prices in the early 1980s, the energy industry found itself in a phase conducive to investment. High oil prices, various nationalizations and industry consolidation created ideal conditions for the industry to open new oil producing provinces. This run of favorable conditions continued into the 1990s, as the push for globalization and the collapse and subsequent opening of the Soviet Union also created new opportunities of which the IOCs readily took advantage.

However, in the past several years, IOC upstream expenditures have been stagnant. During the 1999-2003 period, in spite of very healthy growth in both the earnings and the free cash flow of the IOCs, their total upstream spending stayed relatively flat. For example, in that 4-year period, the compounded annual growth rate in the free cash flow of a group of IOCs (BP, ChevronTexaco, ConocoPhillips, ENI, ExxonMobil, Marathon, Oxy, Repsol YPF, Shell, TOTAL) was well over 50%, while in the same period the compound annual growth rate in their upstream spending was merely 2%. This lagging behind of spending relative to free cash flow in a persistent high price environment is not characteristic of the industry; in fact, it is contrary to customary behavior.

There are several reasons for this stagnation in upstream spending on the part of the IOCs.

First, the traditional, profitable areas of IOC crude oil production (generally in the OECD countries) have become increasingly mature. This means that the technical risks of exploration are considerably higher, while the expected returns in terms of the size of new discoveries, are considerably lower than what they were a decade or two ago. This

also means higher operating costs for existing production, because of the cost of overcoming the decline rates.

Second, IOCs are organized and capitalized to invest in a specific risk-reward environment. And while risks for them have increased, because of the maturity of their production areas, the rewards have not necessarily kept pace. This may sound counterintuitive, given the high oil prices. But high oil prices do not always accrue to the IOCs. Current fiscal terms in most traditional producing areas reflect lower-risk environments, and are designed for $15-$25 oil price range and generally favor government's share of incremental revenues as energy prices rise. Risks have risen, and although prices have also risen substantially, fiscal terms do not allow companies to keep enough of the price upside to offset the higher risks.

Third, some host governments increasingly prefer to rely on their own national oil companies (NOC) to undertake major upstream investments. This is partly because certain NOCs have developed considerable technical and managerial skills in the past decade and can manage large projects better than they used to, and in part because the high oil prices provide host governments with substantial financial resources to invest in their sectors, and thus they no longer need foreign investment as much as a decade ago. This has restricted the quality opportunities for IOCs, as the more promising production areas, with the exception of West Africa and some deepwater projects, are increasingly in countries which are either closed to or have limited openness to outside investment in the oil sector.

Thus, the IOCs face a relatively unusual dilemma: despite high oil prices and substantial free cash, they face limited profitable investment opportunities. Unless NOCs launch a major upstream investment program, or unless there are significant and consequential changes in the fiscal terms of mature producing areas, the crude oil production capacity deficit will not be closed in the next several years.

It is important to stress that preceding analysis applies largely to crude oil. Natural gas presents different opportunities, prospects and risks to both IOCs and NOCs. The combination of a dearth of attractive investment opportunities in the oil sector, a concerted effort on the part of companies to switch to a cleaner source of energy and considerable technical and commercial advancements in the commercializing natural gas, has translated into a shift on the part of the IOCs from oil to gas. Few NOCs have the technical capability and experience to develop large-scale gas projects, and fewer still are prepared to tackle the unique market risks that exporting natural gas presents. Thus, in both very open countries like Qatar and relatively closed countries like Saudi Arabia, IOCs have managed to secure substantial upstream projects in the gas sector.

The Resurgence of NOCs

The predicament faced by IOCs in the global upstream oil sector described earlier turns the focus back to NOCs and governments. Most of the world's reserves are owned and controlled by governments. Traditionally, IOCs have sought access to these reserves by offering to put their superior access to "above ground resources" in the service of the host countries, namely, technology, managerial skills, access to capital, access to global markets, etc. Thus, the NOC-IOC dynamic has always revolved around access to and control of hydrocarbon resources, both above ground and below ground, with NOCs traditionally and typically having the comparative advantage in below ground resources, and IOCs traditionally, but not always exclusively, having the comparative advantage in above ground resources. The relative position of NOCs and IOCs in this dynamic has evolved over time depending on how badly one side has needed the resources of the other. Given the market trends of 2004, and given some of the more fundamental industry trends of the past decade whereby many NOCs spent considerable time and resources improving their access to above ground resources, we have already entered an era where NOCs will find their relative position vis-à-vis IOCs vastly improved.

This does not mean, however, that there is no room for IOCs in the global upstream oil sector. NOCs and governments have their own challenges when it comes to upstream spending. Most NOCs are organized as asset managers, but are not set up to take exploration risk. Governments in general do not understand exploration risk. So, even in cases where the NOC of a given country has the technical and managerial capabilities to undertake complex projects and the government has the necessarily funds to finance such projects, partnering with an IOC may make sense just to diversify technical and commercial risks. Of course, in cases where these capabilities exist and the risks are viewed to be minimal (such as the Saudi Arabian oil sector), then it becomes very difficult to justify foreign investment.

NOCs themselves are not exempt from radical changes in both their operating environment and in

> **Given the market trends of 2004, we have already entered an era where NOCs will find their relative position vis-à-vis IOCs vastly improved.**

the demands put on them by their shareholders, i.e., the producing governments. Depending on specific sectoral conditions, their government's strategies and their own internal capabilities, different NOCs have reacted differently to new demands to take and manage new and higher risks: some have commercialized, introducing strict performance criteria to ensure efficiency and meritocracy in their organizations, and have invested considerably in training and building of a competent cadre of professionals; other are in transition, being forced to change their structure, organization and mandate by their shareholder; still others have basically remained façade organizations and extensions of the government bureaucracy, abdicating most of the new technical and managerial challenges to the foreign companies operating in their countries.

In many ways, the developments of 2004 consolidated the gains made by NOCs in the past decade in the technical and managerial fields by introducing the critical new advantage of finance. What was a relatively slow, evolutionary process leading to the resurgence of NOCs as critical players in the global crude oil market received a huge boost and gained huge momentum in 2004. No oil producing region in the world is more affected by this than the Gulf.

Implications of 2004 for the GCC

The short-term benefits of the 2004 market trends to the GCC countries are obvious: GCC members have been balancing their budgets, building foreign reserves, paying down debt, and increasing both private and government investment. What the governments and NOCs of the GCC need to do now is to build on these short-term successes to position themselves for the new world order in oil markets.

If in fact the global petroleum sector has entered a new era of higher sustainable average oil prices and an era where NOCs have enhanced competitive positions, then OPEC producers, and in particular those of the Gulf, face three broad types of policy opportunities and challenges.

First, the challenge of continued market management in light of different fundamentals and different parameters governing the petroleum markets. OPEC, like everyone else, was taken by surprise by the extent of the trends in 2004. It had not anticipated the strength in demand, nor the slow response of non-OPEC supplies. In fact, until last year, the organization was in a price-defense mode, attempting to steer oil markets through a global recession. Early last year, it was called upon to offset two major supply disruptions, in Venezuela and in Iraq following the chaos in wake of the US invasion. Both these disruptions drained already low private oil stocks and with Western governments unwilling to release official stocks, the Gulf country members of OPEC had to step in and offset the declines. This year with stocks already depleted they were faced with the short run problem of meeting Chinese demand surge and the prospect of longer term severe tightening of market fundamentals.

Now for the first time in OPEC history they are confronted not with the challenge of curtailing production but mobilizing costly investments in the upstream sector to raise crude oil output and production capacity. The problem is more severe than just overall output capacity - the solution also calls for raising light sweet crude oil supplies. There is no excess capacity of light sweet crude. The policy dilemma is two fold: one, what if demand falls as a result of higher prices; and two, there are inter-temporal choices to be made. Should these countries, particularly in the Gulf, save their funds for another period of low oil prices or invest it in capacity which may result in lower oil prices.

Second, the challenge of adapting their NOCs to the new realities of the global energy sector, as well as to the new requirements domestically. The NOCs in the Gulf are currently in strong positions-they have the financial resources, some have advanced technology, especially in the upstream area and they still have substantial reserves. The decision to invest heavily in their own oil sectors is a political and geostrategic one and will be dealt with by their shareholders-i.e., the governments. But there is a unique opportunity to cooperate with other NOCs particularly in the OPEC countries to phase-in investments cooperatively as an organization in order to avoid competitive investments that could undermine prices and to share the burden of using precious financial resources. The Gulf NOCs are relatively new at this because they have been focused on their own oil sectors in a period of financial resource scarcity. Now they have to look overseas and learn the behavior of diverse countries with a variety of strategic objectives and government requirements. Areas of cooperation include: technology and skills sharing, marketing and regional oil market management and portfolio diversification. Such cooperation would enhance their government's strategic importance in a number of new regions. This is important since many Gulf governments are attempting to diversify relations with regions they have traditionally ignored-such as Asia, Latin America and the Former Soviet Union.

Third, the challenge of broader macro-economic and political reforms. After nearly two decades (1986-2004) of economic stagnation, the countries of the Gulf have a unique opportunity to fix many of the structural economic problems afflicting them. Through the lean years, they learnt some important skills of fiscal management, monetary policy stabilization and institutional development. With the current surge in prices, they have more flexible options. They can save funds for a rainy day, they can invest in infrastructure, education and health to improve the quality and effectiveness of their population and they can create the right business climate for their private sectors. Investing in their oil and gas sectors would help the Gulf countries maintain their international strategic importance. Balancing that with using their national oil companies to lead the way in local and international corporate development - skills, diversification of portfolios and deepening diplomatic ties would greatly enhance their domestic economic and global geostrategic presence.

Conclusion

The 2004 oil market is a unique opportunity for the Gulf countries. The bottom line is that they have to rise to all these three challenges by balancing inter-temporal, inter sectoral and international objectives. With the vast financial resources available and the lessons of the past two decades (this is critical if they want to avoid the excesses and lost opportunities of the past), this could well hail the onset of a golden era in the Gulf.

An Overview of the Gulf Economies: Challenges and Prospects in a Global Marketplace

John Sfakianakis

Independent Senior Economic Researcher

Sustainable growth, economic diversification, employment, human capital development and education for a growing population are among the top challenges for current and future generations to come in the Gulf. The pressures for reform, especially from within, will continue to increase yet the momentum for change will continue to vary among many techno-bureaucracies in the region. Not all Gulf economies are alike and as a result not all face the same degree of challenges and options available to them. As a rule of thumb, oil prices will continue to be the most unpredictable commodity. However, contrary to the opinion of some analysts, higher oil revenues will not necessarily lead to a lessening of pressures for reform. On the contrary, high windfall from oil only heightens the citizenry's perceptions that money is available in the states' coffers and it has to be used prudently. The times do not call for investments on glitzy goods and flashy weaponry that lack in interoperability.

The role of the state both in its distributive/spending capacity as well as an employer is predominant in the region. The state plays an important, yet conventional, role as the engine for growth, affecting private sector growth and consumption. As a result, in most cases of diversification, it is the state that takes a leading role instead of the market. All governments in the Gulf expect the private sector to play an increasingly important role in economic development yet much is needed to entice it as well as to allow for a true partnership with the public sector to be established. Some private sector actors have repatriated a segment of their investments back into the region, mainly due to the Post-September 11th climate as well as the boom in regional equities, yet the attraction of more funds will only be ensured if the state becomes more entrepreneurial and imaginative in its dealings with the private sector. Pressures to generate much-needed funds due to high capital investment requirements might compel the state to restructure its incentive towards the private sector in order to cajole it. All of the above challenges are based on modest revenues from hydrocarbons.

The social contract, government allocation of economic patronage and goods in exchange for loyalty from the citizenry in most Gulf countries will have to be rethought. Expectations will continue to rise amongst the citizenry as demographics simply decreases real incomes and puts pressure on governments to invest and deliver more services.

During the past fifteen years, GDP per inhabitant on a purchasing power parity basis rose slightly in Qatar, Kuwait and the UAE followed by a slower rise witnessed in Bahrain and Oman and a decline in Saudi Arabia. Nevertheless, Kuwait, Qatar and the UAE have ample energy reserves to keep real incomes steady, given that there is no population explosion. At the same time, perceptions about wealth creation and real purchasing power capacities are deteriorating as is the rise of income inequality among the more demographically explosive countries like Bahrain, Oman and Saudi Arabia. In these three countries, population growth has averaged around 3 percent per year in the past two decades and rising unemployment rates remain unmanageable for the time being. Heavy reliance on expatriate labor in all sectors, except government jobs reserved for nationals, is a heavy burden on some Gulf economies. Attempts at mobilizing local labor, Bahrainization, Omanization and Saudization, have yet to restructure job markets in a fundamental way.

The phenomenal rise of income that permitted entire populations to literally go from tents to marbled mansions and stay rich is a difficult socio-economic mobilizing factor to replicate under prevailing economic conditions in the region. Governments are under tremendous pressure to create employment opportunities at a time when neither their economies under their current structure nor the international division of labor allows them to be anything but capital intensive and to some degree service oriented. Over the past two years regional equity markets have risen to new heights and the public is overly fascinated with stocks. Heightened anticipations about market investments

Expectations will continue to rise amongst the citizenry as demographics simply decreases real incomes and puts pressure on governments to invest and deliver more services.

that produce soaring returns create a desire to get into the game. When this exuberance dissipates public frustration about their state will amplify. States have an obligation to educate investors to consider looking beyond stocks as a way to diversify and hedge against the inevitable downturn.

The inattention and mismanagement of the above challenges and the solutions offered will give food for thought to various opposition voices, including the more Islamized ones. Moreover, the creation of new institutions or the empowerment of existing ones that can be effective and timely is a challenge for the political economies of the region. Education systems in the Gulf need enormous revamping as they produce unmarketable graduates. The replacement of high-skilled expatriates cannot be carried out without a pool of local experts.

Diversification has been a subject of concern for all regional governments over the years. Clearly, diversification strategies have been marked by a dependence on a limited amount of comparative advantages linked to energy resources. There are three main paths of diversification that are being followed: industrial activities linked mostly to the oil sector (Bahrain, Saudi Arabia), development of gas resources (Qatar) and the growth of the services sector (UAE). Also, most countries try to explore secondary or tertiary avenues of diversification. Tourism, re-exporting, financial services are being explored as additional paths of diversification. However, investment in these others fields depends on revenue from oil. Gulf regimes are quite durable in surviving yet in the past this was done with less pressure for change from without as well as declining real incomes and a growing population from within. Below is a brief review, excluding Iraq and Iran, of the policies and challenges facing the economies of the Gulf.

Bahrain: The Region's Offshore Banking and Financial Services Center

Due to its geographic location, Bahrain has been a natural trading hub for the past two centuries. Unlike its neighbors, Bahrain's oil reserves, estimated to last another fifteen years, have proven to be small, forcing it to make genuine attempts to diversify and become more global and aware of its limitations. Bahrain's economy is closely linked to the economies of its neighbors and to international energy markets. Oil and gas accounts for about 17 percent of the country's GDP.

The services industry is helping Bahrain broaden its options as well as provide much needed employment (in 2003 unemployment was at around 15 percent) for its citizens. In 2002, services accounted for two-thirds of real GDP, compared with 39 percent in 1980. The development of Bahrain's port and airport facilities and a more aggressive Bahrain airways campaign have turned the country into a semi-regional transport hub despite rising competition from Qatar and the UAE. Tourism has also been developed as another revenue and employment alternative that is geared towards visitors from neighboring countries, mainly Saudi Arabia. In 2001, tourism generated some US$500 million in revenue from some four million visitors. Nevertheless, Bahrain's tourism industry faces considerable competition from Dubai, however, it can keep its market position as a weekend destination post for Saudis. Special sporting events based on new venues like the new Formula One race track, inaugurated in April 2004, could also diversify Bahrain's tourism options.

The financial services sector has flourished in Bahrain and in 2003 it accounted for more than 15 percent of its GDP. At the end of 2003, there were 52 offshore banking units and 357 financial institutions were operating in Bahrain. Bahrain's inability to retain its market position in the offshore banking sector will prove detrimental for the economy. The offshore banking sector holds assets roughly ten times greater than the size of the Bahraini economy. Steps have been taken to strengthen even further Bahrain's position as the regions premier financial center and such moves are noteworthy and timely given Dubai's interest to compete in this area. In 2002, the Bahrain Financial Harbor (BFH) project was announced as a residential and commercial purpose center. An attempt to turn Bahrain into a regional insurance hub that will provide conventional and Islamic products remains to be tested in the years to come. Bahrain has undoubtedly developed into a regional center for Islamic banking. More recently, Bahrain was selected as the host for a planned US$1.5bn fund aimed at financing infrastructure and privatization projects in Muslim countries.

Low-cost power and feedstock helped the growth of the manufacturing sector. Aluminum and petrochemical plants benefited from cheap energy inputs. As a result, Bahrain has established its position as a major player on the world aluminum market (aluminum exports currently account for about 15% of total exports). Ship repair and light engineering facilities have also been established to serve the regional oil industry, and if exploited correctly could also widen Bahrain's diversification options. The challenge for Bahrain will be to continue to hold its position as the premier regional financial center as well as find ways to create employment for its citizens in an expanded service-oriented economy.

Kuwait: Oil and More Oil

The Kuwaiti economy is dominated by petroleum. Oil accounts for 90 percent of merchandise export earnings and over 80 percent of budget revenues. The manufacturing sector is dominated by downstream petroleum industries such as oil refining and petrochemicals. Although the government has called for the private sector's greater involvement in the economy not much has taken place. Much of the country's limited private-sector activity is driven by public sector spending.

Efforts have been made to turn the port of Shuwaikh into a free-trade zone (FTZ) strengthening Kuwait's position as a trading hub. Despite the establishment of more than 300 traders, the volume of goods resulting from the number of visit from container ships has been small. Iran and less Iraq, due to the current security situation, are tangible markets for Kuwait. Nevertheless, competition from Dubai's Jebel Ali has disabled Shuwaikh. Public management of Shuwaikh has not helped its performance and outlook and full private management of the planned Abdali FTZ, close to the Iraq border, is projected. Kuwait's small-scale manufacturing which is domestically geared is little match to the products offered by some of its neighbors. The prospects for doing business in Iraq is proving to be less sanguine as initially envisaged by the government. Another factor accounting for Kuwait's inability to expand in Iraq has been the lack of encouragement of US agencies through which aid money can been distributed to subcontract with local Kuwaiti firms.

Oman: Some Oil and Growing Gas Windfall

Oman just like Bahrain is faced with declining oil reserves which at present rates of production - notwithstanding improvements in technology and new discoveries - will terminate in about twenty years. Diversification has been arduous and slow. Oil still accounts for around 30 percent of real GDP. One of the most pressing challenges for Oman is its demographic explosion. Average population growth between the 1980s and 1990s has been around 4 percent, although World Bank estimates for 2002 place it at 2.4 percent. Between 1970 and 2002, Oman's population grew from less than one million to an estimated 2.5 million stretching the already scarce water resources.

The discovery of large quantities of natural gas has brought additional revenue and a possibility to develop strategies of niche diversification in manufacturing that use gas as a fuel and a feedstock. Nevertheless, what exists now is small-scale manufacturing, based on import substitution that has yet to diversify the country's export options and the newly created industrial estates are too few and mostly employ expatriate labor. More recently, Oman made bold attempts in developing a niche in container transshipments with the construction of the Salalah port. Although the port has performed well, especially due to the war in Iraq, rival ports such as Jebel Ali will have to make Oman think hard of its available options. An attempt to develop an FTZ in Salalah as well as in the newly built port at Sohar might offer opportunities for trade and a development of the re-exports sector. In 2003, re-exports amounted to nearly 13 percent of total export earnings. However, any re-export activity necessitates a rise in import spending which affects the country's external account position. The tourism industry in Oman has enormous potential and multiple benefits for the economy. Tourism is a labor intensive activity that generates and multiplies opportunities for a lot of other sectors in any economy. Yet the government is less aggressive in attracting visitors in contrast to Dubai, Qatar and Bahrain.

Natural gas offers a solid option for diversification. Liquefied natural gas (LNG), first exported in 2000, is at the core of the country's plans to export its gas resources. Although LNG prices track those in the broader commodity market, hence revenues are volatile, but provide an enticing windfall. Oman's LNG production capacity is being expanded and exports in natural gas to neighboring UAE commenced in early 2004. For Oman, the challenges are not only to find additional sources of revenue but also create new employment opportunities for a rising indigenous population and reduce its reliance on expatriate labor.

Qatar: From Oil to Gas Windfall

The growth rate of the Qatari economy has fluctuated dramatically over the past several years, reflecting the country's vulnerability to oil price fluctuations. Until today, the economy remains heavily dependent on oil but things are changing. In 2002, the contribution of the oil and gas sector to nominal GDP reached 60 percent.

The local economy as well as the private sector is still dependent on government spending derived from oil revenue. Qatar has the world's third largest gas reserves and expected to last more than 300 years at the current and anticipated rate of production whereas oil is expected to last around

twenty years. Natural gas is a rising source of export revenue that is expected to continue as Qatar expands its capacity in gas-based industries. Exports of LNG, natural gas liquids, petrochemicals and condensates now account for about 50 percent of Qatar's export revenue, with the remainder mainly coming from crude oil sales. Qatar's development strategy is to encourage foreign investment, and the country has been successful in reaching joint-venture agreements with foreign partners to develop the country's gas reserves. Qatar has also attracted investment from international oil companies in the form of innovative production-sharing agreements.

Qatar's dependence on oil income will remain considerable. It has received billions of dollars in external loans to fund the development of its gas and petrochemicals industries. The IMF estimates that by the end of 2001, Qatar's total foreign debt was more than US$15 billion. Until these projects start paying significant returns, Qatar's economy will continue to depend on oil revenue to finance both payments on this debt and other government expenditure.

Attempts at diversifying beyond the oil and gas and its related products is not easy. Qatar has found the tourism industry as an alternative. Unlike Bahrain, Qatar over the past two years has invested a staggering US$1 billion in order to attract foreign tourists. Like Bahrain and Dubai, Qatar is trying to project its image as a tourist destination by hosting various international sporting events. The 2006 Asian Games are going to be held in Qatar. This strategy might bear some fruits yet the level of competition among the three tourist destinations is rising and Qatar's positioning will not be easy. Finally, Qatar's US$5 billion plus project to set up, in the next five years, outposts for Western universities (Education City) in the outskirts of Doha will attract students from the region and beyond. In a nutshell, windfall from gas will be seminal and will permit Qatar to explore other avenues for diversification.

Saudi Arabia: Oil and Petrochemicals

Saudi Arabia is by far the largest economy in the entire Middle East (excluding Turkey). Oil acts as the most important engine of growth for the economy. Around 85 percent of export receipts and 75 of government revenue were derived from oil in 2003. Although Saudi Arabia is a special case several of the challenges it faces are not entirely uncommon to the rest of the region.

Employment generation is among the most serious challenges Saudi Arabia is facing at the present moment, affecting the social fabric of the country. The ratio of job seekers that find employment is low, only three out of every ten that enter the job market each year find work. Although familial and social ties do act as a financial support valve for those who are unemployed or underemployed, economic exclusion will increase resentment over the coming years. In addition, a sense of unrealizable father-to-son wealth gap and diminishing real per capita incomes will only increase dissatisfaction. Under such conditions, perceptions of unfair income distribution could generate a sense of exclusion and further social tension.

Localizing the labor force is not an easy task for any country in the region, and is always countered by two powerful vested interests: the private sector and well-placed rent-takers. Short-term fixes to the employment problem do not come easy. Certainly the mentality of servitude that oil windfall created in the 1970s has not helped. All menial, blue-collar jobs were left for the expatriate labor force and an entire generation was left to ponder of rentier pastures and/or public sector posts. Efforts to localize the labor force cannot be realized if the educational system is inadequate and far from the needs of the private sector. Also generational changes have to occur as Saudis have to become willing and disciplined wage earners. From its side, the private sector will have to swallow the not so bitter pill to incur lower profit margins due to higher wages. Consumers will also have to expect prices to rise due to higher wages but employment opportunities for a larger segment of the population will act as an important buffer against rising prices.

The industrial sector's development is based on the ample availability of hydrocarbons resources, and is strongly influenced by developments in the oil industry. Quite rightly, growth in the oil downstream sector has been led by petrochemicals output, a sector still dominated by the government but with growing private involvement. Moreover, the Kingdom's competitive advantage is based in capital/energy intensive industries which create growth but initiate few new jobs.

Tourism is an area with a high employment ratio and acts as a stimulus for the retail sector that the Kingdom could greatly benefit. Religious tourism, as well as internal tourism, has enormous potential for development. The growth of internal tourism is noteworthy as 100 percent more Saudis spent holidays in 2002 inside the Kingdom than in previous years. The pilgrimage is big business and the Kingdom could benefit greatly in developing its comparative advantage in religious tourism. Other Muslim countries like Jordan, Iran, Morocco, and Uzbekistan are also alerting themselves to the market potential of religious tourism. The challenges the Kingdom faces are numerous. High population growth rates coupled with rising unemployment and a fall of real income over time are not easily solved.

United Arab Emirates: Oil, Free Zones, Palm Cities, and Hotels

Despite recent and vocal attempts at diversifying economic output, oil earnings form the central aspect of government income, with oil revenue determining the public-sector expenditure on which much of the non-oil economy directly or indirectly relies. At the core of the diversification process is Dubai's successful effort at becoming the Gulf's trading and re-export center for markets in South Asia, various republics of the former Soviet Union and the Red Sea states of East Africa. At least half of the total value of re-exports goes unrecorded but recorded re-exports were close to US$14 billion in 2002.

There are two distinct approaches to diversification and development within the UAE. Dubai has ventured into the development of a services sector economy. One of the success show cases of Dubai has been the FTZ of Jebel Ali. It is home to more than 3,000 companies, including major regional distribution facilities for international firms, and have helped increase Dubai's manufacturing output. Due to the business friendly environment, many regional firms, including many from Saudi Arabia, have moved their operations to Jebel Ali. Replicating the success of Jebel Ali pushed the authorities to establish Internet City and Media City, with new free zones under develop-ment focusing on finance, healthcare and outsourcing. Despite some initial appre-hension, Internet City has turned Dubai into a regional hub for e-commerce. However, Media City has yet to establish itself as a media hub for the entire region. The launch in 2003 of Knowledge Village which is also a free zone has enjoyed limited

success partly due to competition from Qatar's Education City.

The above attempts have been complemented as a result of heavy investment in infrastructure, a costly yet successful international advertising campaign (Emirates Airline signed a US$180 million sponsorship deal with the English football club, Arsenal), a city that is characterized by its Western lifestyle, and a risk prone ruling elite with ample capital to spend which are not easily replicable in the rest of the region. The flamboyance of Dubai is evident in its real estate projects which are also linked to its ambitious goals for tourism. A heightened sense of demand gave rise to real estate speculation and windfall profits. Astronomical funds of "Olympic" proportions are being invested in various real estate projects. In total, some US$12 billion will be invested in various "mega" residential and tourist accommodation projects on massive tracts of reclaimed land. A theme park estimated to cost some US$10 billion and the world's tallest tower are also part of the emirate's development plans. The completion of the Burj al-Arab in late 1999 is unlikely to recover anytime soon its construction cost of US$1 billion. Nevertheless, it did help project Dubai's image onto the world stage, which is an invaluable asset with possible high rates of return in the long run.

Tourism forms an integral part of all this flamboyant development and tourists are on the increase as shopping has become a trade mark of the emirate. Dubai's motto "if we build it tourists will come" seems to be working for the time being. For an emirate that offers very little history and culture, its five million visitors in 2003 - the goal by 2010 is to attract some fifteen million tourists - is impressive and competes well with a historically rich destination

Dubai's motto "if we build it tourists will come" seems to be working for the time being.

such as Egypt that attracted a million more tourists during the same year. However, Dubai is not alone in developing aggressive tourism strategies with an eye towards differentiation. There is fierce competition for Arab leisure tourism mainly from Syria, Egypt, Lebanon, Jordan and Turkey. Of particular interest to all regional competitors are Gulf tourists. According to the World Tourism Organization, Gulf nationals and expatriates living in the GCC countries spent in 2003 around US$30 billion on travel and accommodation expenses abroad. Hence, Dubai is rightly targeting tourists from Europe and Asia. With the completion of Dubai Medical city, "health tourism" will attract additional tourists from the region, South Asia and beyond. Overall though, tourism is a volatile industry, extremely sensitive to security issues which Tunisia and Egypt only know too well.

Given its vast oil resources, Abu Dhabi has unsurprisingly been the slowest to pursue economic diversification. In sharp contrast to Dubai, in 2004 Abu Dhabi embarked upon a US$10 billion privatization of significant government-owned industrial assets. Whereas Dubai has targeted services and new technology industries, Abu Dhabi believes its comparative advantage lies in energy intensive industries, particularly petrochemicals, and manufacturing, using both cheap energy from Abu Dhabi and cheap expatriate labor. The diversification experiment that is carried out in both emirates will create success stories but also failures. It remains to be seen if the benefits will outpace the costs in the long run.

Conclusion

Growing population and the high rates of unemployment are among the most formidable challenges facing the GCC States, albeit in varied degrees. In spite of the GCC States' attempts to diversify their sources of income, they still depend largely on oil revenues. Some of the GCC States have started to attach greater importance to various industrial and service sectors as well as to re-export and tourism.

However, political and security developments unraveling across the Gulf region in light of the ramifications emanating from the conditions in Iraq and Iran will probably have palpable implications for the economies of the Gulf countries.

Obstacles to Economic Reform in the GCC

Emilie Rutledge

Economic Researcher, Gulf Research Center

"Financial dependence on volatile oil export receipts has remained high, compounding economic vulnerability to oil price shocks. Economic performance has lagged despite the GCC's enormous potential"

Rodrigo de Rato, Managing Director of the International Monetary Fund
GCC meeting of Ministers of Finance and Governors, Jeddah, October 2004

Increasingly there are calls from GCC business leaders, economists and liberal technocrats alike for the need to diversify away from dependence on oil, reduce the role of the welfare state and privatize state owned entities. Economic reform, in today's world, tends to involve increasing the role of the private sector at the expense of the public sector. Implicit in this is the opening up of national economies to foreign capital and competition, as well as conforming to global standards such as those of the International Monetary Fund (IMF) and the World Trade Organization (WTO). There are also external calls for GCC economic reform, for instance, the US Administration's Greater Middle East Initiative (GMEI) encourages "the growth of an entrepreneurial class which would be an important element in helping democracy and freedom flourish."

To varying degrees, all GCC states are facing similar economic problems: income derived from hydrocarbons no longer covers their fiscal commitments and the public sector is finding it increasingly hard to absorb the rapidly growing populations. The GCC's average population growth rate is estimated to be around 3 percent, in Saudi Arabia for instance, an estimated 60 percent of the population is less than 20 years old and around 100,000 Saudis are entering the job market annually.[1] As the oil industry is capital intensive, it is only able to employ a limited number of people. The public sector can no longer, certainly not productively, employ such large numbers of people.

Perhaps with the exception of Qatar and the United Arab Emirates (whose small populations relative to their substantial hydrocarbon reserves, reduces their immediate need to reform), it is widely recognized

---

[1] Robert Looney, Saudization and Sound Economic Reforms: Are the Two Compatible? *Strategic Insights*, Volume III, Issue 2 (February 2004).

that all the GCC states need to carry out economic reforms in several key areas, and indeed they have committed themselves to such a process, at least in principle. Firstly, there is a general need to diversify economic bases away from dependence on hydrocarbons. Not only does reliance on oil and gas revenues lead to highly cyclical shocks in the economy, it makes meaningful economic planning by the government extremely difficult. Part of the diversification process involves increasing regional integration although this is taking place - a customs union was agreed upon in 2003 - the process needs to be driven forward and more power should be devolved to GCC institutions. Secondly, there is a need to reduce the welfare state which has become extremely large and inefficient as well as reforming the labour market. Other areas of reform will be have to take place in order to mitigate the reduced role of the welfare state - if and when this occurs - such as the increased privatisation of state entities and opening up to foreign investment.

Obstacles to economic reform

Dependence on oil

The benefits from oil that brought about a marked improvement in living conditions in the 1970s and early 1980s and provided a high degree of infrastructural development has failed to generate sustainable economic growth or employment. The capital intensive nature of the oil sector has meant that it is unable to provide sufficient employment for growing national populations. Today, the GCC collectively possesses around 46 percent of the world's proven oil reserves and Qatar alone, has the world's third highest reserves of natural gas.

Following warnings from the International Monetary Fund (IMF) in the mid-1990s, when the oil price was at historically low levels, serious attention was given to the issue of economic reform and diversification away from oil. In Saudi Arabia for instance, several government subsidies were reduced, or eliminated altogether. However, hydrocarbons continue to dominate the GCC economies, on average hydrocarbon exports accounted for 77 percent of total exports, and contributed to 41 percent of total GDP in 2003. Even in Bahrain, which has by far the smallest amount of oil reserves, and where there have been concerted efforts to diversify their economic base by strengthening sectors such as aluminium smelting and financial services, 73 percent of government revenues still come from oil.

Between 2000 and 2003, the average GDP growth rate was 10 percent (average growth rate of 12 percent is expected in 2004). There has also been sustained growth in the region's stock markets in 2003 by an average of 58 percent, and further growth expected in 2004. Primarily, this can be attributed to buoyant oil prices, since 2003 oil prices have remained above US$25 per barrel and in 2004 the average price of oil was around US$40. While greater oil rev-

Table (1) Average GCC hydrocarbon dependence

	2000	2001	2002	2003
% Government revenues	78.8	75.7	74.1	73.5
% Total exports	83.3	76.6	75.5	76.8
% GDP	43.2	38.9	38.0	40.6

Source: GCC National Central Bank reports

enues have helped regional governments balance books, they have also reduced the need to carry out economic reforms. The large revenues earned from oil in 2003 and 2004 have temporarily enabled the GCC states to delay undertaking some of the more painful economic reforms. The impetus to scale back government spending through the reduction of price subsidies and welfare benefits has been weakened and has also reduced the immediate need for increased privatizations.

Oil therefore, could be considered a mixed blessing for the GCC economies and to some extent in itself presents an obstacle to economic reform. When oil prices are low, the need to instigate economic reform is high, yet when the price of oil is high the need to modify the economic status quo is low. Furthermore, the vastness of regional hydrocarbon exports and subsequent exchange rate appreciations have consequently impaired the competitiveness of non-oil exports and at the same time has made it relatively cheaper to import goods as opposed to manufacturing them domestically. This phenomenon, known as Dutch disease, tends to disadvantage locally based non-oil manufactures.

Lack of political will

For GCC governments, economic reform is a sensitive issue. In the limited form that it is already taking place, there is a concern that more fundamental reforms will lead to increased public calls for greater representation. Two areas of particular concern are the reduction in welfare spending and the privatization of state owned entities.

The generous welfare system that the GCC states introduced in the 1960s and the 1970s has become expensive. The high rate of population growth requires a continuing commitment to building new schools, new hospitals, new housing, and providing more electric power, water, and transportation. Any substantial reduction in welfare spending, elimination of subsidies or reduction in the numbers of nationals on the government payroll will present a painful transitional period of adjustment with nationals being made worse-off.

Even though the precise relationship between economic and political liberalization is unclear, in general free market reforms often increase the bargaining power of private sector and their demand to be involved in decision-making processes tends to increase. Privatization is an important step towards broader economic reforms. It enables the public to play a greater role in the economy, rather than relying on the state to facilitate all economic growth opportunities. There is a certain amount of government reluctance to proceed too rapidly with privatizations as it reduces their ability to control financial resources, thus undermining their power and influence. Additionally, the level of privatization will be impeded, at least in the short term, because many state enterprises lack transparency and tend to underemploy too many nationals. Some GCC governments tend to see public sector employment of nationals as a means to distribute wealth rather than a way to get work done in the most productive manner. Firstly, this may deter private investors because the actual underlying value of the given company's assets and profit levels will be unclear. Secondly, privatization may lead to job cuts and this will then exacerbate the levels of national unemployment and could lead to political unrest.

> **There is a certain amount of government reluctance to proceed too rapidly with privatizations as it reduces their ability to control financial resources, thus undermining their power and influence.**

Reforming the labor market may lead to resentment against the region's governments. Many nationals have long taken well remunerated public sector jobs for granted, in a sense seeing such jobs as their dividend of national oil wealth. In 2003, over 90 percent of all Kuwaiti citizens were employed by the public sector, consequently the government will need to create thousands of additional public sector jobs on an annual basis. All GCC states are heavily dependent on foreign expatriate workers. For instance in the UAE, expatriate workers comprise 90 percent of the labor market while in Qatar they comprise 83 percent. A consequence of such dependence has been the insufficient priority given to productivity levels. With little incentive to invest in improving the productivity of the expatriate labor force, it is cheaper to hire more workers from abroad than to invest in the training and technologies that stimulate greater productivity.

The GCC states face the dichotomy therefore of having difficulty in providing employment for the high numbers of nationals entering the workforce every year at the same time as having an increasing number of expatriate workers. Today in Saudi Arabia, the figure of expatriate labor is estimated to be 71 percent of the country's workforce. The unemployment rate, however, among Saudis is 8.2 percent, reaching as high as 32 percent among younger workers.[2]

In an attempt to deal with this many GCC states have adopted a policy of nationalizing the workforce. Emiratization, Saudization and Kuwaitization policies have aimed to replace foreign workers in the public sector and at the same time have stipulated targets for employing nationals in the private sector as well. This is relatively easy to instigate in the public sector but may actually have a negative impact if forced onto the private sector. There is concern that policies such as that adopted by Saudi Arabia of setting targets for the proportion of national employees to be employed by private businesses may in fact negatively impact private sector efficiency and competitiveness which could in turn force businesses to relocate, jeopardizing the growth of private sector businesses.

Objections to external interference

Even though some regional experts contend that external calls for reform have helped to bring about some 'cosmetic changes', economic reform must be seen as first and foremost an internal matter. Indeed, some external pressure could actually present an obstacle to economic reform as it may be viewed as interference. This is particularly the case with privatizing or allowing greater foreign involvement in sectors such as hydrocarbons and when economic reform is linked to social or educational reform.

The example of the Middle East Partnership Initiative (MEPI) is a case in point. The aims of the initiative are to provide support for "economic, political, and educational reform efforts in the Middle East and champion opportunity for all people of the region, especially women and youth." Many GCC citizens, understandably, dismiss such initiatives as hypocritical and imperialistic coming from an administration that provides unconditional support for Israel's occupation of Palestine and whose 'liberation' of Iraq has only added to the region's security concerns. In addition, social and religious conservative elements in GCC societies reject external interference and this poses an obstacle to economic reform. Out of the six GCC states, only Saudi Arabia has yet to join the WTO, a situation that is in part due to the fact that some Saudis are concerned about whether membership of the WTO is compatible with Sharia law. In Kuwait's July 2003

---

[2] Robert Looney, Saudization and Sound Economic Reforms: Are the Two Compatible? *Strategic Insights*, Volume III, Issue 2 (February 2004).

National Assembly elections, the Islamists strengthened their position while liberal-pro economic reform MPs lost many seats. Islamist and populist forces in the Kuwaiti national assembly remain opposed to general liberalisation of the economy, especially any foreign participation in the oil industry. Indeed, Walid Musaid al-Tabtabaie a high profile Islamist member of the Kuwaiti National Assembly, argues against many economic reform policies that he deems as 'un-Islamic'.

Security concerns

There are a range of security concerns, both internal and external which may impede certain types of economic reform. Internal security issues focus on reforms that may disenfranchise the public such as reducing the benefits provided to nationals through public sector employment and the welfare state. External security concerns involve factors such as the possible privatization of the oil industry and affect the ability of the GCC states to attract increased Foreign Direct Investment (FDI).

If the GCC states were to substantially reduce fiscal spending this could have destabilising social and political consequences. As long as welfare benefits are generous and well remunerated and public sector jobs are in plentiful supply, such questions will remain private. If, however, welfare benefits were to be cut, such questions would become less muted. On the one hand, increased poverty can lead to radicalism - a particular concern in Saudi Arabia - but on the other it will disenfranchise the population from the ruling elite and could lead to greater demands for representation and scrutiny of government accounts.

Regional disputes also play a role. Prior to Iraq's 1990 invasion of Kuwait, the country used to participate in GCC sports and cultural activities and since the removal of Sadaam Hussein, Iraq has several times asked to join the GCC. Yet, even though Kuwait and Iraq agreed to restore full diplomatic ties in 2004, the prospect of Iraq's desire to become a member of the GCC will inevitably create some security concerns. There is also the issue of the UAE's dispute with Iran over three islands in the Strait of Hormuz which the latter is occupying. These concerns are compounded by the fact that the US-led occupation of Iraq has resulted in the political map of the region being redrawn. GCC governments are worried about the threat of terrorism and in Saudi Arabia terrorist incidents have increased since the US-led invasion of Iraq. To some extent then, a relationship exists between external threat - whether real or imagined - and domestic change (such as economic reform); where the greater the former, the lesser the latter.

Regional security issues have also, in part, hindered the GCC's ability to attract increased FDI which has been another economic policy priority. So far, levels of foreign direct investment flows into the region have been extremely low. In 2003, the GCC states received just 0.3 percent of global FDI.[3] The GCC states cannot continue to be marginalised from the transfer of ideas and best practices that accompanies FDI since it represents a key driver of economic growth.

Summary

The key obstacles to greater levels of economic reform in the GCC are a combination of several interrelated factors: oil dependency, lack of political will, objections to external interference and security concerns. The region's main challenges - implementing comprehensive economic reforms, ensuring that rates of growth are higher than population growth and creating productive private sector employment - are also interrelated.

The main challenges facing economic reform in

---

[3] United Nations Conference on Trade and Development, World Investment Report 2004.

the GCC is that it will necessarily involve reducing the levels of welfare and subsidies the governments currently provide. This in turn will result in the populations being less satisfied and more likely to call for greater representation and transparency of government accounts. Furthermore, as living costs increase and public sector employment becomes less 'generous' there will be an increased need for greater female participation in the labor market in order to bring home adequate funds for the family unit, which will not necessarily be acceptable to the more conservative elements of GCC society.

Section Three

Defense and Security Issues in the GCC States

Defense Affairs

Musa Qallab

Research Manager, Defense Program, Gulf Research Center

This report covers the most important developments in defense affairs in the GCC countries (Bahrain, Kuwait Oman, Qatar, Saudi Arabia and UAE) in 2004. While relying on the published defense budgets, the unavailability of precise data on the actual defense expenditure in many of these countries, on the one hand, and the incompatibility of such expenditure with the defense budgets as allocated by them, on the other hand, means that more than often the actual defense budgets exceed the published ones. Similarly, defense expenditures as published in other references are mostly only estimates and the figures published refer to past years.[1]

The total of the GCC defense budgets in 2004 amounted to $30 billion compared to $29 billion in 2003 and $28 billion in 2002. In a descending order in terms of spending, the GCC countries can be ranked as follows: Saudi Arabia, Kuwait, Oman, UAE, Qatar and Bahrain.[2] Meanwhile, the total troop level in the GCC countries is 385,000, 40% of which composed of the Saudi army and National Guard. The ranking order again is: Saudi Arabia, UAE, Oman, Kuwait, Qatar and Bahrain.[3]

In terms of armament, sources of procurement were mainly western, especially American. It is worth noting here that the actual need for arms as determined by the threats faced by the GCC countries, whether existing or potential, is only one factor in determining arms purchases. Other

considerations including political, diplomatic, economic, financial and commercial are equally as relevant and have played a role in the finalization of defense deals in one GCC country or another. Overall, taken individually or collectively, these factors have combined to bring about a certain stability in the Gulf defense procurement.

Bahrain

Defense budget
The Bahraini defense budget for 2004 was about $473 million. As this does not include procurement items, there has been an increase of $13 million on

---

[1] It is worth mentioning that the *Military Balance 2004-2005* published by the International Institute for Strategic Studies in London does not list the defense budgets of many countries including those of the GCC due to the lack of accurate information. Likewise, the report presented here does not provide the percentages of the relative defense budgets in relation to GNP since this requires the exact data, figures and statistics that are hard to obtain.

[2] International Institute for Strategic Studies (IISS), *Military Balance 2004-2005* (Oxford: Oxford University Press, 2004), 302-305.

[3] *World Defense Guide 2003-2004,* published in collaboration with the Economic and Business Group and the German Muench Group (Beirut), 16-20.

the 2003 budget and an increase of $42 million on the 2002 budget. The Bahraini GDP for 2003 was approximately $8.2 billion.[4]

Manpower

The total Bahraini military personnel has remained steady at 11,000 soldiers including 8,500 in the army, 1,350 in the navy and coastguard, and 1,000 in the air force. There is an expectation that this figure could increase in the future due to the introduction of new weaponry. The paramilitary force includes about 2,000 policemen. There also is a national guard of 1,000 men established to take up duties of internal security which is independent of the armed forces. Military personnel are all volunteers.[5]

Weapons systems

The American navy has decided to supply Bahrain with a FFG 12 frigate out of its navy surplus or as part of a hire purchase scheme. There has been no confirmation of the deal by the Bahraini authorities.[6] Overall, there has been a tendency in Bahrain to cut down on procurement plans with the parliament deciding to reduce the 2005 defense budget by $10.6 million in order to give priority to development and infrastructure projects.[7]

Present defense data indicate that priority is given to the air force. Bahrain is taking delivery of two F-16 C/D aircraft, together with 10 other aircrafts of the same type that had been purchased back in the year 2000. The air force will also acquire systems for control, surveillance and communication, and it will consider the purchase of additional helicopters. As for training aircraft, sources at British aerospace said that Bahrain had ordered 6 Hawk 200 fighters due for delivering in 2006. There is also an option to buy 6 more aircrafts of the same type in the future.[8] The Bahraini navy, meanwhile, has merely announced its intention of buying sea landing craft. The army's procurement includes the purchase of rocket launchers, something ascribed to the nature of the potential threats and the geography of Bahrain as an island.

Kuwait

Defense budget

Kuwait's defense budget for 2004 was $4 billion, an increase of $200 million on 2003 and $500 million on 2002. The GDP in 2003 was about $ 40 billion.[9]

Manpower

Kuwaiti military personnel in 2004 included about 15,000 in addition to 24,000 reservists. There is an indication that the Kuwaiti army might number about 40,000 in the future. The Kuwaiti National Guard has around 5,000 soldiers and is expected to be expanded and developed along the lines of the Saudi National Guard as a force independent of the army. All salaried Kuwaiti troops are volunteers who have the option to join the reserve force after two years of regular service. No actual increase in manpower exists when compared to 2002 and 2003. Servicemen are 12,000 in the army, 1,500 in the navy and 2,500 in the airforce.[10]

---

[4] IISS, *Military Balance 2004-2005*, 302.

[5] *World Defense Guide 2003 -2004*, 22.

[6] Ibid.

[7] *Defense Magazine*, Beirut, No. 51 (March 2004): 29 as declared by the minister of defense, General Shaikh Khalifah Bin Hamad Al-Khalifah

because of auditioning exerted by parliament as required by the new royal constitution.

[8] *Defense Magazine*, Beirut, No. 50 (January 2004): 25.

[9] IISS, *Military Balance 2004-2005*, 303.

[10] *World Defense Guide 2003-2004*, 41-42.

Weapons Systems

In addition to putting out a tender for 4 to 6 light missile frigates, Kuwait signed contracts to purchase a total of 3 boats for delivery in 2004. Kuwait showed interests as well in buying an unknown number of F/A-18 E/F Super Hornet aircraft to consolidate its naval force. In this context, a Kuwaiti airforce delegation held official discussions with the Boeing company about upgrading the current fleet of hornet fighters including improving their airborne radar operation and power. The Kuwaiti government also discussed with the Raytheon company the possibility of upgrading the Patriot anti-missile system which Kuwait had bought in the wake of the second Gulf war in 1990.[11]

The Kuwaiti army ordered 16 American Apache helicopter gunships, 8 of which are of the Advanced Long Bow variety. Delivery of these helicopters is due to start in 2005 and the deal is meant to consolidate the armored land forces. The Kuwaiti airforce has put on sale around 14 French made Mirage fighters, as well as a 9 Tocano training aircraft, with the intention of modernizing its training aircraft in the future. Negotiations have also been going on to buy 4 American made C-130 military transport aircraft to meet operational and logistical needs.[12]

Strategic alliance

Kuwait saw its status for the US consolidated when the country was designated as a major non-NATO ally, a clear appreciation of the role played by Kuwait in bringing peace to the world and fighting international terrorism.[13] In this context, however, the Kuwaiti defense ministry denied speculation that outside pressures had been applied to buy weapons from particular external sources. Kuwait also quelled rumors that its decision to cancel a purchase of some British military systems represented a downgrading of Kuwaiti-British military ties. It also stressed it was going ahead with plans to build up its defensive force and refrain from threatening any party or country.[14]

Oman

Defense budget

The Oman defense budget for 2004 was $2.6 billion representing an increase of $100 million over both the 2002 and 2003 budgets. Oman's GDP for 2003 was around $21 billion.[15]

Manpower

Omani air forces personnel in 2004 included about 43,000 servicemen in addition to 3,700 non-Omani soldiers. The Omani paramilitary force includes an air wing and a coastguard besides a tribal guard of 3,500 soldiers. As there is no conscription in Oman, manpower numbers have remained steady. The army numbered 25,000 men, 6,000 of whom are in Sultan's guard. Airmen are 5,000 and the navy has 4,500 soldiers.[16]

Weapons systems

Oman invited offers for the supply of two 75 meter long frigates as part of a plan to upgrade the capabilities of the Omani navy and consolidate it with helicopter gunships. In that context, 20 British made Super Lynx helicopter gunships are to be delivered for use for naval survey and surveillance. Oman has also ordered 12 American made F-16

---

[11] *Defense Magazine*, Beirut, No. 50 (January 2004): 26.
[12] *World Defense Guide 2003-2004*, 42.
[13] *Qatar News Agency*, April 2, 2004 quoting a statement by Shaikh Jaber Al Mubarak Al-Sabah, Kuwaiti Deputy Prime Minister and Defense Minister.
[14] Al-Sharq Al-Awsat, July 19, 2004.
[15] IISS, Military Balance 2004-2005, 304.
[16] Ibid, 36-38.

C/D block 50 aircraft to be used for air supremacy. Delivery of these aircrafts will start in 2005. This procurement plan is meant to fulfill the aim of diversifying the sources of arms as most Omani aircraft are either British or French made. There is also a plan to acquire medium capacity transport helicopters to replace most of the existing transport helicopters in the Omani airforce. 15 British made Jaguar fighters have already been upgraded to match other British aircrafts in operation in Oman. An advanced three dimensional S74 radar has also been purchased.[17]

The Sultanate of Oman concluded a 4.3 million UAE dirham deal with the Abu Dhabi Shipyard Company to build 12 boats for the Omani coastguard to be able to undertake joint tasks with the army as well as reduce manufacturing costs.[18] In general, Oman has taken part in all Gulf defense activities, coordinated its policies with their neighbors including Yemen and Iran.

Qatar

Defense budget

Qatar's defense budget in 2004 was around $2.1 billion, an increase of $200 million on 2002 and 2003. The GDP in 2003 was $19.2 billion.[19]

Manpower

The Qatari armed forces in 2004 numbered 12,000 personnel to which one can add a paramilitary force including the Emiri guard under the command of the defense ministry and the police force. No conscription is in force in Qatar, and there

has been no increase in personnel on 2002 and 2003. The army numbers 8,500 men, the navy 1,500 including the air police while the air force has 1,500 airmen.[20]

Weapons Systems

The London IISS Military Balance 2004-2005 makes no mention of any Qatari arms purchases in 2004 or any arms deliveries. The Stockholm International Peace Research Institute also makes no mention of any data on the Qatari defense expenditure. Qatar has invited offers from world manufacturers to build 40 combat tanks to replace their existing French made AMX 30 which are getting old. The Qatari air force has decommissioned and offered for sale a complete squadron of 12 modern Mirage 2000-5 aircraft. Some quarters claim that Qatar may replace these aircrafts with American F-16 fighter jets but no decision has been taken since 2001 on this.[21]

Military security

In order to consolidate the security of its armed forces, the Emiri court issued a decree to establish the first military intelligence department. This department will report to the supreme commander of the armed forces. It will have a head, a deputy head as well as a number of assistants and officers that will be appointed by an Emiri decree.[22]

International conference

One of the most important events in Qatar was the convening on April 20, 2004 of the Doha conference to discuss NATO and Gulf security with a view to establish stability in the Gulf region and find ways for overall development that requires guarding

---

[17] World Defense Guide 2003 -2004, 38.

[18] Emirates News Agency, May 25, 2004.

[19] IISS, Military Balance 2004-2005, 304. The book makes no mention of Qatari arms deals and the time of delivery. See page 107.

[20] World Defense Guide 2003-2004, 40.

[21] Ibid.

[22] Al-Watan (Qatar), May 7, 2004.

against outside threats. The idea for the meeting grew directly out of the experience over the past two decades in which the region experienced a number of threats. As a result, there have been increasing calls for cooperation with influential parties to assist in warding off potential and existing threats.[23] In this context, for example, the rear commands of the American navy and air forces are still stationed at Qatari bases and in Qatari territorial waters.

Saudi Arabia

Defense Budget

The Kingdom's defense budget for 2004 totaled around $ 19.3 billion, an increase of $600 million over the 2003 figures and $800 million over 2002. The defense budget, covering both defense and security, has witnessed successive increases over past years to account for new armament and security plans for land, sea and air requirements. The GDP for Saudi Arabia for 2003 totaled around $ 211.1 billion.[24]

Manpower

The total Saudi armed forces personnel in 2004 was around 160,000 troops which includes the paramilitary force of the National Guard whose servicemen totaled around 75,000, the Coast Guard with 6,000 men and a special anti-terror branch. No significant change to manpower took place since 2002 and 2003. However, an ambitious plan has been announced to increase the armed forces servicemen to 200,000, all of whom volunteers. Although conscription plan is in place, this has not yet been put into effect. The army's

servicemen exceeded 75,000, although the intended number is 90,000. As for the navy, its servicemen totaled 13,500 of whom 3,000 are marine infantry. Servicemen in the airforce are 18,000.[25] The intention to increase the manpower of the armed forces could be part of a plan to establish new formations and enforce existing ones. This is due to internal security requirements as a result of the terrorist attacks in both 2003 and 2004.

Weapons systems

Saudi Arabia intends to buy 65 tanks as a first batch of 150 advanced tanks following the decision to decommission half of its French made AMX-30 tanks due to their age and high maintenance cost. The new tanks will be exclusively US Abrams M1A2, British challengers and French Leclercs. In order to regenerate the national light defense industries, the armed forces received 50 of the Saudi made 8X8 Al Fahid wheeled vehicles. It is possible that another order to acquire vehicles of the same type may be issued. Negotiations are also underway to acquire German made Fuchs vehicles which are capable of detecting weapons of mass destruction. Saudi Arabia intends to replace the old Chinese DF 3A ballistic missiles by a more advanced Chinese or Russian medium range ballistic system[26].

In the air force, the F-15 aircraft have been equipped with approximately 500 advanced medium range air to air missile, and Saudi Arabia has become the first Middle Eastern country to acquire missiles that operate beyond the range of eyesight in order to develop their air-to-air combat missions. British tornado IDS bombers are being upgraded to the level of the advanced GR-4 aircraft for ground attack purposes in relations to its arms system, bomb load and advanced technical

---

[23] *Qatar News Agency*, April 20, 2004, on the opening of a conference on NATO and Gulf changes under the auspices of HRH Shaikh Tameem Bin Hamad Al-Thani, Qatari Crown Prince and Deputy Emir.

[24] IISS, *Military Balance 2004-2005*, 304.
[25] *World Defense Guide 2003 -2004*, 28-32.
[26] Ibid, 30.

equipments. Plans have also been set to upgrade the Apache helicopter gunships to the level of advanced Apache AH-64D in order to support armored units. The Saudi air force is modernizing its five AWACS aircraft with a state-of-the-art electronic system as present systems are antiquated and no longer are compatible with the latest systems of surveillance, command, control and communication. Delivery has been taken of 44 Italian AB-412TP search and rescue aircraft.[27] The navy in 2004 received a third French made Riyadh Lafayette frigate.

Generally speaking, there have been no changes in the defense strategy established for years in conjunction with the GCC countries including in terms of Gulf inter-defense relations. Saudi Arabia is also going ahead with its stable defense policies towards non-GCC neighbors such as Yemen through the demarcation and control of borders.

United Arab Emirates

Defense Budget

No change has been made to the UAE defense budget for many years with the budget staying the same in the years of 2002, 2003 and 2004 at about $1.6 billion per annum. This despite the fact that the UAE's GDP in 2003 had grown to approx. $78 billion. The defense budget, however, did not include additional procurement which greatly contributed to an increase in the estimated annual expenditure of $2.8 billion. This declared expenditure has remained stable for nine years.[28]

Manpower

Armed forces personnel number remained the same between 2002 and 2004 at around 43,400 composed of 40,000 in the army, 1,900 in the navy and 1,500 in the air force.

Weapons system

The American F-16 aircraft deal is the central component of the UAE-US military deals. The first batch of 80 aircraft was to be handed over in April 2004 but delays have postponed that to 2005. All deliveries are to be completed by 2007, the total cost of the project being $6.4 billion.[29] This advanced airpower will be a huge deterrent as it includes advanced aviation and armament systems such as air-to-air AMRAAM missiles, anti-radar Harm missiles, and Hakeem missiles. The aircraft are much more sophisticated than those in the possession of other countries in the region, particularly Iran. The aircraft include an integrated mechanical system for command and control and an advanced command and control system, especially the Hawkeye early warning system from the Northrop Grumman Company.[30]

The UAE air force has also been taking delivery of the first batch of 33 multi-purpose French made Mirage 2000-9 aircraft with enhanced bombing capability. The handover is scheduled to be completed in 2005. This coincided with a process to upgrade the existing Mirage 2000-EAD/DAD to the level of the Mirage 2000-9. The number of such aircraft will reach 63 by the end of year 2005. There is also an order to purchase 14 French made Acoreil AS-350B helicopters to train pilots.

The UAE has purchased 6 French made large boats under the Bainunah program with the first boat scheduled to be built at the dockyards of the French company CMN and delivered in 2008. Other boats will be built at the Abu Dhabi ADSB dockyards so that development can continue and

---

[27] Ibid.

[28] IISS, Military Balance 2004-2005, 301.

[29] Defense Magazine, Beirut, No. 51 (March 2004): 64.

[30] Defense Magazine, Beirut, No. 50 (January 2004): 12.

meet requirements of modern sea warfare. Negotiations also took place to buy 4 EADS Casa C -295 aircraft for sea patrol and the Shaheen-1 system for attack purposes in order to support the navy and collect intelligence on threats at sea. Furthermore, 4 heavy multi-purpose sea landing ships have been ordered. Plans are also in place to upgrade the combat capability of two existing frigates of the Abu Dhabi type.[31]

The UAE and Oman have concluded separate deals with Abu Dhabi dockyards to buy 42 armored boats, 30 of which are for the UAE and 12 for the Omani coastguard. The cost of the deal is 15 million dirhams, 4.3 million of which will be met by Oman as a means to reduce costs.[32]

The French Giat company delivered to the UAE in 2004 the last batch of Leclerc tanks bringing the total to 390. Such tanks have an advanced weaponry system and are suited to the hot and dusty Gulf climate which affects combat readiness and the maintenance of armored vehicles in battle.[33]

Training

In terms of training and cooperation, the German defense ministry announced a cooperation arrangement with the UAE to train Iraqi officers and soldiers whereby Germany would provide the experts for training and the UAE meets the logistical requirements. This deal forms part of the aid program for the Iraqi government. A statement by the German defense ministry indicated that a team of 34 German experts arrived in the UAE in November 2004 on a two-month mission. Experts of the German federal anti-crime department had already trained over two hundred of Iraqi security personnel. The German defense ministry made it clear that its efforts fulfill the decisions taken by NATO at its meeting in Istanbul on January 28, 2004. Germany also sent to the UAE 20 military vehicles to be used in training the Iraqi security forces. Other German experts took part in overhauling and repairing Iraqi vehicles in the UAE. Germany has also offered to send 80 other military vehicles to the UAE to support the Iraqi army although Germany still refuses to participate in direct military tasks in Iraq.[34] The German general Harald Kujat, chief of military works at NATO praised the military cooperation between Germany and the UAE in training the new military units for the Iraqi army.[35] In this context, visits have been made to the UAE by Iraqi officials, notably Defense Minister Hazem Al-Shaalan who visited Abu Dhabi on November 27, 2004 to met senior armed forces officials.[36]

GCC Peninsula Shield Force and joint action

The number of the peninsula shield force is between 5,000 to 10,000 troops depending on the need to raise the combat readiness level in response to the strategic situation in the Gulf region. The GCC countries still intend to gradually increase the number of this force to 20,000 servicemen.[37] Progress has been made improving communications for the force with a military communication cable being laid connecting the air defense centers with an early warning system. A large number of references and training booklets have, as well, been standardized in order to unify the military basics and concepts among the GCC countries.[38]

---

[31] IISS, *Military Balance 2004-2005,* 308.

[32] *Emirates News Agency*, May 25, 2004.

[33] *World Defense Guide 2003-2004*, 18.[34] *Kuwait News Agency*, November 17, 2004.

[35] *The Emirate Gulf Journal*, August 5, 2004.

[36] *Emirates News Agency*

[37] *Gulf News* (Dubai), May 12, 2002.

[38] *Emirates News Agency*, May 6, 2004.

Within the context of cooperation and coordination, a coordination meeting was held in Kuwait at the level of deputy chiefs of staff between April 18 and 21, 2004.[39] This meeting was aimed to coordinate joint exercises and maneuvers and discuss ways to develop the peninsula shield force as a joint defense effort. Joint exercises in 2004 included the Rimah 2 (Lances 2) exercises executed in two stages in Saudi Arabia. These exercises are held every two years and hosted by a member state as part of military cooperation in order to raise the standard of performance and training within the GCC air force.[40]

At the level of decision making, the GCC joint defense board held its third regular meeting in Kuwait on October 4 and 5, 2004 to discuss the joint military cooperation process. The GCC secretariat general said in a statement that the meeting discussed various military issues, notably the following:[41]

o The peninsula shield force and the completion of its development and organizational studies.

o Review and discussion of progress in various joint military projects, including the cooperative belt for search and identification of aircraft, the coded military communications, and the Gulf military surveillance satellite.

o Arrangements for joint exercises on land, at sea and in the air, according to the scheduled yearly exercises.

The effect of the US Military presence

The deployment of US forces in the Gulf region as part of the US-led invasion and occupation of Iraq beginning in 2003 have raised concerns of contributing to overall instability including in Iraq, in Saudi Arabia and Yemen, and the possibility that similar incidents could happen in other GCC countries. The threat is further increased by the presence of around 140,000 US troops in Iraq and the US-Iranian dispute over Iran's nuclear program which includes the possibility of a military confrontation between the two sides, and the possibility of an all out war breaking out in the area with Israel as a party to it. Therefore, it is not expected that the external and internal threats will recede unless the situation in Iraq settles down and unless the US-Iran dispute is resolved as part of a comprehensive settlement to all military dangers that threaten the region.

The uncertainty of the foreseeable future makes it likely that an armament build up will continue to be a top priority for the GCC. This, however, is notwithstanding the need to control defense expenditures and allocate funding for other development programs, particularly since the purchase of expensive weapons systems has not only burdened the budgets over the last fifteen years but have also not succeeded in bringing about a more stable security situation. With oil prices on the rise, this may lead to a further rise in the cost of arms deals thereby adding an additional burden to the existing defense budgets.

Conclusion

The GCC countries are trying to control military expenditure, albeit gradually and slowly, while defense ministries and armed forces are moving ahead with upgrading and modernization projects as well as taking delivery of previously contracted arms purchases. There

---

[39] *Al-Watan* (Oman), April 18, 2004.
[40] *Saudi News Agency*, August 17, 2004.

[41] Press release on the GCC third regular meeting on October 5 as it appeared on the GCC website www.gcc-sg.org/gcc.news

is also a serious attempt underway to raise the standard of collective military coordination among member states and develop the peninsula shield force.

The peninsula shield force consists of more that an armored division backed up by all sorts of land support including artillery, corps of engineers, communication, and logistics. Air and naval support is provided with equipment supplied by marines, air forces, and air defenses of member states. The peninsula shield force, at its present headquarters in the Hafr Al Baten area, gets air and artillery support from the Saudi armed forces. When it is established in any of the GCC countries, the host country will provide support, including air and sea support, in conjunction with other member states that have the required facilities.

Table (1) Data on GCC countries

Country	Population	GDP 2003	Defense budget 2003 (in billion $)
Bahrain	712,000	$ 8.2	$ 460 million
Kuwait	2.4 m	$ 40.3	$ 3.8
Oman	2.6 m	$ 21	$ 2.5
Qatar	624,000	$ 19.2	$ 1.9
Saudi Arabia	22.5 m	$ 211	$ 18.7
UAE	4.0 m	$ 78	$ 1.6
Total	32.8 m	$ 377.7	$ 28.96

Source: IISS, Military Balance 2004-2005

Table (2) Statistics on GCC neighboring countries

Country	Population	GNP 2003	Defense budget 2003 (billion $)
Iran	66	128	3
Iraq	24.7	Unavailable	Unavailable
Yemen	19.2	11.4	797 million

Source: IISS, Military Balance 2004-2005

Table (3) Statistics on other selected countries

Country	Population	GNP 2003	Defense budget 2003 (in billion $)
Israel	6.7	109	7.4
US	291	10.9 trillion	456.2
Pakistan	148.4	69.6	2.8
Russia	143.4	1.31 trillion	10.6
China	1288.4	1.43 trillion	22.4
Egypt	67.6	67.5	1.7

Source: IISS, Military Balance 2004-2005

Security Developments in the Gulf

Dr. Mustafa Alani

Senior Advisor and Program Director for Security and Terrorism Studies, Gulf Research Center

Security developments in the Gulf region over 2004 centered on the internal situations of the Gulf countries. Of significant note were the developments in the four states of Iraq, the Kingdom of Saudi Arabia, Yemen and Iran.

Kuwait and Bahrain

Minor, yet important developments took place in the remaining Gulf States. The Kingdom of Bahrain, for example, battled the internal security challenge posed by opposition forces in the country. Such opposition has manifested itself in the organization of popular marches and other protest activities that strongly criticized the domestic policy of the Bahraini government and also denounced the US's occupation of Iraq and its policy in the Middle East. It must be noted that the evolving climate of increasing political openness in the country over the past few years has allowed for such activities to be possible. There were also minor security developments in the Kingdom: in mid 2004, for example, security agencies detained a number of Bahraini citizens for the purpose of investigating a suspected terrorist plot to attack targets in the Kingdom. At the same time, the American authorities proclaimed a state of alert to all US citizens and US facilities in Bahrain; a number of US citizens were subsequently evacuated. Overall, however, the general security situation in the state remained calm without any serious developments.

Kuwait, however, has faced major problems resulting from the deteriorating security situation in Iraq, largely due to its geographic proximity to it but also because of the emirate's internal situation. Concerns over issues related to Iraq prompted the Kuwaiti authorities at the beginning of the year to build an iron fence over 200 kilometers in length along the line of the Iraqi-Kuwaiti borders in hopes of preventing illegal infiltration of the borders on both sides. In mid 2004, a state of alert was proclaimed in the Kuwaiti ports as a precaution against a possible attack from the sea by a terrorist group.

The depth of the Kuwaiti security dilemma and the implications of developments in Iraq on the country's security and stability were confirmed in July, when Kuwaiti security forces detained a number of Kuwaiti citizens on charges of forming a network to recruit volunteers to fight the American occupation forces in Iraq. This coincided with a handover by the Syrian authorities of a number of Kuwaiti citizens to the Kuwaiti security forces after they had been detained on Syrian territory whilst attempting to cross the borders into Iraq. Over the course of the year, Kuwaiti authorities brought a number of Kuwaiti citizens before the courts on the charge of attempting to participate in operations against occupation forces in Iraq.

Although security challenges this year have included both armed and unarmed activities, the Gulf States were able to bypass any major threat from political opposition groups by resorting to the temporary detention or arrest of active group members in Bahrain, Saudi Arabia and Iran. Thus, the most serious challenges to security in the Gulf States over 2004 continue to arise from armed groups carrying out terrorist acts.

2 Iraq

The situation of chaos and instability in Iraq has emerged as the prime source of some of the most serious challenges faced by the region in 2004. January (which marked eight months since the downfall of the Iraqi regime and the US occupation of the state) was characterized by a serious escalation of violence at all levels. This year has been one of the bloodiest and most violent, with more than 1,000 civilians killed and close to three times this figure wounded or incapacitated. Aside from civilian casualties, there were repeated bloody assaults targeting the recently formed police forces and the National Guard, both of whom sustained an estimated number of 1,000 killed. Considerable losses were also sustained by the occupation forces, which had been targeted throughout the year in intensified and variegated operations.

The increase in the number and variety of terrorist operations in Iraq continues to have serious consequences on the internal security and stability of the surrounding states. The primary concern in this regard is the potential "export" and spread of terrorism to neighboring countries. Thus, the deteriorating security conditions have led the six states surrounding Iraq, three of which are Gulf States, to coordinate their efforts in order to prevent the continued deterioration of the security situation and its subsequent impact upon regional stability. These states have accordingly participated at the

ministerial level in the Sharm Al-Sheikh and Tehran meetings held during the last quarter of the year with the aim of providing assistance in stabilizing the security situation to allow for legislative elections to be held in Iraq.

It is clear that the security crisis will not come to an end along with the year. Rather, the US push for political and constitutional developments for the next year - particularly the organization of legislative elections without a sustained effort to create the necessary conditions to support such developments - will alienate many parties in the Iraqi community. This will consequently deepen the security dilemma in Iraq.

3 Yemen

During 2004, Yemen witnessed one of its greatest challenges to the state's legitimacy since the end of the Yemeni civil war. A major source of confrontation to the Yemeni authorities came from the organization known as the "Believing Youths," which was founded in 1997 and headed by the cleric Hussain Badr Al Deen Al-Houthi. Headquartered in the northern Saada Governorate, initial acts of rebellion from this grouping commenced in June and continued - alternating between political nego-tiations and armed conflict - for a period of more than three months. The Yemeni authorities were not able to put an end to the rebellion until Al-Hothy was killed and a large number of his supporters surrendered in September. It was officially announced that the Yemeni army had lost about 400 of their personnel in confrontations with the rebel forces. The official news, however, did not refer to the number of losses sustained by the rebels; hence, the total number of casualties cannot be estimated.

Moreover, in the perpetual campaign to disarm

Yemeni citizens, the authorities announced that they had spent close to US$50 million on buying weapons owned by citizens.

In other developments, the trial of eleven Al-Qaeda members accused of working for the organization on Yemeni territory began in early 2004. The defendants included six members accused of planning and executing the assault against the American USS Cole in 2000, and five others of being involved in the assault against the French Limburg in 2002. In early December, the court issued preliminary death sentences upon two of the accused and prison sentences of between five and ten years upon the remaining four accused of carrying out the attack against the USS Cole. The decision to initiate the trial came after several hesitations and delays lasting several years for both technical and political reasons.

Saudi Arabia

In Saudi Arabia, the year 2004 brought with it a marked escalation in confrontations between armed terrorist groups and the Saudi authorities. The latter were able to kill or detain a large number of those involved in terrorist activities through a series of raids and armed confrontations that took place throughout the year. Key figures were among those killed, including such men as Khaled Al-Hajj and Abdulaziz Al-Muqren, who were believed to head cells of the Al-Qaida organization in the Kingdom. These remarkable victories for the Saudi security forces did not, however, put a decisive end to the activities of the terrorist groups.

The year 2004 has also witnessed a number of significant terrorist acts that claimed the lives of a number of Saudi citizens and foreigners residing in the Kingdom. The car bomb assaults against the headquarters of the traffic police in Riyadh, which took place in April, marked the beginning of major terrorist operations. This was followed by an armed assault in the coastal city of Yanbu in May, which targeted the headquarters of a Swiss-Swedish petrochemical company. In the same month, the city of Khobar witnessed an armed assault against three residential compounds killing 22 persons, 19 of whom were foreigners residing in the Kingdom; this was one of the largest such acts of the year. Statistics have shown that in the period between May and August terrorist operations in the Kingdom claimed the lives of about 90 persons.

The assault and storming of the American Consulate in Jeddah in December was considered a major shift in tactics from attacking easy civilian targets to attacking fortified foreign targets, considered prime targets for the terrorist groups. In April, American authorities instructed American citizens residing in the Kingdom to evacuate, as they had received information indicating that terrorist operations were likely to be executed against American targets in the Kingdom.

Statistics prepared by the Gulf Research Center indicate that the year 2004 was one full of clashes between Saudi authorities and armed militants in the Kingdom. Sixty-eight victims were killed in these confrontations, including 29 security men, five citizens and 34 expatriates. Casualty statistics indicate that there were 138 victims, including 90 casualties among security men, eight among citizens and 40 among expatriates. The terrorist groups

> **In Saudi Arabia, the year 2004 brought with it a marked escalation in confrontations between armed terrorist groups and the Saudi authorities.**

sustained total losses of 199; 51 were killed, 17 wounded, and 131 detained.

2004 also witnessed a development in the methods employed by terrorist groups. In mid June, one such group kidnapped the American citizen Paul Johnson, making demands that were to be met in return for his freedom. This was the first operation in the Kingdom involving the kidnapping of foreigners rather than simply murdering them, although it now appears that the American hostage was executed within a few days of his detention.

International control efforts targeting the finance of terrorist groups have played an important strategic role in the fight against terror. The relevant authorities in the Kingdom announced a decision in October to close and liquidate the Al-Haramain charity, which was accused by American authorities of financing terrorist groups. No official reason was given by the Saudi authorities for stopping the activities of the institution and liquidating its assets; it must also be noted that the charity denied the American accusations.

As a contribution to Saudi efforts in combating terrorism in the Kingdom, on June 23 Crown Prince Abdullah bin Abdulaziz announced a government amnesty of one month applicable to all those involved in terrorist organizations in order to give them a chance to recant and return to their community without fear of any legal repercussions. The scheme was only partially successful.

Iran

Iran's security dossier contains several potential clash-points in the year ahead, the most important being the cat-and-mouse game between the Iranian leadership and the international community regarding, in particular, accusations of Iran's alleged

attempt to develop a clandestine nuclear program for military purposes. Talks on this subject went back and forth between Iran and the International Atomic Energy Agency over 2004, with the European Union acting as a mediator. Tensions heightened over the threat of a possible Israeli or American military action aimed at destroying Iran's nuclear capabilities. November's developments were a decisive factor in alleviating and overcoming the crisis when an announcement was made that a settlement had been reached.

A further security concern arose relating to the official Iraqi-American statements accusing Iran of intervention in the internal affairs of Iraq. The US accused Iran of attempting to change the political status quo in Iraq, primarily through the alliance with the Iraqi religious groups and political parties historically linked with Iran, which serves the latter's interests and goals in dominating the political life of the state. There was also another accusation which affirmed that Iran was sending a large number of Iranian citizens to Iraq to settle there and seeking to influence its internal conditions in a manner that would serve Iran's strategic interests.

During the year, information emerged concerning the holding of bilateral talks between Iran and the Kingdom of Saudi Arabia and other Gulf States for the purpose of extraditing a number of Gulf citizens held in Iranian prisons to their respective states. An unidentified number of the detainees were believed to be members of the Al-Qaeda Organization who had escaped from Afghanistan and taken refuge in Iran. It is believed that these talks eventually bore fruit when the Iranian security authorities agreed to hand over or deport a number of those who were wanted in the Gulf States.

In the latter half of the year, the Gulf waters were a theater of unfriendly skirmishes in which Iran was a direct party. During the month of June, the Iranian navy held three war boats belonging to the British navy near the joint naval line between Iraq and Iran on the pretext that the boats had entered Iran's territorial waters. They also held eight British soldiers belonging to a British marine unit. The captives were released only after a few days of detention and diplomatic negotiations. Simultaneously and in separate incidents, boats belonging to the coastal guards of Qatar, the United Arab Emirates and Kuwait held a number of Iranian fishing boats on the charge of entering and fishing in territorial waters or in areas of economic benefit belonging to these states without prior permission. In return, Iran seized two fishing boats belonging to Qatar on the same pretext. The developments exacerbated relations between Iran and the three Arab states for a short while before the matter was settled.

Conclusion

Generally speaking, and with the exception of the deteriorating security condition in Iraq and the activities of terrorist groups in Saudi Arabia, the security conditions in the other Gulf States remained relatively stable. Next year, the political and security developments in the Iraqi arena will play a decisive role, either negative or positive, on the stability of the Gulf region. These developments are expected to have immediate and long term strategic effects on security developments next year.

Table (1) Acts of Violence and Terrorism in Saudi Arabia according to Date, Timing, Site Location and Type

Date	Timing	Site Location	Type
January 4, 2004		Riyadh	Defusing a bomb planted at a residential building
January 10, 2004		Switzerland	Swiss security authorities apprehend eight Saudis on wanted list
January 11, 2004			Exchange of a number of wanted terrorists between Saudi and Moroccan authorities
January 12, 2004			Interrogation of eight arrested terrorists and seizure of a quantity of weapons and ammunition
January 29, 2004		Riyadh	Apprehension of a wanted terrorist after an exchange of fire and search of his home
February 4, 2004	Evening	Riyadh	Arrest of a suspected terrorist
February 8, 2004		Riyadh	Arrest of a suspected terrorist
March 15, 2004	Evening	Riyadh	Exchange of fire in a hunt-down operation of suspected terrorists
March 15, 2004		London	The Saudi embassy receives an envelope suspected of including Anthrax
March 31, 2004		Brida	Arrest of an Arab expatriate found giving refuge to a number of wounded suspects
April 5, 2004	Evening	Riyadh	Chasing down and exchanging fire with a number of suspected terrorists
April 9, 2004	Afternoon	Jeddah	Shooting of a police officer
April 12, 2004	Evening	Riyadh	Operation against and exchanging fire with suspected terrorists
April 13, 2004	Morning	Riyadh	Exchange of fire with a number of extremists
April 14, 2004		Riyadh	Operation against and exchanging fire with suspected terrorists
April 17, 2004		Jeddah	Defusing of a car bomb
April 18, 2004			Arrest of Dr. Saeed Al-Zaeer for openly supporting extremists on a TV program channel
April 18, 2004			Defusing of three car bombs
April 20, 2004		Brida	Apprehension of a terrorist suspect
April 21, 2004	Afternoon	Riyadh	Bomb attack against the general traffic directorate
April 22, 2004	Evening	Jeddah	Operation against a terrorist hide-out
May 1, 2004	Morning	Yanba'a	Attack against an industrial complex
May 12, 2004	Dawn	Al-Madinah	Operation against a terrorist hide-out
May 20, 2004	Afternoon	Brida	Operation against on a terrorist hide-out
May 22, 2004	Afternoon	Riyadh	Shooting of a German expatriate
May 29, 2004	Morning	Al-Khobar	A number of wanted terrorists break into a company and a residential complex
June 2, 2004	Morning	Al-Taef	Laying siege around a number of wanted terrorists
June 2, 2004	Morning	Al-Kharaj- Route towards Riyadh	Terrorists shoot at cars driven by nationals and expatriates
June 6, 2004	Late afternoon	Riyadh	Shots against a number of expatriates
June 8, 2004	Afternoon	Riyadh	One expatriate shot
June 12, 2004	Late afternoon	Riyadh	One expatriate shot
June 13, 2004	Evening	Riyadh	One expatriate kidnapped
June 18, 2004	Evening	Riyadh	Shootouts with a number of wanted terrorists
June 24, 2004		Al-Namass	A wanted terrorist, Sa'aban Mohamed Abdallah Al-Yalhali Al-Shahri, surrenders to authorities
June 28, 2004			A wanted terrorist, Othman Hadi Al Makbul Al-Umri, surrenders to authorities

June 30, 2004	Late afternoon	Riyadh	Exchange of fire with a number of wanted terrorists
July 1, 2004		Riyadh	Police raid against a residential villa hosting terrorists
July 1, 2004		Riyadh	Exchange of fire with a number of wanted terrorists
July 3, 2004		Riyadh	Death of a number of injured from the Al-Fayha'a incident on April 12, 2004
July 4 2004		Riyadh	Death of a security officer in a confrontation on King Fahd Street, Riyadh, on June 30, 2004
July 13 2004		Iran	A wanted terrorist, Khalid bin Awada Al-Harbi, surrenders to authorities
July 17 2004		Syria	A wanted terrorist, Ibrahim As-Sadiq Al-Bakri Al-Qaidi, turns himself in to the authorities
July 18 2004			27 Saudis wanted by the security forces are handed over by different countries
July 21 2004		Riyadh	A raid against a terrorist den on King Fahd Street and three other hide-outs
July 22 2004		Syria	A wanted terrorist, Fawzan Nasser Al-Fawzan, surrenders to authorities
July 22 2004		Taef	A wanted terrorist, Fayez bin Rasheed bin Mohamed Al Khashman Al-Dusri, surrenders to authorities
July 31 2004		Riyadh	Arrest of an expatriate living in the Kingdom
August 3 2004	Late afternoon	Riyadh	An Irish expatriate is assassinated in his office
August 8 2004	Evening	Abha	Arrest of two wanted individuals, one of them was Faris bin Ahmad Shwell Az-zhrani
August 11 2004	Evening	Meccah	Raid against a suspect and exchange of fire
August 30 2004		Jeddah	An American expatriate was fired at while leaving a bank. No casualties
August 31 2004		Al Ahsa	A police raid of two suspected sites
September 2 2004			A wanted terrorist, Abdullah Abdulaziz Ahmad Al-Moqren, surrenders to authorities
September 3 2004		Brida	Exchange of fire between the security forces and a group of wanted terrorists
September 5 2004		Brida	Police raid streets south of Brida
September 11 2004	Morning	Jeddah	An explosion caused by a booby-trapped car while driving down a street in Jeddah
September 15 2004		Riyadh	A British expatriate shot dead in a parking lot
September 20 2004		Tibuk	Exchange of fire with one wanted terrorists
September 24 2004	Evening	Tibuk	Apprehension of one wanted terrorists on Al-Muruj Street in Tibuk
September 26 2004	Morning	Jeddah	A French expatriate is shot dead on Al-Zahra' Street in Jeddah
October 12 2004		Riyadh	Exchange of fire with a wanted group on An-Nahda Street in the eastern side of Riyadh
October 31 2004	Morning	Riyadh	Arrest of a group of wanted terrorists
November 3 2004	Morning	Brida	Arrest of one wanted terrorist
November 9 2004		Jeddah	Raid against a terrorist hide-out
December 6, 2004	Morning	Jeddah	Attack against the US consulate in Jeddah
December 27, 2004	Evening	Riyadh	Exchange of fire with a number of wanted terrorists in a residential area
December 28, 2004	Morning	Riyadh	Exchange of fire with a terrorist
December 28, 2004	Morning	Jeddah	Arrest of a wanted terrorist

December 29, 2004	Evening	Riyadh	Explosion of a booby-trapped car outside the ministry of the interior
December 29, 2004	Evening	Riyadh	Explosion of a booby-trapped car outside the premises of the special forces
December 29, 2004	Evening	Riyadh	Exchange of fire with a group of wanted terrorists

Table (2) The Number of Casualties caused by Terrorist Acts in Saudi Arabia during 2004

Casualties								Perpetrators				
Deaths				Wounded								
Security men	Nationals	Residents	Total	Security men	Nationals	Residents	Total	Targets in the incident	The Dead	The injured	The Arrested	Total
												0
								8			8	8
								3			3	3
								8				0
6	1		7	1			1	8			8	8
								1			1	1
								1			1	1
								2	2			2
												0
								1			1	1
								2		1		2
1		1						1				0
1			1	4			4	2	1			1
4			4									0
1			1	1			1					0
											3	3
								1			1	1
								8			8	8
											1	1
5	1	1	7					1	1			1
				1	1		2	8	5		3	8
1			1	18	5	3	26	4	3		1	4
								6			6	6
2			2	1			1	5	4	1		5
		1	1					1				0
	3	19	22			25	25	4		1		1
								2	2			
												0
		1	1			1	1	2				0
		1	1					1				0
		1	1					1				0
		1	1									0
1			1	2			2	16	4		12	16
								1			1	1
								1			1	1

Casualties								Perpetrators				
Deaths				Wounded								
Security men	Nationals	Residents	Total	Security men	Nationals	Residents	Total	Targets in the incident	The Dead	The injured	The Arrested	Total
1			1	6	1	3	10	1	1			1
												0
1			1	1	1		2	2	1	1		2
			1					10	2		8	10
1												0
								1			1	1
								1			1	1
								27			27	27
				3			3	11	2	3	6	11
								1			1	1
								1			1	1
								1			1	1
		1	1									0
								2			2	2
				1			1	1	1			1
								5	1	3	1	5
								1			1	1
1			1	3			3	4	1		1	2
3			3					7			7	7
								1		1		1
		1	1					1				0
				3			3	1		1		1
								1			1	1
		1	1					1				0
				7			7	3			8	8
								3			3	3
				2			2	1		1		1
				2			2	4	1	1	2	4
		5	5	5		8	13	5	4	1		5
		1	1	1			1	2	1	1		2
				4			4	1	1			1
								1		1		1
				6			6	3	3			3
				12			12	2	2			2
				6			6	7	7			7
29	5	34	68	90	8	40	138	212	51	17	131	199

Table (3) Total Number of Casualties in Terrorist Incidents in Saudi Arabia (2003- 2004) until January 1, 2005

	Casualties								Perpetrators				
Year	Deaths				Wounded								
	Security men	Nationals	Residents	Total	Security men	Nationals	Residents	Total	Targets in the incident	Dead	Injured	Arrested	Total
2003	11	13	26	50	47	6	314	367	247	40	2	151	193
2004	33	6	34	73	73	7	40	120	212	51	15	166	232
2005	0	0	0	0	3	0	0	3	4	4	0	0	4
Total	44	19	60	123	123	13	354	490	463	95	17	317	429

Table (4) Number of Iraqi smugglers & infiltrators Arrested (2000 -2002)

Categorization	Year	2000	2001	Difference	2002	Difference	Total
Infiltrators	1885	1871	1871	-14	1993	122	5749
Smugglers	635	822	822	187	658	-164	2115

Table (5) Items seized by coast and border guards in Saudi Arabia (A comparison among the years 2000, 2001, 2002, 2003 up until October 2004)

Year / Description	2000 *	2001 **	Difference	2002 ***	Difference	2003 ****	Difference	2004 *****	Difference	Total
Infiltrators	378382	337733	-40649	474210	136477	642454	168244	379738	-262716	2212517
Infiltrator carrier	0	11	11	50	39	0	-50	0	0	61
Smuggler	3433	4367	934	3654	-713	5429	1775	3532	-1897	20415
Bombs	56	46	-10	54	8	63	9	84	21	303
Kgs/explosive material	0	604	604	209	-395	0	-209	14	14	827
Dynamite	90710	176171	85461	56999	-119172	4465	-52534	22205	17740	350550
Set of explosive wires	84460	176281	91821	56976	-119305	5010	-51966	22070	17060	344797
Various weapons	3632	4082	450	3432	-650	1503	-1929	873	-630	13522
Miscellaneous ammunition	2642043	4102194	1460151	3547801	-554393	1031115	-2516686	1687390	656275	13010543
Cache of weapons	2166	980	-1186	2060	1080	0	-2060	753	753	5959
Kg of hashish	2690	2425.55	-264.45	2689368	2686942.45	5742778	5740352.45	6609.8	-5736168.2	8443871.35
Drug pills	71616	400345	328729	95113.5	-305231.5	129565	34451.5	194540	64975	891179.5
Kg of Qatt	2923863	324286	-2599577	3193512	2869226	4212949	1019437	3242464.36	-970484.64	13897074.36
grams/ marijuana	1840	3656	1816	6000	2344	0	-6000	1.34	1.34	11497.34
Bottle of alcohol/Liter	19159	14033	-5126	+13509 +98.5		1410262	0	7354 +56		
Beer cans	3688	658	-3030	646	-12	3920	3274	1638	-2282	10550
Cars	736	1285	549	1690	405	0	-1690	63	63	3774
Livestock	5262	34038	28776	35435	1397	37075	1640	35294	-1781	147104
Kgs/food items	282025	1666933	1384908	3163909	1496976	2833287	-330622	3248137.5	414850.5	11194291.5

Sources:
* The twenty-seventh Interior Ministry Statistical Book for 2000
** The twenty-eighth Ministry Statistical Book for 2001
*** The twenty-ninth Interior Ministry Statistical Book for 2002
**** *Al Watan* newspaper, issue No. 1310, on March 12, 2004 - report on items seized by border guards during 2003
***** *A lecture delivered on October 24, 2004, by Major General Musfir Saleh Al-Ghamdi,* Assistant Director of Saudi Coastguards, at King Fahd Security College.

Section Four

Women and Civil Society in the GCC States

Higher Education in the GCC States: Current Conditions, Problems and Solutions

Dr. Ibrahim Mubarak Al-Dossari

Advisor for Educational Affairs to the Secretary-General of the Gulf Cooperation Council

This section of the report deals with the march of development experienced by the higher education sector in the GCC countries in addition to monitoring and analyzing the most prominent issues facing it. Following a brief historical background of the inception of higher education in the GCC countries, the quantitative growth of the higher education institutions in these countries and the factors influencing that growth are examined. This, in turn, identifies key issues that must be addressed in the coming years. Finally, the section concludes with a quick reference to the efforts exerted by the higher education institutions in the GCC countries.

The appearance of higher education institution in the Gulf

The development of teachers colleges, technical (industrial, commercial, health and agricultural) education and the gradual progress towards the establishment of university colleges and universities at later stages reflect part of the response of education to the requirements of growth and change witnessed by the Gulf region. The need for teachers in public education schools has led to the establishment of teachers' training institutes at the intermediate and secondary levels. These institutes have gradually developed into colleges that accept students after completion of the secondary stage. The same progression is noticed with respect to technical education in terms of the growth from specialized institutes and schools that serve specific purposes, according to the needs of their supervisory parties, to multi-purpose higher education institutes.

In the face of the increasing need for employees and leaders to work in the different state agencies, the severe lack of indigenous qualifications, and in view of the abundance of secondary stage graduates,[1] the modern university started to appear. Colleges of education kept representing the first nucleus of the university in most cases as seen in the University of Umm Al-Qura, the Islamic University of Imam Muhammad Saud, the University of Bahrain and the University of Qatar. The University of King Saud, established in 1957, the Islamic University (1961) and Kuwait University (1966) were the first government universities, a process that grew to all GCC States with the University of Bahrain and the University of Sultan Qaboos in 1986. There are now

---

[1] The percentages are extracted from the university statistics for the years 2001/2002. Thus, they may vary a little. They are available on the Internet websites of the following ministries of planning and economy www.bahrain.gov.bh/; www.moneoman.gov.om/; www.mop.gov.kw/; www.planning.gov.sa/; www.planning.gov.qa/; www.uae.gov.ae/

18 government universities in the GCC countries. At later stages, the increasing flow in the number of secondary education graduates, and the increasing demand for higher education coupled with the limited absorption capacity of the government universities, led to the appearance of new types of government colleges (specialized institutes and colleges, community colleges), in addition to private sector universities and colleges, and the open university.

At the organizational and supervisory level, there are currently three ministries of higher education (Saudi Arabia, Oman and Kuwait) following the merger of the Ministry of Higher Education and Scientific Research and the Ministry of Education and Youth in the UAE, which is now the Ministry of Education and Youth. Moreover, there are Higher Councils or Councils of Trustees that are responsible for laying down the general policies in the field of higher education or general supervision of universities. Variations exist among the GCC countries in respect of organizing and supervising the Teachers Colleges and Education Colleges. As for technical education, while there are three central institutions each in the UAE (hi-tech colleges), Saudi Arabia (Technical Education and Vocational Training Institution) and Kuwait (Public Authority for Applied Education and Training), technical education in Oman is under the Ministry of Manpower. No technological colleges were established in Bahrain and Qatar that require the establishment by central bodies.

Quantitative Development in the field of Higher Education

1.Numbers of Students

Higher education statistics show that the number of registered students in all higher education institutions of the GCC countries during the year 2002/2003 was a little more than 7000 male and female students (See Table 1). During the period 1990 to 2001, the numbers tripled at the level of the GCC countries with the annual growth rates being 2.3% in Qatar, 4.5% in Kuwait, 7.5% in Bahrain, 11.5% in Saudi Arabia, 19% in the UAE and 22.5% in Oman. Pursuant to these percentages, higher education enrollment is expected to exceed 120,000 students during the next five years.

2.Distribution of registered students by higher education institutions

Official statistics show that the percentage of registered students in the government universities compared to the total number of students registered

Table (1) Numbers of registered and graduate students in higher education institutions

	UAE (02/03)	Bahrain (01/02)	Saudi Arabia (02/03)	Oman (02/03)	Qatar (01/02)	Kuwait (02/03)
Registered						
Male students	22962	6196	219356	22581	2243	11151
Female students	45220	10120	305988	26883	5902	22752
Total	68196	16316	525344	39343	9192	33903
Graduates						
Male students	3462	1131	32688	3029	257	1672
Female students	8035	1708	40919	3183	1021	2943
Total	11497	2839	73607	6212	1278	4615

Source: Compiled by the researcher.

in higher education is somewhat more than 45% in the GCC countries. However, the percentage varies according to each country (from 3% in Kuwait, 22% in Oman and 99% in Qatar) and to the presence of alternatives for university education. The Teachers Colleges that are run as independent institutions in Saudi Arabia (100 education colleges most of which are for female teachers) account for nearly 50% of the number of students registered in higher education in the kingdom compared with about 16% in the case of Oman where there are six teachers colleges. The number of students in the College of Basic Education belonging to the Public Authority for Applied Education represents nearly 16% of the number of students registered in Kuwait.

As for the number of (registered) students in the colleges of technological and technical education, it is still low on the whole compared with the numbers of students registered in all the higher education institutions in the GCC countries. They amount to 80,120 students representing nearly 1.5% of the total registered students, though this percentage again varies from one country to another. In the UAE, for instance, the number of registered students in the hi-tech colleges compared with the overall students registered in all higher education institutions, both government and private, amounted to about 22%, while in Saudi Arabia the figure is less than 97%, in Oman 17%, and in Kuwait nearly 32%.

Except for the UAE, which has between 24 private colleges and universities officially recognized by the competent authorities, and which include about 57% of the numbers of registered higher education students, and Oman which has 12 private colleges and universities that include about 15%, the private higher education share of the total students registered in the government private higher education institutions

remains a modest share in the other GCC countries, where private colleges and universities are still recent or are in the process of being established.

3.Distribution according to gender:

The GCC countries have made wide strides in the field of educating females. This is reflected by the high percentage of the number of registered female students compared with registered males whether in the higher education institutions (67%, 62%, 56%, 54%, 77% and 69% in the UAE, Bahrain, Saudi Arabia, Oman, Qatar and Kuwait respectively - see table No. 1) or in the universities (76%, 60%, 33%, 50%, 77% and 70% in the UAE, Bahrain, Oman, Saudi Arabia, Qatar and Kuwait respectively). However, it is worth noting that most of the female percentages are concentrated in the theoretical colleges and specializations, such as sociology, science and literature. The highest level of concentration is in Saudi Arabia, where there are more than 76% of female students in the teachers colleges that are outside the framework of the universities.

4.Distribution according to specializations:

The percentage of students registered in scientific and engineering specializations (medicine, science, health, science, information technology, computer, agriculture and engineering) compared to the overall students registered in the GCC universities also varies from one country to another. It amounts to 23% in the University of Bahrain, 24% in the University of Qatar, 37% in the Saudi universities and in the University of Kuwait, and 43% in Sultan Qaboos University.[2] These percentages are lower, of course, if compared with the overall students registered in all higher education institutions.

---

[2] Saudi Arabia occupies first position among the GCC countries in respect of its spending on education as a percentage of GDP. These percentages were 7.9%, 9.1%, 8.03%, 9.5% for the years 1999, 2000, 2001 and 2002, respectively (Ministry of Planning and Economy, 2003).

The main problems facing higher education

Higher education in the GCC countries is facing many problems that represent an overall challenge to be addressed at present and in the future. Expansion, appropriateness and quality represent interconnected basic issues around which revolve further items. The problem of expansion is summed up in the presence of a wide gap in demand necessitated by the socio-economic requirements, the growing social need for higher education, and the absorptive capacity of the existing institutions and their low numbers and types. The issue of appropriateness, which expresses the extent of the congruence of the outputs of the higher education institutions with the development requirements and social aspirations, represents an issue of decisive importance, especially in the light of the presence of excessive numbers of expatriate labor, and the emerging unemployment problem among graduates. As for quality, this relates to the level and quality of the educational institutions and their programs, and their congruence with the desired objectives and the acceptable norms and criteria.

Higher education in the GCC countries is facing many problems that represent an overall challenge to be addressed at present and in the future.

Expanding the scope of education

Comparison shows that the percentage of higher education students in the GCC countries is still much lower than its counterpart in advanced and developed countries. While the percentage of higher education students of the age category of higher education in some advanced countries amounts to, or exceeds, 80%, it does not exceed 20% in most GCC countries. Higher education in these countries faces a continuing increase in the community demand and an aggravation of the acceptance problems due to the nature of their demographic structures (high growth rates and the expanded base of the demographic pyramid). It also faces an expansion in general education and rising numbers and percentages of general secondary education graduates, which exceed the current absorptive capacity of the higher education institutions. In Oman, for instance, out of 35,044 male and female students who graduated from the general secondary education in 2001/2002, only 9,416 were admitted in government higher education institutions. If one adds this to the number admitted to private higher education institutions (1,628) and those who pursued their education abroad (3,348), the percentage of secondary graduates able to continue their studies does not exceed 40%.

Several options may be advanced to meet the demand for higher education which is prompted by the development requirements in the GCC countries and the increasing demand for education. The most prominent of these options are:

o Increasing government investment in higher education: Governments in the GCC countries and in many countries of the world remain the principal funding source of higher education. Considering older figures that are available in reports issued by some international organizations, such as the UNDP or the World Bank, as percentages fit for comparison, it may be inferred that the investment rates in education in the GCC countries measured in relation to the total Gross Domestic Product (GDP) or the general spending are not too far from their counterparts in the advanced and developing countries.[3]

But as for investment in higher education, statistics available from the ministries of planning and economy show a difference among the GCC countries in the spending percentages, although if one takes into consideration the individual funding source of the higher education institutions, the manner they spend their budgets and the level of their internal efficiency, one can see that all of them invest (spend) much less than what is required.

o Raising the internal efficiency of the higher education institutions: The issues of organization and management and educational loss are among the most important aspects than can be dealt with within this option for meeting the need for expanding and developing higher education. With respect to organization and management, what is of concern here is perhaps the centralization of decisions and the resulting limited authorities given to the higher education institutions in managing their resources, flexibility in the programs and methods they can innovate to face their special circumstances. Initially, most higher education institutions (or the bodies working within their framework), get their budgets by negotiating with the state financial authorities. Most often, the concerns and needs of these institutions are not given proper attention. In many instances, the higher education institution finds itself compelled to continuously refer to the central authority to get approval for its plans and programs or for bypassing some stern restrictions regarding spending decisions.

Facts indicate that failure to apply modern technology in many higher education institutions is not limited to administrative aspects only, but extends to the academic and teaching aspects as well. Technology is not being made use of in such a manner as to raise the level of internal or external efficiency. The competence of many of the members of the teaching staff, students and administrators need to be improved and developed. In addition, the severe lack of integrated resources among the higher education institutions is not confined to exchanging and organizing information and benefiting from it in the fields of planning, scientific research and sources of learning and teaching. It rather extends to benefiting from new equipment, labs, workshops and libraries that are available in some of them.

As for the issue of educational loss, several studies point to a general loss ranging between 30% and 50% among those registered in the universities of the GCC countries.[4] This means (financially at least) the loss of 30 to 50% of the financial resources of the universities. Certainly, paying more attention to the aspect of internal efficiency would help the higher education institutions in the GCC countries rationalize their resources, lower the actual cost to the student on the one hand, and focus on improving the quality aspects and ability to raise their absorptive capacity on the other.

---

[3] The World Bank (2002, p.82) estimates, based on the experience of the OECD countries, that the appropriate general level for investment in education as a percentage of the gross product ranges between 4 and 6%. Consequently, it is proposed that investment in higher education must be within the limit of 15 to 20% of the total investment in education. However, in our view, this estimate is not consistent with the nature of the funding sources, domestic efficiency, and the size of the corresponding age bracket of higher education, in the light of the expansion requirements in education.

[4] See, for example, the results of the seminar organized at Qatar University by King Abdulaziz University in coordination with the GCC General Secretariat and the Secretariat of the Vice rectors of universities for academic affairs about the status of the educational loss in the universities of the GCC countries (King Abdulaziz University, October 2002).

[5] Given the increasing role of these centers, a standing committee was established at the level of higher education institutions in the GCC countries, with its headquarters in Kuwait, to exchange expertise, experiments and cooperation in this field.

o Diversifying funding resources: There is no room here to illustrate the experience of different universities in the field of scientific research and consultations. However, it must be pointed out that the current resources that are available through these two sources are still low, partly due to socio-economic factors, most of which are beyond the control of the university. As for training, the current experience of the communal service centers that exist in most higher education institutions[5] is a good example that may be expanded and linked to the growing needs in the field of continuous education, which is acquiring increasing importance in the labor markets and modern economies. There is still a need to step up the efforts in the field of diversifying resources through known options, such as donations, grants, trusts, creating academic chairs, and benefiting from the Islamic trust funds.[6]

o Diversifying higher education patterns: Until recently, modern education patterns, such as e-learning, community colleges, the Open University, the virtual university, and private colleges were still new to the region. In view of the wide capabilities of these patterns of spreading higher education and fulfilling the requirements of individuals and society,

At present, communications, information and Internet technology add unlimited potentials in the field of learning outside the traditional framework.

in terms of getting highly-flexible good education, in addition to their capability of absorbing much pressure off the traditional institutions, they represent successful options which circumstances make it imperative to invest in them. At present, communications, information and Internet technology add unlimited potentials in the field of learning outside the traditional framework. Place and distance no more pose an obstacle to access to information or to acquire education[7]. The need for expansion and flexibility calls for moving towards these patterns and providing the necessary potentials for their growth.[8]

o Encouraging the growth of private higher education: On the one hand, private higher education represents an option of low cost to the public budget, and a flexible method in responding appropriately to meet the demand for education, on the other. At present, private higher education contributes very little to higher education in the GCC countries compared with countries like the Philippines, Korea, Japan and Belgium (85%, 80%, 70% and 65% respectively).[9] Without dealing with issues related to private higher education, such as quality, growth controls and compatibility with the

---

[6] The GCC General Secretariat prepared a study on diversifying the funding sources of higher education in the GCC countries in implementation of the decision of the Committee of the Ministers of Higher Education and Scientific Research (General Secretariat, 1998).

[7] For example, there are millions of students studying through the Open University model in a number of developed and developing countries. In the field of e-learning, there were, for instance, in the USA alone, more than 230 higher education institutions (university or college) in the year 2000/2001 that were offering courses to more than three million students in different diplomas and specifications.

There are even a number of e-academic programs and diplomas (NCES 2004).

[8] The study was prepared by a team formed by the Minister of Higher Education in Saudi Arabia based on a decision taken in 1998 by the Ministers of Higher Education and Scientific Research in the GCC countries.

[9] The World Bank, 2000. The increasing contribution of private education in these countries must be taken into consideration when comparing the level of public spending on higher education in the countries where governments are the main financer of education.

needs of society, all of which are undoubtedly highly important and complicated, one can point out that the wide possibilities which it provides in the field of expanding higher education and improving its quality, require that the GCC countries exert strenuous effort to support it and encourage its growth. Financial support is represented in giving loans, grants, financial facilities, land grants, participation in establishing facilities and equipment and facilitating the use of the facilities of government universities and educational institutions as well as bearing part of the students' fees. Such assistance may be linked one way or the other to the level of the students that are admitted, the quality of the programs and outputs, and the extent of integration with the other institutions, etc. so as to assist in developing it in a manner that serves the development objectives. The state may provide its support through easing the restrictions and controls which the responsible parties place in the field of licensing and the measures related to the establishing of the projects of private education institutions, and through focusing instead on quality control once those projects are well established.[10]

The issue of congruence

Congruence relates to many of the important dimensions of the role of higher education in fulfilling communal and individual requirements. There is no room here to deal with these dimensions in detail. Instead, it is sufficient to deal with the supply side in terms of the relation between higher education outputs and the requirements of the labor market, due to lack of space, the presence of a large number of documents and previous studies which addressed the issue in great detail.[11] The importance of this aspect lies in the questions concerning the relation between the surplus of supply from higher education outputs, the high percentage of incoming labor to the markets in the GCC countries, and the problem of unemployment among graduates. The above mentioned quantitative indicators have shown the presence of imbalances in the higher education outputs, most prominent of which were represented in the small numbers and types of technological and technical education institutions, the low number of students registered therein, the disproportion in the distribution of students among the theoretical specializations, and the preponderance of the numbers of higher education female students as compared with the numbers of male students, most of the female students concentrating on theoretical specializations.

Among the other imbalances that may be pointed out are the shortages in the levels of qualification and preparation of graduates in terms of the required skills in the labor market, such as business skills, or the ability of oral and written expression, command of English, skills in using modern technologies, the ability to deal with problems and situations in real life with a certain measure of flexibility and innovation, etc. An examination of the curriculae of general preparation in most higher education institutions would reveal a great deal of cramming, weak concentration on developing those skills, and too much focus on memorization, passive instruction, lecturing and theorizing without giving consideration to developing the student's capabilities of critical thinking, problem-solving, self-learning, and the application of teaching to practical life.

[10] In this respect, reference may be made to a good number of papers submitted to the International Conference about the Twenty-First Century University, which was organized by the Ministry of Higher Education in Oman (2001).

[11] See, for example, the study prepared by the GCC General Secretariat (1989) on the congruence between the education out- puts and the development requirements in the GCC countries; the study prepared by Al-Rashid and Al-Bi'adi (1992) submitted to the Intellectual Seminar of the university rectors and directors (Kuwait, 1992) on the same topic, and the set of working papers on congru- ence presented at the Higher Education Seminar in Saudi Arabia (1998), Ministry of Higher Education.

In addition, there is the weak relation of the higher education institutions to the community institutions in general, and the institutions that receive their graduates, in particular. There is also a shortage in the representation of those institutions in the supervisory bodies and councils of higher education institutions, inadequate benefiting from their ideas or identifying their requirements when planning and implementing the curricula and in developing the educational and training programs. Such drawbacks are more evident in the field of scientific research and the limited role of universities in the service of society and in realizing the objectives of scientific progress and economic and technological development in this field. It is obvious that for improving the level of congruence, the higher education institutions in the GCC countries must redress these imbalances and overcome the existing weaknesses.

The issue of quality

Developing high-level education systems, fulfilling the dire need for expanding higher education and adjusting it to development requirements, necessitates the presence of systems of evaluation and quality control in the higher education institutions without getting involved in discussions of quality dimensions, or their importance with respect to higher education institutions. Suffice it here to refer to some efforts exerted at the collective and individual levels of some higher education institutions in the GCC countries. At the collective

> **Throughout their history, most of the higher education institutions in the GCC countries have not encountered pressures for evaluating their performance, the need to justify their programs and plans, or explaining their performance.**

level, and for over twenty years,[12] several attempts were made through the Arab Education Office of the Gulf countries, and were repeated uninterruptedly over the subsequent years through the committees of the joint education action within the framework of the GCC, for setting up an accreditation and quality evaluation system for higher education institutions. Given the importance of the subject, the Consultative Commission of the GCC Supreme Council has included within its conceptions of the educational and scientific research system in the GCC, a proposal to set up a commission for academic accreditation and quality control of education. The Supreme Council adopted the proposal at the Muscat Summit (December 2001) and directed the competent committees to implement it.

In implementing the decision, the GCC General Secretariat prepared an elaborate study, in cooperation with the UNESCO regional bureau in Doha, for determining the human and financial requirements for setting up the Commission and for laying down its administrative organization and the necessary steps to be taken for its establishment. The General Secretariat, in coordination with the Ministries of Education and Higher Education, have set up an ad hoc committee to follow-up the issue of accreditation. Attempts and efforts continue to be exerted for setting up the committee.

At the level of the individual countries, there are at present three commissions, one in the UAE under the Ministry of Higher Education and Scientific Research,

---

[12] During the 1980s, several studies and proposals were submitted through the Arab Education Office of the Gulf countries and through a number of conferences and seminars about the need for a joint commission for academic accreditation in the region.

another in Oman under the Higher Council of Education, and the Ministry of Higher Education in Oman acting as its secretariat. In Saudi Arabia, an evaluation and academic accreditation commission has been established recently. At present, it is difficult to evaluate the performance of these commissions, their independence or their future role in accreditation, though it is clear that their main function focuses in the first stages on licensing private institutions of higher education. At the level of universities, serious attempts are being made in the field of self-evaluation through the assistance of regional and world expertise. A number of universities in the GCC countries have managed to obtain the accreditation of the programs of their colleges of engineering by the Specialized World Academic Accreditation Associations. However, efforts are still limited at the level of institutional accreditation.

From the above review, it becomes clear that development in the field of academic accreditation and quality control is still in its initial phase. This delay is partly due to the fact that the majority of education institutions are basically governmental. Moreover, they do not have financial and administrative independence and concomitant flexibility to establish independent systems for evaluation and accounting. Throughout their history, most of the higher education institutions in the GCC countries have not encountered pressures for evaluating their performance, the need to justify their programs and plans, or explaining their performance. With the increasing demand for education, the issue of quality, from the perspective of the student or society, becomes secondary compared with the life chance of getting education of whatever level. These two factors will certainly remain an obstacle in the face of the appearance of independent institutions for accreditation and quality control. Most of the efforts deployed by the universities will continue to be based on subjective incentives, and not in response to any outside pressure, at the present time at least.

Conclusion
Joint cooperation among the Higher Education Institutions in the GCC countries

Education enjoys special attention in the development of the GCC. The standing committee of the ministries of Higher Education and Scientific Research supervises the joint action committees. Such committees include, inter alia, the committee of the rectors and directors of universities and higher education institutions, and a large number of committees of the deans of the corresponding colleges, such as the colleges of arts, education, engineering, medicine and others. The General Secretariat assumes the coordination of the Ministers' Committee and the Committees of the Presidents of the University rectors and the Preparatory Committees of its meetings. However, the colleges themselves assume the work of their respective secretariats. All the committees aim at realizing cooperation and integration among higher education institutions, exchanging expertise and information, and benefiting from the available resources and sources.

There are intensive activities in the field of holding scientific seminars, conferences and meetings, student visits, sports and cultural activities. This is not the place to examine or evaluate the joint action process.[13] It is worth

---

[13] There are several reports and working papers in the field of monitoring and evaluating the process of educational joint action. They may be obtained directly from the GCC General Secretariat.

noting that the GCC Supreme Council has adopted a number of important decisions in the field of education. Most important among them are those related to the joint plant for developing the general education curricula (Manama, December 2000), and the views of the Consultative Commission with respect to the systems of education and scientific research in the GCC countries (Muscat, 2001), education trends (Doha, December 2002), the trends contained in the document of ideas presented by HRH Prince Abdullah bin Abdulaziz on the educational side (Doha, December 2002), and finally, the document of the comprehensive development of education (Kuwait, December 2003). The implementation of these decisions is currently in progress.

References

GCC General Secretariat (1989): *Congruence between the graduates of higher education institutions and the requirements of the GCC countries for labor of higher education.*

GCC General Secretariat (1998): *The diversification of the funding sources of higher education in the GCC countries.*

King Abdulaziz University (2002): *The researches and studies presented to the seminar on educational loss*, King Abdulaziz University, Jeddah, October 2002.

Al-Tariri et al (1998): *Patterns of Higher Education in the GCC countries*, Ministry of Higher Education, Saudi Arabia.

Arab Education Office of the Gulf countries (AEOGC) (1992): The Fifth Intellectual Seminar of the University Rectors and Directors in the member countries of the AEOGC (Kuwait University, Kuwait, 1992).

Ministry of Planning and Economy, Saudi Arabic (2003): *The National Report on Human Development*, Ministry of Higher Education in Saudi Arabic, Riyadh, February 1998.

Ministry of Higher Education (2001): The International Conference on the 21st Century University (Muscat, March 2003).

NCES (June 2004), *The condition of Education 2004*, US Department of Education, Institute of Educational Sciences.(www.nces.ed.gov/).

World Bank (2002): *Constructing Knowledge Societies: New Challenges for Tertiary Education*, Washington, D.C. (www.worldbank.org/).

World Bank (2000): *Higher Education in Developing Countries: Peril and Promise*, Washington, D.C. (www.worldbank.org/)

Women's Issues in the GCC States

Dr. Ebtisam Al Kitbi

Assistant Professor of Political Science, UAE University

This part of the Yearbook 'The Gulf in a Year 2004' sheds light on the most prominent developments bearing on women's issues in the GCC countries during 2004 such as women's political rights, their role in politics, their presence in civil society organizations, their role in economic life and their participation in the labor force in particular. Similarly, this paper explores the role of businesswomen in some GCC countries and analyzes the main aspects showing the interest of some Western states and organizations in this issue.

The Political Role of Women in the GCC

It would certainly be no exaggeration to say that 2004 was the year of the "ministerization" of Gulf women. The year witnessed the appointment of a total of five women ministers in the Sultanate of Oman, the Kingdom of Bahrain and the UAE. Sultan Qaboos of Oman issued on March 8, 2004 a decree appointing Dr. Rawya bint Saud al-Busaidi as the minister of education. Al-Busaidi is in fact the first woman to take on a ministerial portfolio in Oman although she had served as undersecretary in the same ministry. The Sultanate took another step regarded as unprecedented when Sheikha Aisha As-Siyatu was appointed as Chairperson of the General Commission of Artisans Industries with the rank of a minister in March 2004.[1] This was followed on June 9, 2004, by a decree from Sultan Qaboos providing for the establishment of a tourism ministry for the first time ever. The decree further provided for the appointment of Rajiha bint Abdulamir bin Ali as the minister of tourism, making her the second Omani woman in the government.[2] Similarly, on October 20, 2004, a third royal decree was issued, appointing Sharifa bin Khalfan bin Nasser Al-Yahyaee as Minister of Social Development, becoming thus the third woman in the Omani government since the beginning of 2004.[3]

2004 also witnessed the appointment of the first female minister in both Bahrain and the UAE. On April 22, 2004, the King of Bahrain issued a royal decree providing for the appointment of Nada Hafaz as the first Bahraini woman minister entrusted with

---

[1] *Al-Hayat*, March 9, 2004

[2] Rajiha Abdul Amir was undersecretary of the Ministry of Statistics in the Development Council in 1988. She is considered the first undersecretary to a ministry in the Sultanate of Oman and in the GCC countries. She was later undersecretary to the Ministry of Development before it was dissolved. Shortly afterwards, she took up the position of undersecretary to the Ministry of National Economy for Development Affairs in 1996 (*Al-Khaleej*, June 1, 2004).

[3] See Oman-based *Al-Watan* newspaper, October 23, 2004; See also, *AFP*, October 23, 2004.

the health portfolio.[4] As for the UAE, the presidential decree, issued in early November 2004, called for a ministerial reshuffle and provided for the appointment of Lubna Al Qasimi as Minister of Economy and Planning. Al Qasimi is the first UAE woman to accede to a ministerial position in the history of the country,[5] bringing the number of women who currently hold ministerial positions in the GCC countries to seven.

At the level of public offices, the government of Kuwait appointed Nabila Al Mulla as the permanent Kuwaiti ambassador to the UN. Al Mulla is thus the first Arab Muslim woman to hold an ambassadorial position in the UN.[6] In Qatar, the government chose a woman to occupy the post of undersecretary to the Ministry of Education.[7] Another Qatari woman was appointed to chair the civil service at the Budget Directorate.[8] An Emiri decree was issued providing for the appointment of Dr. Hassa Al Jaber as Secretary-General of the Supreme Council for IT and Telecommunications.[9] In Saudi Arabia, Hasna Al- Ghamdi was appointed as Director General of

the Tumors Center at the Jeddah-based King Abdulaziz Hospital. She is, in fact, the first Saudi woman to take on such a position at the Ministry of Health.[10] At the judiciary level, five Omani women were appointed as vice general prosecutors, becoming the first group of women to join the judicial corps in the Sultanate of Oman.[11] As far as consultative and municipal councils are concerned, a decree was issued on January 9, 2004 providing for the appointment of seven women as members of the Consultative Council in the emirate of Sharjah in the UAE.[12]

It is worth noting that in August 2004, a federal decree was issued providing for the UAE's ratification of the Convention on the Elimination of All Forms of Discrimination against Women[13] (CEDAW), while the government maintained some reservations about some of the clauses embedded in the text of the convention.[14]

In Bahrain, a royal decree was issued providing for the appointment of Bahya Al-Jashi as member of the Consultative Council to succeed Nada

[4] *Elaf*, April 23, 2004.
[5] See *WAM* (UAE news agency), November 2, 2004.
[6] *Kuwait News Agency* (KUNA), January 18, 2004.
[7] *Ar-Raya*, February 2, 2004
[8] *Ar-Raya*, April 19, 2004
[9] *Qatar News Agency* (QNA), November 12, 2004
[10] *Okaz newspaper*, August 4, 2004
[11] *Al-Khaleej*, April 12, 2004
[12] *Al-Khaleej*, January 10, 2004
[13] *Al-Bayan*, August 16, 2004
[14] Among the articles of which reservations were noted are: Article 2 clause b: To adopt appropriate legislative and other measures, including sanctions where appropriate, prohibiting all discrimination against women; Article 9, Clause 1: States Parties shall grant women equal rights with men to acquire, change or retain their nationality. They shall ensure in particular that neither marriage to an alien nor change of nationality by the husband during marriage shall automatically change the nationality of the wife, render her stateless or force upon her the nationality of the husband; Clause 2. States Parties shall grant women equal rights with men with respect to the nationality of their children; Article 15, Clause 2: States Parties shall accord to women, in civil matters, a legal capacity identical to that of men and the same opportunities to exercise that capacity. In particular, they shall give women equal rights to conclude contracts and to administer property and shall treat them equally in all stages of procedure in courts and tribunals; Article 16, Clause 1: States Parties shall take all appropriate measures to eliminate discrimination against women in all matters relating to marriage and family relations and in particular shall ensure, on a basis of

equality of men and women: (a) The same right to enter into marriage; (b) The same right freely to choose a spouse and to enter into marriage only with their free and full consent; (c) The same rights and responsibilities during marriage and at its dissolution; (d) The same rights and responsibilities as parents, irrespective of their marital status, in matters relating to their children; in all cases the interests of the children shall be paramount; (e) The same rights to decide freely and responsibly on the number and spacing of their children and to have access to the information, education and means to enable them to exercise these rights; (f) The same rights and responsibilities with regard to guardianship, stewardship, trusteeship and adoption of children, or similar institutions where these concepts exist in national legislation; in all cases the interests of the children shall be paramount; (g) The same personal rights as husband and wife, including the right to choose a family name, a profession and an occupation; (h) The same rights for both spouses in respect of the ownership, acquisition, management, administration, enjoyment and disposition of property, whether free of charge or for a valuable consideration; Clause 2: The betrothal and the marriage of a child shall have no legal effect, and all necessary action, including legislation, shall be taken to specify a minimum age for marriage and to make the registration of marriages in an official registry compulsory; Article 29, Clause 1: Any dispute between two or more States Parties concerning the interpretation or application of the present Convention which is not settled by negotiation shall, at the request of one of them, be submitted to arbitration. If within six months from the date of the request for arbitration the parties are unable to agree on the organization of the arbitration, any one of those parties may refer the dispute to the International Court of Justice by request in conformity with the Statute of the Court.

Hafaz.[15] Bahrain also appointed two women as representative members of the Consultative Assembly at the Supreme Council of the Gulf Cooperation Council.[16] In the Sultanate of Oman, nine women joined the State Council, a government body whose key functions lie somewhere between the Consultative Council and the government. Mrs. Thawbiya Al-Barwaniya joined the State Council, raising the number of members to 57.[17] In Qatar, Mrs. Mashael Ad-Darham was entrusted with the responsibility of the Secretary-General of Qatar's Municipal Council.[18]

Qatar engaged in a new constitutional and political phase after the Emir of the State Sheikh Hamad bin Khalifa Al Thani issued the permanent constitution approved by a popular referendum on April 29, 2003 before holding the general elections with the participation of women. The text of Qatar's constitution guarantees the right of men and women to run and vote two-thirds of the Consultative Council members.[19]

In Kuwait, the cabinet adopted on May 18, 2004 a bill for the amendment of the Kuwaiti electoral law, granting women the right to vote and run for membership in the National Assembly.[20] After the Emir of Kuwait signed the bill, it was submitted to the vote of the National Assembly. However, the decree failed to emphasize the urgency of the matter and remains on the agenda of the commission for internal and defense affairs pending a report to be submitted to the speaker of the National Assembly. Only then can the bill be discussed by the members of the parliament.

Some political analysts have pointed out that the Kuwaiti leadership expects the bill to be rejected by the National Assembly, which is dominated by Islamists. Sunni Islamists and members with tribal affiliation, a majority within the Assembly have traditionally opposed granting women any political rights. The government, however, was taken by surprise when the Islamic Constitutional Movement - the strongest Sunni Islamic front in Kuwait - changed its traditional position towards the issue of women's participation in elections by announcing its support for the bill in June 2004. This reversal of position now opens for the way for the bill to win approval since liberal-minded and Shi'ite members have already indicated their support. The bill has also received widespread international and media attention in support of its passing. Since National Assembly members have the right to vote on a bill discussed before the parliament, 33 out of 56 votes are required to have the bill passed. Given the current circumstances, there is a good chance that it will be ratified by the parliament.

On another front the Committee for Public Utilities consensually approved on March 21, 2004, the deletion of a clause from the new municipality law related to women's participation in the municipal council both as voters and candidates. There was a feeling in the committee that the government was not serious about the issue and that therefore women's participation should not be placed within the text of the law in a supplementary manner. Instead, it was argued that the National Assembly should deal with the manner in a straight-forward way as the municipal council is both an executive and technical body.[21] The deletion was

In Kuwait, the cabinet adopted on May 18, 2004 a bill for the amendment of the Kuwaiti electoral law, granting women the right to vote and run for membership in the National Assembly.

---

[15] Al-Ayam, April 27, 2004.

[16] Akhbar Al-Khaleej, May 31, 2004.

[17] AFP, October 21, 2004.

[18] Al-Hayat, October 9, 2004.

[19] Al-Hayat, March 9, 2004.

[20] KUNA, May 16, 2004.

[21] Kuwait-based Al-Watan, March 22, 2004.

regarded by many as a blow to women's political rights.

The move by the committee had come as a response to a decision by the Cabinet in October 2003 to amend the Kuwaiti municipalities to grant women the right to vote and run for office at the municipal council.[22] Following the committee's objection, the government dispatched a letter to the president of the council in May 2004, asking him to hold the project for amending the electoral law for the municipal council for a year so that the government could have enough time to prepare the law accurately.[23]

In Saudi Arabia, a heated debate was sparked off over the issue of women's participation in the partial municipal elections scheduled to be held in successive phases in early 2005. This was surprising as the organizational list issued by the Saudi Ministry of Municipalities and Rural Affairs did not explicitly stipulate that women would be banned from participating as voters or candidates. The organizational list merely defined voters as "any citizen/s that meets the conditions set for the elections" and stresses in its third clause that all citizens do enjoy electoral rights. In both references, there were no conditions associated according to gender. Moreover, the position of the Saudi government was divided. While the Saudi Minister of Interior stated that the participation of Saudi women in the forthcoming elections was not on the cards,[24] the Chairman of the General Committee for Municipal Elections asserted that the electoral regime did not explicitly ban women from participating, although he did say that due to lack of sufficient time it would be difficult to make the necessary arrangements so that women could participate.[25] The Chairman of the Municipality and Head of the Supervisory Committee on Municipal Elections said that women could always voice their opinions through the available channels and attend debates, indicating that the Municipalities and Rural Code that regulates the work of the Municipal Council extends the Council the right to invite any person/s whose attendance is deemed appropriate without necessarily having the right to vote, as is actually the case for women.[26] In fact, though Saudi women are banned from running for municipal office, seven women did submit their candidacy to hold membership in the municipal councils in Jeddah, Riyadh and Qatif.[27]

In 2004, women's issues were also placed on the agenda of the Saudi National Dialogue. From June 12 to 14, the third meeting of the dialogue took place under the title "Women: Their Rights, Duties and its Relation to Education."[28] Some seventy prominent scholars, half of whom were women, participated although women were seated in a separate hall. The conference was marked by an open and heated debate orchestrated mainly by two key and conflicting ideological currents. Yet, it was clear from the moment that the names of

---

[22] For more details on this specific issue, see Ebtisam Al-Kutbi, "Women's Political Role in the GCC Countries," in *The Gulf in a Year 2003* (Dubai: Gulf Research Center, 2004).

[23] Kuwait-based *Al-Watan*, May 31, 2004.

[24] *Elaf*, October 14, 2004 available at http://www.elaph.com/Politics/2004/10/14958.htm

[25] Aman News Center, October 13, 2004 available at http://www.amanjordan.org/arabic_news/ wmview.php?ArtID=15999

[26] *Okaz*, November 9, 2004.

[27] See *Al-Khaleej*, November 1, 2004; also *AFP*, September 21, 2004.

[28] Working papers presented at the conference focused on four themes including the cultural, daily, economic and political life of Saudi women. The first theme included two topics: "Women and Legal Duties and Rights" covering such areas conditions of the political systems, propos-

als of mechanisms for empowering women to gain their legal and civil rights and women's duties; while the second topic centered on the concepts related to women caught between traditions and mores and religious principles. The second theme was entitled "Women and Society" and focused mainly on social problems facing women and the ways to develop social services as well as women's social participation. Another aspect was women's rights and duties towards family and society with participants shedding light on the prevailing conditions and the future prospects of women, together with the issue of household violence. The third theme was entitled "Rules and Systems for Women's Employment: Overview and Evaluation" and discussed the fields suitable for women's employment, particularly the specification of fields and rules. The fourth theme focused on "Women and Education."

participants were announced that the conservative camp within Saudi society would dominate not only the discussions but also determine the results and recommendations of the conference.

As soon as the announcement of the event had been made, the conservative elements within Saudi society mobilized their forces to ensure that discussions would not take an unexpected or too tolerant a turn. For example, the King Abdulaziz Center for National Dialogue, the institutional patron of the event, issued strict guidelines for what the dialogue about to take place. This included references to the way dialogue should be conducted as laid out in the Holy Quran and according to Prophet Mohammed's deeds and sayings. The guidelines were repeated by Sa'ud bin Muhammed Al-Shareem, Imam and preacher at the Al-Masjid Al-Haram, during the Friday prayer that preceded the conference. Al-Shareem urged the participants to stick to the teachings of the Quran and Hadith while discussing women's issues and other related topics.

Shortly before the conference started, a document entitled "The Rights and Duties of Muslim Women" penned by a group of Islamist figures was distributed among participants. The document was nothing less than an outline of the conservative religious approach to women's issues, stressing the concept of justice instead of equality between men and women. Similarly, 32 women from Medina (the city that hosted the conference) issued and distributed a statement alongside the same conservative tone that called upon the participants to frame their debate within religious guidelines and to not allow themselves to be carried away by Western models of reform. Two prominent senior religious clerics were invited to take part in the conference, both of them religious scholars well-known for their stringent view on the subject of women's rights.[29]

In light of such a prevailing atmosphere, the outcome of the conference fell far short of expectations, even as far as the government was concerned, which had hoped to receive support for expanding the role of women in the labor market. In fact, several participants demanded that women's participation be restricted to the education of children and household chores. As a result, the third Saudi Conference for National Dialogue caused a greater amount of controversy than agreement among participants. Both liberals and moderate Islamists underlined their reservations at the recommendations issued at the conclusion of the event as both had made it clear at the outset that they saw tenable reasons for excluding women's issues from the national agenda. While the recommendation included 17 clauses calling for granting women their rights, these were issued in the framework that women remain the caretaker of the family unit.[30] In terms of

---

[29] Ibid.

[30] The final statement set forth recommendations that, according to participants, were based primarily on Islamic precepts. The statement called for the creation of a specialized national authority to be entrusted with the task of supervising women's issues and facilitating their movement across the country, as women do not the right to drive cars. The statement pointed out that participants demanded of concerned authorities to conduct a study of the conditions of women's public transport as well as propose suitable mechanisms to enable women to move easily whenever they need to. Other recommendations included a call for a national document that would clearly separate women's legal rights from their legal duties and their role in the family and society. Participants also demanded that plans for establishing family courts be implemented so that women could at last enjoy their privacy. Other demands included the need to expand women's departments in courts in order to register women's grievances. The statement emphasized the need to include within the educational curricula the legal rights and duties of women in order to propagate tight concepts of women's role and place in society as well as prepare curricula suitable for female students to groom them for social life. In parallel, the statement demanded a review of the regulations that frame, organize and expand women's work, including retirement schemes, leave policy, rotations, work hours and part-time employment, which do not run counter to Islamic precepts. Additionally, the statement called for widening women's participation in public affairs in accordance with Islamic and legal stipulations and in line with the social, economic and cultural changes currently under way, together with "developing and implementing rules against the practice of all forms of violence against women." See Al-Hayat, June 15, 2004 as well as Al-Sharq Al-Awsat, June 16, 2004.

central problems that characterize the lives of Saudi women, recommendations only included vague formulas subject to numerous interpretations. They certainly did not advocate placing women's rights on an equal footing with that of men. Neither did they mention the absence of institutions capable of representing and defending women's rights.[31]

At the same time, the discussion put the agenda of women squarely within the public domain. The fact that the con-ference was able to discuss items previously considered inappropriate or even taboo has to be considered an important milestone in the overall political development of Saudi society. By placing women's issues into the limelight, it has become possible to conduct future discussions in a much more realistic and well-balanced manner.

> **The fact that the conference was able to discuss items previously considered inappropriate or even taboo has to be considered an important milestone in the overall political development of Saudi society.**

The role of women in Civil Society Organizations (CSO)

Women have also become increasingly active in Gulf civil society organizations. The year 2004 saw the selection of three Saudi women to the executive council of the new Saudi human rights association. Ten women were among the founding members with nine of them taking part in the elections.[32] Two Saudi women journalists also gained membership to the board of directors of the Saudi press association.[33] Election results of the first labor committee

set up as part of the Jeddah Chamber of Commerce and Industry gave two Saudi women the highest number of votes among the eligible 26 candidates.[34] Additionally, 12 women were among the signatories of the reform petition submitted to Saudi Crown Prince Abdullah which called for the release of three reformists put on trial for advocating the establishment of a constitutional monarchy in the Kingdom of Saudi Arabia.[35]

In Kuwait, the general constitutional association for the council of the Al-Massila district chose for the first time ever in the history of the district councils two women as part of the board of directors.[36] In mid-December 2004, a woman won the chairperson seat of the Kuwaiti Association of Economists for the first time. In Bahrain, two women won membership seats in the board of directors of the Al-Manbar National Islamic Association also for the first time.[37] At the same time, the announcement of a possible women's union triggered wide debate among the protagonists and detractors within the Ministry of Labor and Social Affairs.[38] While women have tried for many years for the right to establish a union, the Ministry responds by asking them to change clauses within their proposed constitution. This has lead to severe criticism of the ministry's role and to accusations that the Ministry is trying to predetermine the nature of the association itself.[39] In April 2004, the Ministry finally approved the constitutional acts with the provision that the organizations call itself the union of women's

[31] Ibid.
[32] Al-Hayat, March 3, 2004.
[33] Al-Hayat, June 9, 2004.
[34] Al-Sharq Al Awsat, July 7, 2004.
[35] AFP, August 17, 2004.

[36] Kuwait-based Al-Qabas, June 23, 2004.
[37] Akhbar Al-Khaleej, May 9, 2004.
[38] Akhbar Al-Khaleej, April 2, 2004.
[39] Al-Ayam, March 20, 2004.

associations rather than the women's union.[40] This, however, was rejected by the preparatory committee within the ministry in an appeal to the Ministry of Administrative Affairs[41] on the grounds that it should not be forced to change from its original intentions.[42]

On another level, a petition was submitted to the Bahraini king signed by some 1,542 men and women drawn from various Bahraini societal circles in December 2004 demanding an end to the violation of women' rights, and emphasizing the prevalence of negative attitudes towards women among judges in the religious courts.[43]

Improving the Economic Conditions of Women

As far as the economic conditions of women are concerned, the issue of women's unemployment dominated the deliberations of the Saudi Council of Ministers on June 30, 2004.[44] In its decision, the government committed itself to a set of measures that if implemented would constitute the genuine beginning in terms of labor conditions. This included a number of measures and regulations such as granting women the right to set up factories, expanding job opportunities for women in both the public and private sectors, and liberating women form the legal shackles usually regarded as making women dependent on men.[45] One specific item was the allocation by the Ministry of Civil Service of 26 new jobs in the field of administration established within the Foreign Ministry in Riyadh.[46]

The General Directorate of Passports, for its part, announced a plan to create separate women departments in the provincial administrations whereby qualified women employees would manage and take care of processing documents and

---

[40] Akhbar Al-Khaleej, April 28, 2004.

[41] Al-Ayam, May 17, 2004.

[42] Among the goals taken out from the constitutional acts was a proposal put forward by the women's union, namely the need to engage women in political life. Other goals, too, were rejected, particularly when it comes to eliminating all forms of discrimination against women. Another goal related to women's participation in the legislative, executive and judiciary branches of government were rejected. Goal number 10 which focused on protecting the rights acquired by women and women's efforts to gain rights likely to complement their citizenship was also removed. Goal number 11 stipulating that women should participate in cooperation with concerned departments in formulating laws to protect women and empower them to acquire their rights and duties was scratched. Finally, goal number 12 calling for enhanced actions conducted by local and international women's unions was also taken out.

[43] Al-Khaleej, December 14, 2004.

[44] Saudi-based Al-Watan, June 1, 2004.

[45] Measures and regulations were as follows:

o Issuance of licenses allowing women to practice economic activities in accordance with legal regulations and rules;

o Creating special departments and units for women in government institutions that offer services for women; establishing a women's committee by the Council of Saudi Chambers of Commerce and Industry. The committee ought to be made up of people with experience and expertise to be entrusted with the task of encouraging private sector organizations to create employment opportunities for women, creating a motivating environment for women and habilitating and training them for specific jobs, and providing financial support to women on condition that government departments contribute tom

o Allocating sited within cities for the creation of industrial; project that would employ women.

o The Fund for Human Resource Development ought to attach greater importance to training ands employing women as part of its programs and plans; coordinating with the ministries of labor, civil service and social affairs to take necessary measures to implement plans distance work as one option for women's employment, conducting programs for productive families and offering appropriate support to make these programs a success.

o Formulating a well-integrated national plan for women workers by the Ministry of Labor in cooperation with the Ministry of Economy and Planning, and the Ministry of Civil Service in order to determine the needs for women in the field of employment in all specialized fields.

o The Ministry of Labor, the Ministry of Commerce and Industry and the Saudi Council of the Chambers of Commerce and Industry need to conduct a study to grant working women maternity leaves that would give women better incentives for work and in such a way as not discourage employers form taking in women.

[46] Saudi-based Al-Watan, September 13, 2004.

administrative needs of women.[47] The first such department began its work in Riyadh with a second office planned to open in Mekkah. Here, it should be pointed out that this is not a novelty as Saudi women have previously worked at the passport departments. What is innovative is the setting up of independent female sections at the departments.[48]

This was followed by an announcement by the Minister of Labor, Dr. Ghazi Al-Ghosaibi of the establishment of a task force to look more closely into the issue creating job opportunities for women in the private sector. Reports suggest that the Ministry has given its preliminary consent to the idea of allowing women to practice law through larger offices to handle cases that directly involve women. They would not, however, be allowed to plead before the courts, an exercise that would remain reserved for men.[49] Similarly, on the occasion of inaugurating the Academy of Aviation Sciences, Prince Sultan bin Abdulaziz did not rule out the idea of women joining the new academy and made it clear that women play an essential role in supplanting foreign workers. As such, there is no contradiction according to the prince in having women work in Saudi airlines in full respect of Islamic traditions.[50]

At the same time, the Saudi government immediately announced that it would take at least one year to achieve its ambitious plan which has as its target an increase in the female participation in the labor market by over 20 percent depending on the fields that the cabinet commits itself to opening. Other government incentives include a bona fide acknowledgement of the social difficulties faced by women as far as the number of work hours, vacations and maternity leave is concerned. The

decisions taken by the government are in strict line with the recommendations issued by the national dialogue meeting held in June 2004. The Ministry of Trade, for its part, had decided some time earlier to repeal the need for a power of attorney for businesswomen. Meanwhile, the government granted women the right to obtain individual civil cards, part of a number of decisions that recognized the economic importance of women in the employment field.

The decision concerning women were also the direct result of an internal Ministry of Interior study that revealed an overall deteriorating social situation in particular in relation to rising rates of unemployment of both male and female Saudi nationals. While the government tended to side with conservative elements in terms of women's issues, such evidence has initiated a shift in terms of looking at the existing problems from more of a practical point of view. As such, Saudi society as a whole appears to be undergoing a transformation to overcome the stagnation that has characterized society for a long time.

The Emergence of the Role of Businesswomen

Outside of the issue of providing greater employment access to women in the Gulf, women themselves have become increasingly active in the business fields as entrepreneurs and managers. This, in turn, has provided them with additional leverage to galvanize governmental efforts at boosting women's economic opportunities. Official statistics indicate that there are currently over 30,000 trade

---

[47] Ibid, August 2, 2004.

[48] Al-Khaleej, August 30, 2004.

[49] Women lawyers would simply meet with women clients while men

would make the pleas before the court. See Al-Bayan, July 11, 2004.

[50] Al-Riyadh, December 4, 2004.

registrations in the name of women in Saudi Arabia, about 5% of total trade registration. The sectors of wholesale, retail and services come out on top with a capital value of one billion Saudi Riyals (i.e. $266 million).[51] The number of companies owned by women has reached 15,000 medium and small-sized companies, accounting for about 4.3% of registered companies in the kingdom. Women's savings in Saudi banks is estimated at about SR 60 billion representing around 70% of the total value of savings while investments stand at about 21% of total private investments in Saudi Arabia.[52]

In the UAE, women members in the Board of Businesswoman which was established in May 2003 number 10,500 women[53] where they manage investments with a value of AED 12.5 billion.[54] In Bahrain, there are 7,000 women trade registrants. In fact, Bahraini women have succeeded in raising their share in trade registration from 3.24 percent in 2001 up to 6.30 percent in 2002. The number of women members in the Bahraini Chamber of Commerce and Industry stands at 1,145 while Bahraini women account for some 9% of the total labor force in the country.[55]

The growth of women in the business field has led to the creation of a Gulf-wide committee of businesswomen in April 2004. The committee is composed of 12 members and operates under the umbrella of the Union of Gulf Chambers of Commerce and Industry. It is made up of women affiliated with various chambers of commerce as well as members of the various national committees of businesswomen. Some 600 women took part in the first meeting held in Riyadh in October 2004 which was aimed at devising ways to attract and move capital owned by women, estimated at about SR 18 billion deposited in banks.[56]

In March 2004, a women's branch was also opened at the Riyadh Chamber of Commerce and Industry[57] followed by a women's committee to oversee operations in September 2004.[58] In November, the Saudi Ministry of Commerce and Industry allowed Saudi businesswomen for the first time to cast direct votes during the elections for the Riyadh Chamber of Commerce board. While women were not allowed to run for office,[59] their participation in the election was also limited with only 15 women out of an eligible 3,000 casting their ballots.[60] This despite the fact that a center for businesswomen also exists in Riyadh.[61]

The Saudi Al-Watan newspaper reported on December 8, 2004, that the Saudi Ministry of Commerce and Industry was considering allowing women to work in the field of real estate and would add this to the list of commercial activities that women could directly exercise without the need to resort to legal representatives. Licenses will be issued in the future for offices owned and managed by

---

[51] Saudi women's participation in the public sector accounts for 14% in proportion to the total size of the labor force while their participation in the private sector stands at 0.5%. Women's' participation in the labor market is restricted to the sectors of medical and educational services (50%) and the banking service (20%). See Management Institute Newsletter, November 2004.

[52] See the newsletter issued by the Management Institute, November 2004; see also, Al-Sharq Al-Awsat, November 9, 2004; Elaf, April 10, 2004.

[53] Al-Ittihad, March 15, 2004.

[54] Women's representation in the local labor force in 2004 accounted for about 22.4%. Women represent about 66% of the total labor force in the public sector while the rate of national women employed in banks is around 32% in proportion to the size of the total labor force in the sector. See Al-Ittihad, March 15, 2004. Aman News Center, December 6, 2004, available at http://www.amanjordan.org/arabic_news

[55] Laha online, October 26, 2004.

[56] Al-Riyadh, March 22, 2004.

[57] Al-Hayat, September 15, 2004.

[58] Al-Khaleej, November 25, 2004.

[59] Al-Hayat, November 30, 2004.

[60] Al-Riyadh, June 13, 2004.

[61] Saudi-based Al-Watan, December 8, 2004.

women and providing real estate services to other businesswomen and investors in real estate projects.[62] In November, a real estate group was set up by some 30 Saudi businesswomen composed of women investors from different regions of the kingdom. The new firm was launched with a capital of SR 50 million to be invested in the real estate market.[63] It is important to note that women already possess around 40% of real estate assets in Saudi Arabia.[64] Statistics indicate that the size of women investments in this field stands at around SR 400 million while reports point out that 40% of businesswomen exercise the profession through middlemen.[65] In early December, Lubna Al-Olayan became the first Saudi woman to join the board of directors of a Saudi banking organization after she was elected by the general assembly of Saudi-Dutch Bank.[66]

Gulf women were also active overseas with delegations from Saudi Arabia, Qatar, Kuwait and the UAE visiting the United Kingdom, Sweden and Finland in a bid to enhance cooperation between them and their foreign counterparts.[67]

With their growing public profile, a heated controversy was set off at the Jeddah Economic Forum held in January 2004. The forum was marked by a strong and prominent female presence as some 620 Saudi businesswomen attended the meeting. Significantly, their participation extended outside traditional lines including the mixing between males and females and between Saudis and non-Saudis.

Used to participating in conferences but in separate closed-door halls, the Jeddah forum allowed women to participate directly in the sessions on an equal footing with men.

Used to participating in conferences but in separate closed-door halls, the Jeddah forum allowed women to participate directly in the sessions on an equal footing with men. Women were even given the freedom to take off their veils.[68] This fact created a stir when the Okaz newspaper published a picture featuring 26 Saudi women, without their head scarves and standing next to Queen Rania of Jordan, on its front pages. This, in turn, brought about a sharp rebuke from various circles with the Grand Mufti of the Kingdom, Sheikh Abdulaziz bin Abdulla Al Sheikh, noting that that "the mixing between men and women is totally forbidden and highly punishable. It is … the root of every evil and catastrophe."[69] In the wake of the Sheikh's statement, the Chairman of the Saudi Chambers of Commerce, Abdurrahman Al-Jeraisi, criticized what he described as "the errors and transgression committed during the Jeddah Economic Forum." He added that "the worst thing is the participation of women in this manner." One day later, Crown Prince Abdullah bin Abdulaziz stated that "the march of reform will continue but gradually."[70]

The role of Western States and Institutions in promoting women's issues in the Gulf

Right from start, 2004 witnessed wide interest by both Western states and institutions with regard to

---

[62] Al-Sharq Al-Awsat, November 24, 2004.

[63] Al-Hayat, September 15, 2004.

[64] Saudi-based Al-Yawm online, November 8, 2004.

[65] Al-Sharq Al-Awsat, December 2, 2004.

[67] See KUNA, December 1, 2004; Al-Hayat, May 18, 2004; Qatar-based Al-Watan, May 19, 2004.

[68] Al-Sharq Al-Awsat, January 1, 2004.

[69] See Agence France Press, January 21, 2004.

[70] Elaf, October 14, 2004, available at: http://www.elaph.com:9090/elaph/arabic/index.html

the issue of women in the Gulf. As part of the overall focus on reform in the region, numerous conferences and training programs were organized to assist women to take up positions in decision-making circles and improve their overall standing.

From February 14-18, Qatar hosted a special training workshop to enhance the awareness of Gulf women in managing regional electoral campaigns. Entitled "Partners in Participation: An Initiative to Support Women's' Participation in Public Life in the Middle East," the workshop was part of the Greater Middle East Partnership Initiative (MEPI) program supported by the US government.[71] The function was organized in cooperation with both the International Republican Institute (IRI) and the National Democratic Institute for International Relations (NDIIR), non-governmental organizations based in Washington whose mission revolves around encouraging and training candidates and the creation of strong political parties abroad. Around 60 women attended the workshop from all the GCC states with the exception of Saudi Arabia. The program included themes focused on planning electoral campaigns, the relationship between media and communication on the one hand and elections on the other, the ways to convey information to voters, strategic planning, developing skills for fundraising, forming team works, the mechanisms to be deployed in order to expand popular participation, and the relationship between candidates, campaign managers and official departments.[72]

Here it has to be mentioned that the paradigm adopted during the workshop for electoral campaigns was based on US elections, which is quite obviously far removed from the dominant conditions in the GCC societies in terms of general elections and the role of women. As such, the workshop turned out to more of an introductory session to the US electoral system than providing any real training to women participants.

The British Foreign Office meanwhile announced that it would support a three-year project slated to help Bahraini women engage in public life. Accordingly, the British embassy in Manama organized a workshop on 'Women leadership skills' on June 12, 2004, followed by a second workshop held on June 26 with the participation of women's associations as well as a number of other political and social associations operating in Bahrain. According to press reports, London plans to transform Bahrain into a regional center for the empowerment of Gulf and Arab women by training them in acquiring leadership skills.[73]

In the Sultanate of Oman, the Committee for the Coordination of Voluntary Women's Action held in cooperation with the US embassy a training workshop under the title of "Building Efficient Organizations and Collective Women's Action" from September 26 to 29, 2004. The workshop was attended by Mona Al-Manthari, member of the State Council and Chairperson of the Coordination Committee for Women's Voluntary Work. Participants included some 30 women from Muscat who represented various NGOs and government departments.[74]

---

[71] That was a presidential initiative launched in 2002 under the slogan of supporting development efforts in the Middle East region and increasing opportunities available to the people of the region, especially women and children.

[72] See Qatar-based Al-Watan, February 12, 2004; see also, Al-Sharq Al-Awsat, February 16, 2004 and Washington Newsletter, February 17, 2004. There is no existing electoral system in the UAE where women

could participate in. In Kuwait, women do not enjoy the right to run or vote as candidates in elections. In Saudi Arabia, women have no political rights and are not allowed to participate in municipal elections due on February 2005.

[73] Elaf, May 25, 2004.

[74] Oman-based Al-Watan, September 27, 2004.

Conclusion

The developments described above point towards substantive and positive change as far as the position and role of women in the GCC countries is concerned. At the same time, a few clarifications are necessary:

1- Democracy requires equality among all citizens, be they men or women. Enhancing the rights of women, thus, is part of boosting democracy itself. Democracy also entails the establishment of institutions that can be held accountable to the citizens and which can counter-balance the powers of other institutions through a system of checks and balances. The mere establishment of such institutions is not dependent on granting women their rights.

It is a well-established fact that a state cannot aspire to become democratic if it practices discrimination against women. The real hurdle to democracy in the GCC countries does not lie in the discrimination against women, but rather in the limited scope of political rights granted in some countries and the utter absence of these rights in others. The real problem is not simply installing equality between men and women; it is the reform of the entire political system in such a way that all citizens are granted their equal political rights. Democratic nations are by essence nations that have organized political opposition, strong parliaments, an independent judiciary, a political system based on the principle of separating authorities. This does not include nations that grant their women citizens a few public positions or allow them to vote and run for a seat in a weak parliament or council.

2- The situation of women in the GCC States is moving towards further progress and development although the scale of development varies from one country to another. However, it is of utmost importance that women's issues be handled without forcing them out of context, as any such approach would only compound existing complications. In fact, problems facing women in the GCC countries are not widely different from problems facing men, whether in terms of economic rights or political rights. These issues touch women as well as men. In that context, the demands of Gulf women could serve as a mechanism to secure public political rights for all concerned.

3- The ruling elites in the Gulf attach a great deal of importance to projects slated to improve women's conditions, yet such initiatives do not necessarily ensure an effective guarantee for implementation. There is a need therefore for institutional frameworks and channels via which women could express their opinions and organize themselves in unions in order to activate proposed laws and legislations and make them permanent.

4- The socio-cultural environment in the GCC countries, with all its traditions, values and mores, is certainly no incubator or even motivator for genuine female empowerment. Hence, it is almost impossible to isolate women's issues and problems in these societies from their wider social and cultural context. Similarly, enhancing and modernizing women's roles ought to run concomitantly with a comprehensive process of development and modernization of all the socio-cultural components of the existing societies.

Civil Society in the Gulf Region

Dr. Baqer Al-Najjar

Professor of Sociology, University of Bahrain

When broadly defined, the term 'civil society' refers to associations and organizations of a contemporary character in terms of structure and core activities. As a rule, civil society organizations (CSOs) are voluntary, non-profit organizations; that is, those who belong to such organizations join them out of free will and not as a result of sectarian obligations. CSOs do not engage in politics, although their work might intersect with the political realm. Politics are never a core interest or an essential part of the work of such groups as they are with political parties or political organizations. CSOs never seek an active role - be it legislative or of a different nature - in government. Instead, they may embrace a specific position on certain policies or measures enacted by the government or attempt to pressure the government into implementing their suggestions in the legislative process.

One should not assume that because CSOs are contemporary in character, they are removed from the wide social and cultural context within which they operate. The truth of the matter is quite the contrary; CSOs are a product of their environments and as such, they reflect the social and cultural dimensions of the settings in which they operate. They are molded and defined by the social, cultural, economic and even political milieu out of which they came into existence.[1]

The Increase in the Number of CSOs in the GCC Countries

In spite of the emergence of a huge swath of non-governmental and governmental associations in the GCC States, no comprehensive database exists on the number and activities of CSOs. One reserved estimate puts the number at 688 organizations; another report puts the figure at 900 organizations, most of which are based in Saudi Arabia and Bahrain. They are active mostly in the social, cultural, professional, charity, religious and women-related fields. If sporting clubs are included, the number of non-governmental organizations would jump to 1,500; when including Iraq and Yemen, this figure would reach almost 5,000.

Available reports do not mention any fundamental changes in the number of CSOs in any GCC state during the year 2004 save for Bahrain, where the number soared from 190 organizations in 2001 to around 245 by 2003. By the end of 2004, there

---

[1] See, Baqer Al-Najjar, ' Civil Society in the Arab World', paper presented at a symposium on the role of civil society in achieving reform in the Arab world, Alexandria, Alexandria Library, June 2004.

were 386 registered CSOs in the country.

The case of the Sultanate of Oman is somewhat similar to Bahrain's in the sense that an increasing number of CSOs operating in various fields - particularly the professional field - have been established. There are currently 44 CSOs in the country, most of which are active in the cultural and professional fields; other CSOs are involved in special activities, i.e. providing assistance to people with special needs. It must be pointed out that in Oman's past, non-government organizations were almost always women's associations. Over the few past years, however, a remarkable number of professional and cultural associations have come into existence. The ability of such organizations to influence the status quo, however, remains limited for many reasons, including their relative immaturity and their status within the dominant cultural and political context.

Legislation Regulating the Work of CSOs

No major changes occurred in 2004 in the legal texts ruling or the activities and nature of CSOs in the GCC states. With the notable exception of Qatar, the GCC states are still governed by laws 20 to 40 years old. The sole exception to this rule is perhaps the case of Qatar, where a new law was issued in May 2004 recognizing for the first time the right to establish professional associations and labor syndicates. The workers' union includes worker committees set up at the level of work organizations.[2] In this regard, Qatar became the third GCC country after Kuwait and Bahrain to allow the establishment of labor syndicates. The Qatari law, however, also provides for the right to stage labor strikes in the event of an acute dispute between

workers and employers, a provision that is unprecedented in the GCC domain.

In this vein, a group of Bahrainis, including members of the Shura [Consultative] Council, submitted a bill that would regulate the work of non-governmental organizations. If adopted, it would be the most progressive law in this field in the entire Gulf region.

The War on Terrorism and its Impact on CSOs

As a consequence of the sustained war on terrorism and the international efforts slated to freeze possible terrorist assets, specific ministerial decisions were issued in some GCC states in a bid to better regulate the activities of CSOs, particularly those operating in the field of charitable and humanitarian assistance, both domestically and internationally. The cases of Saudi Arabia and Kuwait are probably the most illustrative of this phenomenon.

Following the attacks of 9/11 and the subsequent investigations, Saudi Arabia issued a number of resolutions banning individuals and groups from raising funds at schools or in religious and public places without first securing an official permit. Saudi authorities also made it mandatory to disclose the source and the destination of funds, thus increasing the degree of transparency within such organizations.

In January 2004, four satellite offices of the Al-Haramain charity organization were included in a list of organizations and companies implicated in providing funds for terrorist groups. The list was drawn up by the UN as part of a joint initiative launched by Saudi Arabia and the US administration. The US Treasury affirmed in a statement read out at a press conference held by

---

[2] *Al-Sharq Al-Awsat*, May 21, 2004.

Adel Al-Jabeir, advisor to Saudi Crown Prince Abdullah bin Abdulaziz, at the Saudi embassy in Washington, D.C. on January 22, 2004, that four branch offices of Al-Haramain in Indonesia, Kenya, Tanzania and Pakistan provided financial and logistical support to al-Qaeda and other terrorist organizations[3]. Following that declaration, Saudi authorities replaced the director-general of Al-Haramain, Shaikh Aqeel Al-Aqeel, with Dabbas Al-Dabbasi.

Pressures on the Al-Haramain organization did not emanate from the US alone, but from states across the world, including Saudi Arabia. In February 2004, as US pressures relentlessly mounted, Saudi authorities closed down the overseas[4] offices belonging to the organization. Shortly afterwards and following a decision to freeze the organization's assets overseas, the authorities froze its financial assets in the Kingdom.

Some time after the Saudi authorities decided to freeze the bank accounts of Al-Haramain in the Kingdom, Shaikh Dabbas Ad-Dabbasi - the newly appointed director-general of Al-Haramain - resigned after just 188 days of his appointment, lamenting that he "could not hand out assistance packages to some 53,602 families during the first three months of his tenure." Analysts saw in Shaikh Al-Dabbasi's decision a prelude to the dissolution of Al-Haramain. Indeed, following this incident and four months after an indication given by Al-Jubeir in June 2004, Saudi authorities decided to dissolve the charity organization and its committees operating overseas; the company's assets were to be managed by the newly-established Saudi National Authority for Charity Work. The new authority was to be a non-governmental association charged with the distribution of donations and funds provided by institutions and individuals in the Kingdom. Al-Jubeir observed that the authority was to be subject to stringent legal oversight and was to work in accordance with clear policies in order to avoid misuse of donations raised to help the needy, adding that Saudi authorities "will determine and cut off the sources funding any terrorist organizations."[5]

During the same period, Saudi Arabia, together with the US, submitted a request to the UN to include a number of the satellite offices affiliated with Al-Haramain in the list of individuals and organizations accused of funding terrorism. The offices in question were based in the Netherlands, Albania, Afghanistan, Bangladesh and Ethiopia. In June 2004, US authorities placed the name of Shaikh Aqeel Al-Aqeel on the list of individuals funding terrorism; consequently, his bank assets were frozen and his financial transactions were terminated.[6]

Al-Haramain had operated around 46 offices in Saudi Arabia and another 15 offices overseas. The sum total of the donations it received during 2004 amounted to roughly $62 million while its expenditures soared to $52 million. In the wake of the dissolution, its offices were turned organizations for social services - as happened in Ta'if - or into non-religious charity organizations, as was the case in Jeddah. More importantly, the responsibility for supervising the activities of Al-Haramain shifted from the Ministry of Religious Affairs to the Ministry of Social Affairs in what appeared to be an attempt to

> **In January 2004, four satellite offices of the Al-Haramain charity organization were included in a list of organizations and companies implicated in providing funds for terrorist groups.**

[3] Al-Sharq Al-Awsat, January 23, 2004.
[4] Al-Sharq Al-Awsat, July 14, 2004.

[5] Al-Sharq Al-Awsat, June 30, 2004.
[6] Ibid.

contain the influence of the religious establishment and the Islamists on its activities. Prince Nayef bin Abdulaziz, the Saudi Minister of the Interior, described Al-Haramain as "ill-organized even at the level of its organizational structure and work, a fact that allowed some people who seek to harm the country to get involved in its activities."[7]

In Kuwait, Foreign Minister Shaikh Mohammad Al-Sabah made no attempt to conceal the fact that charity work in his country might be linked to terrorist activities. Shaikh Al-Sabah said that there are "possible links between some charity associations and terrorist organizations." In response, Kuwait's Ministry of Labor and the Ministry of Social Affairs issued a set of decisions determining the rules and regulations governing fund-raising campaigns by strictly implementing the principle of transparency insofar as the sources and destinations of funds were concerned. The new regulations carried a visible impact on the scope of activities conducted by Kuwaiti Muslim charitable organizations, which soundly rejected the policies implemented by the government.

The tighter rules enacted by both the Kuwaiti and Saudi governments led to a reduction in the size of the financial support that once lined the coffers of Muslim charity organizations. Around the same time, Saudi authorities decided to put an end to the work of the so-called "religious tutors" employed in Saudi embassies around the world; these individuals were regarded with a degree of suspicion and distrust in both Western and Arab countries alike.

Civil Society and the State

The relationship binding civil society and the state is subsumed within legislation that governs and shapes the inner character of this relationship. To be sure, even though existing legislation does grant some space for free movement and action for civil society organizations in some specific areas, it also provides the state with an arsenal of legal texts and stipulations that allow it to interfere in and impose regulations on the proceedings of CSOs. In some cases, the legislative texts governing the work of CSOs in the GCC countries are derived from the experience of other Arab states and although the experiences are similar on some levels, the differences between those of the Gulf states and other Arab states are different enough to warrant a separate approach.

It is of utmost importance to point out that some local authorities in the Gulf region sometimes prefer to ignore existing legislation that, when fully regarded, would severely incapacitate CSOs. At other times, however, governments are forced to take a strong stance against CSOs clearly transgressing their boundaries.

Politics often tend to hamper the progress of many non-governmental organizations, particularly those of Kuwait and Bahrain. On numerous occasions, the degree of politicization in fact dominates the scope of the activities in the designated specialized field, if this exists. The cases of Kuwait and Bahrain reflect more so than any other GCC state the vibrancy - if not actual opposition - that characterizes the relationship between politics and CSOs.

It is clear that the presence of political associations in both Bahrain and Kuwait that enjoy a good margin of political freedom has rendered the relationship between CSOs and the state more dialectical in nature and has enhanced the dynamism of the political scene in both countries. In other words, and even though CSOs have at times caused some tension between political associations and the ruling regimes, they contribute to a political

[7] Al-Sharq Al-Awsat, October 19, 2004.

vibrancy unmatched by any other GCC State.

Admittedly, some political opposition groups in Kuwait - and to a lesser extent in Bahrain - have opted to embrace violence in handling their disputes with the government; the Salafist-Jihadist groups in Kuwait come to mind. Over the past few months, Kuwait has been witness to an unprecedented wave of organized violence orchestrated by the Salafist-Jihadist movement against the presence of US troops in the country. Other Islamist groups are striving by various means to 'Islamize' Kuwaiti society.

Along with the unstable security conditions prevailing in Iraq, security developments in Saudi Arabia and the wide Islamist presence driven by deep conservatism and a strong influence in the National Assembly have helped Islamist groups impose their agenda on Kuwaiti society. Furthermore, the policy predicated on maintaining a balance of power pursued by the Kuwaiti government over past decades has pushed the state into making palpable concessions in favor of the Islamists, who do not see the concessions as sufficient to really and fully 'Islamize' Kuwaiti society.

Issues such as the US military presence in Kuwait, the projects aimed at political reform floated by the US administration, women's political participation and the attitude towards terrorist acts in Iraq and other Arab countries constitute the political aspects of the dispute between Islamist movements and the state, just as the same issues stand at the core of the dispute between liberal groups and the government. Other issues, such as the separation of males and females at schools, university campuses and public places, banning singing at functions held at hotels and restaurants, and reforming Kuwait's educational system, constitute a matter for verbal tit-for-tat among the various political and social forces in Kuwait and a fertile ground for what has come to be known as "the war of fatwas [religious edicts]." Some of the fatwas issued so far have been religious in character, but also clearly aim to achieve social and political objectives.

While armed violence characterized the stand-off between the state and apostatizing Salafist groups, newspaper pages, magazines, the Internet and television channels have become the space where the relations between liberal groups and Islamist movements unravel. In this regard, both entities employ the various media available to them in their attempts to turn the state against the other party, as is crystal-clear from the writings published by figures belonging to both groups.

It is worth pointing out here that the forces representing Shi'ite political Islam in Kuwait seem to maintain political positions that are closer to the ideas championed by the liberal opposition. However, when it comes to their social issues, they seem to be closer to the Sunni political Islamists. Shi'ites have in fact supported many Islamist figures serving in the National Assembly, thereby sustaining the conservative streak that drives the relationship between the Kuwaiti state on the one hand and modernity and globalization on the other. This is not unlike the positions held by political forces representing Shi'ite Islam in Bahrain in the sense

Issues such as the US military presence in Kuwait, the projects aimed at political reform floated by the US administration, women's political participation and the attitude towards terrorist acts in Iraq and other Arab countries constitute the political aspects of the dispute between Islamist movements and the state

that in Bahrain, they also remain socially conservative but appear to advocate rather radical political views.

The point is that political Shi'ism in Bahrain has succeeded in imposing its political agenda on other major political opposition groups thanks mainly to its wide-ranging popular base. Take, for example, the Al-Wefaq National Islamic Society. This association is the strongest political organization in Bahrain both in terms of the number of its members and in terms of its capacity to mobilize other opposition groups. On the issue of constitutional reform, Al-Wefaq managed to rally the support of some left-leaning movements, along with other nationalist groups and some small Sh'ite forces, notably the Shirazi movement.

One could briefly browse through landmark developments in the relationship between the state and civil society organizations, some of which were shaped by CSOs while others were triggered and driven by governmental authorities. It is worth noting that most landmark developments were associated with controversial issues, particularly when regarding the relationship between political organizations and the state. Similarly, some women's associations were locked in a stand-off with the state over the issue of creating a women's union. Although the issue was put on the table in 2004, the year came to an end without the project being implemented; this was most likely due to a host of hurdles that surfaced within the female community as well as the positions espoused by a number of new women's associations against such a project. The official stance maintained by the government towards the project, its nature and its activities further obstructed the establishment of a women's union.

Civil Society-Related Developments in Bahrain: a 2004 Survey

From a broad perspective, the most salient developments that unfolded during 2004 at the level of civil society in Bahrain could be summarized as follows:

o The relations binding state authorities and Al-Wefaq was marred by more disputes. In late December 2003, the government banned the association from presenting a play entitled "Abu Al-Aich" under the pretense that the association did not secure a license from the Ministry of Information. In the wake of the dispute, the association's first annual conference faced difficulties in obtaining an official permit. After a long-running tug-of-war within the government as well as within the association, it managed to hold its conference on the scheduled date, January 21-23, 2004. At the same time, the Ministry of Information expressed its willingness, according to a statement issued by the association, to grant the association a license to publish a newspaper. The project has not yet been finalized.

o The constitutional issue, as it has been labeled by the entities that brought it up, was the source of acute disagreement between what came to be known as the quartet coalition and the state over a set of constitutional questions and the scope of parliamentarian power. The quartet coalition included the Islamic National Accord, the National Democratic Action Society, the Islamic Action Society, and the Democratic Nationalist Bloc. The coalition faced some official difficulties while it tried to hold its first conference: the authorities banned foreign participants, including Ahmad Al-Sa'adun, Abdulmuhsin Jamal, Adnan Abdulsamad - all three of whom are Kuwaitis - and Dr. Ali Al-Kawari from

Qatar from entry into Bahrain; other delegations from the UK and France, too, were banned on the pretext that the conference was to discuss purely domestic issues and no foreign participants or experts should hence be involved; and the management of the hotel designated as the conference venue apologized at the last minute for not being able to host the event, forcing the quartet to hold it at Al Uruba [Arabhood] Club on February 14 and 15, 2004. During the conference, the idea of launching a popular petitioning campaign was proposed; this later proved to be a test of strength between the quartet and the state authorities. The petition campaign was 'temporarily' interrupted in return for the release of a group of jailed activists who took charge of compiling signatures. In the meantime, the government launched an initiative to conduct open dialogue with the quartet, though the initiative was cut short by the government after the Bahrain-based Al-Ayam newspaper published reports on alleged meetings held by the leaders from the four associations with the US and UK ambassadors in Manama; all of the parties concerned denied the allegations and the four associations accused the Minister of Labor, who was entrusted with the task of managing the dialogue initiative, of "a lack of seriousness and of obstructing dialogue by issuing controversial statements."[8]

o The bill on political association, submitted for discussion at the parliament by the Independent Bloc, constituted another major dispute between civil society organizations and the State. Sheikh Ali Salman, the president of the Islamic National Accord described the bill on September 16 as a source that could "threaten the structure of the reform project," pledging "not to spare any efforts to stand firmly against it."[9] The proposed bill spurred as much criticism on the part of the liberals and leftists as it did the Shi'ite Islamist groups; all entities regarded the bill as being "closer to the policies framing the state security law" which was abolished by an Amiri decree at the very inception of the reform project in Bahrain in 2002. As a result of the wide and sharp critiques leveled against the bill by various civil society organizations and the press, the Independent Bloc, the submitter of the bill, called upon political organizations to engage in further consultations on the bill's content. The call, however, was surprisingly rejected by the quartet on the basis of its earlier rejection of the 2002 amended constitutional text and the stipulations regarding the elected chamber. Instead, the quartet opted to further study and improve its own position as an alternative to the proposed law.

The socio-political picture in Bahrain appeared at times to have regressed or spun out of control only to be followed by periods of quietude and serenity.

o The socio-political picture in Bahrain appeared at times to have regressed or spun out of control only to be followed by periods of quietude and serenity. Indeed, the symposium on poverty organized by the Bahrain's Center for Human Rights on September 22 and the ideas discussed during the event as well as the fiery speeches delivered, prompted reactions on the part of government authorities that seemed to be slightly harsh. For example, the government decided to close down the Al-Uruba Club for a few weeks and on September 29, the Ministry of Labor and Social Affairs decided to dissolve the Center for Human Rights while Abdulhadi Al-Khawaja, the Center's executive director, was placed under

---

[8] Al-Wasat, October 29, 2004.

[9] Al-Wasat, September 16, 2004.

detention. Al-Khawaja later stood trial on charges of instigating the people to rise against the public order. In the wake of Al-Khawaja's arrest, huge popular demonstrations demanding his immediate release were staged throughout Bahrain. Some demonstrators set police cars on fire and threw stones against anti-riot forces. In many respects, the scene was reminiscent of the events that shook Bahrain during the second half of the 1990s. Sheikh Ali Salman, the president of the largest political association in Bahrain, was rather unsympathetic and criticized the popular rallies as well as the attacks on the government apparatus and its officials. He confirmed that religious scholars condemned all forms of violence, as did the Islamic National Accord.[10] The ruling regime, however, did not desire to have the arrest of Al-Khawaja assume far-reaching implications; a royal amnesty followed only a few hours after the sentence against Al-Khawaja was read.

o The year 2004 culminated with disputes over the nature of a proposal to establish what came to be called the 'moral police.' Although similar forces do exist in many countries both in the West and the East, a number of civil society organizations regarded the project as an attempt to revive the role of the secret police. Official authorities, however, claim that the project is an attempt to correct an ill-founded attitude towards the police and their role in society.[11]

Conclusion

Generally speaking, civil society in the Gulf region has seen a good measure of development in some states, particularly with respect to the number of CSOs and their degree of influence. To be sure, the most outstanding development during 2004 was the official constitution of a press association in Saudi Arabia, even though the Saudi state retains the power to appoint one-third of its members. Another notable development was the official announcement of the creation of a human rights association in Kuwait even though the said association was in fact established a decade earlier.

On the other hand, the year 2004 also witnessed the dissolution of a number of CSOs, as was the case of Al-Haramayn charity organization in Saudi Arabia and the Center of Human Rights in Bahrain. In both cases, state authorities concluded that the organization had overstepped the boundaries set for non-governmental activities inside the countries in question.

Of all of the GCC states, Bahrain and Kuwait remain on the top of the list not only in terms of the steadily increasing number of CSOs - particularly in Bahrain - but also in terms of the strength of the relationship between CSOs and the existing political systems. Although at times the relationship has been rocked by tension and controversy, this only enhances the dynamism of political life in both countries.

---

[10] Al-Wasat, October 31, 2004   [11] Al-Wasat, September 10, 2004.

Section Five

Intra-GCC and GCC-Arab Relations

Intra-GCC Relations

Jameel Mirdad

Associate Professor at the Institute of Diplomatic Studies, Saudi Arabia

According to its charter, the GCC is a regional organization covering political, economic and social issues. The GCC was created to meet the challenges imposed by surrounding circumstances. The geographical proximity of the GCC states and the similarity of their political systems as well as economic and social conditions were additional factors that helped in the establishment of the organization. For the GCC, the year 2004 represented a period of divergence among its members. While until recently, they maintained at least a minimal level of congruency, the accelerated political and security developments, both domestically and regionally, have made it clear that current policies at the political and security levels are insufficient.

Economically, the regional picture was positive. The combined economies of the GCC countries surged by 3.84 per cent in real terms on the back of high oil prices and strong private sector activity. Qatar was the star economic performer with its GDP growing by 8.4% as a result of a steady expansion of its liquefied natural gas (LNG) projects at the mammoth offshore North Field, the world's largest single gas reservoir. Growth was estimated at 4.4% in Oman, 4.1% in Bahrain, 3.8% in Kuwait, 3.7% in Saudi Arabia and around 3% in the UAE. Experts suggest that as last year's growth outpaced the annual increase in the GCC's population, this should allow the countries to reverse the recent upward trend in unemployment. This is however only a temporary relief as oil prices could decline in the coming years and push growth rates back to the 1990s level when regional economies either contracted or recorded minimal growth after a collapse in crude prices.[1]

Patterns of Convergent and Divergent Policies at the Individual State Level

One of the prominent developments of 2004 was the improving relations between Bahrain and Qatar following a period of coolness since the middle of 2002 when the meeting of the joint committee between the two states, headed by the respective crown princes, was suspended. In 2004, the two sides agreed to form a joint higher committee to discuss joint projects, including a bridge that would link the two states similar to the one that exists between Bahrain to Saudi Arabia. Several meeting of the committee were held to follow-up agreed cooperative measures.[2]

---

[1] *Gulf News*, January 21, 2004.

[2] See the news agencies of Bahrain and Qatar on February 12 and April 28, 2004 respectively.

Similarly, the Omani-Qatari Joint Committee held its 8th meeting in Muscat in April 2004 and activated agreements signed in previous years including the diplomatic and consular agreement of 1998, under which Qatari and Omani diplomats are appointed to certain embassies to look after joint interests. There is also a media agreement in place that was signed in 2001. At the economic level, the two countries signed an accord on the establishment of a joint business council as a means to encourage and develop trade exchange and commodity flow between them. A Memorandum of Understanding to open a joint labor office in Doha was signed last year. Other issues included a Qatari proposal to extend joint tourist visas between the two countries to one month, cooperation in the fields of telecommunications, information technology, investments in the oil and gas sector and in petrochemical industries as well as developing relations between security and safety services establishments.[3]

Oman and Kuwait also continued the meetings of their joint committee, tackling both regional and international issues of common concern. The two countries reviewed the existing bilateral cooperation and expressed their appreciation of the high standards that such relations have reached. During the meeting, it was decided to look into ways to further upgrade ties in all political, security, economic, commercial, industrial fields as well as in the oil and gas sector, education, information, manpower, civil service, social affairs, municipalities, environment, civil aviation, youth, sports and cultural affairs.[4]

There were also issues in which GCC states took opposing views. Qatar and the UAE, for example, indicated their support for waiving most of the more than $7 billion Iraq owes them, with UAE President Shaikh Khalifa bin Zayid Al Nahyan stating that the UAE was prepared to undertake talks to write off most of Iraq's debts estimated at more than 14 billion dirhams ($ 3.8 billion). Similarly, an official from the Qatari Foreign Ministry said his country would waive most of Iraq's debts, estimated at $4 billion, and consider writing off the rest. Saudi Arabia and Kuwait in the meantime have been reluctant to waive the debts on Iraq and have provided different proposals calling for investments in Iraq that would be counted against the owed debts.[5] Overall, it can be said that relations between Qatar and Saudi Arabia continued to fluctuate over contentious issues such as the common border, the activities of al-Jazeera and regional policies regarding Iraq and Gulf security.

Another issue concerned the membership of Yemen in the GCC. While Oman and Qatar have supported full membership, other GCC countries have shown different attitudes. UAE Information Minister Shaikh Abdullah bin Zayid Al- Nahyan has stated that Yemen does not qualify to join the GCC in the short term as Yemen is an impoverished republic and the only Arabian peninsula state without a foothold on the Gulf.[6] Referring to the example of the European Union spending hundreds of millions of dollars to prepare countries like Greece and Spain to join, Shaikh Abdullah indicated that the timing was simply not right to consider the issue now. At their December 2001 summit meeting, GCC leaders decided to allow Yemen to join the GCC council of health ministers, a regional education bureau, the council of labor and social affairs ministers and the Gulf football cup as part of a gradual integration process.

---

[3] *Times of Oman*, March 3, 2004.

[4] *Khaleej Times*, August 19, 2004

[5] Iraq is estimated to owe the Gulf countries $45 billion, mostly money given to Baghdad during its 1980-1988 war with Iran. Iraq insists the money from Saudi Arabia and other Gulf countries was given as grants.

[6] *The Peninsula*, January 13, 2004.

In relation to political reforms, GCC States also took divergent stances. While countries like Qatar, Bahrain and Kuwait prefer the speeding up of reforms, Saudi Arabia and the UAE made it clear that their preference is for slow but steady reform measures. Some GCC states are seriously considering legalizing political groupings into political parties. Others do not advocate such option, at least for the time being.

Finally and probably most importantly, the GCC states have shown a great discrepancy in their perception to the existing security arrangements in the Gulf. At the same time that Saudi Arabia saw the removal of foreign troops from its soil, Qatar and Kuwait welcomed those same troops to be stationed on their land. Qatar, Bahrain and Kuwait continue to see the US as the key guarantor for their security while Saudi Arabia has been favoring more regional arrangements based on local, regional and international cooperation.[7] Saudi Arabia has also emphasized the inclusion of Iran, Iraq and Yemen in any security measures in the Gulf, thereby widening the differences with other GCC members. This has led to disagreements of another nature in relations to bilateral agreements signed outside the framework of the GCC, such as the Free Trade Agreement between the US and Bahrain. This has been criticized as an unnecessary divergence from the collective consensus.

the GCC states have shown a great discrepancy in their perception to the existing security arrangements in the Gulf.

Patterns of Convergent and Divergent Policies at Collective-State Level

Looked at from a collective point of view, the issues of security, reform and media are probably the most disputed areas between the GCC states, while the policy towards the Palestinians and the UAE islands are issues where there exists general agreement.[8] For example, the GCC once again urged the US, the European Union and the international community to put an end to Israel's assassination of Palestinian leaders and destruction of Palestinian houses. Also, in July 2004, the GCC General Secretariat expressed its strong denunciation and rejection to Israeli aggressions on the Lebanese territories, which it said terrorized the people and expanded the circle of violence.[9]

The annual summit meeting in December, which was held in Bahrain at the request of the UAE discussed such issues as elections in Iraq, Gulf security, the crisis between Iran and the US over the former's nuclear program, reforms and the war against terrorism. That these are not easy issues had been apparent all year. On January 12, 2004, Qatar's deputy premier and foreign minister, Shaikh Hamad Bin Jasim Al-Thani stated that the Gulf states do not have to feel ashamed for being protected by the United States. By hosting the headquarters of the American Central Command in the Gulf, Qatar is in fact choosing a pragmatic policy in order to ensure the security of its peoples.[10] This, of course, stands in

---

[7] See the press release distributed by Prince Saud Al Faisal, Saudi Foreign Minister, at the end of the conference held in Manama, Bahrain at the Gulf Dialogue Conference, December 5-6, 2004.

[8] The GCC states have continuously supported the UAE in its dispute with Iran over the three strategic islands which Tehran took control of after British forces left the Gulf in 1971. This includes taking the issue to the International Court of Justice if Tehran fails to settle the dispute

through negotiations.

[9] Kuwait News Agency, July 22, 2004. In its statement, the GCC stated that recent atrocities on Lebanese territories constituted a violation of all international norms and charters, as well as a flagrant aggression against a UN member state.

[10] *Gulf in the Media*, Gulf Research Center, January 12, 2004.

contrast to the policy of Saudi Arabia.

In terms of reform, Gulf foreign ministers met on February 29, 2004 to discuss a joint stance on the eve of an Arab League meeting focused on how to reform the state of affairs in the Arab world including future plans for the 22-member body.[11] The meeting also reflected on Washington's "Greater Middle East Initiative" to democratize the region. In that context, the GCC made it clear that they are proceeding with reform in keeping with their own interests and values, and that they would not accept a particular pattern of reform to be imposed externally.[12] To put the reform debate into context, the GCC states collectively endorsed the smooth transfer of power in the UAE to Shaikh Khalifa after the death of his father Shaikh Zayed bin Sultan in November 2003. The immediate support once again underlined the importance placed by the GCC states on maintaining the existing order as part of overall stability and tranquility in the region.

On other particular matters of foreign policy, there was once again general agreement. GCC Secretary-General Abdul Rahman Al-Attiyah described on May 12 the decision by US President Bush to impose sanctions on Syria as unacceptable and contradictory to the promotion of stability in the region.[13] Here it should also be mentioned that the GCC in September announced its support of the UN Security Council Resolution calling for the withdrawal of all foreign forces from Lebanon without mentioning Syria by name.[14] Also, in the case of the Qatar-Russian rift over the assassination of the former president of Chechnya in Doha on March 3, 2004, in which the Qatari government arrested and put two Russian intelligence officers on trial, the GCC expressed its clear solidarity with the Qatari government.[15]

The war against terrorism also cemented relations between the GCC states. GCC interior ministers on May 4 signed a landmark counterterrorism pact calling for concerted efforts to combat terrorists including co-ordination among security agencies and better exchange of intelligence information. The accord, which had been approved at the GCC Summit held in Kuwait in December 2003 was described by Secretary-General Al-Attiyah as the "most important" since the GCC was formed in 1981, stating that such a comprehensive pact" would help security officers in the member states to carry out their mission effectively.[16] Overall, Gulf states have made effective contributions in the global effort to combat terror, although such efforts have remained largely unnoticed.[17]

In the meantime, the state of lawlessness in Iraq adversely affected the security of the GCC states, which have been required to take on additional security measures such as boosting the monitoring of borders to stop infiltrators. Most of the Gulf States, with the exception of Kuwait, held strong reservations to the Iraq invasion but they soon welcomed steps such as the transfer of power to Iraqis in June 2004 in the hope that this would lead to a restoration of security throughout most of the

The war against terrorism also cemented relations between the GCC states.

---

[11] *Arab News*, February 29, 2004.

[12] *Agence France Press*, February 28, 2004.

[13] *Kuwait News Agency*, May 13, 2004. The US contention that Syria supports terrorism and was not adequately cooperating adequately in restoring stability to Iraq was deemed as unconvincing in light of Syria's clear statements on more than one occasion that it rejected all acts of terrorism.

[14] *Arab News*, September 14, 2004.

[15] This came in the conclusion of a meeting of GCC foreign ministers in Riyadh.

[16] *Gulf News*, September 16, 2004.

[17] *Arab News*, May 5, 2004.

country. The GCC characterized the transfer as a step on the right path to building a unified Iraq. Individual Gulf States also expressed their support. The Omani Foreign Ministry welcomed the handover, stating that the move would contribute to development and reconstruction in favor of stability. Qatar noted that the transfer of power was important and necessary for Iraq to recover its sovereignty and independence as well as to realize the security needs of the Iraqi people. The UAE called the handover an important step along the road to the stability of Iraq and urged other countries to aid the new Baghdad government in its effort to bring about stability. Bahrain sent interim Iraqi President Ghazi Al-Yawar a congratulatory telegram telling him that Manama wished to strengthen relations with Iraq.[18] Saudi Arabia, however, cautiously welcomed the handover and questioned how far real authority remained in the hands of the Americans.[19]

> **Most of the Gulf States, with the exception of Kuwait, held strong reservations to the Iraq invasion but they soon welcomed steps such as the transfer of power to Iraqis in June 2004**

Looking at the Performance of the Gulf Cooperation Council[20]

Since the establishment of the Gulf Cooperation Council in 1981, the organization has been plagued by central deficiencies brought about by both endogenous and exogenous factors. This is not to say that the GCC has fallen short of expectations or that achievements have been few and far between. However, the GCC is currently facing some mounting criticisms which centers on the following issues:

o The slow process of decision-making and lack of implementation of taken decisions. It is widely known that collective decisions are hardly processed despite the fact that the average time for taking an ordinary procedural decision is 8 hours. Main essential decisions such as the proposal for an electricity grid linking all GCC states, take a lot longer. In this case, the idea was developed in 1982 but it was not decided on until 2000 and will now not be enforced until 2007.

o Within the GCC States, most decisions are taken at the national rather than the regional levels. In the EU, economic decisions, regulations and rules taken by the European Commission constitute 60 to 70 per cent of those taken at the national level in any single EU member state. For the GCC states, it thus remains a long way ahead to reach such level of integration.

o The GCC continues to be hampered by the overall low level of trade between its member states although it should be remembered that apart from oil and gas, trade exchanges between the GCC states constitute 30 to 40 per cent of their total foreign trade, the highest percentage within the Arab-Arab trading bloc.

o While some observers criticize Saudi Arabia for adopting protectionist measures against other GCC states, the fact is that the kingdom is the biggest

---

[18] *Arab News*, June 30, 2004.
[19] *Al Riyadh Daily* Newspaper, June 29, 2004.

[20] This part, basically, reflects the point of view of Abdullah Al Quwaiz, published in *Al-Wasat* on December 6, 2004.

trading partner for most GCC States and that for example in the case of Bahrain, the trade balance favors the latter. This is because Bahraini sectors such as insurance and banks depend on the Saudi market.

o Within the parameter of banking, three GCC states do not allow other GCC banks to operate on within their jurisdiction, although such a step should be activated in the framework of financial integration. One impact is that in a GCC common currency envisioned for 2010, the use of the US dollar as mediator for transferring money would no longer be needed. This should increase the capital flow and investment between the GCC states and enhance their trade volume.

o The insistence on sovereignty is the main obstacle against a more efficient integration between the GCC states. There is a need to consider relinquishing an entity's sovereignty for the sake of greater integration, but this is basically an issue of political will.

o The quest for security and the continuous need for an external party to maintain the region's security has been a chronic problem. This is a key factor that limits the efficiency of the council.

Conclusion

Within the GCC States, bilateral relations continue to remain prevalent. As such, agreements and/or disputes mainly occur at the individual national level, a phenomenon that can also be noticed by the fact that mediation is still seen as a main avenue to settle disputes between two members. Gulf politics therefore is still to a large extent persons-oriented. Factors like the need for regime survival, sovereignty and the fear

of hegemony can thus be considered main factors that hinder the further integration between the GCC states. Although the GCC charter stipulates equality between the members and consensus to pass a decision, such harmony does not really exist, as can be seen in the various foreign policy decisions regarding regional developments.

GCC-Arab Relations

Dr. Ahmad Youssif Ahmad

Professor of Political Science, Cairo University

A study on GCC-Arab relations bears particular significance in view of the fact that it helps resolve one of the thorniest research dilemmas associated with the relations between the pan-Arab order and its sub-regional counterparts. The dilemma has been in the forefront of the Arab scene ever since the Gulf Cooperation Council came into being in 1981. At the time, it was commonly believed that the creation of such a council would probably lead to the relative isolation of the Gulf region from the wider Arab political order.

This study faces a methodological dilemma that routinely arises whenever relations between two regional blocs are broached and whenever relations between a regional grouping and a given state are approached. Take, for instance, Arab-African relations. An approach to these specific relations presupposes the existence of two separate entities, one Arab and the other African, an assumption that is far removed from fact. There exist in fact many parties to the relation, each holding a separate view. This is especially true when considering that collective entities - in this case the Arab League and the African Union - do not have the upper hand in managing the international relations of these groups.

The same dilemma clearly plagues GCC-Arab relations at the collective level. In 2004, the period considered in this analysis, no remarkable interactions between the Arab League and the Gulf Cooperation Council were witnessed. It would be more appropriate to discuss on one level specific positions expressed by the Gulf Cooperation Council towards certain Arab issues, on another level the Council's collective relations with specific Arab countries and on yet another level the bilateral relations between specific member states of the Council and non-member Arab countries. In this vein, it must be noted that though the bilateral level cannot be subsumed within a study of the GCC-Arab relations, its inclusion certainly helps bring out a number of interesting implications for the collective relations. Following the multi-leveled analysis, the discussion will conclude with an attempt to forecast the possible future prospects of GCC-Arab relations.

The Gulf Cooperation Council and Arab Issues

It is clear that the most prominent issues in 2004 include the Iraqi crisis, an issue that carries direct implications on the security of the GCC states, as well as the Arab-Israeli conflict and the issue of reforming the Arab order.

The Gulf Cooperation Council and the Iraqi Crisis

The GCC held four meetings during 2004 - three of which were convened at the ministerial level - to discuss developments in Iraq; the fourth meeting was held at the summit level. The statements issued at the conclusion of these four meetings reflect the position of the GCC States towards Iraq. The dimensions of the GCC states' stance could be summarized as follows:

1. The emphasis on the need to avoid the de-fragmentation of Iraq, the importance of Iraq's territorial unity and the need to preserve the country's sovereignty and independence as well as the call for non-interference by external parties in its internal affairs. These principles were explicit in the statement issued by the Ministerial Council held in February 2004.[1] The meeting by the Ministerial Council held in June 2004 reiterated the same principles while urging the UN Security Council to exert serious efforts to preserve Iraq's territorial integrity and restore its sovereignty and independence as soon as possible.[2]

2. Welcoming the political process inaugurated by a transfer of power to the Iraqi interim government in late June 2004. During its ministerial meeting held in June 2004, the Gulf Cooperation Council regarded the formation of an Iraqi government as "an important step on the road towards handing over sovereignty to the Iraqis." The statement added that "all the Iraqi people and social groups ought to be equal before the law,"[3] a position reiterated during the December 2004 Gulf Summit. The statement expressed concerns by the GCC States over the possibility of disrupting the political balance of power in Iraq in favor of the Shia community and

all of the ramifications such an outcome could imply for the Gulf region as a whole.

3. Welcoming a UN role in Iraq, as was made explicitly clear in a statement issued in the wake of the February 2004 meeting of the Ministerial Council held. The statement emphasized that the UN should take on a vital role in managing the affairs of Iraq.[4] The same demand was reiterated during the meeting held by the Ministerial Council in June 2004, emphasizing the necessity for UN assumption of a pivotal role by contributing to the preparation of the right conditions for a hand-over of sovereignty to the Iraqis by June 30, 2004, establishing state institutions, and calling on the UN Security Council to secure the preservation of Iraq's territorial integrity and restore the country's independence and unity. Again, the statement called for the need to ensure that all the Iraqis are represented in the forthcoming government while insisting on the equality of all Iraqi social groups before the law.[5] The GCC Summit held in the Bahraini capital of Manama in December 2004 further expressed the hope that "the US administration would work efficiently along with the UN and the international community in a bid to empower all the Iraqi people to contribute to the political process represented by the elections."[6]

4. Denouncing the terrorist acts that destabilize Iraq[7] in general terms but on a level that does not distinguish between terrorism per se and armed resistance against occupation. In this context, one may appropriately say that the Manama Summit

---

[1] See the statement issued at the end of the two-day session of the GCC Ministerial Council held during February 28 and 29, 2004 in Riyadh, Saudi Arabia.
[2] See the statement issued at the conclusion of the session of the GCC Ministerial Council held on June 5, 2004 in Jeddah, Saudi Arabia.
[3] Ibid.
[4] Ibid, the statement issued at the conclusion of the ninetieth session of the GCC Ministerial Council.

[5] Ibid, the statement issued at the end of the ninety-first session of the GCC Ministerial Council.
[6] See the statement issued at the end of the twenty-fifth session of the GCC Supreme Council held on December 21, 2004 in Manama, Bahrain.
[7] Ibid, the statement issued in the wake of the ninety-first session of the GCC Ministerial Council

achieved a modest step towards driving home the distinction between terrorism and resistance by specifically defining terrorist acts as "bombings and terrorist operations that target civilians and religious establishments and kidnapping and torturing of innocent people."[8]

5. Condemning the inhumane treatment to which occupation troops subjected some Iraqi detainees, regarding acts perpetrated by the occupation forces as a violation of the Fourth Geneva Convention and other international treaties related to the treatment of prisoners.[9]

It is worthwhile to point out at this juncture that the dimensions of the position maintained by the GCC states towards the Iraqi question broadly converge with those of the stance held collectively by the other Arab states as represented by the Arab League, with some marginal differences regarding less critical issues.

The positions held by the Gulf states and the other Arab countries set out from a set of principles, as can be seen from the documents issued by both the Arab League and the GCC. The Gulf states and the other Arab states alike stressed the need to preserve the unity of Iraq, its independence and the protection of its territorial integrity. Both entities also emphasized the need for a UN role in Iraq and concurred on the crucial importance of the political process conducted under occupation; in this regard, the GCC States tended to insist more particularly on the need for the political process to involve all the Iraqi factions equally before the law. Both parties

denounced terrorist acts while making it clear that resistance against occupation forces is not terrorism. Finally, both lashed out against the illegal and inhumane behavior of the occupation forces against some Iraqi detainees, though it should be noted that in September 2004, the Ministerial Council of the Arab League decried the "air strikes and other military operations that target civilian Iraqis in different cities and villages, causing the death of many innocent civilians," adding that such acts must cease.[10] In May 2004, the Arab summit held in Tunis again denounced the excessive use of force by occupation troops.[11]

On another level, resolutions ratified by the Arab League attached great importance to the process of reconstruction in Iraq. The Ministerial Council held a meeting in March 2004 urging all the Arab states and the various Arab monetary and financial funds to contribute to the reconstruction of Iraq.[12] The decision was embedded in the statement issued at the end of the following session held in September 2004,[13] though no mention was made of the decision in the statement issued at the conclusion of the Tunis Summit.[14]

The Arab-Israeli Conflict

By looking into the statements issued during the four meetings that determined the position of the Gulf Cooperation Council towards the Iraqi crisis, it becomes clear that there is a qualitative difference between the GCC states' stance towards the Iraqi file and that towards the Arab-Israeli conflict. In the latter case, the GCC states vociferously denounced the aggressive policies employed by the Israeli occupation

---

[8] Ibid, the statement issued at the end of the twenty-fifth session of the GCC Supreme Council.

[9] Ibid, the statement issued at the end of the ninety-first session of the GCC Ministerial Council.

[10] The decisions reached by the Arab League during the ministerial level meeting in its 122nd ordinary session, Cairo, September 2004, the Secretariat-General, the Administration of the Affairs of the Arab League's Council, p. 31.

[11] The statement issued at the conclusion of the sixteenth Arab Summit held in Tunisia on May 23, 2004.

[12] Ibid, the decisions reached by the Arab League during the ministerial level meeting in its 121st ordinary session, Cairo, September 2004, p. 21.

[13] Ibid, the decisions reached by the Arab League during the ministerial level meeting in its 122nd ordinary session, Cairo, September 2004.

[14] Ibid, the statement issued at the conclusion of the sixteenth Arab Summit held in Tunisia on May 23, 2004.

troops against the Palestinian people, urging Israel to pull out from the occupied territories. In the case of Iraq, the GCC Council confined its statements to denouncing the illegal and inhuman practices employed by the occupation forcers without expressly calling for their withdrawal. The various dimensions of the position maintained by the GCC states towards the Arab-Israeli conflict are as follows:[15]

1. The expression of deep concern and strong denouncment of the continued deterioration of the living conditions of Palestinians in the Occupied Territories as a result of Israeli policies that represent a blatant violation of international norms and standards. The GCC States also denounced Israeli practices driven by these policies.[16] It needs to be noted in this context that the statement issued by the Gulf Supreme Council in December 2004 commented on what was termed "the perseverance of the Israeli government in staging aggressive practices against the Palestinian people."

2. The consideration that the only path towards the achievement a comprehensive, just and lasting peace is through bringing an end to the occupation of all Arab land seized since 1967, including East Jerusalem.

3. The insistence on the Arab character of the city of Jerusalem while denouncing Israel's endeavors "Judaize" the city by changing its demographic and geographical character as utterly illegitimate. Even though this position reflects a principled stance long maintained by the Gulf Cooperation Council, it only appeared in the two statements issued at the conclusion of the ninety-first and ninety-second session meetings of the Gulf Ministerial Council.

4. The emphasis on the importance of the Arab peace initiative ratified by the Arab states at the Beirut Summit held in 2002, while insisting on the need to implement the 'Roadmap' as a dual framework within which the Palestinian question can be settled.

5. The recommendation of the adoption of multiple mechanisms to push forward the peace process by insisting particularly on the role of the parties sponsoring the peace process, a point insisted upon during the ministerial meeting held in February 2004, as well as the role of the international Quartet committee, a point emphasized during all the ministerial meetings held throughout 2004. The two ministerial meetings held successively in June and September 2004 stressed the need to set up an institutional link between the work of the Quartet and the Arab peace initiative; the September meeting emphasized the need for a more visible role by the EU, especially as in exerting pressure on Israel. In parallel, it urged the UN, particularly the UN Secretary-General and the International Human Rights Commission, to take notice of the tragic conditions besetting Palestinian prisoners.

In this same vein, the Gulf Ministerial Council called on the US administration to take a more effective role in the peace process. During its June session, the Council called on Washington to exert pressure on all parties involved in the conflict to abide by the stipulations of the 'Roadmap' and desist from taking unilateral measures. The Council further called on the US to pressure Israel into putting an end to its aggressive policies in the Palestinian lands. The September 2004 meeting went a step further by determining the party responsible for not responding

---

[15] For further details, see the statements issued at the conclusion of the ninety, ninety-first and ninety-second sessions of the GCC Ministerial Council and the statements issued at the end of the twenty-fifth and

twenty-sixth sessions of the GCC Supreme Council.

[16] Ibid, see the statement issued at the end of the twenty-fifth session of the GCC Supreme Council held on December 21, 2004 in Manama, Bahrain.

positively to the various calls for a viable solution to the Arab-Israeli conflict. Moreover, the Council called upon the US administration to exert pressures on Israel to commit itself to the provisions of the 'Roadmap'. The summit held in December by the Council expressed hope that the US President George W. Bush would give priority during his second presidential term to Middle East issues in a way that would lead to the realization of the American pledge to help establish a Palestinian state.

6. The demand that the Middle East region be freed of all weapons of mass destruction by calling upon Israel to sign on the Nuclear Non-Proliferation Treaty and subjecting all Israeli nuclear facilities to international inspection. It is to be noted that the Gulf Summit held in December 2004 urged the international community to exert pressure on Israel to join the non-proliferation treaty, considering compliance as a preliminary condition for any future discussions on security arrangements in the region.

7. The response to the myriad developments unfolding in connection with the Arab-Israeli conflict, as was made clear in the statement issued by the GCC Ministerial Council at the conclusion of its June session. The Council expressed its regret over the US decision to impose economic sanctions on Syria as well as the hope that Washington would review its decision and embrace the principle of dialogue in dealing with the Syrian regime. In September 2004, the GCC Ministerial Council decried the Israeli threats against Syria and warned against any act desecrating the scared shrines in Palestine or damaging the Al-Aqsa Mosque. In December 2004, the GCC States denounced Israeli aggressions against Lebanon while they welcomed

the smooth-running process of political transition in Palestine and expressed their well-wishes for the new Palestinian leadership.

Admittedly, the positions maintained by the Gulf Cooperation Council go hand in glove with the broad stances of the other Arab countries as far as the Arab-Israeli conflict is concerned. Still, the positions taken by the Arab countries assume wider dimensions than those held by the GCC States, as made clear by the following developments:[17]

1. All the Arab meetings hailed the Intifada of the Palestinian people and congratulated the elected Palestinian political leadership with Yasser Arafat as its head. The May Arab Summit hailed the legitimate Palestinian fight against occupation in order to gain national rights while participants at the summit emphasized the need to continue offering political, moral and financial support to the Palestinian people in their legitimate resistance against occupation forces.

2. The insistence on the right of the Palestinian refugees to return to their homeland, as it was explicitly affirmed in the two statements issued by the ministerial meetings held successively in March and September. In May, the Arab Summit referred to a "just solution" to the refugee problem in line with international legitimacy, specifically General Assembly Resolution 194 issued in 1948.

3. The Reiteration of the need to provide financial support for the Palestinian people and the Palestinian National Authority (PNA).

Reform of the Arab Order

The issue of reform divides into two major planks:

---

[17] For further details, see the decisions reached by the Arab League during the ministerial level meeting in its 121st and 122nd ordinary sessions as well as the statement issued at the conclusion of the sixteenth Arab Summit.

the reform of the Arab League on the one hand and the domestic reform in each Arab state separately on the other. A study of this issue brings out the absence of a unified GCC stance towards both sides of the issue.

As far as reform of the Arab League is concerned, the GCC States did not announce any position at all, as any such statements are absent from the content of the statements issued by both the GCC Ministerial meetings and the meetings held by the GCC Supreme Council during 2004. Saudi Arabia chose to float a common reform project articulated in association with both Syria and Egypt, but did not wish to submit the project to the GCC Council for ratification as a collective project. Riyadh's choice seems to be in keeping with the idea of that certain states serve in a leadership capacity as promoted by the Saudi press.[18]

For its part, the GCC Ministerial Council refused the adoption of multiple mechanisms to support the tripartite project during the meeting held in February 2004. The statement issued at the conclusion of the meeting simply mentioned that the Council "reviewed the project to reform conditions in the role of the Arab world and improve the work of the Arab League along with the project submitted by the three countries…," adding that the Council listened to a detailed explanation "by Saudi Arabia's Foreign Minister regarding the reform proposal that will be presented for discussion at the Arab League."[19] Such statements make it clear that the GCC Ministerial Council was unwilling to even discuss the project.

Similarly, the Council seemed either unwilling to discuss the Greater Middle East Initiative proposed at the time by the US administration or had actually discussed it and did not reach a unified position towards its terms and demands, as the statement it issued did not refer to the initiative. A number of indications seem to corroborate the notion that the GCC Ministerial Council failed to articulate a unified stand towards the US-proposed initiative. Saudi Arabia and Egypt rejected it in a statement put out at the conclusion of the visit conducted by Egyptian President Hosni Mubarak to Riyadh on February 29, 2004 on the same day the proceedings of the meeting held by the GCC Ministerial Council ended. The other GCC States, notably Kuwait, preferred to keep silent on the initiative while Qatar invited discussions on the content of the initiative, as made clear by the statement made by the Foreign Minister Shaikh Jassim bin Jaber Al Thani in the wake of the meeting held by the Ministerial Council of the Arab League in March 2004. Shaikh Jassim contended that the GCC states "should discuss this initiative with the party that has proposed it and see if it indeed serves the interests of our region. We do not want to keep rejecting initiatives while we do not have any alternatives for our countries."

Following the meeting of the GCC Ministerial Council held in June 2004 shortly after the conclusion of the Arab Summit held in Tunis, a statement was issued restricting its content to the expression of support for Saudi Arabia's position towards the issue of reform in general - perhaps out of courtesy - by emphasizing "the importance of the document of reconciliation and solidarity ratified by the Arab Summit…regarding it as a document with a critical role to play in serving the Umma [Arab nation] and building a serious and credible foundation for any Arab joint action."[20]

During the GCC Summit held in December 2004, indication of unity between the GCC positions and the general Arab stance appeared to

---

[18] See *Al-Riyadh* newspaper editorial published on May 25, 2004.

[19] Ibid, see the final statement issued at the ninetieth session of the GCC Ministerial Council.

[20] Ibid, see the final statement issued by the ninety-first session of the GCC Ministerial Council.

be more evident in the arena of domestic reform. The statement issued at the end of the GCC meeting concurred with the position taken at the Arab Summit, which stressed the need to enact a process of modernization and development in the Arab world that should spring from the countries of the region themselves while taking into account the political, economic, cultural and religious traits of these countries. The statement further affirmed that the incremental accumulation of results deriving from the process of development is likely to improve the stability, security and prosperity of the region.

It should be noted in this context that the statement issued at the conclusion of the Arab Summit was far more detailed in this respect, though the positions held by the GCC States and the other Arab countries remained fundamentally similar.[21]

Bilateral Relations between the GCC and Other Arab States

Besides the positions held by the GCC governments towards a number of broad Arab issues that emerged during 2004, a host of other developments unraveled at the level of the relations binding the GCC states and the other Arab countries, notably Yemen and Lebanon. The former entertains a quasi-institutional relationship with the Gulf Cooperation Council, particularly after the twenty-second GCC Summit held in Muscat issued a resolution accepting Yemen as a potential member in some of the Council's organs. Also, during 2004 a free trade agreement was signed by Lebanon and the GCC.

The Gulf Cooperation Council and Yemen

Ever since the twenty-second session of the GCC Summit was convened in the Omani capital Muscat in December 2001 and the GCC member states accepted Yemen as a member in some of the Council's organs,[22] the issue of Yemen joining the GCC was approached differently by various circles in the GCC States, especially in regards to enhancing functional relations between the two parties in rendering Yemen's membership status complete and comprehensive. It could be said in this regard that 2004 has revealed a number of structural hurdles that could hamper the implementation of this objective.

It is to be observed first that of the documents issued during the three meetings held by the GCC Ministerial Council and the GCC Summit meetings, only one document issued at the conclusion of the ninety-second session meeting held in September 2004 mentioned Yemen. The document pointed out that the Council had reviewed the results of the third meeting held in June 2004 by the joint task force set up by the GCC Council and Yemen. The Council had also discussed the proposals put forth by the task force in order to boost economic cooperation between Yemen and the GCC States without, however, determining the exact character of the decisions. Apart from the reference made within the statement to the support by the GCC Sates of Yemen in its stand-off with the rebellion led by followers of Hussain Badr Al Deen Al-Houthi in the province of Sa'ada[23], no mention was made of Yemen.

To be sure, there are some impediments that could obstruct Yemen's accession to the Gulf Cooperation Council. The statement made by Sheikh Abdulla bin Zayed Al Nahyan, the UAE Minister of Information,

---

[21] Ibid, see the statement issued by the twenty-fifth session of the GCC Supreme Council; see also the statement issued at the conclusion of the sixteenth Arab Summit held in Tunisia.

[22] The Council of Health Ministers, the Council of the Ministers of Justice

and Social Affairs, the Arab Bureau of Education for the Gulf States (ABEG), and the Gulf Football Cup.

[23] See the statement issued by the ninety-second session of the GCC Ministerial Council.

reflects well the limits of the relations between the GCC Council and Yemen. Sheikh Abdulla said that Yemen "is not qualified to join the Gulf Cooperation Council," adding that the Council is not "a closed club, for Iraq and Yemen could be integrated into the Council when and if conditions are met." Sheikh Abdulla mentioned the example of the EU, where some countries which have applied for membership have had to endure years of strenuous restructuring before they could actually join the bloc. Other countries must continue to strive to enhance their economic and political portfolios before they can be admitted into the EU.

Within the same context, Prince Naif bin Abdulaziz, the Saudi Minister of the Interior, declared in an interview given in January to the Egyptian newspaper Al-Ahram that "We reject Yemen's accession to the Gulf Cooperation Council because it is not a Gulf state."[24] Statements such as that of Prince Naif have induced reactions in official Yemeni circles stating that "Yemen is well qualified to join the Gulf Cooperation Council thanks to its historical heritage, human resources and strategic importance for the security and stability of the Arabian Peninsula and the GCC States." Yemeni officials stressed that "the issue of Yemen's habilation before it could accede to membership in the GCC Council is just an excuse that runs contrary to the privileged relations that bind Yemen to the GCC States, ignoring the volume of trade exchange and economic cooperation that serve the interest of all the parties involved."

Several press accounts took the same line, highlighting the prospects of oil wealth in Yemen, its capacities in the agricultural field, its well-developed educational system, its experience in building regional unions through democratic means and in settling border disputes with its neighbors by peaceful means, in addition to the large Yemeni market's ability to absorb Gulf goods and products because of its close proximity.[25]

There are political and economic reasons that invite pessimism concerning the relations between the Gulf Cooperation Council and Yemen. On the economic front, one researcher pinpointed the differences between Yemen's economy and the economies of the GCC states; this led Sana'a to refuse to sign a free trade agreement with the GCC States, as such an agreement would have lifted customs tariffs imposed on national products of both sides. Yemen seems rather concerned about the possibility that low-price but high-quality Gulf products would dominate its local market and thus would demand compensation for the lost tariffs that constitute a large part of its national income. The researcher proposed that the GCC States offer financial assistance to support Yemen's budget and encourage Yemen's exports to the GCC markets.[26]

Moreover, the political relations between Yemen and the GCC states seem to obstruct the inclusion of the former into the Gulf Cooperation Council. Despite Yemen's support for Iraq's invasion of Kuwait, it must be noted that the resolution ratified at the GCC Summit held in Muscat in 2001 implied that important developments have positively affected the GCC-Yemen relations and have moved past the blemish. Yet, the general differences between Yemen's and the GCC States' political systems constitute the real dimension of the political relationship between the two parties. Developments in 2004 in the relations between Yemen and some GCC states further make it clear that the relationships have not yet sufficiently stabilized. Disputes between Yemen on the one hand and both

---

[24] Egypt-based Al-Ahram newspaper, issue published on January 21, 2004.

[25] See, for example, Yussef Al-Sharif, "Yemen and the Gulf Cooperation Council," Al-Bayan newspaper, February 2, 2004

[26] See Dr. Mohamed Al-Assoumi, "Yemen and the Gulf Cooperation Council," Al-Ittihad newspaper, July 6, 2004.

Saudi Arabia and Kuwait on the other are specific examples in this respect.

As far as Yemeni circles are concerned, the year 2004 did not begin well for relations with Saudi Arabia. Yemen's¹ Foreign Minister, for example, was only received by the Assistant to the Saudi Foreign Minister during the visit he paid to Riyadh in late January 2004, thus indicating a sort of downgrading of the relationship. Shortly afterwards, Saudi authorities banned Yemeni pilgrims from crossing the Al-Wadi'a border gate in the eastern region of Yemen; Sana'a, for its part, accused Riyadh of building a border fence. It was not until the end of the year that relations saw an improvement with the signing of a number of cooperative agreements. In terms of Yemeni-Kuwait relations, there were a series of harsh critiques leveled by a number of Kuwaiti parliamentarians against the Yemeni political leadership, recalling the position held by Sana'a towards Iraq's invasion of Kuwaiti as well as Yemen's stance towards attempts at reconciliation between the government of Kuwait and the former Iraqi regime.

Based on the above, it appears that developments throughout 2004 did not contribute much to the progress of the integrative relations between Yemen and the Gulf Cooperation Council, even though the Secretary-General of the Council affirmed in the wake of the GCC Summit held in December 2004 that he would soon visit Yemen in order to discuss the prospect of its involvement in a greater number of GCC institutions.

The Gulf Cooperation Council and Lebanon

The year 2004 witnessed the signing of a free trade agreement between the Gulf Cooperation Council and Lebanon, the first such agreement to be signed between the Council and another Arab country. When the Ministerial Council held its ninety-first

session in June 2004, the agreement was already signed and the statement issued at the end of the meeting welcomed the agreement, which was dispatched to all the member states of the GCC Council for ratification before it could be effectively implemented. The agreement with Lebanon seeks to lift all tariff duties and remove all taxes and non-tariff duties on the goods and products of both parties.[27]

It should be noted that the statement issued at the conclusion of the ninetieth session of the GCC Ministerial Council held in February 2004 called on the member states to respond to the proposal by the Kingdom of Morocco to establish a free trade agreement with the GCC countries and also referred to the beginning of negotiations on the creation of a free trade zone between the GCC States and Lebanon. The buzz about free trade agreements seems to imply that the GCC Council has an 'Arab policy' of its own regarding the creation of free trade zones. Looked at more closely, however, this impression turns out to be unfounded, for the Council's policy seems to have a rather international character and not just an Arab character.

During the nineteenth session, the Ministerial Council announced the establishment of negotiations with India and its willingness to study the proposal advanced by Pakistan to engage in negotiations slated to create free trade zones with the GCC countries. In the ninety-first meeting of the GCC Ministerial Council during which the free trade agreement with Lebanon was welcomed, the Council announced the beginning of negotiations with Turkey to sign a framework agreement for economic cooperation as a preparatory step towards negotiations on establishing a free trade zone.

It is clear from the content of statements issued by the successive meetings held by the Council that there is no such thing as a well-defined policy to set

---

[27] See Beirut-based *Al-Safir* newspaper, June 7, 2004.

up free trade zones with specific countries; rather, it appears that the GCC states merely respond to other nations' proposals to establish free trade zones with the GCC.

Bilateral Relations between the GCC States and the Other Arab Countries

Before the discussion commences, it must be noted that even though this particular dimension of analysis seems to have the least impact on the collective GCC-Arab relations, it nevertheless provides an appropriate platform to better understand these relations. The analysis includes two major cases illustrative of the bilateral relations between the GCC States and the other Arab countries: Saudi-Libyan relations, offering an illuminating example of conflict-ridden interactions, and the bilateral relations binding Egypt with a number of GCC States, which serves as a prime example of cooperative relations.

Relations between Saudi Arabia and Libya

Saudi-Libyan relations have a history of conflict stemming from the interactions between a revolutionary regime and a conservative regime. Within this context, the relations between the two regimes have seen tensions usually associated with statements made by Colonel Muammar Qaddafi, the leader of the Libyan revolution. For example, in 1980, Col. Qaddafi called on all Muslim pilgrims to cancel their pilgrimage to the Holy Shrines in Saudi Arabia, claiming that the Kingdom was under US occupation. Again, in 1982 he called on Saudi people to stage a revolutionary uprising. On several occasions, Qaddafi demanded that the Two Holy Shrines in Mecca and Medina should be internationalized and managed by a Muslim

administration similar to the Vatican. He even accused the Saudi government of breaching the trust of the international Muslim community.[28]

The mediation role assumed by Saudi Arabia and South Africa in finding a solution to the Lockerbie crisis that locked Libya and the West in 1999 led to an improvement in the Saudi-Libyan relations, though this relief was rather short-lived.

In the aftermath of the September 11 events, Col. Qaddafi accused Saudi Arabia on many occasion of being a hotbed for breeding members of al-Qaeda organization. Riyadh reacted to the situation by counter-accusing Tripoli of undermining Arab unity.

The unfortunate scene between Colonel Qaddafi and Saudi Crown Prince Abdullah bin Abdulaziz during the opening session of the Arab Summit held in Sharm el-Sheikh, Egypt, on March 1, 2003 marked the real beginning of a mounting crisis that rocked the relations between Riyadh and Tripoli in mid-2004. The crisis was sparked by an article published on June 10, 2004 by the New York Times, claiming that the Libyan secret services had planned to assassinate Saudi Crown Prince Abdullah. The alleged accusation was based on confessions made by some detainees implicated in the assassination plot, the most prominent of whom was an Islamist activist still under detention in the US. The activist confessed to plotting to assassinate Prince Abdullah with the cooperation of officers working for the Libyan secret services. He also confessed to meeting Colonel Qaddafi twice in June and August 2003 to discuss the details of the plot; this confession was further supplemented by similar statements made by a Libyan security agent apprehended in Saudi Arabia.

On December 23, 2004, Saudi Arabia recalled its ambassador from Libya and the Saudi Foreign Minister, Prince Saud Al-Faisal, declared that Riyadh would ask the Libyan ambassador to leave

---

[28] See the website of Al-Jazeera at www. Aljazeera.net

the Kingdom. He added that the diplomatic measures the Kingdom intended to take would be restricted to recalling ambassadors out of Saudi Arabia's respect for the brotherly Libyan people, especially as the season of pilgrimage was close at hand.

For their part, Libyan authorities categorically denied that Tripoli had anything to do with the purported scheme. The Libyan Foreign Ministry through the Secretariat of the General Popular Committee for Foreign Communication and International Cooperation attributed Saudi accusations to a wave of demonstrations that swept through Saudi cities at the behest of the reform movements based overseas. Libyan authorities also claimed that some Saudi tribes had withdrawn their allegiance to the Saudi ruling family, pledging instead their allegiance to the leader of the reform movement.

Up until the end of the year, no signs emerged to the effect that efforts deployed by the Secretariat-General of the Arab League or by Arab countries, particularly Jordan, to mediate between Saudi Arabia and Libya had achieved any success. This is quite understandable in view of the stringent conditions set forth by the government of Saudi Arabia for any normalization of relations with the Libyan regime. The conditions were as follows:

1. Tripoli should hand over to the Saudi authorities all the Libyan officials involved in the assassination plot before they would stand trial. Libya should also be willing to cooperate with Saudi Arabia's security and judiciary authorities.

2. Colonel Qaddafi ought to apologize publicly and officially for the statements he made on Saudi Arabia and its role regarding the US military presence in the Gulf region and the 2003 Iraq Crisis.

3. The Libyan authorities should take punitive measures against senior Libyan officials for their part in arranging the assassination plot against Crown Prince Abdullah.

Admittedly, the Libyan-Saudi crisis did not spill over into an Arab-wide crisis; Arab countries did not rush to support or oppose any of the two parties. In fact, the majority of the Arab states preferred to keep silent while others have tried to mediate the conflict. More significantly, the GCC states themselves have not adopted any clear-cut position in support of Saudi Arabia; on the contrary, some Gulf newspapers published articles flaying Saudi Arabia's 'wrought-up reaction' to the allegations. One newspaper even went so far as to link the Saudi 'inflamed reaction' against Libya with the reaction evinced by Riyadh towards Bahrain's free trade agreement with the US. All these developments corroborate the reality that there is no unified Gulf position towards issues related to the GCC-Arab relations.

GCC States' Relations with Egypt

At the bilateral level, GCC-Egyptian relations were marked by close cooperation throughout 2004. This is particularly palpable from the numerous summit meetings held between Egypt and the various member states. Egyptian high-level contacts with the various GCC States covered a number of critical issues, most notably the Palestinian issue, the Iraqi crisis and the project for reforming the Arab League. The underlying objective was to bring into existence a common Arab stand towards all these issues.

In this context, it must be pointed out that the Egyptian and Saudi positions towards the issue of reform in the Arab world have been almost identical. In fact, the statement issued at the end of the visit paid by Egyptian Hosni Mubarak to Saudi Arabia on February 24, 2004, reaffirmed that the Arab states would move down the path of reform, modernization and development in line with the interests of their peoples and values, taking into consideration their needs and Arab identity. The statement further revealed that they would not accept any reform scheme imposed on them by any external powers.

Egypt and the GCC States also discussed issues linked to bilateral cooperation, particularly the need to boost Gulf investments in development projects in Egypt, along with the need to enhance the volume of trade exchange between Egypt and every GCC state. A number of technical issues, notably the need to effectively implement the agreement on handing over detainees sentenced to prison in either Egypt or Kuwait, were also agreed upon. Broadly speaking, bilateral relations between Egypt and the GCC States provide a model of cooperation among all the Arab countries.

Conclusion
Future Prospects for
GCC-Arab Relations

It is clear by now that one cannot speak of a collective framework encompassing GCC-Arab relations. In other words, we do not see an institutional relationship between the Gulf Cooperation Council and the Arab League even though there exists a foundation capable of sustaining such a relationship. Any relations thus far have been built on common denominators shared by the GCC Council and the Arab League, as is evident from the various issues examined earlier in the discussion.

Of similar importance are the institutional relations binding the GCC and certain Arab countries, although they seem to unfold within a nascent context. Perhaps the case of Lebanon stands out as a good reflection of this

development even though the relations between the GCC and Lebanon appear to embody a pattern repeated similarly with other Arab countries, thereby implying that the ramifications on the future of the GCC that are likely to unravel from these relations would not be tangible.

For GCC-Yemen relations, the prospects of Yemen's full-fledged accession to membership in the Council seem to be dim; developments in 2004 were quite revealing in this respect. It is already clear that there exist structural impediments that would almost certainly stand in the way of developing GCC-Yemen relations more fully.

On another level, it seems that bilateral relations between the GCC states and the other Arab countries have not developed solely within a cooperative framework, as it is evident from the case of Egypt, or within a conflictual framework, as was the case with Libya. Thus, the GCC-Arab relations are largely similar to inter-Arab relations as a whole in that they do not seem to be qualified, at least not in the foreseeable future, to develop within a collective framework. There are some strong indications, however, that reveal that the stances of the GCC states and the other Arab countries toward the most crucial Arab issues will serve as the hallmark of their unity.

Of greater significance is the fact that even when disputes do break out, they do not unfold on an Arab-Gulf basis; disputes often involve varying stances by different configurations of GCC and other Arab states and rarely pit the GCC states against the Arab states.

At this juncture, the most important issue for the future relations between the GCC states and the other Arab countries is the Iraqi crisis and its ramifications for the GCC states in particular and the wider Arab world in general, together with the issue of US policies towards Iraq and the Arab world. These issues undoubtedly entail consolidating Arab efforts and will prompt the GCC states to arrive at a common stance regarding the future of Iraq and the rest of the Arab world, a stance that currently seems bereft of any clarity from either party.

GCC-Arab Relations: A Global Overview

Sameh Rashed

Free Lancer

This part of the Gulf Yearbook 2004 examines the relationship between the GCC States and the rest of the Arab world and the issues and positions that dominated ties. Attention is paid to the relations at both the bilateral and multilateral level. Certainly, items such as Iraq and the developments in the Arab-Israeli conflict played a major role and as such it is worthwhile to explore the respective positions. But there other items that also need to be considered such as the GCC relations with Yemen in light of the discussions about a possible Yemeni membership to the council.

Iraq

Security Issues

Throughout the year, the GCC States voiced their concern about the unraveling of the security situation in Iraq. Due to their geographical proximity to Iraq, Saudi Arabia and Kuwait were particularly attentive to the various developments as these were bound to have an impact on their own domestic security situation. In this context, GCC governments, alongside that of other Arab states, expressed their readiness to assist Iraq in improving its security and restoring stability. This involved, for example, efforts to help re-build the police and security forces by providing material, financial and logistical support. The UAE, in cooperation with Germany, has taken a leading role in this regard with its training programs for Iraqi security forces.

Kuwait and Saudi Arabia, meanwhile, tightened control of their borders with Iraq in order to prevent infiltrations and arms smuggling. Saudi Arabia and Iraq closely coordinated their security efforts as a means to stop cross-border movement by suspected militants to either side.[1] In May 2004, Saudi Arabia floated a proposal for the deployment of a Muslim and Arab military contingent in Iraq in order to help control the security situation. The initiative was launched under the slogan of providing protection for UN employees and workers of other international organizations operating in Iraq. Reactions to the Saudi proposal varied causing Riyadh to reformulate its initiative. Among the conditions outlined for the deployment was that such a Muslim and Arab force be fall under a UN umbrella and that their task would be to supplant rather than merely complement the US-led coalition forces.[2] Thus, while the demand of such a force had originally come from the US when it was facing deteriorating

---

[1] This appeared as part of a statement by Saudi Foreign Minister Prince Saud Al-Faisal carried by various news agencies and published the following day by Arab newspapers; see, *Al-Hayat*, January 11, 2004.
[2] *Al-Hayat*, August 2, 2004.

conditions inside Iraq, the conditions set by Saudi Arabia made the idea a non-starter as this would have meant the effective termination of occupation and authority would have been handed over to UN peace-keeping forces.

The change in Saudi Arabia's position was the result of reservations expressed by some countries, especially Iraqi officials, who argued that any Muslim and Arab contingent should exclude forces from neighboring countries. Algeria, for its part, categorically rejected the idea of sending troops to Iraq while Egypt reviewed its initial wholesale rejection of the proposal and opted instead for a conditioned deployment of troops. However, the conditions set by Egypt were not unlike those of Saudi Arabia.

At the level of the Gulf region, no collective position emerged as far as the Saudi initiative was concerned, even though there were some unofficial deliberations about sending troops from the GCC to Iraq within the framework of the 'Al-Jazeera Shield.' No clear-cut position, however, was ever taken. In mid-June 2004, Abdurrahman Al-Attiyah, the Secretary-General of the GCC, ruled out any possibility of sending troop from the GCC to Iraq. Kuwait also declared that it would not send any troops to its northern neighbor.

After the Saudi initiative was floated in July 2004, the White House declared on October 19, 2004 that the idea of deploying Muslim and Arab troops in Iraq did not receive the consent of Washington nor did the Iraqi interim government agree to it. The underlying reasons had to do with the refusal of Iraqi authorities to have military forces from neighboring countries deployed in the country. The conditions set by Riyadh were surely another reason.

Political relations

Unlike the security situation, the GCC were in consensus as far as the political situation in Iraq was concerned. The positions taken at both the individual and collective levels were marked by a large degree of compatibility, and at times close coordination. The GCC governments cooperated with the Transitional Governing Council welcoming the measures enacted by the newly founded Council including the adoption of a temporary constitution and the adoption of the Law of the Administration of the State of Iraq. Both measures were part of the process of political transition, which officially began on June 30, 2004. The GCC used numerous forums to make its position clear such as the meetings of the Gulf Ministerial Council (meetings of the GCC foreign ministers), the conference held by Iraq's neighboring countries, including Saudi Arabia and Kuwait, Arab ministerial meetings and the Arab summit conference held in Tunis.

During the 25th GCC summit held in Bahrain in December 2004, the council expressed its concern over the hardships borne by the Iraqi people and the damages suffered by Iraq's infrastructure. The GCC Supreme Council reaffirmed its positions announced in earlier statements, in particular, its sympathy and full solidarity with the Iraqi people. It also reiterated its rejection of any policies or acts leading up to the Iraq's territorial fragmentation and emphasized the need to preserve Iraq's sovereignty, independence and territorial unity. The Council urged all parties concerned with the Iraqi crisis to abide by these fundamental principles. Similarly, it called upon the US administration to work effectively and in coordination with the UN body in order to empower all the political factions in Iraq so that they could contribute to the progress of the political process by enabling all Iraqis to participate in the scheduled elections. In this way, the Iraqi people would be able to shape their political and economic future, ensure the security and stability of their country, and help put Iraq on the track to becoming an efficient and positive player in the Gulf, Arab and international communities, as UN Security Council Resolution 1546 explicitly stipulates. On another level, the GCC States condemned the sabotage and terrorist operations staged against Iraqi humanitarian and religious institutions and the civilian population. They also lashed out against acts of kidnapping and torturing innocent people.

The stand maintained by the GCC States remained unchanged even after the occupation civilian authorities handed power over to the Iraqi interim government on June 29, 2004. The GCC governments hailed the constitution and shape of the new Iraqi political institutions. They also lauded the components of the interim government and the choice of Ghazi Al Yawer as Iraqi president.[3] As for the future of the Iraqi state, the GCC countries upheld their rejection of any measure that would threaten to divide Iraq and reemphasized the need to respect Iraq's territorial integrity.

To be sure, the GCC States have been deeply concerned about a possible implosion of Iraq. Saudi Arabia, in particular, has expressed fear of Iraq fragmenting with Foreign Minister Prince Saud Al-Faisal making it explicitly clear that a divided Iraq would constitute a threat to Saudi security and the security of other neighboring countries.

As part of their support for the political transition process in Iraq, the GCC States agreed to participate in an international conference slated to focus on developments in Iraq. The conference was a joint US-Iraqi proposal announced in September 2004 after Iraqi Prime Minister Iyad Alawi discussed the idea during a tour he conducted across a number of Arab countries. The conference was held in Sharm el-Sheikh, Egypt, on November 23 with the participation of twenty foreign ministers, in addition to the Iraqi delegation. Participants represented Iraq's neighboring countries, the G8 countries,

China, Egypt, Bahrain, Algeria, Tunisia, Malaysia and the Netherlands. Delegates from four international organizations, namely the UN, the EU, the Arab League and the Organization of the Islamic Conference (OIC) also attended.

Participants in general expressed support to the Iraqi interim government's efforts to hold elections and institutionalize political life in Iraq in addition enacting measures to control the deteriorating security conditions. This applied particularly to the military operations staged by occupation forces inside Iraqi cities and provinces against Iraqi insurgents. The GCC States' participation in the conference on Iraq was remarkable and quite effective. Bahrain proposed to host an Iraqi national conference with the participation of the Iraqi government and all other Iraqi political forces willing to engage in the political process. The objective of that meeting would be to contribute to the success of the elections due to be held in Iraq. The Iraqi Foreign Minister approved in principle Bahrain's proposal pending a final decision on the matter by the Iraqi government.[4]

The GCC States also showed themselves ready to resume official and diplomatic relations with Iraq, a process interrupted by the deteriorating security conditions in the second half of 2004. In general, GCC governments regard the accession of an Iraqi interim government to power as fulfilling a prime condition for the resumption of diplomatic relations. As such, both Riyadh and Kuwait announced during a visit by Iraqi Prime Minister Iyad Alawi the resumption of their diplomatic relations with Baghdad although the actual opening of the embassies was delayed until a more suitable time. Kuwait took care to point out that this decision was solely due to security considerations rather than any political reasons.[5]

---

[3] Al Yawer descends for a prominent tribal line that extends to the Shamar tribe whose members are scattered across Iraq and the Arabian Peninsula.

[4] Al-Hayat, November 24, 2004.

[5] Al-Hayat, June 29, 2004.

The resumption of diplomatic ties was also followed by a discussion about the possible accession of Iraq to membership in the GCC. While both sides remained vague and non-committal on such an idea, some GCC States expressed their approval. UAE Minister of Information and Culture, Shaikh Abdullah bin Zayed Al-Nahyan, not only emphasized that Iraq was qualified to join the GCC but he placed Iraqi qualifications as higher than that of Yemen.[6] In late 2003, Bahrain adopted a similar position. The Iraqi interim government, for its part, emphasized in June 2004 that applying for membership in the GCC is a sovereign decision that should be taken by the forthcoming elected Iraqi government.

Economics

The GCC position on the prevailing economic conditions in Iraq falls squarely within the global positions being held with the GCC stressing its willingness to assist Iraq in reconstructing their country and restore Iraq's sovereignty and independence. In this context, the GCC countries made it clear both at the bilateral and collective level that they would be willing to write off at least part of the Iraqi debts. The UAE decided in early 2004 to forfeit repayment of some $4 billion of the outstanding Iraqi debt. Qatar took a similar decision. Saudi Arabia, for its part, announced its readiness to allow for a substantial reduction in the owed debt which hovers around $28 billion. This tougher stance, along with that of Kuwait, must be viewed within the perspective of the damages caused by Iraq's invasion of Kuwait in August 1990 and the subsequent war of liberation that ensued in 1991.

In terms of bilateral economic relations, trade volume between Saudi Arabia and Iraq soared in the wake of the re-opening of the Arar border crossing. On several occasions, the issue of re-exporting Iraqi oil across Saudi territory was also discussed. Riyadh similarly affirmed its readiness to assist in the reconstruction process for Iraq. During the initial meeting of donor countries held in Madrid, the kingdom alone pledged $500 million in the form of loans on easy terms to be extended by the Saudi Fund for Development. There was also a $1 billion pledge to fund exports.[7] Kuwait, pledged funds during the Iraq donor's conference held in Qatar in June 2004 and expressed its strong willingness to support the Iraqi economy in various fields, both through financial and material support. The Kuwaiti position, however, raised some domestic eyebrows. For instance, some members of the Kuwaiti National Assembly criticized the government for its decision to allocate some $500 million to housing projects in Iraq while thousands of Kuwaiti families lack such facilities.[8]

2 The GCC States and the Pan-Arab Political Order

The issue of reform: Throughout 2004, the Arab world faced numerous demands for widespread political reform as a result of the US determination to seek political change and the broader decision by the G8 countries to see political, economic and social reforms in the region introduced. The GCC States approached the issue on the basis of the dominant values and principles that have ruled the people and the governments for many decades. Saudi Arabia, for example, announced that reform has to spring from the concerned countries

---

[6] Al-Hayat, January 13, 2004.
[7] The Saudi financial pledge was announced during the Madrid donor conference at which the international community pledged to grant Iraq

financial assistance amounting to $33 billion. However, only a small part of the pledges has so far been honored.
[8] Al-Hayat, April 3, 2004.

themselves and Saudi Foreign Minister Prince Saud Al-Faisal warned against exerting external pressures in order to speed up the pace of reform in the Arab world. Riyadh also rejected the Helsinki Convention formula previously espoused by the Western world to pressure Eastern European countries to expand public freedoms and show greater respect for human rights. In terms of the Broader Middle East Initiative, the foreign minister simply said that "Nothing has as yet been issued in that regard."

However, Saudi Arabia's reserved stand soon evolved into a more pronounced rejection of the US-proposed reform project. Other Gulf and Arab countries joined the Saudi position. This collective position was confirmed on repeated occasions during official discussion held by the GCC governments and their Arab counterparts. During the first three months of 2004, at a time at when the US reform initiative was already on the cards, the GCC States and the other Arab countries showed greater policy coordination, especially among the three central Arab countries, namely Egypt, Syria and Saudi Arabia. Almost consistently, the three countries set out by first coordinating their positions and then moving to coordinate with other Arab countries. The outcome of this intra-Arab coordination was made clear when Cairo, Riyadh and Damascus announced that they would submit a set of common ideas to the summit of Tunis to be held in March 2004. The proposed ideas included a project for reforming the Arab League and boosting joint Arab action. These suggestions were later widely discussed at the GCC and Arab levels, particularly during the meetings of the GCC Foreign Ministerial Council and the meeting held by the Arab foreign ministers in preparation of the [first] Tunis summit conference. No clear-cut position, however, was articulated, as differences and disputes abounded during the meeting of Arab foreign ministers. As a result, Tunisia's Foreign Minister soon

saw himself forced to announce a postponement of the Arab Summit.

Even after the G8 summit on June 9, 2004 adopted an amended version of the initial US draft, no palpable change occurred in the general position maintained by the GCC States and the other Arab countries. Their responses focused primarily on the positive aspects embedded in the amended reform recipe, which had to be adjusted after many of the initial points caused widespread outcry throughout the Arab world. The version adopted by the G8 attached greater importance to resolving existing conflicts in the region and stipulated that reform should be devised and implemented by the countries of the region themselves. The project also emphasized the need to take into account the differences among the various cases in the region, which, in turn, would entail a more subtle approach.

At the individual and national levels, the majority of the GCC States upheld similar positions towards the Broader Middle East Initiative, rejecting any attempts to impose reform by any external powers while emphasizing the imperative of embracing reform and the necessity of carrying it out. Still, it is possible to draw distinctions among the GCC States, particularly when it comes to specific issues within the reform project. Perhaps the most salient difference was related to the need for a resolution of the outstanding regional conflicts as a pre-condition for the reform and modernization process. Whereas Saudi Arabia emphasized the importance of resolving the Arab-Israeli conflict, Qatar stated that there was no justification to link the reform issue with the Palestinian question. As the Qatari Foreign Minister, Shaikh Hamad Bin Jassim said: "It is irrational to put off reform until Palestine is liberated." It is worth noting in this context that Qatar was the sole Gulf State that did not express any reservations or level critiques against the US project or the initiative floated by the G8. Shaikh

Hamad bin Khalifa, the Emir of the State of Qatar, called on countries in the region "Not to panic because of the reform projects and ideas proposed and instead deal with them with open hearts and minds."[9]

Kuwait, meanwhile, stressed that the first step on the way to reform is to put an end to external attempts to impose reform and change on the countries of the region. Bahrain demanded earlier that any reform project floated by outside parties ought to be first discussed and coordinated with the countries of the region, making it clear that imposing an external approach would not serve the interests of the countries concerned. Here, it should be recalled that Bahrain participated in the meeting of the G8 while Saudi Arabia declined an invitation to attend.

On another level, Saudi Arabia also took care to emphasize the imperative to maintain and protect its own value system and traditions. The Saudi embassy in Washington made it clear that any reforms ought to be in line with the reality that Saudi Arabia is a Muslim country ruled by a monarchical system of government. The embassy's spokesman pointed out that "If reform means separating religion from the state, then Saudi Arabia will never embrace reform."[10]

Broadly speaking, the main policy line adopted by the GCC States towards the reform project can be summarized as follows:

1- Not rejecting the principle of reform.

2- Rejecting any type of reform pattern imposed by external powers without taking into account existing differences among the countries in the region and the peculiarities of each individual country.

3- The countries in the region should alone take charge of the task of implementing reform while rejecting any endeavors in this regard on the part of any external powers.

In association with the reform pressure from the outside, there were a number of theories and strategies articulated throughout the Arab world that meant to address the need for implementing political, economic and social reforms. Admittedly, most of these ideas failed to rally any significant support, a fact that can be attributed to the lack of a common Arab vision about the aspects of reform or the foundation on which reform should be grounded. For example, some Arab states have nourished deep reservations about the fact that domestic conditions would be subsumed under a collective umbrella, even if the undertaking would be conducted within an Arab framework. The Arab Summit held in Tunisia is a true reflection of the differences among the various Arab countries which resulted in the summit being delayed until May 2004.

The Tunis Summit

When it was finally held, the Tunis Summit was the focal point for the events, developments and interactions that bore on the sensitive issues dominating the Arab scene. And even though the events and developments that have unraveled across the Arab world for the past few years, if not decades, are highly significant as well as being unmistakably dangerous, the response by Arab governments fell short in light of their momentous scope and importance. In the aftermath of the invasion of Iraq in 2003, the changes confronting the Arab states have grown even more serious and pressing, as traditional patterns of response, such as soft and conciliatory diplomacy, are no longer proving as useful as they used to be.

Given this new reality, the 2004 Tunis Summit was of utmost importance, just as were the various interactions, positions and developments accompanying it. Since the GCC States were represented as individual states and as a regional

---

[9] Qatar News Agency (QNA), April 5, 2004.

[10] Al-Hayat, June 19, 2004.

grouping, they evinced increased interest in the Summit and the developments that unfolded along with it. During the preparatory phase for instance, more than one GCC State emphasized the importance of holding the summit as soon as possible and the need to adequately prepare for it. Even when differences surfaced that made the postponement of the summit likely, Saudi Arabia conducted various consultations with a number of Arab states in a determined bid to overcome those differences. Riyadh received successively on March 17 and 18 Egyptian President Hosni Mubarak and Syrian President Bashar Al-Assad. Discussions held between Saudi officials and the two Arab presidents revolved around the summit after the decision to delay the meeting was already on the cards. For its part, Kuwait announced that it would not oppose any call for postponing the summit.[11]

Following the official announcement, the GCC States took variable positions regarding the decision. While the Sultanate of Oman expressed its respect for the Tunisian decision, describing it as "serving the general interest," Saudi Arabia along with the UAE emphasized the importance of holding the summit as soon as possible. Both countries thus welcomed the Egyptian proposal along those lines. When the summit did take place in May 2004, the GCC States participated in the two-day meeting held on May 22 and 23. During the subsequent discussions, the Sultanate of Oman and Qatar expressed reservations about the "modernization, development and reform" document and asked for the item to be withdrawn or at least its content to be amended before the Secretary-General of the Arab League could announce that the Arab states have all signed and approved the document.[12]

GCC relations with the Arab League

Besides the debate over the reform agenda, relations between the GCC and the Arab League at the institutional level were dominated by those subjects that were already on the agenda at the end of 2003. In that context, there were no major developments in 2004 indicating a re-orientation in the relation between the two organizations. Generally speaking, the Arab League continues to be hampered structurally as well as functionally by the existing deficiencies in the pan-Arab political order with the result that the League has become simply a theater for intra-Arab disputes. For the GCC states, a major stumbling block appears to have been the personality of Arab League Secretary-General Amr Mousa. In early 2004, Mussa denied any rifts between the pan-Arab body and the UAE after Abu Dhabi announced that it would not deal with him as a direct consequence of a dispute between the two sides during the 2004 Summit. The UAE subsequently paid its financial quota into the League budget only due to the mediation efforts by King Abdullah II.[13] Such tension was also evident with some of the GCC States although these countries remained officially committed to dealing with the Arab League and honoring their pledges as members in the institution. At the same time, the GCC States made it clear that membership in the Arab League did not mean that their right to take individual policy decisions or as GCC members were overridden.

The Arab-Israeli conflict

The GCC States maintained their position towards

---

[11] *Kuwait News Agency* (KUNA), March 24, 2004.

[12] All Arab news agencies and newspapers reported on Qatar's and Oman's

position as part of their coverage of the Summit on May 24, 2004.

[13] *Al-Hayat*, January 20, 2004.

the Arab-Israeli conflict in general and the Palestinian issue in particular by urging a revival of the peace process and calling on the international community to exert pressure on the Israeli government to stop its acts of repression against the Palestinian people and lift the siege imposed on Palestinian President Yasser Arafat.

The Israeli "disengagement plan" floated by Prime Minister Ariel Sharon received negative responses from the GCC States as it was being perceived as a means to divert the direction of the peace process away from the original US-proposed "Roadmap." As such, the GCC reiterated the need for any new peace initiatives to be brought in line with this plan. For many analysts the "disengagement" plan is an attempt by Israel to elude the commitments embedded in the "Roadmap" which, although failing to broach some essential issues such as the future of Jerusalem, does include a vision based on a comprehensive solution and the establishment of a Palestinian state. At the same time, the Israeli plan was approached rather practically. Saudi Arabia, for example, stated that the rejection by Sharon's own Likud party of the disengagement idea confirmed Israel's intention to annex more Palestinian lands rather than focus on bringing about an actual peace settlement. Not only does the plan not fulfill the aspirations of the Palestinians or Arabs to achieve a just and comprehensive peace, the plan does not even have consensus within Israel itself. It was only after a series of bruising debates that Sharon managed to secure approval from the Knesset on October 26, 2004.

There were several other issues that brought about a response from the GCC. The "Separation Wall" built by Israel in the West Bank was the object of much of the GCC States' concern. Here, the GCC States effectively contributed to the efforts deployed by the Arab states to submit the issue of the wall before the International Court of Justice (ICJ) and participated in the presentation of the case before the court. A heated debate also ensued during 2004 over the issue of the Palestinian refugees and their right to return to their homeland in response to the "Geneva Document" formulated by former Palestinian Prime Minister Mahmoud Abbas and Israeli Labor Party member Yossi Beilin. Numerous media reports, for example, pointed to a change in Saudi Arabia's stand towards the refugee question, claiming that Riyadh would accept in principle that Palestinian refugees will not return to their homeland on condition that they are resettled in other countries. Riyadh later categorically denied such reports.[14]

Upon the death of Palestinian President Yassir Arafat in late 2004, the GCC States expressed deep sympathy with the Palestinian people and expressed hopes for forward movement in the peace process. As they had done throughout the year, GCC members called for the implementation of the initiative of Saudi Crown Prince Abdullah which was adopted by the Arab summit held in Beirut in 2003. During the annual GCC summit meeting held in Manama on December 20 and 21, 2004, the Supreme Council expressed its hope that US President George W. Bush would place the issue of the Middle East conflict during his second presidential term on top of his administration's foreign policy agenda. They also called upon Bush to pressure the concerned parties to abide by their commitments and pledges to help establish a sustainable Palestinian state capable of living in peace and security side by side with the state of Israel. The Council hoped that the Quartet would continue its efforts to revive the peace process in the Middle East in compliance with the principles and requirements embedded in the "Roadmap" and the Arab peace initiative,

---

[14] Al-Hayat, January 20, 2004.

together with efforts to assist the unfolding Palestinian political process.

In the end, however, the obstructionist policies pursued by the Israeli government meant that none of these calls were implemented. As such, there were also no palpable developments in the bilateral interactions between the GCC and Israel with the status quo being maintained both for those states that have no official relations with Tel Aviv, such as Saudi Arabia, Kuwait, the UAE and Bahrain, and those, such as Qatar and the Sultanate of Oman, which had previously signed trade agreements with Israel. In one instance, the UAE denied reports published by an Israeli newspaper about ongoing contacts between Tel Aviv and Abu Dhabi about the possibility of establishing representative offices in both countries.[15] For its part, Doha responded to demands floated by some parties that the Israeli trade representation office in Qatar be closed by emphasizing that the office serves to help solve some pending issues between the Palestinians and the Israelis. Qatar's Foreign Minister stated that his country would be ready to close down the Israeli office if it feels that such a step would carry positive results.[16]

GCC Bilateral relations with Arab States

Relations between the GCC States and other Arab countries did not witness any landmark developments during 2004. A major dispute occurred between Saudi Arabia and Libya. In June 2004, reports surfaced claiming that Libya was implicated in an assassination attempt against Crown Prince Abdullah and implying that

Tripoli sought to actively destabilize the Kingdom. The official reaction by Riyadh was initially muted, allowing investigations into the matter to be carried out. In December, however, Saudi authorities requested the Libyan ambassador in Riyadh to leave the country and they recalled the Saudi ambassador from Tripoli. It remained unclear to what degree the incident was related to the verbal tit-for-tat between Colonel Qaddafi and Crown Prince Abdullah that occurred during the Arab Summit held in Sharm el-Sheikh in 2003.

The year 2004 also started on a negative note between Kuwait on the one hand and Yemen and Egypt on the other. Some Egyptian media reports criticized the Kuwaiti Fund for Development after the Fund decided to hold a contest on the occasion of the 40th anniversary of the first financial aid granted by Kuwait to Egypt with the contest carrying the title "Committed to Assisting Others."[17] Egyptian newspapers subsequently launched a verbal campaign against the Fund to which Kuwaiti officials responded with equally sharply-worded reactions. As far as Yemen was concerned, some Kuwaiti politicians accused Sana'a of being informed of the intention of former Iraqi President Saddam Hussein to invade Kuwait, claiming that the Yemeni President encouraged Baghdad to carry out the invasion. Kuwaitis felt incensed after a confidential document revealed that Yemen's President urged the Iraqi President to re-invade Kuwait in 2003. Kuwait's Foreign Minister acknowledged the existence of the document but denied the truth of the reports regarding its content.[18] Sana'a in turn rejected the accusations, but the incident cast a shadow on the relations between the two countries throughout 2004.[19]

---

[15] Emirates News Agency (WAM), June 20, 2004.

[16] Al-Hayat, April 6, 2004.

[17] Al-Hayat, January 3, 2004

[18] Al-Hayat, January 28, 2004

[19] For further details on the interactions between the GCC States and Yemen, see the chapter by Mohammad Al-Jumili in this Yearbook.

Conclusion

GCC-Arab relations in 2004 were dominated to a greater degree by global and regional issues rather than a focus on bilateral concerns. While bilateral relations between the GCC States and other Arab countries were not marked by any prominent developments, pan-Arab and regional issues rallied the interest of both sides on the individual as well as collective-regional level.

The Iraqi crisis and the issue of political reform took up the lion's share of GCC-Arab interactions with numerous contacts, visits and meetings taking place focusing on its implications and developments. As can be expected, the Arab-Israeli conflict formed another important point of concern in particular in regard to the "disengagement" introduced by Israeli Prime Minister Ariel Sharon. With the death of Yassir Arafat, it now appears that a new phase has opened for Palestinian political action and, consequently, for new developments in the Arab-Israeli conflict. Broadly speaking, the challenges that confronted the Arab world have delegated the differences among Arab states and intra-Arab disputes to the backburner. This is particularly the case in relation to reform, the attitude towards the Broader Middle East Initiative and the resulting need for a common Arab position.

In terms of bilateral relations, no notable developments or changes occurred. No movement was visible with regard to Yemen's possible membership in the GCC. Otherwise, GCC-Arab relations were dominated by general-interest issues as outlined above. Tensions were confined to cases such as Libya and Saudi Arabia, and Kuwait and Yemen. In the final analysis, it would be hard to say that the GCC-Arab relations at the bilateral level witnessed a qualitative leap or passed through any major turning- points.

Section Six

The GCC and Regional Relations

GCC-Iran Relations

Prof. Anoush Ehteshami

Head, School of Government and International Affairs, University of Durham

Iran's overall sense of its immediate environment in 2004 was tempered by three key factors: parliamentary elections at home; the continuing political and military tensions in Iraq; and, the absence of security structures in the Gulf region. To a greater or lesser degree, all three factors have left their mark on Iran's relations with its GCC neighbors.

Majlis elections

The political atmosphere was already tense in Iran when the conservative Council of Guardians (CG) announced that it had barred the registration for the 7th Majlis elections of more than 2,500 hopeful candidates, including the president's own brother, some clerics, and another several dozen of the incumbent MPs. The majority of the barred hopefuls belonged to the reformist camp, which caused much consternation. Domestic political turmoil stuck at a time that Iran was already under the spotlight for its undeclared nuclear research and production activities, and for its position on the Arab-Israeli stand-off. It also was already feeling the geopolitical pressure of having the United States as a neighbor on more than one of its borders simultaneously - in Afghanistan, in Iraq, and of course in the Gulf.

Understandably, the domestic and international reactions to the CG's decision, which was taken behind closed doors and without consultation with the national political elite, was one of shock and disbelief. The announcement of the CG's decision was followed by loud protests from the reformist camp, a sit-in in the Majlis itself by a large group of

MPs, public condemnation by President Khatami and the Majlis Speaker (Hojjatoleslam Karroubi), and a request by the Leader (Ayatollah Khamenei) that the CG consider reviewing its decision on all the barred candidates. The CG stood firm, allowing only for the registration of a few 100 of those on the barred list. The trauma of the CG's daring move paralyzed civil society and its many organs, thus depriving the reformist camp of a vital support base outside of the political arena itself.

Externally too, the Council's position was criticized. The Council was accused of trying to engineer the election of a pro-conservative and pro-Leader Majlis. The United States and the European Union countries let their objections be made in public and in strong terms. Many observers could not help but note that the conservatives had chosen a bad time, internationally at least, for 'rigging' the electoral system in their own favor. The domestic and international outcry will only add to national tensions, it was surmised.

In the GCC states, the political divisions in Tehran were viewed with grave concern, raising fears of internal instability spilling over Iran's borders, and worrying that a conservative return, with a strong religious-national make-up will prove to be much less accommodating with its southern neighbors, many of whom were eager to develop their own forms of participatory politics. De-liberalization in Iran was not welcomed by the reform-oriented members of the GCC intelligentsia either, who had hoped that events in Iran could continue to propel reform in their own countries.

Election week itself was marked by an odd mixture of complacency and apathy on the part of many voters, indecision on the part of others, immobility on the part of many pro-reform groups (the bulk of whom had chosen to 'withdraw' from the elections, which was a polite word for a boycott), and a massive media drive, invoking both revolutionary and nationalist images, to encourage the electorate to turn out in force on the 20th of February. The media tide kept hitting the apparently solid wall of apathy until the election day itself. Pundits, inside and outside of the country, were confidently predicting a voter turn-out of 10 percent, or at best 30 per cent. On the other hand, the participating reformists, now led by the Majlis Speaker Karroubi, cobbled together a list of some 120 candidates, confidently predicting a presence of some 100 seats in the 7th Majlis. In the event, both proved to be spectacularly wrong: the turn-out was healthy and the reformists gained far fewer than the expected 100 seats.

The reason for the unpredictability of the election result can be sought in the complexities of the Iranian political system itself. Voters were naturally deeply unhappy about the CG's behavior, but faced a complex dilemma. By not voting they would leave the field free for conservative domination. Yet, by voting they would legitimize the undemocratic behavior of the CG. Moreover, they were already so disappointed in the conduct of the reformist 6th Majlis and the paltry gains of the MPs in terms of progressive legislation, that they were not too sorry to see the reformers punished for their apparent neglect of the popular agendas.

In the event, the conservatives secured over 150 seats of the 290-seat Majlis, and the reform bloc some 60 seats. Turnout was 50 per cent, which was much higher than predicted, but low enough to steal some of the conservative's thunder. The European Union and its key three powers (France, Germany and Britain) saw the process and its outcome as a 'setback to democracy', and the United States condemned it as a sham. Yet, some observers have put a very positive spin on the outcome. They claim that the pro-reform forces were too naive in designing their strategies and setting their agendas. Furthermore, for all their pluralist talk, they actually acted in a sectarian fashion. A period of 'exile' from power will force them to review their past behavior and learn from their past mistakes, it was said. Secondly, while a conservative Majlis may not be inclined to pursue the same socio-political reform agenda of the reformist-dominated 6th Majlis, it will nonetheless have to legislate for the reform of the country, which will inevitably force an opening of society to the rest of the world.

But the real arena to watch was in the field of foreign affairs. It was soon suggested after their victory that the conservative-dominated 7th Majlis will be keen to do business with the West, and is

> **Election week itself was marked by an odd mixture of complacency and apathy on the part of many voters, indecision on the part of others, immobility on the part of many pro-reform groups, and a massive media drive, invoking both revolutionary and nationalist images, to encourage the electorate to turn out in force.**

more likely to effectively pursue dialogue with the United States, pursue peace and stability in the region, and deliver on both. In this regard, it has been suggested, the Iranian conservatives mirror their Likud counterparts in Israel: only they can break taboos and get away with it. In Iran's case, the biggest taboo is that of relations with the United States. If, following the Chinese model, they can deliver on the economy and open up to the US, in a year's time one may be wondering what the fuss was all about. But before being driven down this yellow brick road, it might be just as wise to consider the high price for relations with the US that the Iranian people will be paying: the success of the other Chinese model that the Iranian conservatives favor - a complete separation of political and economic reforms - could of course have repercussions far beyond Iran's own borders and affect the political discourse in the highly charged post-9/11 political environment in the Gulf Arab states as well. The 7th Majlis elections therefore unleashed new forces onto the Iranian political scene, and if they also occupy the presidency in the elections due in 2005 they will surely be in a strong position to fundamentally change course, if that were to be their goal. In the next 18 months, one could possibly see a major review of Iran's external commitments and of its regional role.

The end of Saddam's regime has removed a stiff barrier to closer Iranian links with the GCC states.

2 Political and Military Tensions in Iraq

As was noted in last year's GRC Annual Report, Saddam's fall has directly affected factional rivalries in Iran.[1] Some elements in Iran have pointed to US behavior in Iraq-the imposition of an American political model on a Muslim state, the establishment of military bases, and the control of Iraq's oil wealth-as well as the expansion of military facilities in the small Gulf Arab states of Bahrain and Qatar and the perceived encirclement of Iran through an elaborate network of alliances-as justification to encourage some Iraqi Shi'a forces to assist Tehran in extending its power in Iraq by infiltrating the emerging post-Ba'athist polity. Tehran does have several potentially powerful allies among Iraqi Shi'a (notably al-Hakim's SCIRI and the well-established al-Da'wa party) who are both armed and have an influential political role in the new domestic balance of forces in Iraq. It should also be noted that Tehran has in the past been heavily engaged in providing military training for SCIRI as well as the well-established Kurdish PUK and the Islamist al-Da'wa party. An interesting possibility is that continuing Iranian contacts with a slowly moderating SCIRI could have a reverse effect on the Iranian elite and help in bringing Iraqi Shi'a influences into Iran and encourage fresh thinking on Shi'a issues, thereby endangering the semi-unity of the religious establishment in Iran over matters of state and national political issues (the distribution of power between the three branches, social and political reforms, press freedom, organization of political parties).

Those in Tehran who are deeply worried about developments in Iraq and the domestic and foreign policy consequences of manipulating Iraq's large Shi'i constituency for narrow political ends counsel caution. They desire to protect Qom's place as the beating heart of Shi'ism. They also wish to use the

[1] See my chapter entitled "Iran in the Aftermath of the Iraq War," Gulf in a Year 2003 (Dubai: Gulf Research Center, 2004), 320-326.

opportunity afforded by Saddam's overthrow to deepen relations with the GCC countries. The end of Saddam's regime has removed a stiff barrier to closer Iranian links with the GCC states. Tehran no longer has to worry about the GCC states keeping a distance in fear of Iraqi pressure; and, the fall of Baghdad has allowed the emergence of the 'Shi'a issue into the open. The fears, expressed in 1991 for example, that the removal of Saddam Hussein would somehow lead to the rise of an Iranian-controlled Shi'a-dominated state in Iraq has not come to pass, and the Shi'a dimension of Iraqi society is no longer seen as a direct security threat but a part of the reality of the country. The Shi'a no longer stand in the way of closer relations between Tehran and the GCC states, although with every act of violence in Iraq suspicion of the Shi'a factor has continued to grow in the Arabian Peninsula. In theory, US removal of the Ba'athist regime in Iraq has allowed Arab Shi'ites in that country to make their presence felt, and Iran no longer has to fear a negative fall-out in the Arab world of its own Shi'a identity, or close association with this community across the Arab world.

On another front, the political voice of Iraq's Shia communities has mobilized a strong Salafi and al-Qaeda-type violent backlash. Salafis despise Shi'is by the same measure as they hate the United States. Many see the US intervention in Iraq as part of a bigger conspiracy to promote the 'heretical' Shi'a against the larger Sunni Arab states and communities as a way of strengthening its control of Arab-Muslim lands and resources. The Iraq war,

Although no one in Iran bemoans the fall of the Ba'athist regime in Iraq, there are those in the Iranian elite who do miss the large degree of continuity, predictability, and dare one say stability, that Saddam Hussein had brought to Iraq's post-war relations with its neighbor.

therefore, has changed the character of political Islam itself, and, very broadly speaking, has separated them into the Salafi/al-Qaeda and Shi'a camps. The war, furthermore, may well have unleashed a much wider and deeper inter-communal strife in the Muslim world between the majority Sunnis and the minority Shi'a. The ugly manifestations of this division in terms of inter-communal strife has already been in evidence in Afghanistan, Pakistan and India, but with Iraqi Shi'a now free to enter the fray the frontline of this struggle will have widened and deepened possibly to encompass the GCC in which the West has many vital interests to protect.

Although no one in Iran bemoans the fall of the Ba'athist regime in Iraq, there are those in the Iranian elite who do miss the large degree of continuity, predictability, and dare one say stability, that Saddam Hussein had brought to Iraq's post-war relations with its neighbor. Tensions between the two countries during the July-August 2004 crisis in Najaf exemplify the problem for Tehran. For all the declarations of friendship between the two sides, and Iran's continuing expression of support for the post-Saddam Iraqi leadership, it was Iraq's Interior Minister himself, Falah Hassan al-Naqib, who in mid-July accused Iran of involvement in unrest in Iraq, while his counterpart, the Iraqi Defense Minister Hazim Sha'lan al-Khuza'i, accused Iran of "blatant interference" in Iraq's internal affairs.[2] The Governor of Najaf, Adnan al-Zurufi, said on August 8 that "there is Iranian support for al-Sadr's group,

[2] Al-Khuza'i also said on August 9 that "Weapons manufactured in Iran were found in Al-Najaf in the hands of those criminals, who received these weapons from the Iranian border". He accused Iran of being Iraq's "first enemy", in the same interview with Dubai-based Al-Arabiyah television.

and this is no secret. We have information and evidence that they are supplying the [Imam] Al-Mahdi Army with weapons and have found such weapons in their possession."[3]

Tehran was quite taken aback by the forcefulness of these attacks from senior Iraqi officials and in frustration warned that "Iraqi officials have just begun working and need to be cautious... [as their remarks will] have serious legal and political consequences" for relations between Iran and Iraq.[4] Jomhuri-yi Islami, an influential hard-line newspaper, stated in an editorial (August 8) that the interim government was a "cast of hand-picked actors." The next day, it opined that the Najaf crisis was a "premeditated conspiracy to eliminate the forces of resistance" in Iraq: "the time [has] come for us to get up and go after the crown of Islam, the very existence of the Shi'a, and the national interests of the Islamic Republic of Iran?"[5] The Shi'a file in the hands of the hard-liners can spell disaster for the moderate camp in Iran, further testing its relations with the West (notably the European Union, which is being strained by Iran's activities in the nuclear field), and adding to Iran's problems with Iraq and Baghdad's Western backers.

Absence of Security Structures in the Gulf Region

Indicative of the negative impact that the absence of region wide security structures or networks continues to have on Iran-GCC relations was the potentially serious crisis over the 'fishing boats' dispute between Iran on the one hand, and the UAE and Qatar on the other. The capture of an Iranian

shipping boat and its crew off the coast of Dubai on June 5, and Iran's response by detaining seven UAE fishing boats and their 28 crew members, helped in raising the political temperatures on both sides of the waterway. To Tehran, this was another ploy to assert the UAE's claim to the three islands, while to the GCC it again illustrated Iranian intransigence and Tehran's militaristic approach to problem solving with its southern neighbors. Although disputes of this nature are not uncommon, the ease with which the fishing boat incident escalated is disturbing, particularly as it led to an attack by the Qatari navy on another fishing boat, detention of a further two boats, and the death of an Iranian fisherman. In a short period of time, Tehran had found itself entangled with two of its neighbors simultaneously.

Did the fishing boats incidents disguise deeper security problems stretching across the Gulf? The answer is almost invariably yes. With the UAE, the islands dispute is in danger of becoming a permanent fixture of bilateral relations, but at least both sides have seen fit to 'manage' it. At the same time, however, both sides are suspicious of the other's motives in national security terms and there exists the danger that the islands dispute could ignite a much wider conflict.

The dispute with Qatar is altogether different, but equally dangerous, for here the two countries share a much bigger prize: access to the world's biggest off-shore natural gas reservoir (some seven per cent of global known reserves) straddling their territorial waters. With Iranians warning their southern neighbor that they should moderate their output from the shared field and aim to settle their disputes with Tehran "through negotiations instead of confrontation",[6] one can envisage a situation in

---

[3] *RFE/RL Iran Report*, August 17, 2004.

[4] Remarks made by the Iranian Foreign Ministry spokesman, Hamid Reza Assefi. See *RFE/RL Iraq Report*, July 22, 2004. Iraqi Foreign Minister Hoshyar Zebari told The Sunday Telegraph (July 4, 2004) that as many

as 10,000 foreign spies had entered Iraq since May 2003.

[5] *RFE/RL Iran Report*, August 17, 2004.

[6] Iranian Deputy Interior Minister, Ali Asghar Ahmadi, quoted in *Ettelaat International*, June 15, 2004.

which Doha might seek military support from its resident military ally, the United States, and raise the political temperature almost inadvertently. Such a move would not only startle Iran, but actually force it to take an even harder line in its discussions with its neighbor than hitherto, thus accelerating the cycle of enmity.

The absence of transparent regional security structures, therefore, means that an apparently small incident could unravel what might appear to be cordial relations. In addition, without a framework for security dialogue any moves by the GCC states to improve their links with the West could also be viewed with great suspicion by Tehran. One should note in this regard Iran's rather frosty response to the EU-GCC final statement issued on May 18 in Brussels, which proposed that the three islands dispute be referred to the international court of justice in the Hague. Tehran saw in this statement, opportunistic gains by the two parties. It saw the EU using the EU-GCC roundtable as an opportunity to apply renewed pressure on Tehran over its nuclear activities; and it saw the UAE capitalizing on the broader EU-GCC dialogue for its own narrow ends against Iran. From Tehran's perspective, the growing relationship between the EU and the GCC had added to its security challenges in the Gulf.

Iran's suspicions have grown at a most inopportune time, however, as it finds itself entangled with both the EU and the United States over its nuclear program. The GCC states, of course, also look with great concern at Iran's ambitious nuclear-related plans. Despite these problems, trade and broader economic relations between the northern and southern states of the Gulf have been blossoming at an impressive pace. The volume of UAE-Iran trade had grown by a staggering 2,500 per cent in 2004 and Iranian national statistics show the UAE is now Iran's third most important market (albeit for re-exporting purposes) and its fifth most important

supplier of goods. Iran, by contrast is the UAE's single most important re-export market according to UAE national figures. Less dramatic, but an equally positive trend is also in evidence with regard to Bahrain, Qatar, Kuwait and Oman. With the former country, Iran is emerging as an important partner in the development of its banking industry, for example, and with Kuwait, it could become its main supplier of fresh water within three years.

Conclusion

It is clear that economic relations across the waterway have continued to grow, and this process is likely to continue thanks to the unprecedented rises in oil prices since February 2004. It is ironic, and perhaps not surprising, that at the political level problems have endured. Political uncertainties in both Iran and Iraq in the coming year, where major elections are due in both countries in the first half of 2005, will leave a definite mark on Iran-GCC relations, adding to the unpredictability of relations between the GCC and its northern neighbors. Indeed, so will the strategy of the new US administration with regard to its relations with Iran, its military presence in Iraq, and the wider issue of security arrangements in the region.

GCC-Turkey Relations

Prof. Bulent Aras

Associate Professor of International Relations, Fatih University

With the Middle East being subject to direct US interference through Afghan and Iraqi invasions and through political attempts to transform the region socially, politically, and economically, the region is confronted with a new reality. Calls for reform and renovation have reached an unprecedented level, and indeed, there is a high level of desire and hope for good governance, democracy, and human rights in the Middle Eastern societies. The Gulf region is not independent from the problems of the wider Middle East and thus is a participant in these critical developments. In this context, relations between Turkey and GCC Countries are very positive, avoiding many of the problems associated with such competing agendas. The constructive nature of these relations are prominent considering the conflicts and problems these countries are facing in their immediate neighborhood.

Due mainly to physical distance and different foreign policy orientations, it might be an exaggeration to describe the present situation as being one of a close relationship grounded in mutually beneficial trade. However, the recent period has witnessed a considerable improvement in both political and economic relations between the GCC and Turkey. What is more important in this context is the increasing participation of both sides in international and regional diplomatic activities and forums that aim to address regional and international problems. Here, the critical and conflict-prone situation in various parts of the Middle East is paving the way for greater roles for the stable countries of the region. With that as the point of departure, the key determinants of the relations in 2004 have been the ongoing Iraqi crisis, Turkey's EU membership process, the threat of international terrorism and Al-Qaida, the US-led broad-

er Middle East initiative, increasing business and trade relations, the OIC meeting and issues of the wider Islamic world, and, finally, threats emanating from the nuclear program in Iran.

The Iraqi Crisis

The March 2003 decision that forbade US troops from using Turkish territory in the war against Iraq was a historical turning point for Turkey. Ankara made it clear that it would follow the principle of democratic legitimacy in its regional and international policies and the Turkish parliament prevented the United States from opening a northern front against Iraq on the basis that the international community considered the war illegitimate. Turkey's decision prolonged the process of the Iraqi invasion in turn forcing the US to search for greater legitimacy that would justify its overall decision.

The parliamentary motion that prohibited the use of Turkish territory by American troops saved Ankara from much of the negative impact of the Iraq crisis. The decision was shaped by a powerful consensus in Turkish society on this issue; therefore it can be considered as correct both in ethical and strategic terms. The widely held assertion that Ankara would subsequently be faced with numerous problems in terms of its relationship with the U.S. did not materialize. Rather, the decision served to increase Turkey's prestige at both regional and international levels including within the Gulf region.

Outside of its pre-war role, Turkey has been active in facilitating diplomacy among the countries bordering Iraq, bringing those countries together on a periodic basis. The UN Security Council takes these meetings seriously and has demanded further regional cooperation on the Iraqi question. Meetings have been held in the capital cities of three GCC countries: Saudi Arabia, Kuwait and Bahrain. Within each of these meetings, it has become clear that a convergence of interests in terms of the Iraqi question exists between Turkey and the other neighboring states in the context that each of them favors maintaining Iraqi territorial unity albeit for different reasons. Despite the uncertainty over the eventual outcome in Iraq, Turkey and the Gulf States have come to an understanding of each other's positions and a determination to continue the dialogue process. Thus, on a key strategic issue, Turkey and the GCC are engaging in a mutually beneficial exchange of views.

> **Turkey is emerging as a regional civil power thanks to its modernity, political development, economic capabilities, dynamic social forces, and ability to reconcile Islam and democracy at home.**

Turkey's European Union Process

Outside of the direct issue of Iraq, the possible accession of Turkey to EU membership has received significant attention within the GCC countries. On this front, reform in the Turkish political and legal infrastructure and its progress toward European Union membership have made it a unique country in the Middle East.[1] While Turkey is accustomed to balancing between the chaotic Middle Eastern system and the peace and stability of Europe, it now appears to be moving closer to the EU. As a result, even Turkish foreign policy now pays serious attention to societal demands.

Turkey is emerging as a regional civil power thanks to its modernity, political development, economic capabilities, dynamic social forces, and ability to reconcile Islam and democracy at home. This civil power is among one of the very limited sources of change from within the Middle East. Furthermore, Ankara's foreign policy moves are in line with both the EU's foreign and security policies and its recent regional policy. Turkey has showed that the current instability and chaos is neither destined nor irreversible for Middle Eastern countries, a lesson which is also relevant for the regional states. For example, the British ambassador to Saudi Arabia underlined that reform calls are noteworthy in the Gulf region and that Turkey is a good example of this as it bids for EU membership.[2]

The Turkish aspirations are in line with the separate efforts of the GCC States to further develop their

---

[1] See Volker Perthes, America's Greater Middle East and Europe: Key Issues for Dialogue," *Middle East Policy* 11, no. 3 (October 2004).

[2] *Arab News*, October 6, 2004.

own relationship with the EU. The new security environment in the aftermath of September 11 and the Iraqi war have pushed the two sides together to adopt common positions but they have also underlined the fact that security in the region is intricately related to the security situation back inside EU borders. While the current status of the relationship is less than impressive, the potential gains from cooperating are significant. Considering the Euro-Mediterranean Dialogue and New Neighborhood Policy of the EU, there is a need to create new mechanisms to improve relations. Energy security, the nuclear threat in Iran, and the normalization of Iraqi policy are only some examples of potential areas of cooperation. Turkey's active involvement in the EU mechanisms will facilitate this cooperation. Indeed one has seen some early signals of this future cooperative relationship. For example, the EU, GCC, and Turkey adopted the same policy line against the problems associated with a nuclear Iran in the Gulf region. All three want a nuclear-free Iran-and also a nuclear-free Middle East-but oppose a U.S. attack on Iran. They have been in favor of diplomatic efforts, and if necessary, economic measures against Iran.

The Greater Middle East Initiative

Although its origins can be traced to the early 1990s, discussions on the Greater Middle East Initiative have gained prominence both in political circles and in academic analysis. The US administration presents it as a new project that will create order and stability and promote stability in an area that consists of the countries from North Africa to the Indian subcontinent and from Saudi Arabia to Central Asia. In plain English, this project is a part of the Bush administration's attempts to

transform the globe into a safer place for itself.

Since September 11, 2001, the only country that has promoted both security and freedom at home in the greater Middle East region has been Turkey. During the recent visit of Turkish Prime Minister Recep Tayyip Erdogan to Washington in 2004, Ankara recognized another high point in Turkish-American relations that is not likely to end in a short period of time. Turkish economic and democratic developments are positive signals that are not widespread in this region. The NATO summit and G-8 meeting in June 2004 supported the idea that Turkey has reached a point at which US and European interests overlap in many respects. In this sense, GCC countries may make real and constructive contributions if they are assured that this project does not mean a one-sided imposition of US will and interests. Rather, it is necessary to get all sides to agree on the modes of involvement through common analysis of problems and the required measures to resolve current deficiencies.

The GCC countries have great potential in terms of reconciling economic development and modernity in the Gulf region, which may serve as an example for other regions. The GCC is also active in providing funds to a number of infrastructural programs outside the Gulf area. Turkey is a natural key to any plan or concept that aims to promote democracy and raise living standards, thanks to having both European and Middle Eastern identities, its political and social modernization as well as increasing democratic standards. There is a message here for other Muslim states, particularly in light of the fact that a large majority of them opposed the initial Greater Middle East Initiative even after it was rewritten (and toned down) at the G8 summit into the Partnership for Progress and a Common Future with the Region of the Broader Middle East and North Africa. When a government is democratically elected, as in the case of Turkey, it has the leeway to decide whether external projects are appropriate for the country, and can accept or reject them as it sees fit.

Wider Muslim World

Turkey and the GCC Countries have all been victims of international terror and the threat of further terrorism is likely to continue considering these states' active participation in the war against terror. There are also US and British diplomatic, economic, and military assets across the Gulf and Turkey that are direct targets of the Al-Qaida network and international terror. This common threat increases the motivations of both sides to cooperate in building common fronts against the terror phenomenon.

Yet, it has to be recognzied that the Muslim world is at a critical turning point and that the issue of terrorism cannot be seperated from the internal dimension of Muslim societies. The problems emerging from within Muslim countries are now transnational in character and most have a global reach. In return, Muslim nations are facing outside reform plans that may well affect their futures for decades to come.

In June 2004, the Organization of the Islamic Conference (OIC) held a meeting of foreign ministers in Istanbul and addressed a hefty agenda of problems. What was clear from the discussions was that the internal tribulations of the countries of the Muslim world certainly surpass the present external ones. The absence of democratization is a common problem. The relationship between state and religion and the place of religion in the public sphere is another. Secularism is subject to many interpretations in the Muslim world and is sometimes a source of tension between state and society. Globalization has also posed challenges, initiating an identity crisis and fostering a lack of self-confidence in the Islamic world. In addition, intercommunity violence and ethnic problems run deep in many Muslim countries.

The OIC meeting was never going to resolve even some of these issues. Most of the latter are systemic and their solution requires much time and effort. In their final statement, the OIC foreign ministers declared the need for the full sovereignty and political independence of Iraq, issued a declaration backing the Palestinian cause, and expressed support for the Turkish Republic of Northern Cyprus, which recently emerged from its international isolation. The participants also agreed there was a need for reform in the Muslim world and they condemned terrorism. Turkey and the GCC countries share the same concerns and are actively involved in a number of constructive attempts to address these questions. These include a number of joint attempts such as Manila ambassadors of Turkish and Gulf countries visit to Autonomous Region in Muslim Mindanao in September 2004.[3] Turkey and Saudi Arabia are also active members of the Kashmir Group of the OIC.

Turkey seeks to be more active in the OIC and may offer a fresh source of dynamism to the organization. Ankara said "no" to the US before the Iraqi invasion and has also repeatedly brought the Palestinian question to the fore in its public pronouncements. Turkish Prime Minister Erdogan has openly criticized the Israeli government's actions in the Occupied Territories and has called on Israel to stop what he

---

[3] *Manila Bulletin*, September 25, 2004.

referred to as state terror. At the same time, Turkish Foreign Minister Abdullah Gul declared before the OIC summit that Muslim countries were in desperate need of reform and he argued that the Palestinian question should not be used as a pretext to delay this. A Turk, Ekmeleddin Ihsanoglu, has been chosen as the OIC's secretary-general, which could be a positive development for the Muslim world. With Ihsanoglu at the head of the OIC, perhaps opportunities for constructive developments in the Muslim world can now be exploited.

Trade and Business Relations

Turkey's main trade partner among the GCC countries is Saudi Arabia. Total volume of trade between two countries was $1.2 billion dollars in 2003 and reached that level in the first eight months of trade between the countries in 2004. Considering that these countries are emerging markets and have the will to increase trade, this volume could double in the coming year. The United Arab Emirates stands in 13th place on Turkey's export list with an export volume that reached $714 million in the first half of 2004.

There are significant numbers of Turkish workers in various countries including about 100,000 Turks in Saudi Arabia. In addition, 200,000 Turks travel to Saudi Arabia each year for Hajj and to visit the holy places. For the GCC states, Turkey is a natural tourist destination, and Kuwaiti and Saudi citizens have been buying properties in Yalova and Bursa in Western Turkey.

Turkey's dynamic business sector has throughout 2004 focused its attention increasingly on the GCC markets also in order to take advantage of the economic boom occurring in many of the Gulf States. In 2004, the main active business sectors for Turkish companies were in the fields of textiles, construction and food services. For example, Turkey's leading food and beverage group, Ulker, has investments in Saudi Arabia.[4] The Turkish construction company, GAMA, is active in this region while the textile company, Minteks, sells its products in GCC markets. Turkey's finance sector is also undergoing a major transformation and is seeking active participation in GCC financial markets. For example, Yapi Kredi Bank has opened a branch in Bahrain.[5] Overall, participation by Turkish companies in international trade and business fairs in GCC countries is increasing including in international trade fairs.[6]

Conclusion

The year of 2004 has been promising for future close relations between the GCC States and Turkey. The relations are improving under the strains of a number of international and regional problems as both sides are recognizing that an increasing partnership is beneficial in terms of issues like Iraq or international terror. Trade and business relations are likely to develop at an accelerated pace with the sectors of food, textile, construction and finance holding the most promise. A key will be the regular exchange of views through existing and emerging forums leading to closer personal relationships and better institutional ties. On that level, GCC-Turkish relations could soon take on a qualitative aspect that has been missing so far.

---

[4] *Turkish News Digest*, September 20, 2004.

[5] *Turkish News Digest*, January 14, 2004.

[6] *Saudi Arabian News Digest*, September 24, 2004.

GCC-India-Pakistan Ties

Dr. N. Janardhan

Gulf Research Center

About five million expatriates, over $7 billion in annual remittances (see Graph 1) and a potential $20-billion-plus trade bill in 2005 form the edifice of the Gulf Cooperation Council (GCC)-India-Pakistan relations. The verdict for 2004 is that the GCC finally realized the significance of reinforcing and expanding co-operation with India, while maintaining its strong ties with Pakistan, a key element that was missing in its diplomacy armor in the past. This marked a big leap in the GCC's new "Look East" policy.

It appears that the countries involved have realized that economic sense is common sense and that where politics can fail, trade can build bridges. In April, the GCC chambers of commerce and industry called for giving priority to activating economic cooperation with Asian countries with large populations and developing economies, especially India

Graph (1) Total transfers by all expatriates between 1993 and 2002 (Billion US$)

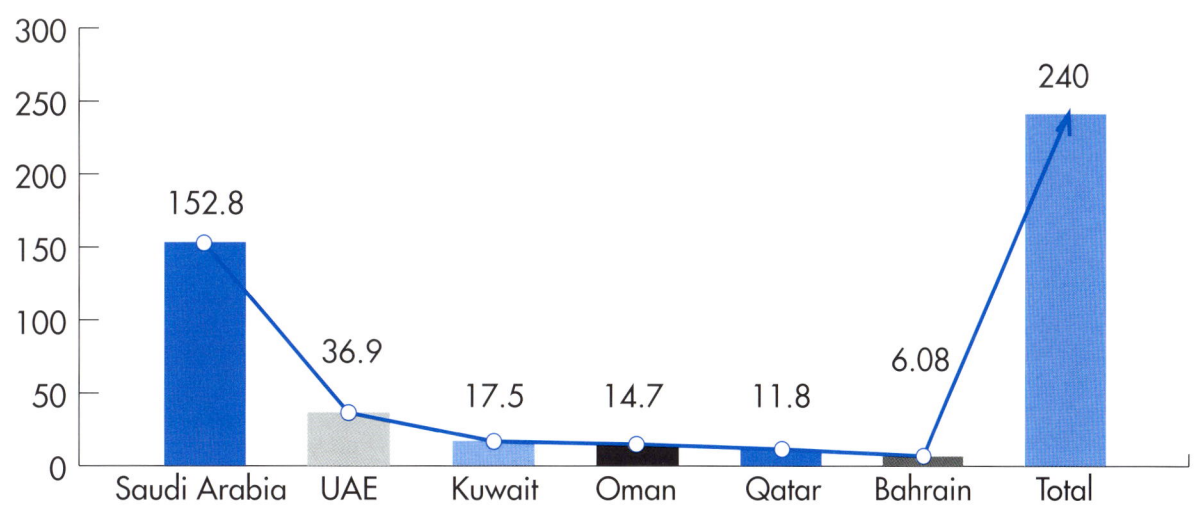

Source: Figures from the Arab Monetary Fund, Abu Dhabi
Notes: (1) The funds accounted for nearly 9% of the GCC's combined gross domestic product. (2) Given that foreigners in GCC countries siphoned out nearly $28 billion in 2002, India and Pakistan together received about $60 billion in remittances between 1993 and 2002. India presently receives approximately $6 billion every year. (3)There are about 11 million expatriates in the GCC countries.

and China. As a result, after years of hesitation, ideology - in the form of Islamic solidarity - took a backseat and the GCC dealt with India and Pakistan on a level playing ground by signing a framework agreement on economic cooperation that will ultimately help create free trade areas between the GCC and India and the GCC and Pakistan.

In acknowledging that the existing GCC-India cooperation was not proportional to their historical ties, geographical proximity, and historical interactions between their people, and signing the ground-breaking framework agreement, the two sides indicated that they were ready to move away from oil and rhetoric, and not allow political and ideological differences to puncture economic ties. Equally important was the GCC's recognition of India's advancement in a number of key areas and its political willingness to learn and benefit more from India. At the same time, signing a similar preliminary agreement with Pakistan indicates that the GCC has graduated to the next level of diplomatic maturity in dealing with the two countries on an equal footing.

Table (1) Oil consumption pattern

Thousand barrels per day	1990	Percentage of world	2003	Percentage of world	Change (%)
China	2,384	3.6	6,254	8	162.3
India	1,211	1.8	2,426	3.1	100.3
US	16,988	25.7	20,071	25.7	18.1
Brazil	1,274	1.9	1,817	2.3	42.6
World	66,227	–	78,112	–	17.9
World (excluding India and China)	62,632	–	69,432	–	10.9

Source: *BP Statistical Review of World Energy* (June 2004)

Graph (2) Indian oil imports (Main GCC countries, million US$)

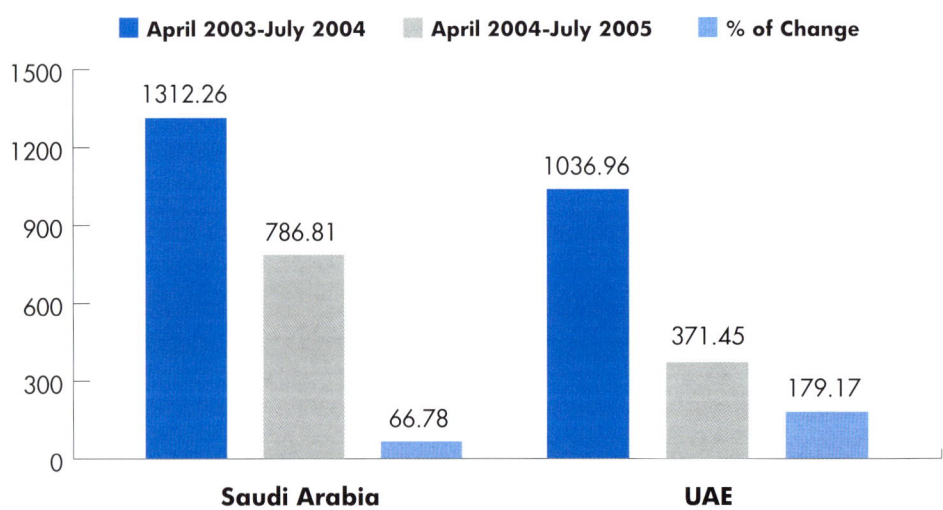

Source: Adapted from the website of the Ministry of Commerce and Industry, Government of India

GCC-India ties

The most important event of the year was the negotiations for a free trade agreement (FTA), which could sharply boost the growing non-oil trade bill of $12.5 billion in 2002 to over $15 billion during 2005. The talks with India were first mooted at the inaugural GCC-India Industrial Conference in Mumbai in February 2004, which served as a springboard to transform a traditional relationship into a robust one.

The India-GCC Framework Agreement, which was signed in August, would enable exploration of possibilities of mutually beneficial economic and industrial cooperation, with particular emphasis on supply of energy, oil and natural gas to India, development of small- and medium-scale enterprise sectors, meaningful privatization programs, Indian participation in the petrochemical and energy-intensive industries in the GCC and tie-ups with Indian information technology (IT) companies. A clause that would prevent another fiasco like the Saudi displeasure with the Bahrain-US FTA was also inserted - "individual member states are free to undertake bilateral activities with India in various fields." After the last round of talks in Delhi, the GCC Secretariat is hopeful of a free-trade zone agreement by the end of 2006.

During 2003-2004, India's exports to the GCC totaled $7.02 billion and imports, excluding oil, touched $3.25 billion (see Graph 3). India buys two-thirds of its oil needs from the Gulf, while it also has the world's biggest gas purchase agreement with Qatar to buy nearly one billion dollars worth of liquefied natural gas (LNG) for 25 years. India is and will continue to be one of the largest markets for GCC energy products. India's oil demand is projected to grow by four percent annually from 2.4 million barrels a day (mbd) in 2003 to 5.5 mbd in 2025 (see Table 1). In the fiscal year that ended in March 2004, the country's consumption of petroleum products was estimated to be 108 million tons. While the demand for oil in 2004 increased by about 140,000 barrels a day, the energy import bill from the GCC countries is about $6 billion (see Graph 2).

India's relations with Bahrain received an impetus when Prime Minister Shaikh Khalifa bin Salman Al-Khalifa made his first official visit to the country in January. The two countries signed an extradition treaty, denying a haven to international terrorists and criminals, and reviewed ways of enhancing bilateral trade, which stood at around $186.8 million at the end of 2003. The other agreements signed were aimed at mutual legal assistance and judicial co-operation in civil, criminal and commercial matters, bilateral investment promotion agreement and avoiding double taxation. Two Indian banks, the Industrial Credit and Investment Corporation of India (ICICI) Bank and the State Bank of India, were granted an offshore banking unit license and a restricted full commercial bank license in Bahrain and Oman respectively.

With India studying about 100 commercial contracts with major contractors in Iraq, economic ties with Kuwait assumed greater significance. The kidnapping in Iraq of Indian truck drivers employed by a Kuwaiti company tested the political and diplomatic circles of the two countries, but yielded the desired result with the three hostages managing a safe passage. During Kuwaiti Foreign Minister Shaikh Mohammed Sabah Al-Salem Al-Sabah's visit to New Delhi, three agreements were signed - an extradition treaty, one on mutual legal assistance in criminal matters and the third to bolster trade and economic links.

Oman and India celebrated the 50th anniversary of the establishment of diplomatic relations. The signing of an extradition treaty with Oman marked a significant step forward in bilateral relations. A five-pronged Oman-India alliance was also initiated for further study in the IT, tourism, education and human resource development, healthcare and small- and medium-scale enterprises sectors. The visits by Minister of State for External affairs E. Ahamed, Minister of State for Overseas Indian Affairs Jagdish Tytler and External Affairs Minister Natwar Singh to Muscat in one year reflected the deep-rooted ties.

It was all about gas between Qatar and India. Petronet LNG, India's first liquid natural gas venture with a capacity of five million tons (mt), received its first shipment from Qatar's RasGas in January as part of a 25-year deal worth $859 million annually. The first delivery heralded the culmination of efforts that spanned over four years, during which time both nations witnessed the construction and development of massive infrastructure projects. Petronet imported 2.5mt from Qatar in 2004 and is looking toward 5mt in 2005. India expects the volume of gas supplied from Qatar to be substantial, covering around 25 percent of its requirements. India's projected requirement for natural gas in 2020 is likely to be around 80-90mt, with the share of natural gas in the country's energy basket projected to grow from eight percent to about 20 percent by 2025. Indian gas available for sale at present is around 80 million cubic meters a day, which meets only about 70 percent of the country's demand. In the fiscal year ending March 2004, India's overall gas output was 31.39 billion cubic meters, an increase of 1.8 percent over the previous year. With India set to sign an agreement to import 7.5 million tons of LNG from Iran under a 25-year agreement beginning 2009, it is important for the GCC countries to safeguard their business interests with India with regard to the 'fuel of the future.

The campaign undertaken by the Ministry of Labor to achieve 100 percent Saudiization in the gold and the travel agency markets continued to test Saudi-India relations with several instances of harassment and humiliation reported by Indian workers. But that problem has to be internalized and looked beyond given that Saudi Arabia is bound to vigorously pursue its 10 percent unemployment-alleviation drive. At present, the kingdom is the 13th largest market for Indian exports with the GCC member also being the source of 5.5 percent of India's total imports. India is the fourth largest market for Saudi exports and ranks 10th in the Saudi imports market list. It is the largest source of crude oil to India, supplying more than 450,000 barrels per day and a total of 23.55 million tons, which is 23 percent of the total crude requirements.

The volume of Saudi-Indian bilateral trade in 2002-03 stood at $5.1 billion, up 13.7 percent over the previous year. Saudi exports totaled $3.65 billion, while India's exports to the kingdom were around $1 billion. India's major export item was IT, which, with an export value of $170 million, is poised for further growth. Many Indian companies have taken advantage of the new Saudi laws which allow 100 percent foreign-owned projects in the kingdom. The Saudi Arabian General Investment Authority awarded licenses to Indian companies to establish 62 joint ventures or 100 percent Indian-owned companies in the kingdom in different sectors such as management and consultancy services, construction projects, telecommunications, IT and pharmaceuticals. These companies are expected to bring investments totaling $360 million into the kingdom. In India, there are about 47 joint ventures in designing, consultancy, financial services, software development and others.

One of the key results of the two-day visit to the UAE by Natwar Singh was an agreement to boost economic cooperation through reviving a joint economic commission. In 2003-04, trade between India and UAE was $7.2 billion, up by about 70 percent from $4.2 billion in the previous year. While the Indian exports to the UAE reached $5.1 billion, the UAE exports to India accounted for $2.1 billion, making the UAE the second largest trading partner of India after the US. The non-oil imports from the UAE surged to $1.78 billion from $850 million, up

Graph (3) India's trade with GCC countries

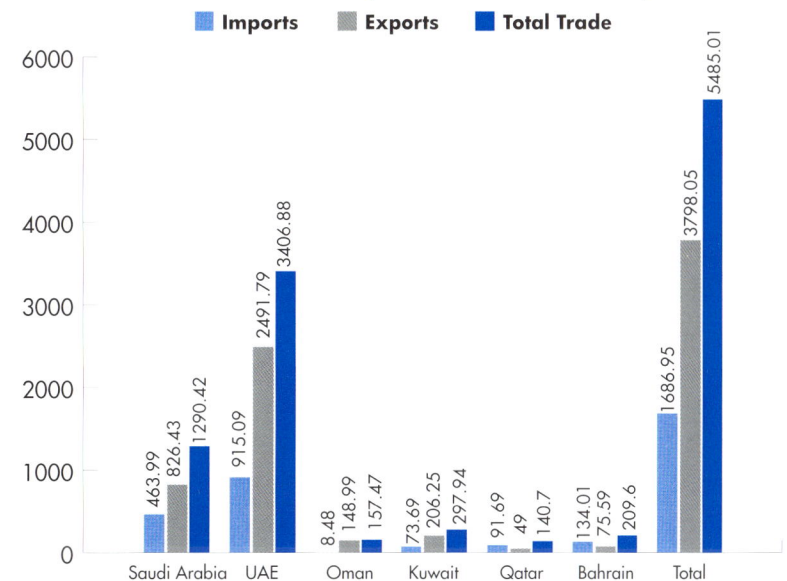

India's trade with GCC countries: April 2001 - March 2002 (in US$ million)

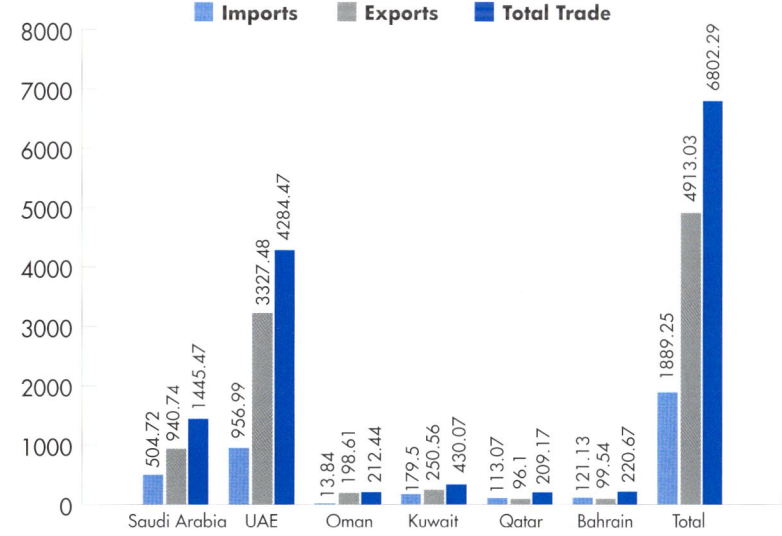

India's trade with GCC countries: April 2002 - March 2003 (in US$ million)

* The above figures of Indian imports do not include imports of crude oil and petroleum products. During 2002-03, India imported crude oil worth approximately $5.76 billion, a major portion from the GCC countries.
Source: Adapted from the website of the Department of Commerce, Government of India

108 percent. The UAE has the distinction of being the largest trading partner of India in the GCC followed by Saudi Arabia, Kuwait, Qatar, Bahrain and Oman. Boosting the trade ties was the UAE's first trade exhibition in Mumbai at the end of 2003 where it managed contracts worth $140 million. India signed two memorandums of understanding between the chambers of commerce and industry of Dubai and Sharjah in March, opening the doors for UAE investment in Indian infrastructure, where close to $20 billion worth projects are in the pipeline, and vice-versa.

A large number of Indian IT firms are targeting the fast growing Middle East IT market through the UAE. India's electronics and software exports to the Middle East increased by more than 70 percent from $163 million in 2002 to $275 million in 2003. Currently, the region accounts for about 2.5 per cent of India's software exports, and in value terms, the software and electronics exports will be in excess of $360 million. The UAE is the top destination for India's electronics and IT exports in the Middle East. During 2004, the electronics and software exports to the UAE accounted for $149 million, up from $102 million the previous year.

Among the other big contracts was the Dubai Ports International (DPI) winning a 38-year concession to manage, operate and develop the Rajiv Gandhi Container Terminal in Kochi on a build-operate-transfer basis. The DPI won the $450-million container transshipment terminal, offering 33.3 percent revenue to Kochi Port Trust annually. This was the DPI's second successful bid, following a 30-year contract for the Vishakhapatnam port. The recent decision by the Indian government to lift the $100 million limit on overseas investments is expected to pave the way for many of the country's large corporations to set up shop in the UAE, especially in Dubai's free zones. Not many companies might be keen to set up outside the free zones since UAE

company law does not allow foreign entities to own more than 49 percent of a local company. That is also the reason why more Indian companies, especially in the manufacturing sector, are eyeing Saudi Arabia, as the kingdom grants 100 percent ownership in its manufacturing sector.

For the future, India could be an important source of semi-finished products, which can be improvised and packaged by the GCC countries as a way of enhancing domestic trade. But the more conventional approach of viewing India as an extension of GCC markets and not as an investment destination has to change. The GCC countries should explore investment in Indian infrastructure projects like highways, airports and ports. Tourism is another sector where the hotel industry is in need of capital.

The impact of the GCC granting the "dialogue partner" status to India - the first from the developing world and only the fourth country in the world other than the US, European Union and Japan to get that privilege - and the success of the FTA talks will depend on how the two sides deal with the future prospects. With a targeted annual growth of eight percent over the next five years and foreign exchange reserves worth $115 billion, the transformations in India will make it an economic, industrial and scientific power. That, combined with availability of cheap and skilled labor, and assured political stability, should make India the most favored destination for investment. The fact that India will co-operate on the basis of equality and mutual respect is a bonus.

GCC-Pakistan ties

Apart from the framework agreement on economic cooperation, the GCC signed a deal with Pakistan in August giving it "dialogue partner" status in order to promote trade, exchange of information and encourage technical cooperation.

Kuwait and Pakistan inked three memorandums - one encouraging bilateral political consultations between the foreign ministries, the second on cooperation in the fight against trafficking narcotics and psychotropic substances, and the third, an executiv program of cultural cooperation. In a sign of Pakistan's importance to the region, Oman's Foreign Minister Yussef bin Alawi Abdullah called for a new Gulf economic grouping, uniting the six GCC countries with Yemen, Iraq, Iran and Pakistan.

Pakistan's ties with Saudi Arabia remained as strong as before. Bilateral trade between Pakistan and Saudi Arabia has increased from $1.5 billion during 2001-02 to $1.7 billion during 2002-03. In October, Pakistan and Saudi Arabia underscored the need for enhancing military cooperation between the two countries by agreeing to hold joint military exercises and enhancing military interaction through exchange of visits by military officials. Currently some 150 to 200 Saudi servicemen are being trained at a time in Pakistan, but this number is likely to increase after a Saudi decision to send more soldiers for training in naval, air and military services. The meeting between Saudi Assistant Minister of Defense for Military Affairs Prince Khalid bin Sultan bin Abdulaziz and Pakistani Defense Minister Rao Sikandar Iqbal discussed the possibility of setting up of a joint venture in the production of arms and ammunition, armored vehicles, ANZA missiles and Al-Khalid tanks. Pakistan will deliver 14 home-made Super Mushak warplanes to Saudi Arabia in 2005 under an arms deal signed in 2002 to deliver 20 jets. The Royal Saudi Air Force is already using six Mushak trainer planes. The Saudi

The UAE is Pakistan's second-largest global trading partner (after the United Kingdom), and its largest trading partner in the Gulf.

Army will also receive Al-Khalid tanks for trial soon.

Pakistan and the UAE formed a trade promotion group to increase bilateral trade, which touched $2.5 in 2004. The UAE is Pakistan's second-largest global trading partner (after the United Kingdom), and its largest trading partner in the Gulf. Pakistan's exports to the UAE grew to nearly $1billion during 2003-04, an increase of over 125 percent over the previous year, while Pakistani imports from the UAE was $1.5 billion. The UAE is not only Pakistan's second largest trading partner but also contributed the third largest chunk of foreign direct investment (FDI), which rose six percent during 2003-04 to $130 million from $113.7 million the previous year. The UAE's share in total FDI and foreign private investment during July-December 2004 stood at $34.5 million, making it the fourth major country outside the US and EU after Netherlands, Japan and Hong Kong.

During the same time, remittances from Pakistanis in the UAE declined. About $598 million was remitted during the financial year through banking channels, which was considerably lower than the previous year's remittances of $838 million. The monthly average remittances for the period July-December, 2004, from the UAE, Saudi Arabia and the other four GCC countries amounted to $57.66 million, $49.86 million and $42.38 million respectively. The decline in remittances by nearly 30 percent could be due to two factors: the lack of attractive investment options that compels them to retain their money in the UAE, and using the speedy alternative route or hawala system. Pakistan is currently looking for further investments in sectors such as mineral development, oil and gas, IT, agro-based industries, housing and tourism.

In a new trend, the UAE emerged as one of the main countries attracting investment from Pakistan. The foreign account holders of the commercial banks preferred to transfer their investments to the UAE to set up businesses, and lease real estate. Newspaper reports estimated that about $10-15 million was being exported through unofficial channels every day.

During UAE Deputy Prime Minister and Minister of State for Foreign Affairs Sheikh Hamdan bin Zayed Al-Nahyan's visit to Pakistan in March, the two sides signed an extradition treaty, reached deals on loans for six infrastructure and hydropower projects in Pakistan, and agreed to take steps to enhance two-way tourism and cooperate in the spheres of information, archaeology, music and sports. A UAE-based Arab investor, Yusuf Muhammad Yusuf Al-Najeebi, signed a $1.7-billion agreement with Pakistan in June to launch a water and electricity provision township in Pakistan-administered Kashmir. The new township will be situated at Chattar Kalaas on River Neelum (Jhelum) and the project will generate 1,000 megawatts of electricity plus a reservoir around which a modern mini city will be built, and will be completed in five years.

In April, Dubai-based TransAsia Gas and Interest Gas Company of Pakistan signed a memorandum of understanding to form a joint venture company in gas pipelines projects, which would explore the possibility of investment in the petroleum sector of Pakistan in general and pipeline infrastructure development for import of gas into Pakistan from any of the neighboring countries in particular. Accordingly, TransAsia Gas, a sister company of Al Ghurair Group, reached a deal in May to have a 40 percent stake in the new $1.3-billion joint venture project to build a gas pipeline bringing gas from Turkmenistan/Iran to Pakistan and India. The gas import project is scheduled to be completed by 2009.

Another UAE-based company, Warid Telecom, won the $291-million bid to introduce a new cellular phone in Pakistan and the Abu Dhabi Group signed a $200-million agreement with a consortium of 18 Pakistani banks to finance its telecom project in Pakistan. Saudi Arabia and the UAE also assured Pakistan more assistance to help develop its economy and infrastructure.

Conclusion

In tune with the realities, the developments in 2004 - a healthy break from the past - promise robust GCC-India-Pakistan ties in the years ahead. The new approach appears to be aimed at building the GCC-Indo-Pak relations on sound economic and human factors that will not only open up promising horizons for the future, but will also rejuvenate the heritage of the pre-oil era.

Moreover, the age of expatriates remitting all their earnings in their home countries is fast becoming a thing of the past. With recent decisions of Bahrain allowing expatriates with more than 15 years working experience and a healthy bank balance to reside in the country even without work permits, Dubai allowing ownership of real estate to foreigners, and the possibility of stock exchanges allowing trading by non-nationals, the money that was hitherto siphoned as savings will be put back in the form of investments in the GCC countries. This will begin to alter the edifice of the GCC-Indo-Pak ties, because the fruits of engagement will no longer be shared by just the labor exporting countries, but will be seen to be mutually beneficial.

Add to it the wealth of resources the subcontinent has on offer for the GCC countries in the realm of knowledge economy, and the equation of complementarities is complete. India alone has more than 380 universities, 11,200 colleges and 1,500 research institutions; the knowledge workers in the software and service industry increased from 6,800 in 1986 to 650,000 in 2003.

Given that the GCC countries, India and Pakistan also have several commonalities, with terrorism topping the list in the present environs, maintaining closer interaction becomes inevitable and even acquires a sense of urgency given the subcontinent's volatile security milieu and the critical developments in the Gulf, including Iraq. The repercussions of Sept. 11, 2001, have been a catalyst. The region's disenchantment with the Taliban and the Al-Qaeda extremists that have proved to be a source of instability in the region are now identified as a common threat and impediment to peace.

Aiding the process is the change of political guard in India. As part of the Congress Party-led coalition government's stated policy of reverting to more traditional ties with the Arab world, as opposed to the former government's perceived close relations with Israel, the ideological barrier has and should incrementally make way for constructive dialogue and mutually-trustworthy relationship between the two sides. The seriousness of Prime Minister Dr. Manmohan Singh's government to cement its credentials was evident in Natwar Singh's visits to Oman and the UAE in December. The minister's scheduled visit to Bahrain had to be cancelled at the last hour due to the emergency arising out of the Asian tsunami.

With India viewing the Gulf, South Asia and Central Asia as "strategically interactive and interrelated regions", it is time for the GCC to reciprocate in a commensurate way. Given the prevailing anti-West sentiment among Arabs, it is the appropriate time for upgrading Indo-Gulf economic ties. With a view to strengthening and diversifying relations, it is imperative for both to acquire fresh dimensions to consolidate their positions in a fast-changing socio-politico-economic world. Further, with Indo-Pak peace talks at their constructive best in a long time and the possibility of more rapprochement than hostility very likely, the prevailing conditions should act as the foundation for further cooperation between and integration among the three sides. The road ahead should seek to continuously diversify relations, with all the parties acquiring fresh, systematic, multi-dimensional and strategic dimensions to consolidate their positions.

The GCC and the Red Sea Basin States

Muhammad Yusuf Al-Ju'aili

Affiliated Researcher, Gulf Research Center

In the year 2004, relations and interaction between the GCC States and the Red Sea Basin states were characterized by a certain degree of vitality and dynamism with progress being achieved in a number of political, security and economic fields. This is particularly true of Yemeni-Saudi relations, which have witnessed a qualitative shift reflected most directly in the completion of the border delineation between the two countries pursuant to the provisions of the Jeddah Agreement signed in the year 2004. The first half of this year was also characterized by the intensification of contacts and interactions between the GCC States and the Sudan, particularly in the economic and investment field, following the Peace Agreement reached by the Sudanese Government and the Rebellion Movement in the South of the Sudan. On the other hand, relations with the remaining states of the African Horn in 2004 were characterized by limited interactions as compared with the preceding year.

Yemeni- Saudi Relations

Yemeni-Saudi relations have clearly achieved constant progress in the political and security fields. This was reflected in the intensity of mutual visits between the two countries at the highest level, the conclusion of a number of agreements and protocols, and in fact that both sides displayed the required political will to resolve pending issues between them, and, finally, by the joint coordination in respect to regional and international issues of common interest.

1. Political and Security Cooperation

The year started ominously with tensions rising due the Saudi decision to construct a concrete barrier along the border between the two countries. This action triggered various reactions in Yemeni political circles with opposition forces considering it a violation of the border treaty signed by the two sides in June 2000 in Jeddah. However, the matter was quickly brought to an end with the visit of Yemeni President Saleh to Saudi Arabia when officials in the kingdom agreed to halt any further construction. The fact that the issue was not allowed to escalate is a reflection of the seriousness and awareness on the part of the both political leaderships to solve pending problems through negotiations and dialogue.[1]

On most other issues, such as the challenges faced by the war on terrorism, developments affecting the Palestinian cause and the debate over political reform, the views of the two countries were largely identical. Particularly on the issue of reform in the Middle East, both Yemen and Saudi Arabia stated that this is a process that must emanate from the will of the people and be consistent with their political, cultural and ideological peculiarity.[2]

The participation by Prince Abdullah bin Abdulaziz in the celebration of the 10th National Day of the Republic of Yemen confirmed the strength and solidity of relations between the two countries. Thus, the bilateral relations witnessed a qualitative shift through the activation of the Security Agreement signed by the two sides, as a result of the visit paid to Sana'a by Prince Muhammad bin Nayef bin Abdulaziz, Deputy Minister of the Interior for security affairs in Saudi Arabia, and the visit paid by the Yemeni Deputy Minister of the Interior to Riyadh to discuss the aspects of bilateral cooperation in the security field, particularly in the field of training and preparation.[3] In this context, Yemen condemned the terrorist acts that targeted various areas in Saudi Arabia while Saudi Arabia condemned the terrorist acts perpetrated by Hussein Bader Eddine al-Houthi and his followers in the Governorate of Saada. Such cooperation is indicative of the realization by both sides that they represent a strategic depth of the other and that their security is an indivisible whole. Within the framework of the exchange of detained persons, Saudi Arabia handed over 14 Yemenis that had been detained in the Kingdom on security charges whereas Yemeni authorities handed over a number of individuals wanted by Saudi authorities.

Illegal border crossing continued to be a main problem with Saudi border forces arrested more than 51,000 infiltrators during one month.[4]

2. The delineation of borders

The delineation of the borders between Saudi Arabia and Yemen encountered some early obstacles as mentioned above. Sana'a was of the opinion that the barrier being erected by Saudi Arabia would have encroached on certain areas designated as pastures by the border treaty in addition to negatively affecting the border trade between the two countries.[5] Exports of Yemeni products to Saudi Arabia through the Al-Boqa' and Ulab outlets in 2004 amounted to $25 million as compared to Yemeni imports from Saudi Arabia which totaled $270 million.[6] For its part, Riyadh considered the barrier as being within Saudi territory and argued that it was principally to stop smuggling and the infiltration of the extremists suspected of being affiliated to Al-Qaeda.

In this connection, the Saudi committee concerned with the delineation of the borders at Saada Governorate was fired at by tribes of the Al-Otaif in protest against the delineation work that they believed crossed their territory. Moreover, Razeh tribes opened fire in protest against the delineation processes that crossed their territory, dividing such territory into two parts, one Saudi, and one Yemeni.[7]

Despite all these obstacles, the first half of the year 2004 witnessed the setting up of 800 basic and secondary border signs by the German firm entrusted with the job in the year 2001. With this, the field activities of border delineation were completed with the only remaining items being technical issues including the printing of the maps. This is expected to

---

[1] See the statements made by Prince Sultan, Saudi Minister of Defense, on this matter to *Al-Khaleej Newspaper*, February 11, 2004. See also Albawaba.com, February 17, 2004.

[2] See also the statements made by Prince Saud Al-Faisal, the Saudi Foreign Minister in *Al-Khaleej*, June 22, 2004.

[3] *26 September Newspaper*, June 22, 2004.

[4] *Al-Watan* (Saudi Arabia), May 10, 2004.

[5] Albawaba.com, February 17, 2004.

[6] *Al-Khaleej*, April 14, 2004.

[7] Ibid.

be completed in the middle of next year.[8] In this context, the process of handing over of some areas and facilities by the two parties was completed in an atmosphere of full cooperation and brotherhood. Yemeni authorities received from Saudi Arabia the Al-Badeea airport and the areas associated therewith, as well as the Al-Hargah Center. Yemen was also handed over the Al-Kharkeer Center and Al-Wajeb force at Al-Badeea, the power plant, the communications building and the Sardab Emirate Center, as well as the Umm Ghareb Center, Al-Akhasheem Center, Dhahiyyah Center and Dhahiyyah Village.[9]

3. Economic Cooperation

The Yemeni-Saudi Coordination Council is the mechanism entrusted with the setting up and implementation of policies, agreements and memoranda of understanding in all fields, particularly in the economic field. The Council holds an annual meeting in the respective country and is usually preceded by several meetings of committees to ensure that resolutions adopted by the Council in its previous session have been followed up with and that preparations for the upcoming council meeting are moving ahead.

The 16th session of the 2004 Council General Meeting was held in the Saudi capital Riyadh on December 11 and 12 and resulted in numerous agreements being signed between the two sides.

The 16th session of the 2004 Council General Meeting was held in the Saudi capital Riyadh on December 11 and 12 and resulted in numerous agreements being signed between the two sides. At the political and security level, the two sides agreed to continue the security cooperation between them within the framework of an earlier security agreement. In addition, there were cooperative measures signed in the field of youth, sport, religious matters, endowments and cultural cooperation, as well as in regard to petroleum and mineral wealth exploitation, management of hazardous waste, the desalination and rationalization of consumption of water, customs cooperation, and land, and sea transport. In the health field, it was agreed to continue cooperation in the field of combating malaria in border areas, while continuing to implement the 110 annual treatment grants to Yemeni patients at Saudi hospitals. In the development field, a grant agreement by the Saudi Government was signed for financing the rehabilitation of Aden Hospital, amounting to 50 million Saudi Riyals, together with a loan agreement by Saudi Arabia designated for participation in the Yemeni social security fund project, amounting to SR75 million.

Saudi Arabia has also agreed that the Saudi Development Fund allocate the equivalent of $150 million for priority development projects, including those provided for the reconstruction of the areas damaged as a result of the recent events that had taken place in the Saada Governorate, and to allocate $100 million to finance Saudi exports used in Yemen's regional projects. A grant was also allocated to Yemen's national program for the elimination of mines (for the second phase) amounting to $1.5 million for a period of 3 years at an annual rate of 500,000.[10] Furthermore, consultations are in progress for selecting a consultation firm from among 9 firms for starting preparations of a study for the electric linking of Yemen with Saudi Arabia. The findings are to be submitting to the Arab Development Fund for possible financing considerations.[11]

---

[8] Al-Watan, May 28, 2004.
[9] Al-Sharq Al-Awsat (London).

[10] See www.alwatan.com
[11] 26 September Newspaper, May 13, 2004.

Overall, it can be stated that the meeting of the 2004 Yemeni-Saudi Coordination Council constitutes a qualitative shift in the bilateral economic relations as it confirmed the seriousness of the Saudi side in supporting Yemen in all fields.

4. Yemen's relations with other GCC states

Security matters overwhelmed Yemen's interactions with the other GCC states, particularly Qatar and the UAE. In his visit to Yemen on May 30, 2004, the Qatari Minister of State for Internal Affairs discussed ways and means of consolidating cooperation in the security field including joint coordination in combating terrorism, the appropriate mechanism for activating the security agreement signed by the two countries and the development of its provisions as a means to strengthen the security and stability of both countries.[12] In the meantime, the UAE expressed its readiness to provide support for the completion of infrastructure and technical equipment for the Yemeni Coastal Guards Authority as well as having Coast Guard members participate in training at the Emirates Naval College.[13] Finally, within the framework of relations between Yemen and the Sultanate of Oman, the ratification documents pertaining to the Sea Borders Delineation Agreement between the two countries have been exchanged.[14]

Yemen and the Gulf Cooperation Council

The year 2004 did not bring about any noticeable developments in Yemeni-GCC relations barring the approval of Yemen joining the Gulf Industrial Consultations Organization and the Gulf Standards and Measurements Committee,[15] and the participation of Yemen in the 17th Gulf Football Cup. This was Yemen's second participation following the resolutions of the Muscat Summit in December 2001, which approved the joining by Yemen of some Council institutions, particularly in the fields of education, health, sports and social affairs.

On the other hand, the question of Yemen's joining the GCC remained marred in conflicting statements and views expressed by officials, in turn provoking certain sensitivities and tensions. In this context, the Saudi embassy in Yemen distributed a statement denying remarks attributed to Prince Nayef bin Abdulaziz, Minister of Interior, that Yemen could not join the GCC because it is not a Gulf state.[16] Prince Saud Al-Faisal, the Saudi Minister of Foreign Affairs, stated during his visit to Yemen in July that the matter was being discussed by the Republic of Yemen and the GCC, that the discussion would not harm cooperation between the two sides and that there were some basic things that must take place before Yemem could be considered for membership. "This was something of which both Yemen and the GCC are convinced," said the Foreign Minister.[17] In the same context, the Yemeni Minister of Foreign Affairs affirmed that Yemen's joining the GCC has not been decided on by the Gulf leaders, as there are reasons connected with the constitutions of some of the states, although Yemen was not in hurry to join the GCC and that it would eventually join because it is part of the texture.[18]

The issue of Yemen joining the GCC has to be considered within a practical and rational framework which recognizes the magnitude of the economic

[12] Al-Raya (Qatar), May 31, 2004.

[13] 26 September Newspaper, July 29, 2004.

[14] 26 September Newspaper, May 13, 2004.

[15] Al-Ittihad (Abu Dhabi), July 6, 2004.

[16] Al-Bayan (UAE), January 27, 2004.

[17] Al-Thawra Newspaper, July 11, 2004.

[18] 26 September Newspaper, November 4, 2004.

difference between Yemen and the GCC states. Given present economic condition, Yemen needs substantial assistance and economic, legal and legislative reforms for it to merge in the Gulf economic system. Without such reforms, which Yemen has promised to carry out, and without substantial financial and economic assistance, which the GCC states must provide, the process of Yemen's joining the GCC is bound to take a long time.

Relations of the GCC States with the African Horn States

1. Relations of the Sudan with the GCC States

The relations between Sudan and the GCC states witnessed a development which was reflected in the revival and activation of the joint ministerial councils and committees as well as in the conclusion and signing of several bilateral agreements. Moreover, the year 2004 witnessed a great interest by the private sector in the GCC states of investing in Sudan.

Sudanese - Saudi Relations

A. Political Relations: At the political level, the view of both countries became identical regarding several Arab and international issues, particularly those related to the combating of terrorism. Thus, Sudan expressed sympathy with and support for the Kingdom in its anti-terrorist efforts and condemned the series of explosions that occurred in the Kingdom. Sudan also expressed its appreciation for the Kingdom's effective role in achieving security, peace and stability in the Middle East Region and the support of the peaceful practical efforts. Both countries also agreed in terms of the policies required

to carry out political reforms in the Middle East.[19]

With regard the domestic developments in Sudan, the Sudanese Government has seen to it that the Saudi leadership is acquainted with the totality of political developments taking place there, particularly in relation to the peace agreement signed by the government and the Southern Rebellion Movement. The kingdom has expressed its support for the agreement and promised to contribute to the process of development and reparation of the destruction caused by the war. In respect to the developments in the tumultuous Darfur Province, Sudan was keen on acquainting the Saudi authorities with the developments taking place therein, particularly with the Security Council Resolution which provides for the imposing of sanctions on the Sudanese Government in case it failed to put an end to the conflict in the province and to curb the armed militias. The Kingdom has expressed understanding of the developments of events in Darfur and its monitoring of the same.[20]

B. Economic Relations: Economic relations between Sudan and Saudi Arabia have seen substantial progress. In the first half of 2004, the Sudanese-Saudi Committee held its first round of meetings which resulted in the conclusion and signing of several bilateral agreements and memoranda of understanding including investment programs in such fields as roads, bridges, education, and cooperation programs between Sudanese and Saudi universities. There were also agreements related to cooperation in legal and security fields and the setting up of the Council of Businessmen in both countries. The visit paid by the Saudi Minister of Agriculture and the accompanying delegation to the Sudan on March 2, 2004 gave new impetus to Saudi-Sudanese relations as it called for the setting up of a joint investment committee for

---

[19] See statements made by the Sudanese President Omar Al-Bashir to that effect in *Al-Riyadh* Newspaper, April 29, 2004.

[20] See *Al Ray Al-'Aam* (Sudan).

meeting the Saudi market requirements of animal and vegetable products. The two sides have also secured the entering into a large scale economic partnership for activating the Trade Agreement signed by them.[21] The Saudi private sector was also encouraged to invest in Sudan.[22]

In the context of the Saudi Development Fund, a murabaha agreement was signed by and between the Marwi Dam Project Execution Unit and the Saudi Exports Program amounting to $50 million for the purpose of building residential compounds for accommodating those affected by the construction of the dam. Moreover, a financing contract was signed between the Saudi Exports Program and a number of Sudanese banks, including the Two Niles Industrial Development Bank, the Saudi-Sudanese Bank and Um Darman National Bank, under which the banks would receive financing for the execution of murabaha transactions for the purchase of commodities and Sudanese exports worth millions of dollars.[23]

2004 also witnessed increasing interest by the Saudi private sector in investing in Sudan. This was reflected by the successive visits paid to the Sudan by Saudi business companies and groups. In this connection, the Saudi Al-Salam Group, concluded a memorandum of understanding with the Sudanese Government for developing the Salam City Project in Khartoum, which involves preliminary investments estimated at $1.5 billion.

The Sudanese-Saudi Committee held its first round of meetings which resulted in the conclusion and signing of several bilateral agreements and memoranda of understanding including investment programs.

The project constitutes a fully-fledged city that is extended along the Nile bank and comprises tourist areas, residential quarters, various government agencies, universities, specialized colleges, embassies, sport cities and other services.[24] Furthermore, a MoU was signed for the financing of the new Khartoum airport between the Sudanese Government and the "Rayat Aliyat" Group which is owned by his Prince Faisal bin Abdullah bin Abdulaziz. Prince Faisal also expressed the readiness of his Group to finance the sector of roads and bridges directly through a "BOT" arrangement or through Arab funds, and to enter into investments in the field of agriculture and the manufacturing of building materials and the hide industry.[25]

Meanwhile, Sudanese meat exports to Saudi Arabia rose noticeably to 200 tons after exports were opened through other companies than the sole agency that until then had monopolized the export of Sudanese meat. Thus, the quantity is expected to rise also in order to meet a gap that has arisen during the monopoly period.[26] The Islamic Development Bank, which is based in Jeddah, affirmed its intention to set up investment projects in the field of animal wealth in order to satisfy the needs of the Bank in terms of cattle during the season of gifts and sacrifices that amount to 500,000 heads. The Bank is also considering the possibility of Sudan becoming the main source for meeting these requirements during the future period.[27]

[21] Al-Anbaa (Sudan), October 5, 2004.
[22] Al Ray Al-'Aam (Sudan), March 5, 2004.
[23] Al-Anbaa (Sudan), June 21, 2004.
[24] Al-Watan (Saudi Arabia), May 24, 2004.
[25] Al Anbaa (Sudan), June 19, 2004.
[26] Al Anbaa (Sudan), October 5, 2004.
[27] Al Anbaa (Sudan), June 19, 2004.

UAE-Sudan Relations

Sudanese-UAE relations made forward progress, primarily in the economic field with the meeting of the joint ministerial committee in Abu Dhabi in the first week of June and discussions in connection with investment opportunities in the various industrial and economic sectors and with the importance of encouraging the UAE private sector to invest in the Sudan, particularly in the fields of the sugar industry, cement, power generation, the cultivation and manufacturing of fodders and other agricultural products.[28] Many UAE companies and business groups have expressed their desire to invest in Sudan. The Sistar Company, for example, has bought 8.77% of government shares in the Rebec Cement Factory for a sum of $15 million, with a view to raising the capacity of the present production line up to 800 tons daily. Sistar Company has cooperated with the Government in financing various projects, the most prominent being the Qari Power Project.[29] Moreover, the UAE Sharara Company expressed its interest to invest in the field of agriculture in an area estimated at 200,000 feddans (acres) in the agricultural Waha Project in the Al-Mahass Katrang Area.[30] The Department of Economic Development of the Dubai Government, has also expressed its plans to invest in the Khartoum Governorate.[31]

In the bank sector, UAE investors and businessmen have obtained a license from the Bank of Sudan (the Sudanese Central Bank) to establish a bank that operates pursuant to the provisions of Islamic Shari'ah, with a capital of $50 million.[32]

In connection with the extension and development of the communications sector in Sudan, the Canartel Coalition, led by the Emirates Communications Institution, won a license to operate the second network of land communications in Sudan, which amounts to 300 million Dirhams. The previous contract comprises the provision of all land telephone services and internet services.[33]

In terms of the crisis in the Darfur province, the UAE was among the first GCC states to respond to the human crisis by providing an aircraft loaded with food supplies and necessary materials for those affected. This support was in line with the assistance extended in the previous period.[34]

Sudan-Kuwait Relations

2004 witnessed the return of Sudanese-Kuwaiti relations to the pre-Second Gulf War status. Agreement was reached between the two sides to set up a joint ministerial committee during the visit of the Sudanese Foreign Minister to Kuwait on April 2, 2004, where he headed a delegation of representatives from the sectors of investment, agriculture and animal wealth.[35] The year also saw the resumption by the Kuwaiti Fund for Arab Economic Development of its activity in Sudan. The Fund is reported to have extended funding to 18 development projects amounting to $450 million including the Marwa Dam project for $150 million.[36] The Marwa Dam Project is expected to provide electric power in July 2007. The Fund granted Sudan an additional loan of $50 million to meet the basic items of the Marwa Dam Project such as transmission lines and hydromechanic equipment. Other development projects could also be

---

[28] Al Anbaa (Sudan), June 7, 2004.
[29] Al Anbaa (Sudan), May 12, 2004.
[30] Al Anbaa (Sudan), June 19, 2004.
[31] Al Anbaa (Sudan), June 2, 2004.
[32] Al Khaleej - Economic Supplement, April 20, 2004.

[33] Al Khaleej - Economic Supplement, February 12, 2004.
[34] Al Anbaa (Sudan), June 17, 2004.
[35] Al Ray Al-'Aam (Sudan), April 29, 2004.
[36] Al Ray Al-'Aam (Sudan), May 30, 2004.

supported after the signing of a recent framework peace agreement by and between the Government and the Popular Movement in Kenyan Nevasha, particularly in the road and land transport sector[37].

Sudan-Bahrain Relations

2004 witnessed the holding of the first meeting of the Sudanese-Bahraini Ministerial Committee, which ratified several agreements, particularly in the field of tourism, air transport, agricultural investment, in addition to the Cooperation and Coordination Agreement between the foreign ministries of the two countries. There was also an agreement for precluding taxation duplication and protecting investment between the two countries, and a general agreement in the field of electricity and water[38].

2. Relations of the GCC States with Other African Horn States

Relations between the GCC states with the remaining African Horn states were characterized by limited interactions and communications. With regard to UAE-Djibouti relations, the Djibouti port began to be operated by the Dubai Ports Authority in June 2004. This authority has the right to manage the port for a period of 20 years. Saudi Arabia drew up an ambitious plan for developing the strategically situated Jeezan Port in the Gazan area in the south of the Kingdom to become an outlet for Saudi and Gulf exports to the densely populated African Horn area, and, conversely, to prepare the port to receive the cattle shipments coming from the African Horn states, by constructing silos for crops and barns for cattle.[39]

At the political level, the interactions of the GCC states with the successive events and political developments witnessed by the African horn did not intensify despite the fact that stability in this area is linked to the security of the GCC states. For many decades, Yemen has borne the political, security and economic implications of the crises of the African Horn and has sought to preserve security and combat terrorism in the southern Red Sea area. Yemen has established the Sana'a gathering which includes Yemen, Ethiopia and Sudan as a means to combat terrorism and strengthen cooperation among the states of the area, despite the reservations and criticisms made by Eritrea.

Conclusion

During the year 2004, relations between the GCC states and the Red Sea Basin states were characterized by vitality, regularity and close views concerning many of the issues and threats confronting the region. Regarding Yemeni-Saudi relations, it can be stated that the closure of the file of the borders delineation between the two countries, which had kept casting its shadows on the bilateral relations ever since the Taif Agreement of 1934, represents an unprecedented qualitative shift in the course of the bilateral relations, as it confirmed the existence of the political will on the part of the leaderships of both countries and their recognition of the nature of the security threats and challenges that confronted both, as well as the need of joint coordination and cooperation to confront the same.

On the other hand, the détente that took place in the relations between Sudan and the GCC states confirms the recognition by the GCC states of the importance of Sudan in view of its unexploited resources and wealth, particularly in the fields of agriculture and animal products in

---

[37] Al-Anbaa (Sudan), May 25, 2004.

[38] Gulf News (Bahrain), April 26, 2004.

[39] Al-Riyadh Newspaper, June 5, 2004.

which the GCC states can invest. However, the challenge facing Sudan is to reach a stage of political stability through a just and durable peace based on finding a political equation for the ruling of the country - an equation that is acceptable to all political forces, provided it shall be based on a fair division of power and wealth, affecting a balanced development, and increasing the support for the less developed areas.

Section Seven

The GCC States' International Relations

GCC-U.S. Relations

Prof. F. Gregory Gause, III

Associate Professor of International Relations and Director of the Program of Middle East Studies, Vermont University

Relations between the United States and the countries of the Gulf Cooperation Council in 2004 were not characterized by the drama of 2003, when GCC states' positions on the war in Iraq were vitally important elements of the American war strategy. Relations were, in many ways, more "normal" in 2004. But "normality" does not mean complete tranquility. The most important bilateral relationship, that between the United States and Saudi Arabia, was characterized by the mix of close cooperation and public disputes that has been the case since the September 11, 2001 attacks on New York and Washington. No longer is the Saudi-American relationship one of close cooperation across the board, conducted largely outside the public arena, as it was before 9-11. 2004 saw the solidification of a new equilibrium in the relationship, where close cooperation on some issues, such as the "war on terrorism," continues despite public disputes on issues like Saudi domestic political reform and Saudi oil policy. American relations with the other countries of the GCC were not as contentious. The smaller GCC states have tied their futures, and their policies, much more closely to Washington, and cooperate with the US much more readily. But, as is the case with Saudi Arabia, the new American scrutiny of domestic political issues in the other GCC countries holds out the prospect of tensions with governments and public opinion backlashes against the US.

Security and the "War on Terrorism"

American relations with the GCC states in the area of security and the "war on terrorism" during 2004 were extremely cooperative. The security issue was not nearly as high-profile as in 2003, when GCC cooperation in the American war in Iraq was vital and when American forces were withdrawn from Saudi Arabia. With the American security focus almost exclusively upon the insurgency in Iraq, it would be easy to assume that security relations with the GCC states were no longer an American priority. However, American troops continue to be based in Kuwait, Bahrain and Qatar, with no sign of withdrawal. The American military continues to have access to important facilities in the UAE and Oman. In January 2004 Kuwait was named a "major non-NATO ally" of the United States, entitling it to a new level of military cooperation with Washington.[1] It is difficult to imagine the US being able to maintain its considerable forces in Iraq without the logistical system established in the smaller Gulf States. While American forces are no longer stationed in Saudi Arabia, Washington receives cooperation from Riyadh in securing the long Saudi-Iraqi border and American training missions remain attached to many parts of the Saudi military establishment, including the air force and the National Guard.[2]

If security issues were not as prominent in 2004 as they were in 2003, "war on terrorism" issues continued to be a major part of the US-GCC relationship. This is particularly true in the case of Saudi Arabia. 2003 saw a major change in the level of cooperation between Washington and Riyadh on the "war on terrorism," and that cooperation continued in 2004. Saudi security forces continued their crackdown on al-Qa'ida elements and their sympathizers in the kingdom. The violent Islamist opposition organized a number of attacks on Westerners in the kingdom during 2004, underlining the common interest the two

countries have in defeating this challenge. Saudi Arabia took a number of steps during the year to respond to American demands that it more actively police the transfer of funds from the kingdom to possible terrorist groups.

The most prominent of those steps was the decision, announced in June 2004 and implemented in October 2004, to close down the al-Haramayn Foundation, one of the major charitable organizations in the country, and establish a new governmental commission to supervise charitable fundraising. Al-Haramayn had been accused by Washington of acting as a cover for the transfer of funds to radical Islamist groups.[3] Saudi Arabia has established a direct intelligence sharing operation, on the ground in Riyadh, with American intelligence officials from the CIA, Department of Defense and National Security Agency.[4] Officials of the US Treasury Department and the Financial Action Task Force of the G-8 summit praised Saudi efforts during the year to counter terrorist financing.[5] While Saudi cooperation with the US on the "war on terrorism" remained a controversial topic,[6] the overall tenor of American-Saudi relations on this issue during 2004 was summed up by the State Department's Coordinator for Counter-Terrorism in a Congressional hearing in March 2004: "Their performance has not been flawless, and they have a large task before them, but we see clear evidence of the seriousness of purpose and the

[1] "Kuwait welcomes role as America's non-NATO ally," *Gulf News*, January 20, 2004.

[2] Anthony Cordesman, "Ten Reasons for Reforging the US and Saudi Relationship," January 30, 2004, www.csis.org/press/ma_2004_-0130_notes.pdf. See point 6.

[3] Susan Schmidt, "To Thwart Terrorism, Saudis Outline Controls on Charities," *Washington Post*, June 2, 2004. On the closure of al-Haramayn Foundation, see Mustafa al-Ansari, "hal mu'assasat al-haramayn al-khayriyya fi al-sa'udiyya," *al-Hayat*, October 6, 2004.

[4] Douglas Frantz, "Once Indifferent, Saudis Allied with U.S. in Fighting Al Qaeda," *Los Angeles Times*, August 8, 2004.

[5] See testimony of the Assistant Secretary of the Treasury for Terrorist

Financing and Financial Crimes before a committee of the US House of Representatives on September 30, 2004. Excerpts available at: www.saudi-us-relations.org/newsletter2004/saudi-relations-interest-10-06.html. The FATF report, including recommendations where Saudi policy in this area could be improved, is available at www1.oecd.org/-fatf/pdf/AR2004-Annexes_en. PDF

[6] See, for example, the report issued by a task force of the Council on Foreign Relations in June 2004 that, while acknowledging progress in Saudi efforts against terrorist financing, says there is much more to be done in the area before Riyadh reaches an acceptable level of cooperation. www.cfr.org/pdf/Revised_Terrorist_Financing.pdf.

commitment of the leadership of the kingdom to this fight."[7] The report of the US commission appointed to investigate the 9-11 attacks, issued in June 2004, exonerated the Saudi government from any direct involvement in financing the 9-11 attacks.[8]

The other GCC states also continued their cooperation with the US on terrorism issues, though with a lower public profile than Saudi Arabia. In August 2004, the UAE captured an important al-Qa'ida operative in Dubai and transferred him to Pakistani authorities, amid indications that the organization was still using Dubai as a transit point and financial center.[9] Security issues surrounding terrorism remained a major issue in US-GCC relations, with Washington evacuating personnel from Saudi Arabia in April 2004 and Bahrain in July 2004. However, there were no indications that these evacuations stemmed from a lack of cooperation on the part of the local governments.

Oil and Economic Issues

American-Saudi relations on oil and economic issues in 2004 were mixed. Saudi Arabia generally adopted oil policies in line with American preferences, with one notable exception in early 2004. At the February 2004 OPEC meeting, Saudi Arabia took the lead to push for immediate production cuts of 1.5 million barrels per day (b/d), with a commitment for further cuts of 1 million b/d at the end of March[10]. Riyadh feared that demand would decrease as the year progressed, and wanted to avoid a price decrease. With prices moving well beyond the OPEC band of $22-$28 per barrel, Saudi Arabia pushed at the March 31, 2004 OPEC meeting for implementation of the next round of production cuts. Washington publicly expressed its displeasure at this move, with Saudi Ambassador Prince Bandar called to the White House for consultations on the oil issue.[11]

As the year progressed, it became clear that the Saudis had miscalculated the market, particularly demand growth in East Asia.

As the year progressed, it became clear that the Saudis had miscalculated the market, particularly demand growth in East Asia. Rather than softening, oil prices took off in the second quarter, approaching $40 per barrel, and reaching $50 per barrel in October 2004. With prices far exceeding the OPEC band, Riyadh shifted policy, announcing a unilateral production increase of 700,000 b/d on the eve of the June 2004 OPEC meeting.[12] From that point, the US and the Saudis had the same goal: to halt the upward price spiral. However, prices continued to increase. In late September 2004, Saudi Arabia announced another production increase of 1.5 million b/d, putting Saudi production very near to its maximum capacity of approximately 11 million b/d.[13] It remains to be seen whether the Saudi moves can bring prices down, but it is clear that Washington and Riyadh were back on the same page regarding oil issues. However, their differences in the early part of 2004 indicate that Saudi and American interests on oil are not identical.

---

[7] Quoted in Michael Janofsky, "Saudis Aiding U.S. in Cutting Off Terrorism Funds, Panel is Told," *New York Times*, March 25, 2004.

[8] Susan Schmidt, "Saudi Arabia Did Not Directly Finance 9/11, Panel Says," *Washington Post*, June 17, 2004.

[9] Paul Haven, "Senior Al-Qaida Operative Captured in the UAE," *Associated Press*, August 8, 2004; Tarek al-Issawi, "Bin Laden's Operatives Still Use Dubai," *Associated Press*, September 2, 2004.

[10] *Petroleum Intelligence Weekly*, February 16, 2004, pp. 1, 4.

[11] John Burgess, "OPEC Votes to Trim Output," *Washington Post*, April 1, 2004.

[12] Peg Mackey and Jonathan Leff, "OPEC Raises Efforts to Control Oil Prices," *Reuters*, June 2, 2004.

[13] Jad Mouawad, "Saudis to Boost Oil Production Capacity as Prices Hit $50," *New York Times*, September 28, 2004.

Saudi Arabia needs increasing amounts of oil revenue to fund its government, and that need will occasionally clash with American desires for lower prices. At $50 per barrel, both countries agree that prices are too high. It is not certain, however, that they could agree on what an optimal price is.

More generally, economic relations between the US and Saudi Arabia reflected the new tensions in their bilateral ties since 9-11. In the first quarter of 2004, Riyadh finalized gas deals with foreign energy companies from Russia, China and other countries, but not the United States, whose companies had dropped out of the bidding in 2003. In May 2004, Citibank, an investor in Saudi Arabia for nearly 50 years, sold its shares in the Saudi-American Bank. The attacks on expatriates and energy companies in the kingdom during 2004 by Islamist militants were clearly aimed at driving Western business, investment and workers out of the country.[14] Meanwhile, negotiations between Washington and Riyadh on Saudi accession to the World Trade Organization, the last step before Saudi Arabia can join the WTO, dragged on. Despite Saudi hopes that they would be finished before the end of 2004, a source in the Office of the US Trade Representative said in September that an agreement is not imminent.[15]

American economic ties with the other GCC states were much more positive and less complicated than those with Saudi Arabia. The other major GCC oil producers, Kuwait and the UAE, unlike Saudi Arabia, opposed the oil production cuts of the first quarter of 2004[16] The UAE moved quickly, with Saudi Arabia, in June 2004 to increase its oil production in the face of rising prices, and both Kuwait and the UAE supported the quota increase adopted at the June OPEC meeting. Bahrain completed negotiations on a free trade agreement with the United States in May 2004.[17] Qatar awarded a $2.5 billion contract for construction of a new airport to American contractor Bechtel in January 2004, and an offshore oil deal with American energy firm Anadarko in May 2004.[18] Emirates Airline, bucking the global industry trend toward Airbus, purchased four Boeing aircraft for its fleet in July 2004 in a deal amounting to almost $3 billion.[19] The continued close political and military ties between the smaller GCC states and the US were reflected in the economic area.

Domestic Political Reform

The most serious and enduring change in American policy toward the GCC states to come from the attacks of 9-11 is a new focus upon their domestic politics, particularly in Saudi Arabia. The US now publicly criticizes Riyadh for purely domestic policies, and encourages greater political freedom and more representative politics in all the Gulf States. The rhetorical change is clear. The extent to which Washington will sacrifice its other goals in the region - stability, oil, strategic access - to promote democratic values is not. The issue of political reform introduced new tensions into American relations with the GCC states in 2004, and also produced signals of a potential backlash from the Gulf States if Washington pushes too hard. As of yet, these tensions have not derailed close cooperation

[14] Simon Romero, "Attacks in Saudi Arabia Raise Market Concerns," New York Times, May 30, 2004.

[15] Muhammad Khalid, "jadwal a'mal dhakham wa asbab faniyya wara' ihtimal ta'khir al-mufawadat al-tijariyya al-'amrikiyya al-sa'udiyya," al-Hayat, September 18, 2004.

[16] "Saudi Arabia faces Gulf opposition to April cuts," Reuters, March 31,

2004.

[17] "Bahrain, US reach free trade agreement," Reuters, May 29, 2004.

[18] "Bechtel in $2.5 billion deal to build Doha airport," Gulf News, January 25, 2004; Petroleum Intelligence Weekly, May 24, 2004.

[19] "Emirates orders Boeings in $3 billion deal," Agence France Presse, July 20, 2004.

in other fields, but they will remain an irritant in US-GCC relations for some time. How much of an irritant depends upon how much Washington pushes for real political change in the Gulf.

The clearest signal of Washington's new approach on political reform during 2004 was the pointed criticism directed at Saudi Arabia on a number of occasions. In his March 2004 visit to Saudi Arabia, Secretary of State Powell publicly criticized the detention of a number of Saudi reform advocates, following up a public State Department rebuke to Riyadh on the issue.[20] In September 2004, the State Department for the first time designated Saudi Arabia a "country of particular concern" in its annual report on international religious freedom.[21] These criticisms were matched by praise from Washington for Riyadh's decision to conduct municipal elections in 2005 and by reassurance of the strong ties between the two countries. However, they marked an unprecedented level of public attention from Washington to domestic Saudi politics. Criticism of Saudi Arabia in the Congress and the media in the US for its lack of political and religious freedoms far exceeded that coming from the Bush Administration.

The Saudi leadership, and other Gulf states' leadership, sent their own signals that they did not appreciate outside pressure to reform their political systems. Crown Prince Abdallah very publicly turned down an invitation to attend the June 2004 G-8 summit meeting that adopted the "Broader Middle East and North Africa Partnership for Progress and a Common Future," calling for political reform in the region.[22] Of the Gulf rulers, only Shaikh Hamad, the king of Bahrain, attended. Even Kuwait, in many ways the Gulf state most closely tied to the United States on security issues, declined to attend, despite frequent expressions of American support for the extent of political participation and reform in the Kuwaiti political system. However, during the year most of the GCC states took steps to portray to their own people and to the outside world that they were moving forward with political reform plans, even while they sometimes adopted measures to limit political speech and intimidate political opposition. Saudi Arabia announced plans for municipal elections; Qatar formally implemented its new constitution; parliamentary politics continued in Kuwait, Bahrain and Oman.

While Gulf elites signaled that they would resist overt American pressures for political reform, signs emerged in the Gulf States that more open politics might not always work to America's advantage. Bahrain saw major demonstrations against American policy in Iraq in March, May and August 2004.[23] Public opinion polls in the Gulf States continue to reflect general public opposition to American policy in the region. Qatar, a very close American ally which is moving ahead with political reform plans, was very pointedly not

> **In September 2004, the State Department for the first time designated Saudi Arabia a "country of particular concern" in its annual report on international religious freedom.**

---

[20] Steven Weisman, "Powell Asserts Saudi Bond Despite Rift," *New York Times*, March 20, 2004.

[21] See Saudi section of International Religious Freedom Report 2004 at www.state.gov/g/drl/rls/irf/ 2004/35507.htm.

[22] In a joint statement with President Mubarak of Egypt, the Crown Prince in March 2004 said that the region would not accept reform "imposed on Arab and Islamic countries from the outside." Guy Dinmore and Roula

Khalaf, "Many in the region are concerned with the survival of existing regimes," *Financial Times*, March 23, 2004.

[23] Mazen Mahdi, "Bahraini protest at US embassy turns violent," *Gulf News*, March 28, 2004; "Bahrain demonstrators clash with police," *Reuters*, May 21, 2004; Mazen Mahdi, "Massive Rally in Bahrain to Protest US Blitz in Iraq," *Arab News*, August 14, 2004.

invited by Washington to attend the G-8 summit meeting that adopted the Broader Middle East and North Africa Partnership. Bush Administration officials were sufficiently upset with al-Jazeera broadcasts to leave Qatar off the invitation list, raising questions about how committed Washington is to press freedom in the area.[24] It is clear that Washington is still working out how it is going to relate its calls for greater political freedom in the GCC states with its other, more traditional foreign policy goals and its historically close relations with the ruling regimes.

Conclusion
The American Elections and the Future of US-GCC Relations

The American presidential election campaign has highlighted the fact that, despite a number of steps to cooperate with the US in the "war on terrorism," Saudi Arabia continues to be viewed with suspicion and mistrust by large sections of American public opinion. Sen. John Kerry, the Democratic nominee for president, repeatedly criticized the Bush Administration for its close relations with Saudi Arabia. In his acceptance speech to the Democratic convention in July 2004, he called for an energy policy that freed America from its dependence on Middle East oil, saying "I want an America that relies on its own ingenuity and innovation - not the Saudi royal family."[25] In a speech in late September 2004 he vowed to "do what President Bush has not done: I will hold the Saudis accountable" for financing terrorist groups.[26] Clearly, the Kerry campaign

believed that they could gain votes by taking an anti-Saudi position and by tying President Bush to the Saudis.

The centrality of Saudi Arabia as an issue in the American presidential campaign should not be exaggerated. There was not a single mention of Saudi Arabia in the first debate between the candidates in late September 2004, even though the debate was devoted to foreign policy. However, Kerry was not the only American politician who detected this trend in public opinion. In July 2004, the US House of Representatives voted 217 to 191 to remove a symbolic grant of $25,000 to Saudi Arabia from the 2005 foreign aid bill. Approval of the measure would have meant millions of dollars of discounts to Saudi Arabia for hardware and military training. One lawmaker said: "I don't want my taxpayer dollars going to the Saudis and I don't want anyone else's to."[27] American politicians would not be taking anti-Saudi stands if they did not detect a continuing negative undercurrent toward the country in American public opinion.

It should be noted that there is no negative American public opinion sentiment toward the smaller GCC states, just toward Saudi Arabia. This public opinion pressure, much like the anti-American public opinion pressures that have developed in GCC states, is an important element in the new relationship between the US and the GCC. On a wide range of issues, common interest continues to bring the two sides together. That was clear in 2004 as cooperation between Washington and the GCC capitals was extensive. There is no sign that cooperation will

---

[24] Steven Weisman, "Bush Plan for Group of 8 to Hail Democracy in the Middle East Strains Ties with Arab Allies," *New York Times*, June 6, 2004.
[25] www.johnkerry.com/pressroom/speeches/spc_2004_0729.html.
[26] www.johnkerry.com/pressroom/speeches/spc_2004_0924.html.
[27] Anna Willard, "U.S. House votes to block aid for Saudi Arabia," *Reuters*, July 15, 2004.

wane in the near future. However, as long as public opinion on both sides is negative toward the other, it will be difficult to maintain a strong public relationship. The public opinion issue remains the largest question mark in the US-GCC relationship, on both sides.

With George W. Bush re-elected in November 2004, one should not expect large-scale changes in American policy toward the GCC States, or in the Gulf more generally. The American war in Iraq will continue, emphasizing the importance of the network of bases the US has in the GCC states. The Bush Administration has been careful to maintain Saudi-American relations even in the face of public pressures against Saudi Arabia in the US, and can be expected to do so over the next four years. The two major uncertainties regarding US-GCC relations in the second Bush term are: 1) how seriously Washington will push for domestic political reform in the Gulf States. If the first term is any indication, the rhetoric of democratization will not be matched by real pressure on the Gulf rulers for major domestic changes. The Bush Administration will be satisfied with small steps (like the Saudi municipal elections); and 2) how Washington will deal with Iran. If the second-term Bush Administration chooses a path of direct confrontation with Iran, it will expect the GCC states to support it. This will places all six GCC capitals before a very difficult choice.

GCC-EU Relations

Dr. Christian Koch

Program Director, GCC-EU Relations, Gulf Research Center

If one were to measure success by concrete results, the relationship between the member states of the Gulf Cooperation Council (GCC) and those of the European Union (EU) would appear to have once again fallen short of expectations during 2004. While there were a number of positive statements about the need to elevate the mutual relationship, both sides continued to grapple with the difficulty of defining an implementable action plan or to agree on a concrete list of steps that could pave the way forward. Moreover of course, issues closer to home dominated the agenda of each respective side with the EU preoccupied with the accession of 10 new member states in May 2004 and with the GCC having to grapple with the regional crisis of Iraq and its mounting instability.

Yet, it was the issue of Iraq that also served as a catalyst for both the GCC and the EU to look closer at the status of relations and to contemplate over how to overcome the stalled momentum that has typically characterized relations in the past. With the opening of a European Commission Office in Riyadh, the release of the "EU Strategic Partnership with the Mediterranean and the Middle East" report in June 2004 and indications that the long-awaited Free Trade Agreement would finally be concluded in 2005, it can in fact be argued that substantial progress has indeed been made in 2004 and that the GCC-EU relationship has carried forward some of the progress already achieved in 2003.[1]

A key year for the European Union

From an internal EU perspective, three key events defined the year 2004. First, with the accession of 10 new member states on May 1, 2004, the EU created a single market of over 450 million people producing a quarter of the world's GDP (€8,800 billion), solidified its position as the world's largest trading bloc and underlined its role as a positive force in world politics. The EU now spends more than €500 million a month in assistance projects throughout the globe, a figure that is unmatched. The expansion of the EU will not only mean that the trade volume with the GCC is bound to increase

---

[1] See the chapter on "GCC-EU Relations" by Giacomo Luciani in the previous *Gulf in a Year 2003* report (Dubai: Gulf Research Center, 2004), pp. 258-264.

further, building on top of the annual increase occurring with the old EU-15 states, but also that the GCC countries as a whole will be drawn into closer association with the EU member states due to the increased contact at various levels and the fact that previous bilateral relationships with the new 10 EU members will now also be conducted through a multilateral framework. Mutual trade volumes had reached a value of over 56 billion in 2003, a figure that is likely to touch on 60 billion through the end of 2004.

The second key event was the signing in Rome by all the 25 EU states and the 3 candidate countries (Bulgaria, Croatia and Romania) of the European Constitution on October 29, 2004. The constitution will still have to go through a lengthy ratification process in all the member states before going actually into force, including the fact that a single no from any member state would scuttle the process. Yet the signing ceremony itself was evidence of a continued movement towards a "One Europe" from monetary union through enlargement towards constitutionally. If the constitution is ratified by the end of 2006, the EU would then have one EU Foreign Minister supported by an integrated EU foreign service. In the words of one commentator this, in turn, could then "mark the coming of age of a more assertive and self-confident Europe."[2]

Finally, the prospect of a common border between the Gulf and the EU was made more realistic by the decision of the EU Council of Ministers on December 16, 2004 to begin accession talks with Turkey beginning in October 2005. With the possibility of Turkish membership, the broadening of the EU's Middle Eastern geopolitical perspective is bound to become even more necessary.[3] And while actual Turkish membership is still at least over a decade away, the fact that actual accession negotiations will now begin in 2005 means that Middle Eastern and also Gulf issues will become

Table (1) Evolution of inter-regional GCC-EU Trade 2001-2003 (in billion Euros)

		EU15			EU25		
		2001	2002	2003	2001	2002	2003
Bahrain	Imports	0.521	0.385	0.345	0.525	0.385	0.346
	Exports	0.932	0.933	0.942	0.941	0.943	0.955
Kuwait	Imports	2.38	1.809	1.927	2.384	1.812	1.93
	Exports	2.747	2.91	3.067	2.791	2.953	3.128
Oman	Imports	0.283	0.434	0.236	0.285	0.435	0.238
	Exports	1.441	1.367	1.278	1.454	1.387	1.295
Qatar	Imports	0.668	0.46	0.849	0.669	0.461	0.85
	Exports	1.935	1.891	2.199	1.943	1.906	2.215
Saudi Arabia	Imports	13.13	12.35	12.948	13.159	12.383	12.997
	Exports	13.229	14.007	13.346	13.418	14.258	13.568
UAE	Imports	2.798	2.829	3.797	2.852	2.907	3.91
	Exports	13.779	14.189	15.703	14.082	14.675	16.467
Total GCC	Imports	19.311	18.27	20.1	19.87	18.38	20.27
	Exports	34.06	35.3	36.54	34.63	36.12	37.63

Source: Eurostat, Official Statistics of the European Commission

[2] Abdullah Baabood, 'The outlook for GCC-EU relations under the new Commission," GRC Research Bulletin, GCC-EU Research Program, Issue 1, March 2005 available under www.grc.ae

[3] Roberto Aliboni, "An Italian Perspective on Future EU-GCC Relations," GRC Research Bulletin, GCC-EU Research Program, Issue 1, March 2005, op.cit.

part of the regular agenda for the EU and its member states. From these three perspectives then, the GCC and the EU have in 2004 inevitably moved closer to one another.

Broadening the Dialogue

Driven by internal EU developments but also due to the regional dynamics in the Gulf region, the most significant development in the GCC-EU relationship during 2004 was the injection of a degree of political priority to boost further cooperation. With the Gulf and Middle East region dominating headlines as a result of the events in Iraq, the most critical component was the growing realization within both European and Gulf circles that a further deterioration in security and stability in the Gulf region is detrimental to both sides. To avoid such a pitfall, there is a need for a more collaborative and substantive relationship between the two organizations.

From the GCC perspective, there was the growing realization throughout the year that the continued sole reliance on the United States as the guarantor for stability and security in the region was proving increasingly inadequate. The US failure to even modestly handle the reconstruction process in Iraq, including its complete unwillingness to consider shortcomings in its policy approach to the country, led some in the region to suggest alternative paths including a greater degree of convergence with European partners. The statement by Saudi Arabia's Foreign Minister Saud al-Faisal in December 2004 that "security in the Gulf needs international guarantees which cannot be ensured by a singly party, even by the sole superpower" should be seen in this context.[4] In addition, the announcement of the US Middle East Partnership Initiative in December 2002 followed by the "Partnership for Progress and a Common Future' for the broader Middle East and North Africa presented at the G-8 summit in June 2004, coupled with the almost universal rejection of these initiatives from within the Arab world, have led the GCC states to look for other avenues in terms of domestic political reform than the forceful US approach. As a result, while acknowledging that reform is necessary and fundamental, the GCC states are increasingly looking to the EU as an example to follow on this issue.

On the EU side, there was also an increasing awareness that the deteriorating security environment in the Gulf did carry with it consequences for the security situation in Europe proper and that therefore a closer engagement with the region was not only necessary but desirable. More than anything else the terrorist attack in Madrid in March 2004 drove this point home. In terms of a response, the EU took a number of key steps including the opening of an European Commission delegation office in January 2004 in Riyadh. This was followed by a more ambitious attempt to integrate the GCC component into a broader framework of an "EU Strategic Partnership with the Mediterranean and the Middle East," of which the final report was issued on June 23, 2004.[5] The

> **The most critical component was the growing realization within both European and Gulf circles that a further deterioration in security and stability in the Gulf region is detrimental to both sides.**

---

[4] See "Gulf States seek greater independence from U.S.," *Agence France Press*, December 9, 2004.

[5] Euromed Report, "EU Strategic Partnership with the Mediterranean and the Middle East: Final Report," Issue No. 78, June 23, 2004.

Strategic Partnership concept initially grew out of an idea put forward by France and Germany and can be characterized as the European response to the US reform plans. The idea of this initiative was to have a complementary yet distinct approach to the overall reform impetus towards the region, an approach that would build on the already established political relationship and the existing institutional framework.[6] What cannot be denied however is the fact that the US call for democracy and reform in the Middle East has acted as a wake-up call for the EU to come up and devise its own program.[7]

The Strategic Partnership concept builds on the contractual relationship that has already served as basis for dialogue even on political and security issues. In that context and as far as the EU is concerned, a dialogue with the GCC is the most promising one in terms of its engagement with the Middle East. Unlike the countries of the Euro-Mediterranean Partnership or the Arab League, the GCC is a relatively unified block in terms of political systems, economic development and social and religious background[8]. Similarly, as far as the GCC is concerned, expanding the partnership with the EU has the advantage of allowing for an alternative approach to that of the US. In that context, the GCC shares with the EU common views on core issues which make it not only a commercial partner but also a political one.

That these are no longer just ideas was made clear

in the Strategic Partnership document where the "EU commits itself to advance its partnership with the countries of the Gulf" including considering bilateral political initiatives with those GCC members that display a desire to move forward more rapidly. Specific aspects to be achieved include the intensification of a dialogue under the relevant political instruments of the GCC, the establishment of a framework for dialogue and confidence-building at the regional level, the conclusion and implementation of the Free Trade Agreement, feasibility studies of technical assistance programs in terms of the restructuring the administrative frameworks in the Gulf, and, finally, youth exchange and university cooperation programs.[9]

How such statements can be turned into concrete policy approaches was made clear by the action of the EU-3 (France, Germany and Great Britain) and its dealings with Iran over that country's nuclear program. As far as the GCC states are concerned, an Iranian military nuclear program is considered unacceptable as it will likely bring about an arms race in the region that only further increases the region's insecurity. Equally, however, a US military strike to prevent an Iranian nuclear program coming online is also objectionable as it would leave GCC states vulnerable to Iranian retaliation. Therefore, a third option is required, an option that was presented through the EU initiative to undertake a negotiation strategy with the Iranians. In the end, a compromise was brought about whereby Iran

[6] Bernard El-Ghoul, "Towards a New Political Partnership between the EU and the GCC: The Challenges of the new European Commission," GRC Research Bulletin, GCC-EU Research Program, Issue 1, March 2005, op.cit.
[7] Gonzalo Escribano-Francés, "An International Political Economy View of EU-GCC Partnership," Paper presented at the "International Conference on Challenges of Economic Development for the GCC Countries," Kuwait City, January 29-31, 2005 organized by the Kuwait Institute for Scientific Research (KISR) and sponsored by the World Bank.
[8] El-Ghoul, op.cit.
[9] See Euromed Report, "EU Strategic Partnership with the Mediterranean

and the Middle East: Final Report," op.cit., pp. 8-12. In addition to such official statements, the call for concrete initiatives was voiced at numerous meetings throughout the year. See, for example, the conference report "Arab Reforms and the challenges for EU policies," Heidi Huuhtanen, Philip Holzapfel, Bente Scheller and Toby Archer, The Finish Institute of International Affairs, September 16-17, 2004, available under www.upi-fiia.fi and the conference summary of a workshop entitled "A Window of Opportunity: Europe, Gulf Security and the Aftermath of the Iraq War," organized by the Gulf Research Center, the Bertelsmann Foundation and the Center for Applied Policy Reseach, Dubai, November 23-25, 2004, available under www.grc.ae

agreed to suspend its uranium enrichment activities in exchange for EU incentives in trade, security and technology. While skepticism remains on whether Iran will eventually stick to the agreement, the EU approach nevertheless provided an alternative that at least for the moment prevented a greater crisis from developing in the region. It is from this perspective that the GCC states have also favored a greater in-volvement by the EU or even NATO in Iraq as a means to foster a more stable political transition process in that country. With security in the Gulf remaining fragile, broader discussion between the GCC and the EU on such issues are likely throughout 2005.

With the coming into force of the GCC Customs Unions in January 2003, the key obstacle towards the signing of the FTA had been removed and as such negotiations began to focus on the more specific outstanding issues.

Solidifying Institutional Ties

In the meantime, the broadening of the dialogue between the GCC and the EU has also been accompanied by a solidifying process in terms of already existing institutional ties. Much of 2004 continued to be dominated by the status of the long awaited Free Trade Agreement (FTA). With the coming into force of the GCC Customs Unions in January 2003, the key obstacle towards the signing of the FTA had been removed and as such negotiations began to focus on the more specific outstanding issues. On April 19, 2004, discussions led to progress on central regulatory issues. EU officials subsequently indicated that an agreement on the FTA could be reached fairly quickly.[10]

Similarly, Kuwait's Foreign Minister Shaikh Mohammad al-Sabah indicated in early May 2004 that an agreement had been reached on a "mechanism to resolve all outstanding issues."[11]

The subsequent joint council meeting in May then agreed to "incorporate in the FTA agreement clauses on human rights and migration" a key element of the EU strategy to include such issues within the ne-gotiations. While the GCC had been re-sisting such demand, it relented after being assured that the GCC states were not being targeted and singled out by such an inclusion. Shaikh Mohammad of Kuwait subsequently stated: "They assured us that we are not targeted by such demands and that such issues are under discussion with all other countries … I believe that we have no differences with the EU on such issues as terrorism, human rights and weapons of mass destruction … so we are in full agreement with them on these matters … we only told them that such issues should not be part of the trade agreement and we have already reached a formula on this."[12] As such, a further two rounds of negotiations took place in June and July with the result that most issues were resolved, particularly Saudi Arabia's removal of its double pricing system on gas in return for the EU's commitment to eventually remove its duties on aluminium and petrochemical products. As a result, the path appears clear for a conclusion to the negotiations in 2005.

Apart from the discussions over the FTA, and as already mentioned, the GCC and the EU held their 14th Joint Council and Ministerial Meeting in

---

[10] "EU optimistic about GCC free trade accord," *Gulf News*, May 6, 2004.

[11] "Kuwait sees free trade accord with EU this year," *Gulf News*, May 3, 2004.

[12] Ibid.

Brussels on May 17, 2004. It continues to be significant that as has been the practise in the past, the meeting was attended by respective high-level delegations from both sides including Brian Cowen, the Foreign Minister of Ireland in his capacity as the EU's President, Javier Solana as the EU's Chief Representative for Foreign and Security Policy and Chris Patten as the Commissioner responsible for External Affairs. From the GCC side, the Foreign Minister of Kuwait, Shaikh Mohammad al-Sabah, as the rotating President of the GCC council and the GCC Secretary-General, Abdulrahman Hamad Al-Attiyyah, led the delegation.

In the communiqué issued at the end of the meeting, it was once again emphasized that "trade, energy and economic cooperation constituted the critical domains on which to further develop and enhance EU-GCC economic and political relations."[13] By 2003, the GCC-EU trade volume has gone beyond 55 billion composed of about two-thirds GCC imports as compared to one-third EU imports. The GCC is the EU's fourth largest export market while the GCC serves as the fourteenth largest source of imports for the EU. As a result, economic ties remain central, an emphasis made clear by the determination to promote greater institutional ties on the economic front. Following the first meeting of the GCC-EU Economic Dialogue in November 2003, 2004 saw the 7th meeting of the Energy Experts Group in Brussels in February and the second session of the Economic Dialogue in October also in Brussels.

Yet, as evident by the discussion above, it was also stressed that there existed "shared political will to further relations and cooperation beyond trade and economic issues."[14] The chances for this to be actually translated into something concrete are assisted by the fact that broad agreements exist between the GCC and the EU on key regional issues including the EU support for the initiative of the Saudi Crown Prince Abdullah with regard to the Arab-Israeli conflict and the commitment of both sides to the principles of the roadmap process, on Iran's nuclear program and on the security situation in Iraq. All of these issues were confirmed in the Joint Council Communiqué. Furthermore, without a significant shift of the US regarding any of the issues, it is likely that both the GCC and the EU will continue their efforts to establish common positions and coordinate their policy approaches.

Prospective Outlook

In terms of the way forward, Luxembourg's Deputy Prime Minister and Minister of Foreign Affairs and Immigration Jean Asselborn has already listed the elections in Iraq and the continuing negotiations with Iran as key priorities for the Luxembourg presidency of the EU which runs until June 30, 2005. Similarly, the new EU Commission President José Manuel Barroso has emphasized the importance of the EU's neighborhood policy while the High Representative for the Common Foreign and Security Policy Javier Solana has specifically stated "that the EU is also keen to strengthen its relationship with several countries beyond its immediate neighborhood of the Southern Mediterranean particularly with respect to the countries around the Gulf."[15] Similar

[13] The 14th EU-GCC Joint Council and Ministerial Meeting, CE-GOLF 3502/04, Joint Communiqué, Brussels, May 17, 2004.

[14] Ibid.

[15] See José Manuel Barroso, "The European Union and the Emerging World Order: Perceptions and Strategies," Speech at the 7th European Community Studies Association World Conference, Brussels, November 30, 2004 available under http://europa.eu.int/comm/external_relations/news/barroso/. See also Intervention by Javier Solana, EU High representative for CFSP at the Forum for the Future, Rabat, Morocco, December 11, 2004, available under http://ue.eu.int/solana

pronouncement has also been made from the GCC side.

The year 2005 will prove whether such statements continue to be mere rhetoric or whether they actually represent a shift in attitude and commitment. To be sure, there continue to be a number of obstacles including the prevailing US-EU differences on the Middle East, the significant trade volume asymmetries, as well as the lack of a strong GCC institution that can speak authoritatively on behalf of the six GCC members. Much of the progress in fact will be contingent on bilateral initiatives, not necessarily between individual EU and GCC states but also between the EU and single GCC member states. Here, it should be mentioned that alongside the developing GCC-EU relationship, there were numerous bi-lateral initiatives that were acted upon throughout 2004, for example, the close cooperation between Germany and the UAE in terms of training Iraqi security forces just to mention one example. Such programs will undoubtedly continue and they will be important for the overall status of Gulf-Europe relations. However, if coupled with substantive progress on overall GCC-EU relations, the impact will be all the more significant.

GCC-Japan Relations

Yoshiki Mickey Hatanaka

Director of the Middle East and Energy Program, International Development Center, Tokyo, Japan

This part of the Gulf Yearbook 2004 discerns and analyses the relations between the GCC States and Japan. It tackles some aspects of the political scene which affected relations in general, specifically the role of Japan in Iraqi developments and the issue of Japanese troops as part of the US-led coalition. Since Japan depends on the Gulf region as a main source of its energy needs, the issue of energy security is a key determinant of Japanese policy towards the region. In that context, some of the other related economic developments will also be discussed.

The Political Scene

The consequences of the Iraq war, especially the impact on oil and the spread of terrorism, shaped the Japanese's policy towards the region during the year 2004. Starting on January 9, 2004, a contingent of troops from Japan's Ground Self-Defense Forces (GSDF) was ordered to leave for Iraq. Although the Japanese government officially claims that the GSDF is not an army, the GSDF has similar characteristics associated with armies in other countries. Therefore, it is hard to substantiate that most of the people who welcomed them in Iraq interpreted their character in the way that the Japanese government does. Although the forces were initially sent to stay for a year, the Japanese cabinet decided on December 9, 2004 to extend their humanitarian mission to Iraq beyond the initial December 14 deadline for another year.

Following the decision to send its troops to Iraq, the Japanese role as part of the coalition forces administering the country was highlighted in the world media. However, most of these news reports about Japan's involvement were fragmented in nature therefore allowing few people to get a comprehensive idea about what the Japanese actions was all about. The situation was exacerbated when Japanese citizens began to be taken as hostages in Iraq thus indicating that there was a direct cost to bear.[1] In essence, Japanese policy can be categorized into four groups: (1) its obligation as a member of the international community (2) its overt support for the US (3) the actual dispatch of its forces and (4) the legislative arrangements that had to be made in terms of its own security policy. As a result, Japanese-Gulf relations have undergone a tremendous shift although this is an unintended consequence as far as Japan's security policy is concerned.

Due to the fact that Japan, even after its economic

[1] A group led by al-Qaeda ally Abu Musab al-Zarqawi showed the beheading of Japanese hostage Shosei Koda in Iraq while he was lying on top of a US flag in an Internet video. The al-Qaeda Organization of Holy War in Iraq said that Tokyo had offered a ransom of "millions of dollars" for the hostage. It warned Japan to withdraw its forces from Iraq or "drown in the hell of the mujahideen" along with "crusader forces." Japanese officials confirmed that the body and severed head of a man found in the Iraqi capital of Baghdad was that of Koda. Zarqawi's group had given Tokyo a 48-hour deadline to save Koda by withdrawing its forces from Iraq, a demand which the Japanese government refused.

recession in the 1990s, still retains influential economic power and has a deep relationship with the GCC countries, which is centered on oil and gas, it is necessary to place the intentions of the Japanese government in their proper context. In fact, the economic aspect of security policy has played an important role, not only in terms of energy security but also, for example, in the form of Official Development Assistance (ODA), particularly technology cooperation such as vocational training. The Japanese government has a clear and comprehensive vision that reconstructed independent and democratic Iraq in the future will eventually play a vital role in stabilizing the region as a whole. As such, Japan has been consistent in giving assistance and participating in reconstruction activities in Iraq.

Meanwhile the military aspects of Japan's security develop its own parameters during this period.[2] For example, prior to the war, Japan was urged in a joint seminar with the GCC States to play a larger role in the maintenance of the security in the region in particular in light of the threat perceived from Iran and Iraq by the GCC states.[3] The threats were of course a more serious security problem for the GCC states than for Japan despite the fact that Japan continues to depend heavily on oil from the region. Yet, among the GCC states, only Kuwait was among the initial 49 members of the 'coalition' on the US side.[4] Taking into account the domestic and international factors that made the GCC states reluctant to overtly support the US, the reasons for the Japanese government to support the actions of the US must also be looked at more closely. In addition, simply to say that the US enjoys a heavy influence on

both the Gulf region and Japan would appear as insufficient. This is because despite having a common ally, the potential for a greater disagreement between Japan and the GCC states on critical issues exists.

Here, it is important to make a distinction. While most Japanese consider the assistance provided by the self-defense forces in Iraq as limited to civil work, most people in the region perceive the Japanese action in terms of military role, including as being part of a Japanese military assistance project. This stands in contrast to the fact that GCC-Japan relations in the past have been defined by the unique inability of Japan to provide any military support including arms sales.[5] Therefore, it is natural for some to interpret Japan's decision as part of a new movement towards a greater serious commitment to the security on the region. This possibility cannot be completely denied, although at this stage it has not materialized further.

Energy Security and Economic Relations

The Japanese version of the Diplomatic Blue Book 2004 mentions energy security as one of the key reasons for the Japanese position towards the Iraqi issue. It states that for a country which depends on its oil supply from the Middle East, the stability and reconstruction of Iraq is considered essential for the energy security and overall prosperity of Japan.[6]

More than 90 per cent of Japan's energy requirements are met through imports, conventional oil being a major component. At present, Japan

---

[2] There have been a number of opposition moves in Japan against the initiative of the government during the period concerned. For example, the then Japanese Ambassador to Lebanon sent two official telegrams to Tokyo in March 2003 presenting his opposition to Tokyo's position on the Iraq War. Opposition has also been expressed, for example, in the Diet as well as in the form of social movements.

[3] This was reported by the MOFAJ in its summary and assessment of the second GCC Security Seminar held on March 4-5, 2003. See the web-

site of MOFAJ.

[4] See the website of the White House.

[5] See Sonoko Sunayama, *GCC- Japan Relations* (Dubai: Gulf Research Center, 2003), pp. 22-29.

[6] On the Energy Security of the Japanese government, see the Japanese Agency for Natural Resources and Energy, Ministry of Economy, Trade and Industry (2003).

imports almost 100% of its crude oil, nearly 88% of which comes from the Gulf region.[7] Because of a combination of rising oil prices and regional risk, Japan's crude oil imports fell 20.9 percent in June 2004 from a year earlier to 108.31 million barrels, marking a ninth consecutive month of decline. Imports from the Gulf accounted for 88.6 percent of the total, up 3.6 percentage points from a year earlier. The United Arab Emirates remained Japan's largest oil supplier, though imports from the country declined 22.2 percent to 24.34 million barrels. Saudi Arabia was the second top supplier with 24.28 million barrels, down 9.3 percent. Iran remained in third place with 16.61 million barrels, down 16 percent, followed by Kuwait with 11.45 million barrels, up 56.8 percent, and Qatar with 10.63 million barrels, down 28.9 percent.[8]

Outside of oil, the economic relationship between Japan and the GCC also continues to improve. In Qatar, Japan has consolidated its position in gas production. Japan first began negotiations to import liquefied natural gas (LNG) from Doha in the middle of 1980s which eventually led to the decision in 1991 to import Qatari LNG. In 1996, Tokyo went ahead and sealed a 20-year deal to import Qatari gas, the first country to do so, for six million tonnes of LNG a year. Currently, nine Japanese companies, including the Chubu Electric Power Company, are importing LNG from Doha and Qatar is the fourth largest exporter of natural gas to Tokyo after Indonesia, Malaysia and Australia.[9]

By comparison, Kuwait has re-consolidated its relationships with Japan after the ouster of the Saddam's regime and both sides have agreed to promote bilateral ties and cooperate in Iraq's rebuilding and the Middle East peace process. Kuwait has been at the forefront in supporting the Japanese decision to dispatch its self-defense forces to Iraq. In terms of their bilateral relationship, Japan and Kuwait agreed to carry out more effective and efficient cooperation in economic and environmental areas. Japan, for example, is going to provide assistance in environmental conservation, especially the pollution of Kuwait Bay.[10] Economic projects are also proceeding in the other GCC States. In Saudi Arabia, Japan has been one of the top investing countries in the Jubail development project with total investments amounting to SR57.61 billion.[11] In Oman, where the Toyota Motor Corp. has already completed a nation-wide state-of-the-art service networks, Nissan has recently re-emerged as a competitor starting its own service centre in Nizwa, the commercial center of Oman's interior.[12] In Bahrain, Batelco has signed a new bi-lateral commercial roaming agreement with Japanese telecoms giant, NTT DoCoMo, Inc., enabling Batelco mobile users to make and receive calls while traveling in the East Asia.[13] Finally, the United Arab Emirates remains the

> **for a country which depends on its oil supply from the Middle East, the stability and reconstruction of Iraq is considered essential for the energy security and overall prosperity of Japan.**

[7] Policy Planning Division, Natural Resources and Fuel Department, Japanese Agency of Natural Resources and Energy, Ministry of Economy, Trade and Industry (2004). Japan and China are already among the largest energy consumers after the United States. This explains why Saudi Aramco does almost half of its business in Asia and has more offices there than anywhere else in the world. Saudi Arabia considers Asia a strategic market with growth potential that will only increase over time. Recently, the Saudi government concluded a deal with Shell to acquire an interest in Showa Shell, a large Japanese refining company.

[8] *The Japan Times*, July 31, 2004.

[9] The amount of LNG imported from Australia and Qatar are almost equal. See *The Peninsula*, November 3, 2004.

[10] *Kuwait News Agency*, November 26, 2004.

[11] *Arab News*, November 5, 2004.

[12] *Times of Oman*, November 29, 2004.

[13] *Bahrain Tribune* , December 4, 2004.

largest partner to Japan in the region being the largest oil supplier to Japan as well as the largest importer of Japanese goods in the region.

Conclusion

The third Gulf War and its ramifications had major effects on Japan's policy towards the Gulf region. Japan supported the US-led invasion of Iraq and has supplied troops to carry out civil and humanitarian tasks. Regardless of the dispute about the real nature of those forces, this development represents the beginning of shift in Japanese legislation when it comes to issues of internal security. It is also part of an overall interest on behalf of Japan to take on a clearer role in the Gulf region. With energy security and overall economic relations bound to take on an increased importance, bilateral relations will likely see a continuous improvement in the coming years.

GCC-China Relations

Li Guofu

Director of the Department of South Asian, Middle Eastern and African Studies, China Institute of International Studies

2004 can be identified as a significant year for China's relation with Arab countries in general and the Gulf Cooperation Council (GCC) countries in particular. At the beginning of 2004, during Chinese President Hu Jingtiao's first state visit to Egypt, Chinese Foreign Minister Li Zaoxing along with Arab League Secretary-General Amr Moosa officially launched the China and Arab Cooperation Forum. Both sides also promised to double their efforts to strengthen the long-time friendship between the two countries. This was followed in early July by the visit of the six financial ministers of the GCC countries and its Secretary-General to China. A few days later, Kuwaiti Prime Minister Shaikh Sabah Al-Ahmad Al-Sabah came to China on an official visit. During each of these stays, Chinese Prime Minister Wen Jiabao and numerous other officials held talks with the visitors from the Gulf on how to broaden the fields and scopes of cooperation between the two sides. As a number of agreements were signed, it can be argued that relations have taken on a higher qualitative dimension. Finally in September, Chinese Foreign Minister Li Zaoxing made a trip to the GCC countries. The frequent exchange of high level visits between China and the GCC countries has not only further strengthened political and economical relations between two sides, but also has laid the solid foundation for the cooperation in the future.

China's relations with GCC countries in the past and at present

China's relationship with the GCC countries can be traced back to ancient times. The famous sea route from China to the Arabian Peninsula was regarded as the second "Silk Road", through which the Chinese and Arabic people exchanged ideas, commodities and learned from each other. The relationship entered into a new stage after the founding of the People's Republic of China in 1949 with China supporting the Gulf States in their quest for independence. While official ties between China and the individual Gulf States were not established until later, China was among the earliest countries to recognize the Gulf Cooperation

Council. On May 27th, 1981, two days after the founding of GCC, Chinese foreign minister Huang Hua sent a congratulatory message to GCC Secretary General Abdullah Bishara. In July 1990, official diplomatic relations were established with Saudi Arabia.

Since that period, China and the GCC countries have attached increased importance in developing their relations. Despite differences in their political systems and cultural and religious background, both sides have observed the principles of mutual respect, mutual benefits and non-interference in each other's internal affairs. As a result, China has firmly supported the GCC policy of unity, consolidation and development among its members as well as appreciating the role played by the GCC countries in pushing forward the Middle East peace process, enhancing the unity of the Arab world, safeguarding peace and stability in the Gulf area and promoting regional economic cooperation. GCC countries meanwhile have been a staunch supporter of China's "one China policy."

The frequent exchange of high level visits has helped the leaders to build a closer personal friendship and better understanding. Since China established diplomatic relations with the GCC countries, Chinese Presidents, Prime Ministers and other senior leaders have made good-will visits to all the GCC countries, and in return, all the leaders of the GCC countries have visited China. Through such visits, leaders of both sides have gotten to know each other, exchanged views on the major international issues and discussed ways for concerted efforts to cope with problematic issues. The relationship entered into a new stage in 1998 when, for the first time, the GCC Foreign Ministers Council during the 66th meeting adopted a resolution calling for strengthening the relationship with China. One year later in October 1999, Chinese President Jiang Zemin, during his state visit to the Kingdom of Saudi Arabia, held talks with

GCC Secretary-General Jamal Hujailan.

The result has been the implementation of a number of mechanisms through which a regular exchange of views has become possible. Since 1990, Chinese foreign ministers have held annual meetings with their counterparts in the GCC countries. In 1996, China and the GCC decided to establish a permanent dialogue on economic issues as a means to enhance bilateral economical cooperation. This resulted in the signing of agreements like "the Economic and Trade Agreement" and "the Accord of Investment Protection." Moreover, high level joint economic and trade committees have been set up.

Bilateral trade and economic relations started to pick up rapidly in the 1990s leading to a ten-fold increase in trade volume between the period of 1991 and 2001. While in 1991, the total amount of trade was about $1.5 billion, by 2002 that figure had increased to $11.57 billion with Chinese exports of $5.55 billion and imports of $6.02 billion. In the period from 1998 to 2002 alone, the annual growth rate of bilateral trade averaged 28%. In 2004, China's trade with the GCC countries amounted to $17 billion, a further increase of 46 per cent from 2002. The major products China exports to the GCC countries include mechanical and electrical products, clothing, textile, shoes, and the daily necessities. In terms of imports, China imports include oil and oil related products. At present, the GCC countries are China's eighth largest trade partner, eighth largest export destination and ninth largest import source worldwide. About 65.2% of the trade of all 22 Arab countries, according to Chinese statistics, comes from the GCC States.

The driving elements for closer relations

The rapidly evolving relationship is due to a number of factors including mutual benefits for both sides and a rapidly changing world situation. More than anything else, the fast expansion of globalization and advancement of high technology has provided China and the GCC countries with both opportunities and challenges. In particular as far as China is concerned, it has made tremendous strides in terms of its policy of reform and opening up to the outside world with the result that the Chinese strategy for development, known as "the Chinese Model", has become a model for others to follow especially among developing countries.

Within the GCC states as well, the continued instability of the past decades and the reverberations of the events following September 11, 2001 have made the region more open to broadening their relations. While the Gulf continues to rely on the United States to provide them with security, the reliance on the US is increasingly being questioned, leading to efforts to strengthen relations with countries such as India and those of ASEAN, in particular China. China, as the permanent member of the UN Security Council, has been very much concerned about the situation in Iraq and has shared the worries of GCC countries. Both for example believe that the United Nations should play a leading role in the political arrangement and economic reconstruction of Iraq; that Iraqi territorial integrity should be respected and preserved; that the future government in Iraq should be based upon broad representation of all segments of society; and that the foreign occupation should end as soon as possible. In that context, China would like to work closely with the GCC countries on the Iraqi issue as well as expand the cooperation on the issues of anti-terrorism and security.

China of course also wants to establish a stable relationship in the energy area as oil has become increasingly important for China's future economic development. In 2002, China imported about 20 million tons of oil from the GCC countries, excluding Iran, which accounted for 30% of the total imported oil. According to China's strategy for development, China will make efforts to achieve an annual growth rate of 7-8% within next two decades. This would mean that China's oil consumption would have to increase at a rate of 5.7% annually if targets set for 2020 are to be met. While China has worked hard to economize its use of oil, the trend of increasing demand is set to continue. As such, the uninterrupted flow of oil at reasonable prices will be very crucial for China's sustained economic development strategy. The Gulf region here is a major element in terms of providing oil to China in the future.

Besides energy cooperation, China would also like to broaden economic and trade relations with GCC countries. Although in recent years bilateral trade volume has grown rapidly, current figures are still small compared with each side's total trade volume. According to the official statistics, China's share of the Gulf market is less than 5 per cent of the region's trade volume. It should not be forgotten that China is a newcomer to the Gulf market. Chinese garments, fabrics, electronic and telecommunication facilities on the one hand and the GCC countries' oil and natural gas and chemical products on the other represent those items that are of great demand on each side. Another important area of Chinese interest is the issue of investment where China is hoping to attract more GCC enterprises to invest in the country, especially in hydropower, energy, mining, transport and telecommunication.

the fast expansion of globalization and advancement of high technology has provided China and the GCC countries with both opportunities and challenges.

China-GCC relations in 2004

As stated from the outset, 2004 saw important visits taking place which proved instrumental in moving the interests as outlined above forward. In early July, at the invitation of the Chinese government, a delegation consisted of GCC Secretary-General Abdulrahman Al-Attiyah and all 6 GCC countries' financial minister visited China from July 4 to 7. The delegation coincided with the eight-day official visit to China by the Kuwaiti Prime Minister Sheikh Sabah Al-Ahmad Al-Sabah, as representative of the GCC rotating presidency. During their stay in China, Chinese Prime Minister Wen Jiabao, State Counsellor Tang Jiaxuan, and other Chinese senior officials held the discussions with both delegations on how to promote bilateral ties.

The Chinese Prime Minister praised the fruitful cooperation between China and Kuwait in such fields as energy, chemical industry and labor, as well as the increasing bilateral trade. He also thanked Kuwait for its one-China policy and expressed the hopes that the two countries would further strengthen cooperation in international affairs in the spirit of political mutual trust and equal treatment, in addition to expanding economic and trade cooperation. The Chinese Prime Minister reassured his counterpart that the Chinese government would always support Kuwait's just cause to safeguard independence, sovereignty and territorial integrity, and would make its own efforts to ease the tensions in the Gulf region. He cited the China-Arab States Cooperation Forum, set up in January of 2004 during Chinese President Hu Jintao's visit to the headquarters of the League of Arab States in Egypt, as an illustration of the Chinese government's attention to the development of its relations with Arab countries.

Wen stressed that it is the Chinese government's fixed policy to forge the overall development of its relations with the Gulf countries. He also hoped that both sides could reach an agreement on building a free trade area at an early possible date. China would push for the establishment of long-term, steady, and cooperative relations of mutual benefit between the two sides, hoping to continue bilateral high-level contacts, further strengthen their coordination and cooperation in international affairs and expand bilateral cooperation in various fields.

The Kuwaiti Prime Minister responded by praising the status of bilateral relations, stating that these enjoyed a sound development momentum and broad prospects. He said the two countries boast very good political relations, satisfactory economic and trade ties and good cooperation of mutual benefit in many fields such as oil and port construction. He said the Kuwaiti side hoped for the establishment of a partnership with China to strengthen bilateral cooperation also in the areas of politics and international affairs.

During the visits, China indicated that it would welcome the setting up of a GCC office in Beijing. Both sides also decided to establish a "free trade zone" in the GCC region through where Chinese products would be transported to the Middle East region and European countries. A framework agreement on economic co-operation in economy, trade, investment and technology was signed in which the two sides consented on establishing a joint committee to oversee the implementation of the agreement and other pacts or protocols signed on the basis of the agreement. To encourage and facilitate trade of commodities and services, the two sides agreed to launch talks on the establishment of a China-GCC free trade area (FTA) with the first round of talks to be held in China as soon as possible. The FTA will include tariff reductions and simplification for flows of goods and facilitation of mutual investments.

In a follow-up visit, Chinese Foreign Minister Li Zhaoxing went to the region on an official visit in September 2004 to discuss current developments and to monitor the progress of the economic and trade agreement signed earlier. In a meeting with GCC Secretary-General Abdulrahman Al-Attiyah, Li said China, as a reliable friend and cooperative partner of the Gulf countries, would strengthen bilateral coordination to benefit the people of both sides. China thus showed itself willing to develop friendly cooperation with the GCC in all relevant aspects.

Conclusion

Thanks for efforts made by both sides, the relationship between China and the GCC countries has entered a new era, with mutual high level visits taking place both politically and economically. China strongly believes that China's high technology and the GCC's rich funds are a good match that can benefit both sides. The establishment of a FTA, expected by the end of 2005 will further forge a more stable base for long-term cooperation and become a good example of South-South cooperation. It is also expected that bilateral trade will continue to dramatically increase over the coming five years as a result of the FTA. As such, the relationship between the two sides is strong and the prospects bright.

GCC-Russia Relations

Dr. Alexander Shumilin

Center for the Greater Middle East conflicts, Moscow, Russian Federation

During the year 2004, Russia steadily boosted its presence in the Gulf region. In brief, it can be stated 2004 was the year of "Russia's return to Iraq" following the end of the warfare there and the start of the normalization process and the year of further strengthening economic ties with Iran and Saudi Arabia as well as with some other countries in the region. As such, it can be argued that the year witnessed the rather successful implementation of Moscow's strategy towards the Gulf region, which is officially described as aiming "to raise the level of economic cooperation with local actors and to promote a political dialogue between Russia and the GCC states." This means that the Gulf is still an important political area for Russia that is increasingly complemented by growing economic activities. This is in line with Russia's development since the collapse of the USSR, where economic cooperation has been given greater priority over previous geopolitical and ideological determinants.

The year 2004 can also be seen as significant in relation to events concerning Iran and Iraq. One year after the official end of warfare in Iraq, it has become clear that Russian commercial companies will not suffer the expected losses and instead have been able to preserve some interests within the Iraqi economy. As for Iran, the nuclear crisis and the need for a diplomatic solution have brought about the possibility of a Russian mediation effort. For Russia, the current situation is an acceptable one, as its economic interests inside Iran are largely preserved and secured while its political role is on the rise. Russia has expressed and asserted its full political solidarity with the "European Troika" of Great Britain, France, Germany and is supportive of a process whereby Iran stops its program to produce nuclear weapons.

The frameworks of Russian-GCC ties

With the headquarters of the GCC located in Riyadh, the main task to develop contacts with officials is assumed by Russia's Ambassador in Saudi Arabia (currently Dr. Andrei Baklanov). Outside of this channel, another framework has been recently introduced - the regular meetings of the Russian Foreign Minister with the Secretary General of the GCC in New York during the course of UN General Assembly meeting in September/October every year.

There are also regular consultations between the foreign policy offices of Russia and the GCC states, the day-by-day affairs being handled by the diplomatic missions located in every GCC capital.

The declared political goal in the Gulf as far as Russia is concerned is the establishment of a system of collective security (SCS) which is seen by Moscow as ever more urgent in the wake of the overthrow of the Saddam Hussein regime in Iraq. This is not to suggest that Russia aspires to any kind of guardianship over the SCS members. However, due to Moscow's efforts to promote this idea, Iran and Yemen have shown a growing willingness to participate in a possible SCS.

The political agenda of Russia is driven to an increasing degree by Moscow's economic ambitions in the area. The economic interests can be listed as follows:

a) providing adequate conditions for Russian oil and oil-related construction and engineering companies to promote their business in the GCC states including setting up joint ventures and raising investments for oil sector development in Russia;

b) promoting Russia's presence in terms of defense contracts and military supplies;

c) preserving the presence of Russian companies in Iran - especially those related to the Russian Nuclear Energy Ministry but operating in Iran;

d) in general further develop trade and economic ties.

The major Russian economic operators currently active in the area include the oil company Lukoil (in Iraq and Saudi Arabia), the construction company Stroytransgaz (Iraq, Iran and Saudi Arabia), the state-owned military sales company Rosoboronexport as well as a number of companies affiliated to the Nuclear Energy Ministry in Moscow.

> **Russian President Vladimir Putin ... has actively encouraged the maintenance and expansion of strong economic relations with both Iran and Iraq.**

Yet even within this increased importance placed on economic relationships, Iran and Iraq have remained the main focus for Moscow. This is because Russia has long-standing and impressive economic ties with these two states, a situation that Russia is not about to sacrifice because of external pressures and wide-ranging instability. Of particular relevance has been the personal role played by Russian President Vladimir Putin, who has actively encouraged the maintenance and expansion of strong economic relations with both Iran and Iraq.

Russia-Iraq: Political recognition vs. oil contracts

Following the handover from the US provisional authority to the Iraqi interim government in June 2004, Moscow extended recognition to the new Iraqi authority and declared its readiness to contribute to the normalization process in the country. This by itself marked a transition in Russia's approach to Iraqi affairs whereby the focus was placed on promoting constructive interaction with the new authorities in Iraq. President Putin did not conceal his hope that the new Baghdad government would share his concern over the role of Russian companies in Iraq and their corresponding interests. Putin made it clear that "the prevailing Russian interest in Iraq" were tied to the Lukoil company and the need to legalize the enormous exploration contract for the "West Kourna-2" wells signed in 1997. The contract calls for joint exploration on the basis of sharing production for a 23-year period including a $4 billion investment by Lukoil. It is worth mentioning that the Kourna-2 deal is regarded as the largest deal ever struck by a Russian company abroad.

The other landmark event in re-establishing Russian-Iraqi ties was the visit of Iraqi interim Prime Minister Allawi from December 6 - 7, 2004. Alawi's talks with Putin included political issues such as prospects of internal normalization in Iraq following the January 30, 2005 elections. This, in turn, meant the start of a political consultation process between Moscow and Baghdad and can be seen as a reward to Russia for its decision to write off 90% of the debts inherited by Baghdad from the Soviet years. The meeting in the Kremlin was attended by a "third" president, Vagit Alekperov of the Lukoil company. This was followed by a statement from the Vice-President of Lukoil Leonid Fedun on January 24, 2005 that Lukoil is prepared to proceed with the exploration works in Kourna-2 "the next day after the establishment of the legitimate Iraqi government."

Overall, it can be said that all the major problems in the relationship between Russia and Iraq have been settled in 2004 on the basis of a clear trade-off: political recognition by Moscow of the new Iraqi authorities and writing off 90% of previous debts for the re-legalization by Iraqi authorities of the Lukoil contract pertaining to the West Kourna-2 project.

Russia-Iran: Preservation of major contracts

The maintenance of the $1.5 billion contract for the Bushehr-1 nuclear station remained the number one priority for Russia with regard to Iran in 2004. This issue is seen in Moscow as the cornerstone for preserving and eventually extending Russia's presence in the Iranian economy as a whole. In that context, all of the involved Russian agencies have been mobilized to find "a complex and adequate solution" in order to avoid increased tensions with both the US and Israel.

One such "solution" was the role for Russia as "a unique and trusted mediator" between the European Troika and Iran. On the one hand, Moscow clearly expressed its concern over the prospects of Iran acquiring a nuclear military capacity and fully supported the IAEA inspections in Iran. On the other hand, Moscow vocally disagreed with Washington's insistence to quickly transfer the Iranian dossier to the UN Security Council and argued for Tehran to show greater cooperativeness toward the IAEA. This included President Putin's declaration on September 24 that "Iran does not need to acquire nuclear weapons" and that "Tehran has to meet the IAEA demands," issued shortly after the IAEA Director's meeting on September 13 that was highly critical of the Iranian position and the visit of Foreign Minister Lavrov to Iran on October 10-12 which resulted in the signing of the imported protocols obliging Iran to return the recycled uranium from the Bushehr station to Russia so that the spent fuel could not be diverted for other purposes. The aim here was to first alleviate Western concerns but also to delay discussions on the referral of Iran to the UN Security Council.

The effort was also recognized within Iranian circles as being effective in lowering tensions with the West. Tehran, for example, invited President Putin to visit Iran, with the exact dates to be confirmed later. In the end, this was precisely the outcome of the negotiations in November when Iran accepted most of the IAEA's demands but the file was kept away from the UN.

Russian companies successfully completed their commitments with regard to the Bushehr-1 plant and they further received an offer to participate in the Bushehr-2 construction project.

Relations between Russia and Saudi Arabia: A better understanding on Chechnya and counterterrorism

If the year 2003 marked a breakthrough in Russia-Saudi relations with Crown Prince Abdullah being the first Saudi ruler to visit Moscow in 70 years, 2004 witnessed the gradual implementation of some of the agreements that were signed during this visit. Among the key issues on the bilateral calendar were the situation in Chechnya, the stabilization of the oil market, coordination over countering terrorism and the participation of Russian Muslims in the annual hajj.

In January 2004, Chechen President Ah-mat Kadyrov visited the Kingdom accompanied by a large delegation of

> **Among the key issues on the bilateral calendar were the situation in Chechnya, the stabilization of the oil market, coordination over countering terrorism and the participation of Russian Muslims in the annual hajj.**

Chechen businessmen. The direct contact between the two sides certainly contributed to a better understanding of the respective positions. From a Saudi perspective, the fact that the kingdom was experiencing its own challenge from extremist terrorism may have led to a softening of views.

In that context, counterterrorist measures and strategies were the focal point of active political consultations between Riyadh and Moscow, a process that will culminate in the international conference on counter-terrorism to be held in Riyadh in early February 2005. Moscow is considering Riyadh as its main partner in promoting the signing of a protocol for political dialogue and cooperation between Russia and GCC countries in terrorism efforts. Moscow strongly believes that such a document, in addition to Russia's gradual involvement in the Organization of Islamic Conference (OIC) activities, will contribute to overcome the still existing dichotomy between Russia and the Gulf monarchies on the Chechnya issue.

On the issue of the oil market, consultations between the two sides went on throughout the year, although no agreements or specific mechanisms were agreed upon. On more practical terms,

Russian energy conglomerate Lukoil substantially extended its presence in the Kingdom after having won a tender on January 26. On March 7, Lukoil President Alekperov and Ali Al-Naimi, Minister of Petroleum and Mineral Resources of the Kingdom, signed an upstream agreement for exploration, development and production of non-associated gas and condensate in the Rub al-Khali for a 40 year period. A joint venture named "LUKOIL Saudi Arabia Energy Ltd. (LUKSAR) with Saudi Aramco was established to implement the project with Lukoil holding an 80 percent share. Thus, it is to be expected that Saudi-Russian relations especially on the energy side will continue to be close in 2005.

Finally, Russia substantially increased the number of Muslims going on the hajj with more than 12,000 pilgrim participants in January 2005. Moscow considers the hajj an important channel for further improving its relations with Riyadh.

Russia - Yemen relations: A return to traditions

In 2004, Yemen took the initiative to reactivate political and economic ties with Russia by stressing the long history of bilateral relations between the two states. The move by Yemen can be seen in the context of US pressure to cooperate on regional counter-terrorist measures and Yemeni fears that the country could become the next target of the US. The move towards Russia can therefore be seen as an attempt to find a protection cover. A Yemeni delegation headed by the President Ali Abdallah

Saleh visited Moscow in early April in which the talks centered on one topic - the regional impact of the American operation in Iraq. On the economic side, Yemen offered Russia a number of projects to operate within the free economic zone in Aden In return, Sergey Chemezov, the Director-General of the Rosoboronexport State Corporation visited Yemen in November 2004. Here, it should not be forgotten that the Yemeni army remains equipped with material stemming from Soviet times.

Russia - Smaller Gulf States Relations

Relations between Russia and the smaller GCC member states were largely quiet. In the UAE, the ties were most noticeable due to the large influx of Russian tourists to the Emirates. Russian-Qatari relations were focused to a large extent on the scandal provoked by the arrest in Doha of two Russian intelligence officers accused and sentenced to life for the assassination of former Chechen President Zelimkhan Yandarbiyev in Qatar in February 2004. The dispute was settled largely due to President Putin's intervention and his direct discussion with the Qatari ruler. In following, both officers were handed over to Russia in December 2004 on the provision that they would finish their jail terms in Russia. Overall, the matter did not have any lasting impact on broader Russian-Gulf relations. This was confirmed by the condolences for the Beslan tragedy expressed on September 23 to Russian Minister Lavrov by all his Gulf colleagues. The company Rosoboronexport also took part in 5th International Exhibition of special types of weapons held in October 2004 in Doha.

In general, US pressure on several Gulf States pushed those countries to look for alternative channels thus opening the door for consultations with Russia. Meanwhile, Moscow was increasingly aware of the chances that such opportunities presented themselves. It is to be expected that such a trend will continue in 2005.

Section Eight

Developments in Iraq, Iran and Yemen

Developments in Iraq

Dr. Mustafa Alani

Program Director, Security and Terrorism Studies, Gulf Research Center

The year 2004 began in what can be termed as the "New Iraq" era of violence and bloodshed. The first of January was marked by a car bomb explosion at a restaurant in the capital of Baghdad where people were celebrating, killing and wounding about 40. This was but one example of what would become an almost daily phenomenon in Iraq over the year. 2004 started with a bang less than eight months after the downfall of the Iraqi regime and the assumed end of the US war on Iraq. According to US predictions prior to the war, 2004 would be the year in which the beginnings of stability and prosperity would emerge in the country. It was asserted by many within the pro-war group of the Bush administration that no more than six to eight months would be needed to establish "stability" following the end of military operations.

The assumption, according to the war planners in Washington was that 2004 would witness the emergence of an "American Iraq" - a new Iraq which (as conceived by the American neoconservative right) would adopt American political and economic values and become a font of American wisdom for the Middle East region. Analysts agreed that developments over 2004 would be critical in determining the destiny of the Iraqi state and community and in determining the future of US policy not only in Iraq, but also throughout the whole Middle East.

But 2004 began and ended not with the emergence of the new stable and prosperous Iraq but with the downfall of the Bush administration's vision for the country. In its place came the collapse of state authority, the spread of crime, terrorism and the rule of lawlessness. The limited success of the Iraqi, American and international efforts to reconstruct the state has worsened the situation. Thus the hope of the hawks in the US administration to restructure the Middle East politically and strategically, through the imagined model of a successful and liberated Iraq has been dissipated.

The actions of the American occupation authorities throughout the year have vindicated the belief which became widespread shortly after the occupation that the Americans and their allies had fallen into a dangerous quagmire and that the Iraqi experiment has taken a wrong direction due to grave miscalculations on the part of the US. The war has not only led to the dismantling of the previous regime, but also to the dismembering of the state and its apparatus without there being convincing evidence that the occupation authorities are able to reconstruct the state or to impose political and economic stability.

Security

At the security level, the state has witnessed one of the most serious crises in its long history. It is a crisis of multiple dimensions in terms of the unprecedented violence that characterized it, the number of victims who have lost their lives as a result of these operations, and its temporal and geographic scope.

Examples from the events of this year all indicate the severity of the security vacuum in Iraq. April was among one of the bloodiest months for the occupation forces and for Iraqi citizens. During this 30 - day period no less than 130 American troops were killed, in addition to 1,014 wounded. No less than 700 Iraqi citizens were killed and 1,000 others wounded. Since April, the monthly average of attacks and violent operations has been close to 2,000, including the operations of actual assaults and attempted assaults or violent actions. The serious escalation of the number of operations, attempted assaults or sabotage are exemplified by the month of September, in which more than 2,300 assaults or attempted assaults were recorded.

Paradoxically, the beginning of the year also witnessed a rising number of personnel operating in the new Iraqi armed forces. The National Guard and the branches of police forces amount to 109,000 - the majority of which are Iraqi police forces (close to 67,000) while the National Guard forces number close to 20,000. The border guard forces are approximately the same number.

Despite the massive increase in armed security forces in Iraq, there was a large and noticeable increase in the number of people involved in resistance operations. According to estimates provided by the Brookings Institution in Washington, during January 2004, the number of those involved in resistance or terrorist operations was estimated at between 3,500 and 5,000 individuals. In July of the same year, the Brookings Institute estimates that the number of people who joined the resistance operations rose more than fourfold in comparison to the beginning of the year. The new figure was put at close to 20,000 fighters. At the end of the year, estimates pointed to more than 20,000 insurgents, 3,000 of whom are believed to be non-Iraqis. There was also an increase in the number of American troops from 122,000 in June to 138 thousand in September, coupled with 50 thousand American troops based in the states surrounding Iraq, in addition to 25 thousand multi-national forces.

Security disturbances this year have been marked by certain striking characteristics. Of particular note is the wide geographical expanse of the resistance and terrorist operations which affected most cities and provinces of the state. Large scale operations were executed in the Kurdish self-rule region, which had previously been one of the most stable Iraqi provinces. On the first of February, no less than 105 persons were killed in a simultaneous double-hit operation which took place during the first day of the Eid in the cities of Arbil and Sulaymaniyah. Although Baghdad and the western region of Iraq were the main centers of violence, other regions of the country were not fully stable throughout much of this year.

The targeting and assassination of Iraqi officials also intensified this year. The most high profile example was the murder of the President of the Iraqi Interim Governing Council, Mr. Izzedine Salim in April. There were also tens of successful or aborted assassination attempts targeting senior administration officials. These included a number of ministers and deputy ministers as well as mayors and governors of major Iraqi cities including the directors of official departments.

The wide ranging phenomenon of suicide operations and the fact that they have become a basic method used by armed groups in Iraq is the most striking security development in the country. The majority of violent acts in the country this year have been carried out through suicide attacks or car bombings. It is estimated that the number of suicide operations executed during the year against multinational forces, the interim Iraqi government and against the headquarters of political parties have exceeded 147 carried out or attempted operations, i.e. an average of close to one operation every week, killing 1,430 people and wounding 3,000.

The basic aim of targeting individuals and institutions from the Iraqi armed forces is clearly to de-mobilize the setting up of any local security or military establishment capable of assuming security responsibilities effectively.

This year was also characterized by the phenomenon of large-scale assaults against Iraqi police forces and the new National Guard. Throughout the year armed groups have carried out operations consistently targeting Iraqi police stations as well as volunteering and training centers for the national guards in a series of suicide operations, car bombs, and rocket attacks. These operations have claimed the lives of numerous victims from the new Iraqi armed forces, numbering close to 800 dead with thousands of injuries. This has partially paralyzed these newly formed units, limited their capacity and undermined the morale of their members. The month of October witnessed the largest collective killing of individuals from a military establishment, when 49 volunteers of the new National Guard were kidnapped and executed by an armed group. The basic aim of targeting individuals and institutions from the Iraqi armed forces is clearly to de-mobilize the setting up of any local security or military establishment capable of assuming security responsibilities effectively.

Despite the noticeable escalation of activity from armed groups throughout the country, the armed Iraqi resistance movement is still without any apparent political leadership. There is no political face to the militant groups to explain their political goals or to carry out negotiations for the purpose of realizing these goals or demands. This has made the possibility of solving the security crisis by diplomatic means highly unlikely.

The escalation of the armed resistance movement against the occupation forces and against the interim Iraqi government institutions has given rise to many criticisms being leveled at the right or legitimacy of other groups (that are allied with the US) to acquire weapons and have armed militias, for example amongst the Kurdish groups. Critics point out that there is little difference between these and the armed resistance groups operating in the Sunni areas of Iraq on the side of Al-Mahdi army, which is affiliated with the Shiite leader Muqtada Al-Sadr. Reacting to these criticisms, the Kurdish parties that are close to the Supreme Council of the Islamic Revolution in Iraq, which are the groups that officially and publicly have armed militias, announced an agreement in March which stipulates the disbanding of all their armed militias. These are the Kurdish Peshmerga forces as well as the Badr Brigade. This agreement was not effectively enforced. In July, the political leaders of the armed militias promised the American occupation authorities to dissolve these militias but did not respect their commitments.

Al-Sadr's Movement

In March 2004, observers witnessed one incident that sparked a large scale confrontation between Muqtada Al-Sadr's group, on the one hand and the American forces of occupation and the Iraqi interim government on the other. On March 28, the Iraqi authorities, supported by the occupation authorities, closed the newspaper "Al-Hawzah Al-Natiqah" - a daily newspaper that represented Al-Sadr's group - on grounds of instigating violence. This step followed a gradual escalation of tension between the two sides. The decision by the CPA to detain some Iraqi dignitaries connected with Al-Sadr aggravated the situation, prompting Al-Sadr to announce, on April 4, that it is the duty of his followers to resort to jihad in order to "terrorize the enemy". This call was followed by the beginning of a large-scale confrontation between the armed militias of Al-Sadr (Al-Mahdi Army) and the American and Iraqi forces. Al-Sadr's militias attempted to assume control of government institutions in many southern governorates. The latter developments prompted the American governor of Iraq, Paul Bremer, to brand Al-Sadr an outlaw and issue an order to arrest and detain him and a number of his followers. The operations carried out by Al-Mahdi's militias were a serious threat to the security of the American occupation forces and constituted a great challenge to the authority and prestige of the interim Iraqi government. Hence, putting an end to the confrontation expeditiously and at any price was supported by the majority of leaders within the interim government.

The rebellion and resistance scenario in Najaf was not different from its counterpart in Falluja, where the situation fluctuated between violent military confrontation and attempts to reach cease-fire agreements. But although several such agreements were reached together with agreements on withdrawal from cities, the majority of these were not honored.

The actual campaign to put an end to the rebellion of Al-Sadr's organization began during the first week of August. On the seventh of the month, the American forces, supported by some Iraqi National Guard units, clamped a strict siege on the cities of Najaf and Falluja. The campaign ended successfully in October, when an agreement was concluded between the leadership of Al-Sadr's organization under which their militias were dissolved and their weapons seized and they themselves were driven out of the center of the main cities in the south of Iraq and out of "Al Thawra City" (Sadr City) which is situated in the suburbs of Baghdad. This was followed by a weapons handover campaign in return for financial compensation.

Falluja

Although the western region of Iraq, particularly the cities of Falluja and Ramadi had been a traditional arena for resistance operations against the occupation forces during 2003, the events of March 23 of that year transformed Falluja into the center of US military operations. On that day, a group of individuals in the center of the city of Falluja killed and mutilated four American citizens who worked for a security company operating in Iraq. This caused great embarrassment for the American authorities, who demanded that the city's dignitaries and religious leaders hand over the perpetrators, failing which the city would be punished. When the leaders of the city refused to submit to US conditions, a strict siege was enforced as military operations started to liquidate the pockets of resistance there. Despite US efforts, the armed militiamen were able to strengthen their control of the city and its suburbs. Falluja was no longer under the control of the central government. In early February 2004, the American forces clamped a siege on Falluja as a prelude to beginning an assault against the city, which started on October 10. The city was re-occupied after a week of bloody fighting and immense destruction.

This situation was repeated in the city of Samurra where armed groups taking the center of the city as their base were able to wrench it from the control of the authorities. Operations continued until October, when the Iraqi authorities decided to re-impose their control of the city supported by American forces. The operation lasted ten days.

According to information from the Iraqi Ministry of Health, the number of citizens killed since the beginning of the occupation in April 2002 and up to the middle of the year 2004 as a result of terrorist acts and resistance operations was close to 3,200. During the same year, the well-known London-based medical Journal "Lancet" carried a report at the end of October which estimated that the number of Iraqi victims since the beginning of the US invasion of Iraq and up to the date of publishing the report exceeded one hundred thousand people.

The Phenomenon of Kidnapping

The phenomenon of kidnapping foreigners in Iraq emerged during 2004 as a new and highly effective insurgency tactic. The first case of an organized political kidnapping incident occurred in the first week of April with the abduction of three Japanese citizens. By the end of April, 43 operations of political kidnapping of foreign citizens were recorded within a period of 20 days. This is one of the highest rates of kidnapping in the world. In mid-May the kidnapping cases assumed worrying and inhuman proportions when the American journalist Nicholas Berg was killed and decapitated. Similar incidents were repeated almost every month.

The demands of the groups that carried out these kidnappings ranged between demanding that states participating in the multi-national forces withdraw their troops from Iraq, demands for the release of Iraqi prisoners, and demands for the departure of foreigners working in Iraq. These were the demands put forward in September when

twelve Nepali citizens as well as Egyptian and Turkish drivers and others were executed. There were also undisclosed demands of ransoms amounting to millions of dollars. In some cases both kinds of demands were made. Although there has been a noticeable reduction in the number of kidnapped foreigners during October and November and up until the end of the year, the number of foreigners kidnapped during the year is nonetheless believed to be close to 160. One third of this number has already been killed. On the other hand, there were many more kidnappings of Iraqi citizens by criminal gangs spread on a large scale throughout the country, as well as murder and robbery at a monthly rate of between 70 and 90 cases in the Governorate of Baghdad alone.

As a result of this critical security dilemma, Prime Minister, Iyad Allawi signed a resolution in July giving the interim government exceptional powers to deal with the deteriorating security situation - including the right to declare a state of emergency. A state of emergency was officially declared during operations in Falluja. This included the closure of the Iraqi borders with neighboring countries, the closure of Baghdad Airport and the imposition of curfews.

The Abu Ghuraib Scandal

The scandal of torture and mistreatment of Iraqi prisoners at the Abu Ghraib prison located outside the Iraqi capital exploded at the end of September. The American press published a series of pictures showing American soldiers violating the basic human rights of Iraqi prisoners including acts of torture, humiliation and beating. This has developed into a legal and political crisis for the American occupation authorities and as a result those involved have stood trial in military courts in an attempt to mitigate the anger of the Iraqi people and the Arab world.

Foreign Interventions

Explicit allegations emerged during the year that foreign parties were attempting to intervene in Iraqi internal affairs. In addition to the statements made by American military and political officials affirming this, prominent members of the interim Iraqi government repeatedly accused a number of neighboring states, in particular the governments of Iran and Syria, of attempting to disrupt security and stability in Iraq and of aiming to interfere in the elections scheduled to be held in January 2005. These accusations were rejected by both governments. The problem of controlling the borders and putting an end to the infiltration of armed militiamen into Iraq was one of the most difficult tasks faced by the Iraqi government this year. It is believed that factions of Iraqi resistance and terrorist groups operating in Iraq exploit the laxity of the security situation in neighboring states in order to send more volunteers across the borders to participate in insurgency movements. The Sharm El-Sheikh Conference held in November was an international attempt to make Iraq's neighboring states commit themselves to not interfering in Iraq's internal affairs and to supporting the efforts of the state to restore security and political stability.

Developments accelerated during August when the Iraqi National Conference was held for three successive days nominating 100 people to form the interim National Council or parliament.

Political Developments

On the international stage, the beginning of this year saw admissions from both American and British leaders that the main and declared reason for the war, namely the attempt to destroy Iraq's weapons of mass destruction (WMD), bears no credibility and that it is clear that Iraq did not possess such weapons or the potential of producing these weapons when the war broke out. The collapse of the original case put forward to legitimize the invasion of Iraq was followed by an announcement by the American and British governments in February to set up a special committee to investigate the work of the intelligence agencies and the reasons for these serious intelligence failures (for which the governments and the political leaderships were not, in the final analysis, declared responsible.)

During the year, the statement made by UN Secretary General Kofi Anan in September came to reinforce the crisis as he condemned the war as being illegitimate and illegal under International Law.

However, Security Council Resolution No. 1546 which was adopted in early June was among the most important events of the year, as it authorized the occupation authorities to transfer "full sovereignty" on June 30 to the interim Iraqi government and at the same time made provisions for the multi-national occupation forces to continue to supervise the security situation until legislative elections are held and a constitutional government assumes its responsibilities. These developments are expected to be completed in early 2006. UN support for this measure came when the UN Secretary-General appointed Mr. Ashraf Al-Qadi, the former ambassador of Pakistan to Washington as Representative of the Secretary-General in Baghdad in order to oversee political developments in Iraq.

In a major political development this year, the Iraqi Governing Council, which was subsequently dissolved, passed what is referred to as the basic law (the interim constitution) in March. Towards the end of this month, Iyad Allawi was selected as the first interim Prime Minister and Ghazi Ojail Al-Yawer as the first interim President of the state since the downfall of the former regime. Developments accelerated during August when the Iraqi National Conference was held for three successive days nominating 100 people to form the interim National Council or parliament.

A pressure campaign against Iraqi politician Ahmad Chalabi began to gather pace in May. He was accused of passing on sensitive information to the Iranian intelligence agencies. His residence and the headquarters of his party were subsequently raided and matters escalated in early August when the Iraqi authorities issued an order for his arrest on charges of forging currencies and documents. This decision was subsequently not implemented for undeclared reasons.

The year was also characterized by the emergence of the Shiite religious leadership in Najaf as a major public player in the state's political arena. This role was reflected in the fatwas (religious edicts) and several statements ascribed to the top authority, Ayatollah Ali Al-Sistani, as well as the other Shiite religious leaders. These fatwas were aimed at influencing political developments in the country and at unifying the "Shiite house". The result of these efforts were reflected in the decision taken by Al-Sistani to intervene publicly in supporting the demands to hold elections at their designated date and to prepare a unified list of the names of the candidates supported by the religious leadership. However the office of Al-Sistani has subsequently denied having prepared the election list.

In April, US governor Paul Bremer announced a radical change in American policy which was supported by a number of Iraqi politicians and a number of members of the interim government to abandon the policy of "uprooting Al-Baath." This opened the way, at least theoretically , to the return

of thousands of civil servants to their jobs and reduced the state of resentment and hostility that had prevailed in the community since the downfall of the former regime.

March also witnessed the beginning of the fragmentation of the coalition forces operating in Iraq under the US umbrella. The governments of Spain, the Dominican, Honduras and the Philippines announced their decision to withdraw their forces from Iraq. Moreover, a number of other states announced their intention to withdraw their forces from the country in 2005.

Top leaders of the former regime stand trial

On July 2, deposed leader Saddam Hussein, after custody of his person had been officially transferred to the interim Iraqi government by the occupation authorities, was brought to trial before an Iraqi judicial body on a number of political and criminal charges.

The announcement made in mid- December by interim Iraqi Prime Minister Allawi to the effect that the interim government intended to conduct the first trials of a number of officials of the former regime before the end of the year indicated the intention of the Iraqi authorities to delay the trial of the former Iraqi president Saddam Hussein until after the trials of his deputies. This would help the authorities obtain enough evidence and legal testimonies from the top leaders of the former regime to help build the case against Saddam. Trial sessions took place in December during which accused members of the former regime stood trial before the Iraqi judicial body.

There have been continued efforts throughout 2004 to arrest the top leaders of the former regime. From the list of 55 wanted persons, which was announced after the fall of the regime, only 12 remained at large by the beginning of the year with four more captured by the middle of the year.

Sab'awi, Saddam Hussein's half brother, remains at large.

Sectarian strife

The violence that occurred this year was characterized by a noticeable intensification of operations aimed at escalating sectarian and religious conflict in the country, such as the attacks on religious buildings and religious celebrations, including blowing up Sunni mosques, Shiite institutes and Christian churches. These were coupled with the assassination of clerics of all sects, particularly those who openly called for the cessation of resistance or for supporting the sect to which they belonged. 180 citizens were murdered in March during the Shiite celebrations on Ashura Day as a result of a series of simultaneous suicide operations executed against the religious sites in Karbala and Baghdad. In August, there was a series of explosions in churches and Christian places of worship in Baghdad and Mosul using car bombs and killing a number of citizens. The two car bombs in Karbala and Najaf towards the end of December came as a signal of the determination of certain groups to continue to carry out their plan of stirring up sectarian conflict aimed at starting a civil war.

Economy

The introduction of the new Iraqi currency, the new dinar, into the market was the first and most important feature of economic development for the state. This had positive effects on the economic conditions of the country and helped stabilize the exchange rate of the Iraqi dinar.

The World Bank decided to recognize the legitimacy of the interim Iraqi government, which qualifies Iraq to obtain international loans. Despite all attempts to reactivate the economy, the basic problems are dominant: the unemployment rate is close to 40% of the total labor force, the provision of basic services are still at unacceptable levels due to chronic problems such as power failure, the provision of basic fuel materials for citizens, coupled with the deterioration of health and education services. This has had negative effects on the stability of the state and on the welfare of its citizens, as well as seriously damaging the legitimacy of the interim government and casting doubts on the intentions of the occupation authorities. Charges of political and financial corruption against a number of Iraqis made things even worse. Similar charges were leveled against a number of American companies that deal with the materials required for rebuilding the infrastructure. The US Congress has to date allocated $153 billion to cover the cost of the US war in Iraq.

This year has witnessed intense international and Iraqi campaigns aimed at canceling or reducing Iraq's substantial international debts or at dealing with the other financial obligations inherited by the former regime. However, substantial success in achieving total, immediate and unconditional cancellation has not been achieved to date. The total amount of debts due by the state is close to $117 billion. During the meeting of the members of the "Paris Club" which was held in November of this year, the participants reached an agreement to gradually cancel 80% of the debts subject to certain conditions. 30% of Iraq's debts would be cancelled immediately, while another 30% would be cancelled after the World Bank's approval of the economic reform and reconstruction plan in 2005, 20% would be cancelled after Iraq's application of the reform plan approved by the World Bank by 2008. The remaining debts would be paid by Iraq to the "Paris Club" states on an installment basis during a period of about 23 years. The American authorities announced in December the total cancellation of Iraq's debts that are due to the United States, estimated at more than $4 billion. This is the first precedent of its kind, whereby a creditor state announces the total cancellation of debts.

Attacks on Oil Facilities

During May, there was a noticeable escalation in the number of acts of sabotage on Iraqi oil facilities. During the first four months of the year, Iraqi oil facilities came under an average of four monthly attacks. This escalated to 21 operations in August. These included three attempted suicide attacks executed by using small naval boats. The attacks aimed to destroy the floating naval platforms used in exporting Iraqi oil through the country's outlets on the Arab Gulf waters. The export lines of Iraqi oil in the north and the south of the country were exposed to repeated sabotage and destruction operations, which led to the cessation of Iraqi oil exports to world markets throughout the year. Sources at the Iraqi Ministry of Oil estimated the total losses resulting from the cessation of oil exports as a result of sabotage operations at about $1.94 billion during October while the average loss during the remaining months was estimated at $1 billion.

In a mid-year report the US intelligence agency, the National Intelligence Council issued a pessimistic assessment of future security conditions in Iraq. The predictions outlined in this report are in direct conflict with the positive assessment by the US administration on the situation in Iraq and the process of restoring stability and security. The report has affirmed that - in the best case scenario - stability in Iraq during the next 18 months (up to the beginning of the year 2006) will at best be tenuous. The more likely scenario is that the situation degenerates into civil war if the security crisis is not brought under immediate control.

Future Developments in Iraq

Dhafer Al-Ani

Research Manager, GCC-Iraq Relations, Gulf Research Center

To say that the future of Iraq is open to all probabilities does not represent an attempt to evade putting forth an approximate or clear-cut answer about the future political developments in Iraq, for a heavy fog shrouds the real and declared intentions of all the parties, domestic or external, concerned with the ongoing political process in Iraq. In fact, the main players on the Iraqi political scene are many and events keep unfolding fast and in highly unpredictable ways. Hence, to predict any future development is, no doubt, a mind-boggling task for any specialist in Iraqi affairs, no matter how sagacious.

However, for the sake of methodological reasons, and out of a desire to anchor the Iraqi issue to a set of academic moorings and embrace an objective and broad-based approach to the current conditions in Iraq, it could safely be said that there are basically three probable scenarios along which the future of Iraq might unfold. The three scenarios are hereunder discussed in detail, along with their conditions and dimensions in the foreseeable future.

Civil war breaks out and security conditions deteriorate dramatically

The majority of Iraqis, including eminent academics and politicians, deny the possibility of such a scenario based on their long-standing experience and social traditions. They tend generally to lean back on historical facts, citing explanations such as the structural cohesion of Iraq and the close social relations binding Iraqis, facts which, in their opinion, have contributed to the development of an Iraqi social attitude marked by tolerance and acceptance of the 'other', whatever their ethnic or religious affiliations may be. In fact, this group of Iraqis believes that Iraqi social relations have evolved to the point of socially fusing the various components of Iraqi society, namely the Arab Shi'a, the Arab Sunnis, the Kurds, the Christians, the Yazidis and the Mandeans.

However, what this group seems to ignore is that Iraq today is no longer what it was prior to April 9, 2003. Occupation has indeed not only destroyed previous realities, but has also created a new reality unlike anything Iraqis were used to in the past. Occupation has taken away the light cloak of social cohesion, inducing Iraqis to fall back on their primal ethnic, religious, sectarian and tribal references after the state, with its central and authoritarian character, was almost completely annihilated. Nothing could better illustrate this new reality than the fact that the majority of political parties and organizations today depend for their strength on ethnic, sectarian and tribal allegiances.

Moreover, taking evidence from the past to corroborate the social tolerance of Iraqis is in essence eclectic, for Iraq's history is not free of domestic conflicts or of simmering popular tensions. What is noteworthy is that the environment in which these conflicts erupted was not unlike the current environment, marked as it is by an agonizing central regime or by pronounced external interference. To be sure, the current environment feeds sectarian and ethnic partisanship. Still, the question needs to be asked: who might have a vested interest in an Iraqi civil war?

It is a well-known fact that the diverse ethnic groups of Iraq have a geographical outreach into neighboring countries. In light of this reality, many political analysts point out that whenever some proximate countries find that it is their interest to move or instigate Iraqi groups with whom they have close connections at the expense of other ethnic or sectarian groups or against the central authority, they do not hesitate to do so. One or more of these states could possibly pave the way for an Iraqi civil war, particularly if they become convinced that their strategic interests would be secured by triggering such an event as a way to compound US diffi-culties and thereby put off the possibility that they might be targeted by the US military machine. This analysis holds true especially in the case of Syria and Iran, both of which figure high on the US list of possible targets once the situation in Iraq cools down.

Iran might choose such a course, particularly as the instruments for such a project, such as strong groups and political parties that feel emotional and religious allegiance towards Tehran, are readily available. In fact, scores of Iraqi groups entertain long-standing relations with Iran and many have been the recipients of financial, political, armament and intelligence support from it. The Supreme

Council for Islamic Revolution (SCIRI), the Al-Da'wa [Call] Party, Hizbullah, and to some extent the Moqatada Al-Sadr Movement as well as the Al-Fadeela [Virtue] Party, all have been receiving Iran's support, as have other Shi'ite groups. In fact, Iran's support does not stop at political forces, but also extends to popular Shi'ite circles.

Syria, in the meantime, could always offer support for Iraqi Ba'athists on ideological and political grounds, as many Iraqi Ba'athists feel today that their ideological and political reference is found in Damascus, particularly since the anti-war stance championed by Syria has deepened that feeling.

Turkey, too, might step in to lend support to the Turkomens of Kirkuk if Ankara sees that they are being subjected to unjust treatment or in the event that the oil-rich city falls into the hands of the Kurds, thus enhancing their secessionist drive.

Arab Sunnis, for their part, enjoy wide multi-dimensional support among fundamentalist organizations and leftist parties across the Arab world, all of which provide support to the Iraqi armed resistance af-filiated with Sunnis. Po-litical squabbles might lead to civil strife due to external interference in view of the fact that the majority of ethno-political factions in Iraq have their own armed and well-trained militias.

Harbinger signs that a civil war might erupt in Iraq could be felt in many current conditions. Ethnic allegiances dominate the Iraqi scene while nationalist feelings seem to recede. National and secularist parties are losing much of their clout to the benefit of sectarian and nationalist parties. The wave of political assassinations and retaliatory killings has proliferated in the aftermath of occupation. Most assassinations are perpetrated out of sectarian and

Occupation has taken away the light cloak of social cohesion, inducing Iraqis to fall back on their primal ethnic, religious, sectarian and tribal references.

partisan motivations. Some hard-line Shi'a have assassinated members of the Sunni Association of Muslim Scholars (AMS), while groups representing Sunni fundamentalism have killed Shi'ite icons belonging to the Supreme Council for Islamic Revolution and the Da'wa Party. Moreover, accusations have been directed at external forces such as Abu Musa'ab Al- Zarqawi or towards some hard-line Iranian figures and forces. In other words, the external factor seems to have the upper hand in moving events in Iraq. In light of unshackled insecurity, the absence of border control and the limited response on the part of neighboring countries to help secure borders, the whole situation seems poised to worsen.

A number of recent political reports point out that there are blatant interferences in the internal political affairs of Iraq by a number of neighboring states. The interim Iraqi government has already expressed complaints against Iran. The Iraqi Defense Minister has described Iran as Iraq's enemy number one. The Iraqi President, too, declared that Iran is responsible for a series of assassinations against intelligence officers, accusing Tehran of inflaming sectarian sentiments.

On another level, there is the possible scenario that in the event that multinational forces deployed in Iraq pull out due to resistance or in reaction to popular and international pressures, a civil war might break out in the wake of the security vacuum that would result from the inability of Iraqi security forces to control the situation. In that case, armed groups might be tempted to stage a rebellion. Ex-Ba'athists might, for their part, re-mobilize, particularly in Sunni-dominated provinces, which might incense conservative sectarian and nationalist

Harbinger signs that a civil war might erupt in Iraq could be felt in many current conditions. Ethnic allegiances dominate the Iraqi scene while nationalist feelings seem to recede.

political forces, ultimately leading to a civil war.

On a similar note, voices calling for secession can be heard. Some have called for the establishment of a Shi'ite state to be built in the south. Wide demonstrations have been held in the Kurdish region demanding secession, not to mention the intermittent, but highly significant, armed confrontations in Kirkuk. Many Kurdish officials have been assassinated in cities where different ethnic groups co-exist, mainly in Mosul, Kirkuk and Diala.

Fortunately for Iraqis, the scenario of a civil war is thwarted by a number of conditions and factors. The first factor is geographical. All the major ethnic Iraqi groups are isolated from each other: the Kurds live mainly in the north, the Shi'a in the south and the Sunnis are based mostly in the central provinces of the country. As such, total confrontations are less likely with possible frictions restricted largely to those regions with ethnically mixed populations, notably the capital Baghdad, Kirkuk, and to a limited extent Diala. Second, the US certainly does not seek a civil conflict under its watch as that would mark the end of its grandiose political project to build a democratic model to be matched by other countries in the region. Third, Iraq's social relations are mostly built on relations by marriage and lineage among various ethnic groups and sects. Thus often times, members of the same tribe may belong to more than one ideological current and the hierarchical order remains dominant, a reality which undermines the possibility of a civil war scenario, though it does not categorically exclude it.

The escalating wave of violence sweeping across Iraq in the post-occupation period has fed - and continues to feed- on existing conditions. Certainly, violence is not expected to come to an end any time soon as military occupation continues to incite feelings of resentment among Iraqis even though the political process is also underway. The aggressive military operations launched by the US against rebel cities compounded by the abuse practiced towards the civilian population has created deep feelings of hatred. Economic and living conditions, too, have not seen any palpable improvement. Many Iraqis today are still without a job while corruption and graft are endemic in many government departments. More significantly, security and military forces have failed to better their performance and are still unable to fill the security vacuum. Occupation will also represent a key factor in heightening religious sentiments among Iraqis, many of whom are enlisting as volunteers in fundamentalist groups to wage a war against US troops. The insurgents appear to have the organizational and logistical capabilities to fight even though their combat performance has been on the decline as a consequence of sustaining hard blows dealt by occupation forces.

Taking all these factors into consideration, violence will likely flare up across Iraq unless serious efforts are deployed to remedy the causes giving rise to such violence.

Stabilization of the political and economic conditions leading to an end of violence

The US administration is bent on completing the political process started in Iraq in June 2003 by transferring power to Iraqis regardless of any negative repercussions that might accrue from the entire process. For their part, Iraqi political forces represented in the interim government are also intent on making the political process a success. The political process will kick off at the end of January 2005 and could be completed by the end of the year. It is set to include the election of a national council and an elected government along with the creation of a national assembly to take charge of drafting a permanent constitution for post-Saddam Iraq. The entire process would culminate in general elections by the end of 2005 or the beginning of 2006. Iraqis thus seem poised to be busy throughout 2005 organizing and completing the political process. Notably, Grand Ayatollah Ali al-Sistani, the most senior Shi'a authority in Iraq, issued a fatwa [a religious edict] urging all Iraqis to participate in the elections. The Kurds, too, are rather enthusiastic about engaging in the political process in order to consolidate their demands for federalism. Any procrastination would certainly not serve their interests.

At the same time, some political parties, particularly those with leftist and nationalist orientations, have called for a boycott of the elections. On the whole, they put the end of occupation as a sine qua non condition before consenting to any electoral participation. They also demand that conditions for holding elections be improved. However, these political forces have only limited influence, save for the Association of Muslim Scholars, which threatens to issue a fatwa calling for the boycott of elections in case military operations continue to target Iraqi cities still locked up in confrontation with foreign and governmental troops. The threat might not actually have much impact, as Sunnis have never been known for their deference to religious fatwas when it comes to political matters in stark contrast to the Shi'a community. Hence, the political process seems to have positive resonance among the majority of Iraqis who are apparently tired of the insecurity engulfing their country and the rising toll of killed civilians. Most Iraqis indeed do support the political process.

At the same time, some political parties, At the same time, some political parties, At the same time, some political parties, At the same time, some political parties, At the same time, some political parties, At the same time, some political parties, At the same time, some political parties, At the same time, some political parties, At the same time, some political parties, All indicators point to the possibility of the current process sustaining the formation of a new government, especially since the electoral system adopted is built on the principle that the whole country is a unified and single electoral constituency. The candidacy system based on electoral lists gives the political parties merged into the current governing coalition a real chance for victory in the elections. In fact, these parties are the strongest in Iraq as they are better organized, better financed and more firmly supported by many countries than any other political formations. The cabinet of Premier Iyad Allawi seems confident of its victory in elections. As a matter of fact, the cabinet behaves today as though it is not merely an interim government, as mentioned by the UN Security Council and as embedded in the Law of Administration for the State of Iraq, but as the permanent government. Certainly, the Allawi government does also not behave as a caretaker government, as the special envoy of the UN Secretary-General, Lakhdar Brahimi, labeled it.

In spite of the critiques some Iraqis have about the performance of the current government, particularly its connection with US policies and the ubiquity of administrative graft, the interim government represents an acceptable option for the majority of Iraqis, especially given the fact that the other alternative is chaos. The maintenance of its present formation also ensures a measure of continuity as it includes a wide palette of political figures representing various political and religious forces. Up to this point, the Allawi government has not behaved in an ideologically biased manner nor has it favored any specific group. It handled the rebellions in Fallujah and Samarra (both Sunni cities) in roughly the same manner as it handled the insurgency in Najaf and Sadr City (both Shi'ite cities).

All indicators point to the possibility of the current process sustaining the formation of a new government.

Such an approach might assuage Sunni concerns over eventual marginalization. Even Ba'athists might feel relieved that the Allawi government is more lenient towards them than other political forces that might hold the reins of power. In fact, Iyad Allawi was among the staunchest opponents of the US decision to conduct a 'de-Ba'athification' campaign. Allawi's party, the Iraqi National Accord, includes a number of former Ba'athists in its ranks and Allawi himself is a former Ba'athist. Military officers, too, seem rather satisfied with the policy choices of the Allawi government, which was the first to warn occupation authorities against the ill-advised US decision to dismantle the military establishment. At present, Allawi strives hard to rehabilitate former military and security officers and integrate them in the newly-created establishments.

To be sure, the stability of conditions in Iraq depends in large part on the ability to work out sustainable solutions to the socio-economic problems that beset the war-battered country. Solutions include executing development projects, reconstructing damaged infrastructures, creating jobs for the masses of unemployed Iraqis, improving the purchase capacities of ordinary functionaries, and boosting education and health-care conditions. In the post-election period, demands for such improvements will probably become even more pressing. The government response could probably be more forthcoming, particularly as oil prices have risen and many countries have pledged to provide financial grants and investments in Iraq.

Stabilizing and restoring security to Iraq is not just an Iraqi desideratum; in fact, it is the desire and ambition of many regional and international players. International powers have vital and strategic interests in the Middle East region and seek to support peace and stability in Iraq; the alternative is an entire region faced with violent developments that could completely get out of hand. Arab states adjacent to Iraq, except perhaps Syria, look forward to seeing Iraq back on the path towards stability and security, largely out of fear that the overwhelming wave of insecurity in Iraq might spill over into their own countries, and lead to a proliferation of extremist groups.

As such, the popular and official Iraqi desire embraces an international desire to invigorate the political process. Regional powers, such as Iran and Syria, which might choose to instigate domestic tensions in Iraq, could be deterred by the US. There are scores of dossiers that the US could bring up against either Iran or Syria in case they fail to abide by their commitments to steer clear of any interference in Iraqi internal affairs and desist from adding confusion to the situation in the country.

For this scenario to materialize, elections must be held and institutional structures properly built in such a way as to undermine the motivations and justifications floated by Iraqi resistance groups. Eventually, resistance groups will find their resonance declining among the populace, leaving Iraq to retrieve its lost peace and stability.

This scenario carries a great deal of optimism, but is not totally denuded of realism.

Setting into motion the political process while violence wanes

Because they derive their existence from entrenched social and power attitudes, the conditions contributing to the rise of violence and to the possibility of civil strife are unlikely to end in the coming year, making the end of violence and resistance unlikely as well. Also, as domestic policies and international interests, particularly US interests,

are not expected to change dramatically over the next year, in particular after the re-election of President George W. Bush, the scenario most likely to unravel in Iraq is a combination of the previous two. In other words, the political process, driving toward Iraq's stabilization, will continue while violence will gradually be confined to particular regions across Iraq.

In fact, the political process seems to be moving towards consolidating the policy principles adopted in the aftermath of Iraq's occupation. Political representation based on sectarian and nationalist proportionality, resting on inaccurate estimates of the demographics of each Iraqi ethno-sectarian group, will probably deepen the feeling of Sunni Arabs that they will be marginalized. Tensions might continue between Sunnis as a formless group and other Iraqi social forces.

On another level, upholding the occupation the way it is today by deploying military forces in the main Iraqi cities and waging retaliatory operations will do nothing to erase the conditions that sustain national resistance which feeds on a dual ideological platform derived from Islamic Jihadist ideas and from the proud Iraqi nationalist spirit that resents living under occupation. Tribal motivations and vindictive sentiments against the inhuman practices conducted by occupation forces against Iraqi civilians are still rife. A number of Iraqis whose private interests and standing were associated with Saddam Hussein's regime might also like to perturb the domestic scene and seek revenge.

Even though the above-mentioned factors will no doubt help sustain violence across Iraq and even create popular rejection of the status quo, resistance seems to be steadily on the wane. Some resistance groups have opted to put down weapons and engage instead in peaceful political opposition, as is exampled in the case of Moqtada Al Sadr's Movement, which represents Shi'a resentful of occupation. Indeed, many elements from Al Sadr's Movement handed over their weapons to the Iraqi interim government in return for sums of money. Other resistance groups are starting to lose popular support as the toll of the dead and injured among Iraqis increases. The fact that military operations staged by some resistance groups have targeted Iraqis more than the foreign presence has led to many Iraqis looking upon the resistance with suspicion, thereby placing the blame squarely on the shoulders of alien infiltrators.

Furthermore, the slew of measures enacted - and those expected to be enacted- in the near future by the government will probably help reduce the underlying causes giving rise to violence. Governmental measures include improving the living conditions of a good proportion of Iraqi society, particularly public servants, as they represent the largest social group, disbursing appropriate salaries for retired employees, and integrating a number of security and military officers into newly created departments. Capital funds for Iraq's reconstruction will likely flow in substantial volume in light of the recent rise in oil prices, which augurs well especially if the oil money is appropriately exploited for the creation of job opportunities and reducing unemployment.

Just as important, the political process, however imperfect it may seem, will probably contribute to containing extremist violence, especially as the majority of Iraqis are keen to engage in the political process. Hence, tension spots, having shrunk in number over the past few months, might continue to shrink over the coming year. Obviously, violence will not end overnight and resistance will continue so long as occupation rules the day and foreign military troops are visibly deployed in the main Iraqi cities. However that does not preclude Iraqis from nourishing the conviction that the cost of resistance is exorbitantly high and those who pay the cost are mostly Iraqis. Such conviction undermines the support lent to resistant groups.

Overall, this scenario is the most likely.

Conclusion

Given the prevailing conditions in Iraq today, the future seems open to all probabilities despite the difficulty of accurately predicting the exact nature of future developments. Still, the scenario most likely to unfold in the foreseeable future would probably see a continuation of the ongoing political process while the wave of violence overwhelming Iraq would begin to slowly decline as well as become more localized. This development depends, of course, on the ability of the concerned parties, be they Iraqis or foreigners, to secure the right conditions that would steer developments along the path for greater stabilization and security.

Developments in Iran

Mahmood Sariolghalam

Associate Professor of International Relations and Research Director of the Center for Scientific Research and Middle East Strategic Studies
National (Shahid Behesti) University, Iran

Two important issues stood out in Iran's domestic affairs and foreign policy during 2004. One was the parliamentarian elections and the gradual closing of the Khatami presidency while the other was Iran's nuclear standoff with the International Atomic Energy Agency (IAEA) and the Western world.

The Khatami presidency: an assessment

The Khatami presidency (1997-2005) led to sharp divisions within the Iranian elites and Iranian society at large. As the president changed his agenda, orientation, priorities and mood, his presidency also declined in relevance and effectiveness. In essence, the Khatami presidency reflects the usual divisions that occur within a revolutionary order as it matures. The pursuit of democracy in a revolutionary order was clearly an illusion. A long history of despotism was also a serious impediment to such a pursuit. President Khatami and his entourage underestimated the institutional power and the social bases of the revolutionary and conservative groupings in Iran. Moreover, is has to be understood that the idea of democracy was and has been an intellectual luxury in the Iranian educated circles. Iran's political system in the post-revolutionary period might allow limited electoral process as it is known in the West and is only understood within a Shii tradition, yet a state-dominated economy and disorganized popular politics impede a Western style democracy to emerge in Iran. In that context, democracy and economic privatization serve as two sides of a coin and greatly reinforce and necessitate

each other. While under the Khatami presidency, Iranian society experienced greater openness, dialogue and media competition, the change was mostly accomplished in the mindset of the average person rather than a sustained institutionalization of the social settings in the country.

Khatami sought to bring about reason and lawfulness into the Iranian order. But the mechanisms he utilized such as philosophical dialogue, oratory power, ethical discussions and sentimental appeals were not effective tools for greater political organization and competition in the country. In this idealistic process, he was discouraged, defeated, defied and disillusioned. Khatami, an idealist, sought justice without power and overlooked the essence of power. No system will volunteer to be just. Justice is achieved through counterbalances and structural competition. Khatami constantly complained about obstructionism but he did not realize that no politician is granted full support; instead all politicians need to rely on organization, skill and incremental work to achieve their objectives.

For the most part, Khatami made use of his oratory power and made emotional appeals to govern and reform. Yet, what is not often realized is that the Khatami presidency also further consolidated his opponents by bringing more organizational discipline into their political pursuits and undermining the intellectual and modernist elements of the Iranian society for some time to come. Furthermore, the Khatami presidency pursued another illusion of far greater magnitude, that is, the pursuit of Islamic democracy. While Islam has its own framework and can be envisioned as a social, economic and political order, its logic, underpinnings and overall direction is philosophically and structurally distinct from a democratic disposition. The pursuit of Islamic democracy by Khatami was a theoretical fabrication that many of the political activists in his entourage understandably ignored. At a time when developing countries such as South Korea, Malaysia, Brazil, UAE and Turkey underwent intensive processes of national wealth accumulation, the Khatami presidency focused on accomplishing reason in a revolutionary order during which the inflation rate in the country quadrupled and populists furthered their political gains and controls.

The parliamentary elections of 2004: the beginning of a new era

The complete immobility of the Khatami approach was made evident in the parliamentary elections of February 2004. Through the constitutional mechanisms of screening candidates for public office, much of the reformist camp was purged from even standing as possible candidates in the elections. According to the Iranian constitution, any person seeking public office must conceptually agree and practically demonstrate his or her affinity to the precepts of the constitution. In this spirit, the overwhelming majority of the candidates from the reformist camp seeking reelection to the parliament had expressed opinions and pursued conduct contrary to the Constitution of the Islamic Republic of

Iran during the 2000-2004 parliamentary term or the sixth Majlis. The constitutional body of the Guardians Council only endorsed candidates who had displayed loyalty to the country's political and ideological principles. Some former reformists with milder views on the constitution and less affiliated with the organized sectors of the reformist movement were ultimately endorsed.

As a result, the outcome of the election was clear before the votes had even been cast. A look at the breakdown of seats in the new 7th parliament as opposed to the previous 6th parliament shows the dominance of the conservative side after the screening process:

	Seventh Parliament	Sixth Parliament
Conservatives	189	60
Reformists	48	190
Independents	44	35
Religious Minorities	5	5
Total	286*	290

* Four seats are yet to be determined because of cancellations during the elections by the Guardians Council. The four members will be elected during the presidential elections in June 2005.

With this dramatic shift in place, there can be no doubt that the 2004 parliamentary elections had a number of consequences. First, it blocked out the Islamic left from the legislative body and weakened their prospects for influencing national politics. The sixth parliament dominated by the Islamic left and pro-Khatami members concentrated on confronting the right establishment in the country and in the process partly neglecting the economic needs of the average citizen with the result that they ultimately lost their political support. The political result of the screening process of the Guardians Council and the purge of the left was more or less public indifference and apathy.

Second, the composition of the new parliament consolidated the conservative and the revolutionary establishment of the country. Third, a conservative legislative body will have a decisive capacity to influence the presidential elections of June 2005. Fourth, though the definite nature of the post-Khatami presidency is not clear, it appears that the overall direction of national politics and policy formulation processes will be substantially influenced by the political needs and desires of the conservative and revolutionary establishment of the country. Fifth, a conservative takeover does not necessarily translate into policies that are contrary to Iran's national development, moderate foreign policy and relaxed social rigidities. Sixth, the new speaker of the Iranian parliament, Dr. Gholamali Haddad Adel, a philosopher turned politician, has vigorously attempted to reach out to the various elements within the 7th parliament, the Khatami government and the society at large to demonstrate accommodation, moderation and understanding.

How these consequences have translated into practice can be seen by the actions that the new parliament has taken since the election. In its five months in operation, the parliament has impeached and unseated the minister of transportation of the Khatami government, has projected more interest in foreign policy decision making processes, has initiated greater supervision over the executive branch and has displayed far more rigor in carrying out its responsibilities. It further appears that the 7th parliament will play an important complementary role for the pursuit of the objectives and the implementation of policies of the conservative establishment in the next four years.

The Iranian nuclear program: confrontations and challenges

Besides the domestic developments, Iran also provoked scrutiny in its foreign policy dealings. Of particular concern was the continued development of the Iranian nuclear program and the possibilities of a heightened confrontation with the United States. To help put the debate into perspective, some context is useful.

Under the Shah, Iran began a nuclear program with the help of the Germans and the Japanese. In 1975, Stanford Research Institute (SRI) concluded that Iran needs a 20,000 Megawatt nuclear power station that can be completed in 20 years for the purposes of technical and economic development of the country. Moreover, British and French companies made arrangements with the Shah's regime to establish a major nuclear center in Isfahan that would account for a nuclear fuel cycle. At the same time, during the Shah's reign, Iran signed the Non-Proliferation Treaty (NPT) on July 1, 1968 and ratified the treaty on February 2, 1970. The treaty's comprehensive safeguards agreement entered into force on May 15, 1974.

Following the 1979 revolution, the Germans and the Japanese terminated their activities in Iran's nuclear reactor program. Subsequently, the Soviet Union and then Russia agreed to complete Iran's reactors in the southern city of Bushehr. Furthermore, Iran signed an Additional Protocol to its Safeguards Agreement on December 18, 2003, the provisions of which it has implemented although official is still pending in the Iranian Parliament. Under the NPT regulations, member countries have the right to pursue civilian nuclear technology for the purposes of producing electricity and engaging in scientific endeavors.

Throughout the 1980s and the 1990s, Western governments, particularly the United States alongside Israel maintained a policy of suspicion towards Iran's nuclear activity. As Iran's program underwent consistent supervision of the IAEA, however, sufficient assurances were made that the Iranian nuclear program was under the agency's control and that Iran was solely interested in complementing its domestic energy needs given its increasing oil and gas consumption. Ironically, among the 135 members of the IAEA, Iran has consistently ranked seventh or eighth in receiving technical assistance amounting to about one million dollars annually from the UN nuclear watchdog. Nonetheless, as early as 1980, American intelligence agencies as well as Israel had maintained that Iran is slowly but effectively pursuing a nuclear weapons program under a civilian umbrella. Even the official American policy of rapprochement towards Iran under almost all U.S. administrations maintained the termination of the nuclear program as a major precondition.

The political crisis between Iran on the one hand and the IAEA, the EU and the United States on the other began in 2002 when it was revealed that Iran was in the process of uranium enrichment and that Iran's technical expertise was far greater than expected. The IAEA declared in June 2003 that there is a time gap between Iranian nuclear activities and its reporting to the agency under the provisions of the NPT. Earlier, it was understood that Iran's cooperation with Russia only concentrated in the Bushehr power plant and it did not involve enrichment and heavy water activities. Furthermore, the Chinese signed a contract with Iran in the early 1990s to provide technical know-how for the Isfahan UCF plant; a plant that processes UC08 derived from uranium. In the mid 1990s, the Chinese under American pressure terminated these nuclear agreements with Iran. Thereafter, Iran pursued an indigenous technological program relying on its own highly trained engineers and

scientists to proceed with the enrichment process. This process has raised concerns that Iran has acquired the capability to gradually complete its nuclear fuel cycle that involves uranium, enrichment and reprocessing of plutonium.

Western governments through the IAEA provisions have tried over the last two years to convince Iran to forego the option of engaging in nuclear fuel cycle indigenously. Though the Atomic Agency has not found any evidence that Iran is pursuing a nuclear weapons program, Tehran's capability and continued efforts to complete a nuclear fuel cycle raises the suspicions that Tehran will ultimately be able to produce weapons since through enriched uranium, the main ingredients of a nuclear explosive device will be supplied.

The time gap between Iran's nuclear activities and its legal reporting to the agency has resulted in a "dilemma of trust" between Iran as a signatory of the NPT and the agency, fueling the suspicions raised earlier by the United States. Perhaps empowered by a sense of fulfillment through the indigenous technical successes, Tehran feared political backlashes in the United States and Israel if its technological advancements were revealed. The Non-Proliferation Treaty does give its signatories the right to develop nuclear programs including the enrichment of uranium. Iran has maintained that the international community must recognize Tehran's right to enrich uranium for power stations. Furthermore, Iranian diplomats have argued that Iran was being unfairly penalized. In an attempt to counter these perceptions, Iran proposed the Middle East to be a nuclear-free zone although Israel which is believed to have 200 nuclear warheads has never

In an attempt to counter these perceptions, Iran proposed the Middle East to be a nuclear-free zone although Israel which is believed to have 200 nuclear warheads has never signed the NPT and has not accepted the IAEA inspections.

signed the NPT and has not accepted the IAEA inspections. While in the aftermath of the problems between the IAEA and Iran, the agency carried out more than a dozen unannounced inspections of Iranian nuclear facilities, mistrust and suspicions however mount over Iran's actual capabilities and its future intentions.

On October 21, 2003, the foreign ministers of the United Kingdom, France and Germany signed an accord with the Iranian chief nuclear negotiator, Hassan Rouhani, indicating that Iran has the right to enjoy peaceful use of nuclear energy and that Tehran can secure long term access to high-tech including nuclear technology. In return Iran agreed to voluntarily suspend all activities related to nuclear enrichment. Iranians were hopeful that through the good offices of the European powers, the agency and the United States could be convinced that the Iranian program is indeed intended for peaceful purposes and acknowledge that Iran had to think ahead and plan for its long term energy needs in the face of increasing population and rates of economic growth. Tehran's expectation was that through greater supervision and unlimited suspension of activities, the Iranian dossier would subsequently be closed at the agency.

Iran maintains that it can develop its needed nuclear fuel supplies and that it is unnecessary to incur heavy costs while the country has the capability to produce its own indigenous nuclear fuel. In this spirit, the Iranian government announced on June 23, 2004 that it would resume the manufacture of centrifuge and the preparation of uranium hexafluoride, the feed material for enrichment. Also, Iran declared that it would begin with the conversion of 37 tons of uranium ore or yellowcake, the initial material for enrichment.

With an agreement back in place at the end of 2004, the central issue remains as to how confidence-building measures can be established between Iranian intentions on the one hand and its capabilities on the other. Equally important is Iran's right under the NPT to the nuclear fuel cycle. Ultimately, Iranians are caught between their capability to engage in nuclear high-tech and the political and economic consequences of maintaining a dispute with the IAEA. Iran argues that it is illogical and uneconomical to have nuclear power stations and not nuclear fuel.

Having discussed the aforementioned technical, legal and institutional details, it appears that the focal point in the dispute between Iran and the IAEA is of a political nature. On September 20, 2004, the United States government announced that it trusts India as a nuclear power and that it is removing its ban on technology exports to India's civilian space agency, the Indian Space Research Organization (ISRO).The word "trust" in this statement is a crucial one. The fact of the matter is that Iran as a Middle Eastern country and now neighboring almost all countries that have strategic relations with Washington has no diplomatic relations with the United States and the two countries have mutually developed a "complex network of animosity and distrust." Moreover, the Israeli-American strategic relationship and the Iranian official policy of calling for the destruction of the state of Israel, directly relates to the American and partly European opposition to the Iranian nuclear program. The strategic viewpoint in the West is that all nuclear powers need to have transparent political structures. The Iranian political system is not well-understood by Westerners and the U.S. has no direct and official contacts with the Iranian elites. In further complicating the political matrix, one can raise the issue that the Iranian security apparatus is not accessible to the Western world. Iranian military officials also make provocative statements regarding their capabilities and intentions in confronting American power and influence in their neighborhood. While Iran labeled the United States, 'The Great Satan," Washington reciprocated by incorporating the Islamic Republic as a member of the "Axis of Evil."

In nuclear terminology, intentions are far more significant than capabilities. Given the political and security contexts between Tehran and Washington, it is therefore evident that despite Iran's declared policy of limiting its nuclear program to civilian use, its rhetoric will dominate the threat perceptions it shapes and the suspicions it raises regarding its intentions in the Western world. If Iran became a nuclear power, the strategic map of the Middle East will fundamentally be altered and Israel will lose its strategic superiority. It is no surprise then that Israel is much more active than even the Europeans in terminating Iran's nuclear program and is perhaps the most single important player behind the scenes in confronting Iran. A nuclear Iran will raise fundamental problems for American power and influence in the Middle East. As American neoconservatives have asserted, a nuclear Iran will obstruct American designs for the Greater Middle East. The United States believes that Iran intends to become a nuclear power to deter American security threats.

From the Iranian side, Iran continues to differentiate between its foreign economic relations and economic development on the one hand and its security perceptions and national security doctrine on the other. Had Iran viewed the two as linked and intertwined, Iranian foreign policy would have evolved in different directions. The Islamic Republic of Iran is essentially a revolutionary order with historical sensitivities to its national sovereignty and political independence. The security consequence since the early days of the revolution has been that it has remained in isolation. This revolutionary inertia is maintained by a revolutionary generation that feels it has a historical responsibility to uphold independent and revolutionary credentials for the Islamic ideology and its own raison d'etre. Therefore, self-sufficiency in security matters is a fundamental objective.

Conclusion

In conclusion, Iran's nuclear stand-off with the IAEA as a UN adjunct and the Western world, mobilized and motivated by the United States, is a reflection of the uncertainties involved regarding Iran's political system and the intentions of its revolutionary elites on the one hand and the Western desire to maintain its power in the Middle East and deter threats to Israeli security in the region on the other. This confrontation became more intense after 2002 when Iranian indigenous capability to proceed with enrichment processes surfaced. While Iran has the right under the NPT to produce nuclear fuel, the controversy centers on its future intentions. There are a number of scenarios regarding this confrontation. One would be Iran's agreement to a longer term suspension of the enrichment process and a transfer of Iran's nuclear sovereignty to external providers of nuclear fuel. Another scenario would be Iran's renewed defiance of the IAEA demands which would in turn escalate the confrontation and bring about a new crisis between Tehran and Washington. This scenario will involve the UN Security Council dynamics between the permanent members. Though there are many uncertainties and limitations as to what degree the Security Council may impede the Iranian nuclear program, its potential decisions will clearly constitute major political and economic difficulties if not crises for Iran. A third scenario envisions the continuation of the dialogue with the EU 3 - Great Britain, France and Germany and a gradual expansion of economic and political benefits to Iran in exchange for a continued suspension. To be sure, politics on both sides will eventually determine the outcome of the conflict although the breakout of more severe consequences remains a real and deeply troubling option.

Developments in Yemen

Hussein Abdullah Al Amri

Professor of Yemen Contemporary History, Sana'a University

The year 2004 was marked by the consolidation of both Yemen's security and regime stability at the domestic and international level. Domestically, the government was able to eliminate a serious insurgent attempt in addition to bringing a number of suspected persons to justice for engagement in terrorist activities. At the regional and international level, Yemen cemented its relations with key actors, including promoting unprecedented understanding and cooperation with Saudi Arabia and the other GCC states. On the economic front, while the increase in oil price contributed to bridging the existing deficit in the government budget, standards of living remained low and unemployment rates as well as poverty levels saw little appreciable decrease. Therefore, improving the economic and social condition of the country constituted the main priority for the government in particular in order to attract foreign investments and refurbishing the country's image that was devastated by the terrorism.

Political and Security Developments

Politically, Yemen did not undergo any major constitutional amendment or legal changes. The relationship between the parliament (Majlis al-Nuwab - Council of Deputies) and the government was, however, anything but smooth throughout the year. In April, parliament succeeded in thwarting a dubious government agreement to sell 60% of its share from an oil field arguing that the agreement was in violation of the law. Over 120 MPs threatened to withdraw their confidence from the government if the agreement was not abolished.

Following the summoning of the Minister of Oil to discuss the matter, and a report conducted by a parliamentary committee that uncovered illegality of the agreement, the government relented and cancelled the arrangement.

Another controversial issue arose in December 2004 with the presentation of the 2005 budget. As it included a number of austerity measures, including a reduction in subsidy payments, the government counted on its parliamentary majority to get the budget passed Yet, a number of ruling party MPs decided to stand along with the opposition, stating that they considered the reforms as being socially catastrophic and lambasting the government for proceeding with the budget despite its own awareness of the risks. As an example, the government proposed to reduce the subsidy on oil derivatives to YR 44 billion from YR 120 billion allocated the previous year. This, in turn, would mean that the price of diesel will double to YR35 per liter from the previous YR17, the price of petrol will increase from YR35 to YR52.5 per liter, while the price of kerosene will rise from YR22 to YR40 per liter. Such increases are certain to meet with public outrage.

Despite the contentious atmosphere between the government and the parliament, Yemen continued on its reform path by promoting the work of the free press, allowing political organizations to operate and strengthening its respective legal framework. This was manifested in a number of conferences that were convened on the subject of good governance; for example one on January 12, 2004 on democracy, human rights and the role of the International Criminal Court.[1] Another event was held in Sana'a on August 21 on the rights of women in Islam in which it was agreed that women should participate more actively in local council elections, the next ones scheduled for two years from now. Already, the presence of Yemeni woman is prevalent in all state institutions, with the result that the awareness between men and women of their respective roles is increasing.[2] On December 6, it was then announced that Sana'a would serve as a permanent headquarters for the democratic dialogue center, which will have the task of boosting democracy in the Middle East and North Africa. The project of establishing the center in Yemen came in response to a recommendation from the foreign ministers of Yemen, Turkey and Italy, countries which had been nominated by the G-8 summit, held in Sea Island, US, in June 2004 to sponsor democratic developments in the region. It should also be mentioned that the government in March formed a higher national committee for eliminating the revenge act phenomenon.

Nonetheless, there were some political setbacks. In March, the government went back on its promise of granting opposition parties a license to organize a large demonstration on the occasion of the first anniversary of the US-led invasion of Iraq. In April, a court in Sana'a banned the correspondent of the Quds press news agency and Secretary of the Journalists' Union in Yemen from practicing journalism for six months and ordered him to pay a penalty of 5,000 Yemeni Riyals (USD 28).

In terms of the internal security situation, 2004 was overshadowed by the rebellion of Hussain Badr Al Deen Al-Houthi, an anti-US Shi'ite cleric, and hundreds of his supporters in the Marran mountains of Saddah province in the northwest of the country. Al-Houthi was a parliamentarian from 1993 to 1997, after which he took over the "believing youths" forum, a group which had split from the opposition Islamic al-Haqq party. In recent years, Yemeni authorities accused Al-Houthi of provoking sectarianism and damaging national unity and peace. On June 18, fighting erupted in full force and lasted for three months. During the period, Al-Houthi was killed after the security forces and armored vehicles imposed a three-day siege on a series of caves in Haidan where he had been hiding out. Al-Houthi's brother, Abdul Malik, was subsequently killed during violent confrontations in August, while another brother, Abdul Karim, was detained. In addition to Al-Houthi, 200 of his supporters were also killed by security forces.

Meanwhile, it was the war against terrorism that received the rest of the headlines. In April, Yemeni authorities brought six persons to trial in the case of the American warship USS Cole and five in the attack on the French Limburg oil tanker. 16 US sailors were killed and 39 wounded in the USS Cole attack in October 2000 while one person was killed

[1] *Gulf in the Media*, January 12, 2004.

[2] *SABA News Agency*, December 12, 2004.

and another wounded in the Limburg case in October 2002. Following the trial's conclusion on September 30, two Yemenis members of the al-Qaeda organization were given the death penalty in the USS Cole case while the others were given jail terms. In the Limburg case, the Attorney General in Sana'a asked on October 11th for the death penalty for all five defendants but an elementary court imposed 10 years imprisonment on each instead.

Following an almost four-year absence since the USS Cole attack, the commander of the American joint forces for fighting terrorism in the Horn of African, Mastin Robeson, announced in April 2004 that the US forces would resume using the port of Aden as a station for fuel supplies.[3] On the occasion, the US handed over seven patrol boats to the Yemeni Coast Guard in the form of a donation. The boats are to contribute to ensuring the safety of Yemen's coasts as well as substantiate the efforts made by Sana'a in the fight against terrorism. The announcement by the US came in light of the government seeking international loans from Italy and Poland in order to secure required additional patrol boats for the Yemeni Coast Guard. Prime Minister Abdul Qader Bajamal stated that Yemen is in need of $700 million to ensure the security of its waters, but that the state budget could only provide for 2% of this sum.[4]

Regionally, Saudi Arabia and Yemen exchanged a number of suspects in the context of expanded security cooperation between the two countries. In May 2004, Saudi Arabia handed over first 14 and then 21 Yemeni citizens, including some suspected of involvement in the Limburg case. Yemeni authorities meanwhile handed over numerous suspected members of the al-Qaeda organization that had been detained inside Yemen. The exchanges occurred within increased Saudi-Yemeni cooperation and contact. On May 4, for example,

Yemeni President Ali Abdullah Saleh received Prince Muhammad Bin Nayef, the Saudi Deputy Minister of the Interior for Security Affairs, and discussed with him bilateral relations between the two states, especially in the security field.[5]

In conformity with the border agreement of 2000, Saudi Arabia, on July 11, 2004 handed over a military airport and two border guard posts in the al-Kharkhir area on the southeastern part of the Kingdom. The three items are among thirteen sites that have been handed over to Yemen up to this point. In total, this includes some 40,000 square kilometers, an area equal to the total area of Switzerland or four times the size of Lebanon. In conjunction to these developments, it was announced on May 27 that the German company Hansa Luftbild had completed the border demarcation between the two states as stipulated by the Jeddah treaty,. What remains are technical items such as the finalization of maps which are expected to be completed by the middle of 2005.[6] The work by Hansa Luftbild also overcame the misunderstanding over the Saudi construction of a barrier fence, which Yemen argued violated the Jeddah agreement. During a visit by President Ali Abdullah Saleh in February to Riyadh, Saudi Arabia agreed to stop building the barrier in exchange for increased joint border patrols. Subsequently, Saudi and Yemeni military officials held talks focusing on "security arrangements designed to tighten border security" in March 2004.

Regional and International Relations

In terms of Yemen's regional and international position, the year 2004 held some promise as far as

---

[3] *Yemen Times*, April 12, 2004.

[4] Ibid.

[5] *'26 September' Newspaper*, May 10, 2004. It is important to note that

the discussion here focused on wanted or known extremists and not the general infiltration of illegal workers.

[6] *Okaz*, May 28, 2004.

Yemen was concerned. On April 10, President Saleh signed into law the maritime border agreement between the Sultanate of Oman and Yemen that had been concluded in Muscat on December 14 the previous year.[7] The Yemeni Consultative and Deputies Chambers subsequently endorsed the pact in a joint session.

Relations with the other GCC states also showed continual improvement in a number of political, economic and social aspects.[8] Most important was the announcement by Saudi foreign minister Saud al-Faisal in December 2004 calling for the inclusion of Yemen into the GCC. Saudi Arabia and Yemen signed a total of 11 agreements on political and economic cooperation on December 13, 2004. The items covered included customs cooperation, oil and mineral resources, cultural cooperation, sports and youth welfare, postal services, transportation of goods by land and sea and agricultural cooperation. Riyadh also extended a loan of SR75 million to Yemen's Social Fund for Development as well as a SR50 million grant to develop Aden Hospital. Other support from the Kingdom include SR28 million for a technical institute in Sana'a which is part of a financial aid package of SR188 million from the Saudi Fund for Development (SFD) to set up 19 technical institutes in several of Yemen's provinces.

Yemen also fostered its relations with Arab countries and stressed the importance of the Syrian, Egyptian, and Saudi initiative to reform the Arab League,[9] which it deemed as important to overall joint Arab action and consensus. In February, the Yemen-Egypt summit was held to promote bilateral ties in the fields of investment and trade. The bilateral trade level currently stands at $80 million but it is expected that cement and building materials exports to Yemen will rise dramatically in 2005. Egypt also hopes to increase its exports of pharmaceuticals, textiles and leather goods to Yemen.[10]

On another note, the President of Eritrea, Asyas Afourki, paid a sudden visit to Sana'a between December 8-10, the first since Eritrea's forces occupied the Yemeni greater Hunaish island in 1998. The summit came in the course of efforts made by Yemen to solve differences between the two countries in particular after Eritrea's boats had entered the Yemeni territorial waters in November. The end result was that on December 28, President Ali Saleh called for the immediate inclusion of Djibouti, Eritrea and Somalia into the Sanaa Grouping of the Red Sea and the Horn of Africa, which already includes Yemen, Sudan and Ethiopia.

Internationally, Yemen consolidated its relations with Europe and the US. The Yemeni President visited the major European countries during 2004 and signed a number of important economic agreements financed by the concerned countries to help developing Yemen. The US also provided tangible assistance in the field of defense and security concentrated mainly on equipping the armed forces and training as well as improving the capabilities of the Coast Guard.

Economic Developments

Yemen continued to be plagued by a number of economic shortcomings in 2004 although the relentless efforts to stabilize and restructure the

---

[7] *Oman News Agency*, April 10, 2004.

[8] The only exception is with Kuwait as there still exist some misunderstandings inherited from the second Gulf war. Some Kuwaiti request an explicit apology for supporting Iraq in its invasion of Kuwait in 1990, similar to the apology presented by Mahmud Abbas, the head of Palestinian Authority in December 2004.

[9] *Al Watan* March 3, 2004.

[10] *Arabic News*, February 7, 2004.

economy have begun to show some positive outcomes, particular as far as capital flows are concerned. In that context, Yemen took a number of steps to develop different economic sectors also as a means to facilitate the integration of the Yemeni economy into the international fold.

For example, the banking sector in Yemen has embarked on drafting procedural and executive measures relating to Yemen joining the banking network of the GCC states. A Yemeni banking delegation visited both Saudi Arabia and the UAE to become acquainted with the electronic banking and information network at the Saudi Arab Monetary Fund and UAE banks. Such familiarization is advocated by various international organizations and builds on Yemen's policies to liberalize trade, allow free movement of capital, remove all restrictions that impede imports, and open up bank credits necessary for trade and trade exchange operations. The successful preparations will ultimately facilitate the cooperation processes between various banks in Yemen and their counterparts in the GCC.[11]

The government also adopted a plan for the establishment of industrial zones in order to contribute to development and to be able to distribute industrial activity over the various regions of the country. The idea is also to create an environment in which local investment can be attracted. Yemen's cabinet has, for that purpose, called upon all investors and industrialists to invest in the new industrial zones, participate in the construction of their infrastructure and benefit from privileges the government would make available for them. In following, the council of ministers approved a decree for three zones to be built in Aden, Hudeida and Mukalla.[12] The industrial zone project is also formulated in conjunction with the development of coastal areas, as Yemen has significant sea outlets that can be utilized for both economic and tourist purposes. In accordance with Yemen's other strategic plans, this is considered a key focus for the overall economic development of the country.

Moreover, there are projects being pursued in conjunction with the private sector to promote job creation and support infrastructural projects. The total cost of planned projects amounts to $96 million and the World Bank contributed $23 million in the first year alone, approximately 90%. In addition, there are secondary sources of finance being offered, for example, by the Saudi Fund. Negotiations are also being conducted with the Arab Fund for the project of a sea bridge linking the area of Khour Maksar to Al-Mansoura.

Internationally, the first round of talks were held with the WTO in preparation for Yemen's possible accession to the world body.[13] In addition to the fact that globalization and the information age make the accession of the country to the WTO a necessity, membership is also seen as establishing an international umbrella to protect the country's economic interests against regional cooperation among other WTO members. The government thus hopes to steer investment into the area of production for export rather than have it simply be used to increase local consumption. An increase in Yemen's credibility with foreign investors is another tangible benefit of membership as is the possibility of increasing trade among the Arab members of the WTO.

---

[11] *Al Thawrah Newspaper*, November 16, 2004.

[12] *Arab News*, December 05, 2004.

[13] *Yemen Times*, December 9, 2004.

Conclusion

Yemen's positive accord with neighboring countries will not only allow it to better handle the challenges stemming from the threat of terrorism but will also enhance the opportunities to improve its economy. Relations with countries such as Saudi Arabia, the US, Germany, France and the Netherlands will remain key in that regard. In addition, the role of international institutions such as the International Monetary Fund (IMF) and the World Bank in driving government's economic policies will remain crucial. The government current account surplus due to the high price of oil has already helped in improving the economic performance of the country. Yet, this only underscores the need for a continued reform effort so that Yemen can be put on the path to greater tranquility and prosperity.

Section Nine

Foreseeable Conditions in the Gulf Region

Gulf Patterns and Trends

Prof. Bahgat Korany

Professor of Political Science, American University of Cairo

In this limited space, devoted to an overview of Gulf patterns and trends, the emphasis is on seven aspects: the challenge of normalizing Iraq; the problem of instability; the prevalence of the need for reform; the issues of terrorism and anti-terrorist measures; regime legitimacy issues and the politics of fatwa; and finally, oil and its economics/politics.

In analyzing the Gulf in 2003/2004, the primary factor is the presence of the US. Though obvious, this still needs to be emphasized. Out of trade with the US totaling more than $37 billion, the GCC countries plus Iran and Iraq have a surplus of $17 billion. Moreover, the US is still the major arms supplier in the region and has as of September 2004 a total number of troops of 193,200 stationed in or around the region. As a consequence of this massive military presence, the US is no longer a virtual power in the Gulf, but a real one. It is physically present on the borders with Iran and Syria, with direct strategic impact beyond the Gulf region itself. For instance, Syria finds itself squeezed between American, Turkish, and Israeli troops. Syria's freedom of movement is therefore bound to be curtailed, as seen in Security Council resolution 1559 on Lebanon. Syria rejected this resolution officially but finally decided to "redeploy" its forces.

As part of its strategic plan in the Gulf, the US is making some changes in its military presence in the region, e.g. moving many of its military installations/logistics system from the territory of traditional allies like Saudi Arabia to newer ones like Kuwait and especially Qatar. This strategic restructuring on the ground is part of Imperial America's "here to stay" intention. The obvious base - military as well as political - is Iraq.

Encouraged immensely by the unexpectedly easy fall of Baghdad in March 2003, the US went on with its campaign of "normalizing Iraq." Determined to use Iraq as a showpiece for restructuring the Arab world as a whole, the first measures of the invading forces were to do away with the bases of power in Saddam's ancien régime: party as well as police and army. Even before the arrival of retired US General Jay Garner on April 20, 2003 as the new governor of Iraq, General Tommy Franks, Commander of the US invading forces, prepared the ground for the dissolution of the Ba'ath party, which the occurred on May 11, 2003. In addition, prominent ancien régime personalities were pursued: on April 24, 2003, Tariq Aziz surrendered; on August 19, Taha Yasseen Ramadan, the former Vice-President was captured; and on September 19, Sultan Hashim Ahmed, Saddam's last defense minister gave himself up. On July 22, the photos of the corpses of the formerly all-powerful sons of Saddam, Uday and Qusay were broadcast on all TV screens.

At the same time in July, a group of Iraqi political parties and former exiles agreed on a list of 25 personalities representing a range of political, ethnic and religious backgrounds to form the Iraqi Governing Council. On August 23, 2003, the first internet café opened in Tikrit, symbolizing the end of the extreme information restrictions of the ancien régime. This was followed with economic liberalization measures announced on September 21, 2003 for all major state industries, except oil, as part of an overall program of economic reform. Optimism about pacifying Iraq was common currency: on June 27, 2003 acting Iraqi Oil Minister Thamer el-Ghadban stated that Iraqi oil production should reach prewar standards by the beginning of 2004. Then on July 13, 2003, the newly-formed Iraqi Governing Council in its first official act abolished all former Iraqi state buildings and declared April 9, the day Baghdad fell to coalition forces, as the new national Independence Day.

This exaggerated optimism, however, was soon to be checked. Instability was rampant. Just over a month in August-September 2003 saw the following events.

o On August 13, a purported defiling of a Shi'a religious flag resulted in riots in Baghdad's Sadr City.

o A few days later, the Kirkuk-Turkey oil pipeline and a Baghdad water main were sabotaged on August 16 and 17, respectively.

o Car bombs were detonated in Baghdad outside the Jordanian embassy (August 7) and the UN headquarters (August 19), the latter killing UN Special Representative Sergio Vieira de Mello.

o Ayatollah Muhammad Baqir al-Hakim and at least 75 other Shi'a were killed by an August 29 car bomb in Najaf.

o On September 13, American soldiers, believing they were being attacked, killed eight Iraqi policemen and one Jordanian security guard outside the Jordanian hospital in Falluja.

o Two days later, Khaldiya chief of police, Colonel Khudayr Mikhlif 'Ali, was attacked and killed by masked assailants in broad daylight.

o And on September 20, in the first assassination attempt on a member of the interim government, nine gunmen shot 'Aqila al-Hashimi, who died from her wounds five days later.

Amid ethnic (Arab-Kurdish) and religious (Sunni-Shi'a) conflicts, even US-appointed leading personnel did not seem trustworthy. On July 1, 2003, American military forces arrested the mayor of Najaf and 62 of his aids on charges of kidnapping and corruption. Later, Ahmed Chalabi, initially considered as the US appointed President, was to be arrested. Still, while the new regime was admitted to the Arab League (June 6, 2004), Washington seemed glad to transfer authority to the new Iraqi government (June 28, 2004) and to escape the stigmatic responsibility of another Abu-Gharib torture scandal.

Instability, however, as is well known, is contagious, sometimes fuelled by desperate regime attempts to cope with pressures for liberalization. For instance, on May 13, 2003, Iran - while trying to control the negative international fallouts of the assassination of the Canadian-Iranian journalist Zahra Kazemi - closed 15,000 websites for their pornographic and especially political content. On September 23, 2003, Saudi police arrested dissident Abdel-Aziz Tayyar who was planning a first meeting of independent reformers. On October 9, 2003, 220 Bahraini prisoners started a hunger strike that lasted for 13 days to protest prison conditions and violation of basic human rights.

These events, taken at random, obviously reflect a deeper malaise. In the same month in Bahrain, on October 22, 2003, Shi'a protesters clashed with police to protest the "un-Islamic" performance of the Lebanese singer Nancy Ajram. And Yemen seemed be a chronic case of sociopolitical instability. It tried to make up with the US for the effects of the 2000-attack against the destroyer USS Cole by elements of al-Qa'ida using Yemen as a base, but Yemeni governmental control over territory outside big urban centers is uncertain, as instances of kidnapping of foreigners and tribal rebellion prove so frequently.

Regimes are obviously under strain, a strain increasing because of external pressures and domestic demand for overdue reform. Despite opposition to US (and G8) condescending comments on reform, Kuwaiti Prime Minister Shaikh Sabah Ahmed al-Sabah on February 20, 2004 called upon other Arab states to "understand" US and EU political and economic reform initiatives, and warned against clinging to older traditions keeping Arabs "in the circle of backwardness." The same day, the Qatari foreign minister said more or less the same thing. In the meantime, Iran was trying and retrying to cope with reformers/conservatives factionalization. The Council of Guardians' decision to disqualify around half of those intending to run for the February 20 parliamentary elections provoked mass resignations and a vow by the Islamic Participation Front - Iran's largest pro-reform political party - to boycott the elections. Although subsequent reviews by the Council reinstated 1,160 candidates, this move was seen as insufficient by President Khatami and other reformists. Moreover, the day before the elections, two major reformist newspapers were shut down by conservatives. With the boycott still in force, election results brought about a conservative parliamentary majority amid voter turnout that was 17% lower than that of 2000. Even Saudi Arabia, whose motto is still "the Koran our constitution," saw itself pushed into the reform direction with the announcement of

municipal election in March 2004. In the same month, King Fahd decreed the creation of a National Human Rights Association, with ten women among the Association founding members.

While regimes demagogically (ab)use domestic mistrust of foreign-induced pre-prepared plans for reform to derail necessary changes, the US and Gulf governments come closer together in their fight against terrorism. Either by the carrot or by the stick, the US is extending its anti-terrorism international agenda to the Gulf. For instance, on April 15, 2004, the US undermined the credibility of the Saudi government to maintain domestic law and order by asking its citizens and "non-essential" diplomatic personnel to leave that country. It also continued its pressure for the control of charity organizations, allegedly associated with al-Qa'ida and using "good faith" funds to finance terrorist activities. Saudi Arabia finally complied. In March 2004, both the Bush administration and the Financial Action Task Force praised the enactment of the new Saudi "anti-terrorist" laws to curtail "terrorist funding." Either on its own or profiting from external help, Saudi forces killed Hazem el-Sha'ir, al-Qa'ida's operational chief for the Arabian Peninsula in a Riyadh shoot-out at a police checkpoint. On June 18, 2004, Saudi forces killed Abdul Muhsin Al-Muqrin, leader of al-Qa'ida in Saudi Arabia.

The "anti-terrorist" campaign was even more systematic and forceful in Yemen, deemed a hotbed of al-Qa'ida terrorism. For example, on January 9, 2004, Yemeni security forces captured the alleged leader of the "Lackawana six" cell in the US, Jaber al-Baneh. On March 3, around a dozen al-Qa'ida suspects, including 'Abd al-Ra'uf Nassib and Sayyid Imam Sharif, were arrested. Moreover, USS Cole bombing suspect 'Ali Muhammad 'Umar Shurbajy

> **Regimes are obviously under strain, a strain increasing because of external pressures and domestic demand for overdue reform.**

was apprehended on March 15, while the last two suspects out of the ten who had escaped from prison in April 2003 were seized on March 21, 2004.

Either by conviction or coercion, governments have tried to bolster their anti-terrorist campaign by providing it with a basis for legitimacy. Thus on August 17, 2003, the Saudi Council of Senior Ulama issued a fatwa condemning terrorism as "un-Islamic" and pledged support for the government. In this case, the fatwa might well be bona fide and justified. But in many Islamic countries and across history, some fatwas have been part of governmental instrumentalism to promote political control, especially in times of crisis and in the face of controversial and painful decisions. Thus the government of Iran, after so many oscillations, is now edging toward the fatwa declaring nuclear weapons and their production as "haram." The issue of WMD has obviously been the leitmotif of Iraq's invasion. The government in Tehran could not be completely insensitive to threats of intimidation, sabotage or indirect/direct invasion in the era of a "pre-emptive" strategic doctrine by both the "Neo-cons" in Washington and the Likud in Tel Aviv. This is why the nuclear issue has been not only prominent but also divisive in Iran's political landscape. President Mohammad Khatami's February 9, 2003 announcement of Iran's intention to seek independent nuclear fuel cycle capabilities created substantial alarm, despite repeated assurances that the country's nuclear program was strictly peaceful and in no violation of the Nuclear Non-Proliferation Treaty (NPT). Thus, an October 21 deal forged with the troika (the UK, France and Germany) to suspend uranium enrichment and sign the Additional Protocol to the NPT - under which the International Atomic Energy Agency (IAEA) can launch increased

Either by conviction or coercion, governments have tried to bolster their anti-terrorist campaign by providing it with a basis for legitimacy.

inspections - brought considerable relief to the US and Europe. However, less than a year later, a strongly worded statement by the IAEA prompted Tehran to announce that it would resume its enrichment activities and the manufacturing of centrifuges (July 27, 2004). Concurrently, Iranian officials warned that any pre-emptive attack - Israeli or otherwise - against the country's nuclear facilities would be met with forceful retaliation.

Most recently, on September 18, 2004, the IAEA Board of Governors issued a November 25 deadline for Iran to fully account for its nuclear program and suspend its uranium enrichment. Iran rejected this call, warning that it would consider withdrawal from the NPT if the matter was referred to the UN Security Council - something that the US had hinted at repeatedly. In October, the troika offered a revamped incentive package, including access to nuclear fuel and economic assistance to the civilian nuclear energy program, in exchange for suspension of enrichment activities. By the time of the meeting in November, and after contentious negotiations with the EU-3, Tehran accepted the deal although it was made clear that the freezing of the enrichment activities were temporary and subject to progress in the overall package negotiations with the Europeans that began in January 2005. Meanwhile, the global system has been conditioned to reject any obstacle to its "war on WMD and terrorism", however loosely defined and politically used.

Another convergence of interests between the Gulf countries and the US-dominated global system is the question of oil. The Gulf is still the biggest exporter of oil and possesses more than two-thirds of world reserves. Indeed, a dominant "theory," inside but also outside the Arab world, is that the most important US motivation of the US invasion of Iraq was not WMD or even the removal of Saddam Hussein's regime, but rather the control of oil. Petrol-guzzling America still consumes a quarter of the world's petroleum.

World demand for oil is soaring and consumption is growing at around 3% in 2004, up sharply from the level of recent years. China's booming economy sucks up oil, but America's European allies as well as Japan are still very much dependent on Gulf oil. Any disturbance in this respect could negatively affect both the world economy and its international politics - a potential that the US is determined to control. Washington is especially determined to keep the oil market dollar-based despite OPEC's losses due to the dollar depreciation in the face of the yen and especially the euro.

The rise in the oil price beyond the $50 mark thus comes at the right juncture to compensate for economic problems within Gulf countries. The projected budget surplus for Kuwait for 2004 is above $10 billion, over double that achieved in 2003 when the surplus reached $4.96 billion. In fact, it is estimated that the recent price increase will hand the six oil economies of the GCC countries at least $300 billion.[1] These countries, especially Saudi Arabia, will use part of their windfalls to reduce their debts and balance their budgets. But they will also be able to do much more since the surplus this year and next could be $70-80 billion, or between 10% and 15% of their GDP. There would then be plenty of surplus left to finance infrastructure projects, buy capital goods and arms from abroad, and also invest in developed countries and financial markets. Official statistics on the ownership of American Treasury bills, for example, show that OPEC countries' holdings are around $44 billion, $8 billion less than two years ago. Thus could therefore be the time to reverse the downward trend. The US,

however, has to compete with Europe - and even Asia - in attracting this new influx of petro-dollars. In 2003, OPEC imports from the euro zone were up by 25% while those from the US were only up by 8%. The evolution of the situation in Iraq as well as US overall Middle East policy toward the Arab-Israeli conflict, terrorism and reform could determine the level and direction of the new petro-dollars. Where these petro-dollars will be invested could be the Gulf countries' big leverage both on the US and internationally and thus transform financial and economic assets into political ones.

---

[1] *The Economist*, US Edition, September 25, 2004.

Future Prospects for the Gulf Region

Prof. Giacomo Luciani

Professor of Political Economy, Mediterranean Program
Robert Schuman Center for Advanced Studies, European University Institute

The past 12 months marked a major surprise in store for the member countries of the Gulf Cooperation Council and Iran: while all analysts expected that oil prices would decline because of growing competition from non-OPEC producers, prices have actually climbed - at the time of writing the gain is 60% relative to the beginning of the year. This simple fact is bound to profoundly affect political developments in the region as well as the attitude of outside actors.

The fact that expectations have been proven wrong is especially important, and has a profound psychological impact. Until well into the first quarter of 2004, the unanimously held view was that OPEC would need to reduce production in order to prevent serious weakness in prices. OPEC did decide to reduce production, although the cuts were never implemented. But contrary to the expectations and declarations of experts, companies and governments alike market prices moved higher and higher.

The cause of the surprise is on the one hand a higher-than-expected increase in demand, especially in the US and China and, on the other hand, the realization that although additional reserves might be physically available in several non-OPEC countries, actually bringing additional supplies to the market is a slow and sometimes difficult process.

Progressively, analysts have proposed the notion that the continuing hike in prices is not a short-term phenomenon, but rather a "paradigm change". Although the consensus vision remains that prices are bound to decline from the levels they have reached, it is nevertheless now commonly accepted that they will not return to within the target band of $22-28 which still forms part of the official policy of OPEC.

This contrasts sharply with the previous consensus view, according to which prices were expected to hedge downwards in the second half of the decade, forcing OPEC to surrender some of their market share. The downward pressure on prices was expected to come from non-OPEC production as well as from increased production in Iraq forcing OPEC to redistribute quotas. The combination of weaker prices and possibly reduced quotas was expected to put pressure on the financial equilibrium of some OPEC countries, notably the GCC member countries and possibly create tension across the Gulf, as Iran would not have been willing to reduce production to accommodate Iraq.

In fact, throughout 2004, the governments of the industrial countries, including the US, as well as international organizations such as the IMF and the World Bank, have been calling on the GCC countries to increase their production and urgently invest in increasing their capacity in order to contain the rise in prices. The latter is expected to be especially damaging for the developing countries, notably India.

Consequently, the GCC member countries find themselves in a new strategic environment, in which their domestic fiscal sustainability is essentially assured (although they are not all in the same position: Bahrain in particular may face some problems and Oman as well) and prospects for the future are reassuring. It is now almost universally expected that the recovery of Iraqi production will be slow, even in the optimistic scenario that sees the country making rapid progress towards political stabilization and the establishment of a legitimate, democratically elected government. Thus, the danger of a squabble over oil quotas again spoiling relations between Saudi Arabia and Iran has faded, and the idea that Saudi Arabia might be marginalized as a global supplier of oil, thanks to increased production in Russia and Iraq, has disappeared from the screen.

The renewed inflow of oil revenue has come as important comfort to the incumbent ruling families in the GCC. But challenges persist, and the need for reform - political and economic - continues to be high on the agenda. Still, the aftermath of regime change in Iraq has so far not irradiated in the region to constitute a threat to the stability of incumbent regimes. One is tempted to say that, quite to the contrary, Iraq has instead acted as a "sink", attracting a lot of the attention and capabilities of violent opposition in the region. This may be a purely temporary phenomenon, the situation in Iraq remains extremely unpredictable. There is no certainty about the outcome of the elections in January 2005 or if the re-election of President Bush might affect the future course of American policy in Iraq and in the region. To be sure, considerably less

The renewed inflow of oil revenue has come as important comfort to the incumbent ruling families in the GCC. But challenges persist, and the need for reform - political and economic - continues to be high on the agenda.

optimism is displayed than in the past about Iraq becoming a stable democratic state and that, by virtue of its example, this will highlight the need for political reform and democratization throughout the region. It is just as probable, if not more so, that Iraq's democratic transition will remain fragile or unfinished for some time to come, thereby sending the opposite message that the path to democracy must be threaded with great caution to avoid falling into a vicious circle of instability and extremism.

The last year has also seen an intensification of political violence in Saudi Arabia, but the net outcome of it is yet unclear. Terrorist attacks that have become progressively less selective ended up alienating a very large part of public opinion from the activities of Islamic militants. The government scored some important successes in the repression of militant groups, and the intensity of terrorist activity appears to have abated. The expatriate community remains nervous, but the objective of the militants - which was to "starve" the regime and the Saudi economy of foreign expertise by precipitating a mass exodus - has not been achieved.

In the meantime, the National Dialogue launched by Crown Prince Abdullah brought to the fore certain basic cleavages in Saudi society and polity; comments in the media were not extremely positive, with more people complaining about the debates not being public or participants being representative of the moods within the populations. Simply expressing satisfaction about the conclusions appears insufficient. The issue of the role of women in society, in particular, exposed the existing polarization. This appears to have been received by the leadership as a sign that further prudence is required and progress should be slow and cautious. Yet the announcement that municipal elections, initially scheduled to begin in November 2004, will not begin until February 2005 and that women will not be able to participate, makes it clear that these are issues that cannot possibly disappear, or that the solution can once again be bought with oil money.

In parallel, economic reform is progressing perhaps more slowly than some people may have expected or wished but progressing nevertheless. The cumulative impact of reforms in the past four or five years, together with the expectation that more is in the making, and the feeling of strength that is given by high oil prices, contributes to sustained growth in the private sector. The Saudi stock market index increased 50% since the beginning of the year after increasing 76% in 2003. This is a sign of abundant liquidity chasing a limited supply of assets and opens the door to the possibility of further privatization and/or reorganization of private sector ownership patterns.

Real growth has not yet sufficiently picked up to reabsorb the unemployment problem, which remains a serious concern and a potential source of instability. As a result, further reform progress is required in order to fully mobilize the potential of the Saudi private sector and achieve real growth rates in the order of 6-7%. This objective is not impossible to reach.

Elsewhere in the Gulf, the economy is doing equally as well. The relentless Dubai boom continues apparently unabated, and has a pulling effect on the neighboring Emirates as well. The combination of increased oil revenue in Abu Dhabi and the continuing growth machine of Dubai has created a unique equilibrium and "division of labor", which translates into continuing positive results. The UAE stock market rose by 24.2 % in 2003, and at the time of writing had risen by 47.6 percent in 2004.

The picture is therefore hardly one of critical conditions, although certainly not everything is positive. The inflow of oil revenue has visibly decreased the zeal to implement economic reform, and even minor difficulties are sufficient to postpone action for long periods.

One very important aspect, that needs to be underlined, is the uncertainty surrounding the future of the GCC as the key regional organization. The GCC must face up to several challenges. While it has officially inaugurated a customs union, the practical implementation of this historical decision is seriously lagging. The problem may not be just temporary, as it involves acceptance of the fact that the GCC must become to some extent supranational, and the member countries must surrender to the GCC their sovereignty in matters related to international trade.

The key difference between a customs union and a free trade agreement is not just that the parties establish a common external tariff, but that they jointly define their external trade policy. In this respect, the fact that Saudi Arabia still cannot succeed in gaining membership in the WTO is a problem, albeit presumably a temporary one. Meanwhile, the fact that the US is offering individual members of the GCC free trade agreements also appears to be in contradiction with the cohesion of the GCC.

The GCC therefore faces a challenge of deepening and acquiring the capabilities required to reach the goals that it has set for itself. At the same time, there is a challenge of membership, with the prospect of Yemen and - in a scenario of political stabilization - Iraq becoming members of the group.

> **The picture is therefore hardly one of critical conditions, although certainly not everything is positive.**

On the one hand, an enlargement to Yemen and Iraq would serve the purpose of balancing the otherwise inevitably excessive weight of Saudi Arabia. On the other, however, it would substantially transform the nature of the group, and require a much greater institutionalization of relations than has been achieved so far.

The dilemma of the GCC is but one aspect of the continuing uncertainty surrounding the ability of incumbent regimes to face up to the challenges of globalization and the rapidly evolving international environment. The recent record of the GCC member countries underlines the paramount importance of leadership in the regional and global context. Those GCC member countries that have managed the transition to a new generation of rulers with vision and leadership have enjoyed much better results. The remaining members are suffering from the feeling of precariousness and fragility that the old age of their rulers inevitably transmits to their bureaucracies and societies, independently of the personal qualities of the incumbent - and this frequently leads to paralysis.

Indeed, the biggest cloud on the horizon of some of the Gulf countries is that they will be unable to implement some of the changes that very clearly are required to address the challenges of the future. The enhanced availability of oil revenue may generate complacency - i.e. the temptation to bid for time and wait until circumstances will reduce the pain of finding a solution. Yet, it is by no means clear that simply letting time go by will facilitate a solution.

The problem of the Gulf today is not lack of opportunities. The tide is not moving against the region, both economically and politically, but the region must seize the opportunity to overcome its idiosyncrasies, and more positively integrate in the global environment. The way ahead is shown by the more successful cases in the region, but the overall political will to engage in the required reforms is not necessarily evident.

Outside actors are baffled by the political paralysis gripping the region. The Bush Administration attempted to set in motion a wave of change by removing Saddam and distancing itself to some extent from Saudi Arabia, while in parallel putting pressure on the Saudi regime to undertake a set of reforms. Clearly, this policy has run into much more serious difficulties than were initially expected. The Iraqi adventure has not been a success so far, and Washington has not been in a position to exert the all the intended pressure on Saudi Arabia - or, for that matter, Iran. Neither, however, it is clear that outside pressure necessarily leads to rejection and ends up being counterproductive. Simply accepting the status quo and acritically supporting the incumbent regimes does not appear to be a very promising alternative. But in the end, change must come from within if it is to succeed.

The Gulf...Where to?

Prof. Hasanain Tawfiq

Professor of Political Science, Cairo University

In spite of the numerous steps taken in past decades to study future developments, such an activity in the Arab world in general and the Gulf region in particular has been characterized by a great deal of precaution. This could be ascribed to the acute complexity of the situation in the Gulf region which itself is a product of many varying factors internally, regionally and internationally. As a result, this paper aims to provide a general overview of the situation in the Gulf in the coming years by identifying the most important factors that will have a bearing on the future outlook.

Factors impacting the future of the Gulf

Among the key issues that are bound to impact on the future direction of the Gulf, the following can be identified:

The demographic imbalance in the GCC states and its consequences

The GCC countries suffer with varying degrees and in different forms from an imbalance in their population structure. Firstly, there exists an imbalance in the proportion of nationals to expatriates, the latter which are dominantly Asian and who make up the majority of the population. Regardless of the reason behind this imbalance, it is one of the key challenges faced by the GCC countries, particularly because of its economic, social, political and security consequences. Although GCC countries have tried to implement programs to rectify the imbalance, results have been modest in countries like the United Arab Emirates, Qatar and Kuwait. Secondly, there is the imbalance in the various age groups. Young people and children form the majority of the population in the GCC countries thereby increasing the strains on the current generation in the form of breadwinners having to feed many more mouths and imposing a heavy current and future burden on government in terms of the needs in education, health, leisure, jobs, housing etc. Thirdly, there is the imbalance manifested in the large number of expatriate workers and the rocketing rates of unemployment among the nationals. In this context, it should be emphasized that there exists a correlation between unemployment and the emergence of extremism, violence and terrorism.

Continuing internal and international pressures for reform

The development which the GCC countries have been witnessing in the form of economic and political change over the past decade is the outcome of both internal and external factors pushing in the direction of reform. These pressures, especially those externally related, have increased since the attacks of 9/11 in relations to the shift in Washington's attitude towards the need for democracy in the Arab and Islamic worlds. A continuation and possibly even escalation in the foreseeable future for further reform measures is to be expected thereby making reform a central component of developments in the GCC region. At the same time, governments in the region will find it increasingly difficult to ignore or circumvent these pressures.

The second oil boom and its impact

Regardless of the speculation about alternatives to oil and the possibility of a decrease in the external demand for Gulf oil, numerous studies have concluded that this is not a likely development in short or medium term. In fact, demand for oil will continue to increase over the next two decades, with the Gulf holding a central position since the region holds about 60% of proven world oil reserves. Due to its strategic importance, oil will remain the main locomotive of the Gulf economies, in particular as diversification efforts have only had a modest impact so far. Moreover, the current price development in the oil markets, where a barrel of oil has traded above $50, translates directly into increased revenues for the oil-producing GCC countries thereby allowing for a relaxation in terms burgeoning budget deficits, high unemployment and high foreign and internal debts.

Yet, there are legitimate questions about what repercussions the oil price rise will have on the reform debate within the GCC States. One danger is that, similar to what occurred after the first oil boom (from the mid 1970s to the mid 1980s), a revenue mentality at the level of both states and individuals in the Gulf will take hold in turn helping to reinforce the status quo and delay both political

and economic reform measures. It should, however, also be remembered that the reform process in the GCC countries has partly become connected with factors other than oil revenue, for example the growing strength of political forces such as groupings and societies. Moreover, there is the emergence of new leaderships that have adopted the reform agenda to argue for the establishment of a new basis for political legitimacy. Added to this, of course, is the existence of an international environment that supports reform. Therefore, a more likely scenario is that the allocation of the increased oil revenues to resolve economic and social problems in the Gulf States will also pave the way for additional steps in the way of political reform.

The situation in Iraq

The future situation in the Gulf will surely depend, to a certain extent, on what will happen in Iraq. In other words, the future of Iraq will leave its traces both on the Arab region in general and the Gulf region in particular. Currently, there are two main scenarios for a future Iraq. The first is the country being put on the right track towards independence, democracy, and development. The second is an Iraq sliding into chaos and insecurity ultimately leading to civil war, partition and the disintegration of the country as a political entity.

Judging by what is happening on the ground in Iraq, the country is likely to witness instability in the foreseeable future, particularly because the holding of elections in January 2005 will not mean an end to the Iraqi crisis. Rather, the outcome is also connected to other considerations such as the future of the American military presence in Iraq, the extent of an agreement between the main political forces on the future of the political and state system, and the progress that can be achieved to further the reconstruction process politically, economically and socially.

Iran between internal challenges and external pressures

Just as the situation in Iraq is going to be an essential ingredient of the future scenario in the Gulf, present developments in Iran are going to be an important factor, particularly in view of the internal challenges facing Iran and the external pressures being exerted against it. The semi-constant tension between reformists and conservatives, which recently produced a clear victory for the conservatives in the last legislative elections, has put the reformist program as represented by President Mohammad Khatami at risk. This in turn is also reflected in the continuation of tension between the US and Iran, which are additionally burdened by such issues as the Iranian nuclear program and the role played by Iran in internal Iraqi developments.

In light of this, Iran might in certain circumstances be a source of regional instability especially if domestic developments begin to unravel or if the relations between Washington and Teheran slide into confrontation. In such an eventuality, Iran may use various methods to target American interests in the area. In contrast to that, however, Iran could also be a force for regional stability in the Gulf although such a scenario would depend, among other factors, on an Iranian reformulation and involvement in a collective arrangement for security in the region.

The lack of a stable structure for security in the Gulf

The Gulf region lacks a stable security structure, a situation that has led to numerous conflicts in the past and forced GCC countries to establish links with outside powers, particularly the US in terms of security arrangements. In the wake of the Iraq war, which resulted in the overthrow of Saddam Hussein and the Anglo-American occupation of the country, the region is now faced with a new situation in that

one of the main factors for instability of the past decades has been eliminated. At the same time, developments that have followed the occupation of Iraq, notably the disbanding of the Iraqi army and the dismantling of the state institutions, have certainly contributed to a strategic imbalance in favor of Iran. Furthermore, with its role inside the country, Washington has emerged as the principal international power in the region. In these circumstances, the lack of any stable security structure in the Gulf is likely to remain one of the future characteristics of the region. The multitude of visions by the parties concerned and the essential conflict between Iran and the US makes the task of formulating a stable security system in the Gulf difficult if not impossible.

Bush's winning of a second term and its bearing on the American role in the Gulf

The US has emerged as the de facto power in the region with over 130,000 troops in Iraq and with the largest US embassy in Baghdad making the American presence look like a parallel Iraqi government. This is supported by a prominent military presence throughout the rest of the Gulf whether in the form of bases, facilities, depots or otherwise, in addition to the security accords that are in place with various countries in the region. The US has also adopted a strict policy towards Iran which it places in the now infamous "axis of evil." American administration figures have consistently maintained that all necessary means will be used to prevent Iran from acquiring weapons of mass destruction including the use of military force if diplomatic efforts fail.

With President Bush winning a second term in office in November 2004, there is likely to be a continuation of the past policies, in particular since the changes made within the administration have increased rather than lessened the dominance of the so-called "hawks." The appointment of Condoleezza Rice as Secretary of State also indicates that any changes in the US Gulf policy in particular and the Arab world in general will be marginal at best. This also means a continuation of the large US presence in Iraq since, as President Bush has indicated on more than one occasion, the US forces will only withdraw until their mission in Iraq has been accomplished. Of course, it remains up to Washington to define such a mission and the form it is going to eventually take. Similarly, the strict policy towards Iran will continue, particularly if diplomacy fails to solve the nuclear program issue. In the meantime, no significant change is expected in terms of the general American military presence in the region, especially in the smaller Gulf States.

Future Trends

In light of the above, one can draw some preliminary conclusions and point towards what might most likely be some of the more prominent trends expected in the Gulf in the coming years.

1. Continuation of restricted political openness without applying democracy

Rising political pressure is expected to continue throughout the region including the development of political legislatures and support of the political rights of women in those countries where such rights are still lacking. Political parties may be allowed in countries like Bahrain and Kuwait alongside a general improvement in their respective human rights records. Yet, it is unlikely that the political reform process will lead to a genuine democratic change as some have hoped for as such process is a long-term development that requires certain

conditions to be met. This does not mean that countries in the region will necessarily witness rising political tensions leading to an outbreak of violence. Still an escalation in the strife between reformist and conservative forces in Iran or a rising dispute between authorities and the opposition in a GCC country remains a possibility.

A further deterioration in the Palestinian and Iraqi arenas could lead to protests in some countries, a situation that has previously led to clashes between demonstrators and security forces. Whereas the Saudi authorities have managed to some degree contain the militant and extremist groups carrying out attacks in the country, the challenge for the kingdom will be in tackling many of the political, economic and social root sources leading to militancy and extremism. The experience of many countries shows that force on its own is not enough to root out such a phenomenon.

2. Gradual and slow economic reform through diversification of the sources of income

In the last few years, GCC countries took varying steps in the way of economic reform. This is expected to continue in the foreseeable future, particularly in the field of privatization and reforming the public sector. However, it is unlikely that such reforms will bring about a quantum leap of diversification in the sources of income as oil will continue as the backbone and drivers of the national economies, particularly in the light of high oil prices and increased revenues. The modest ability of the GCC countries to make some progress in diversification measures is likely to keep unemployment at their present level although current demographic trends point towards rising unemployment rates as new graduates enter the job market. In fact, GCC states already suffer from veiled unemployment for both nationals and expatriates.

3. Living with an unstable Iraq

Iraq will suffer instability for years to come as present developments underline. The US operation in Fallujah in November 2004 to root out the Iraqi insurgency and to teach those that oppose the US presence in the country a lesson has only managed to weaken the resistance for a short period. The holding of elections in January 2005 will also not guarantee stability, even if the main Iraqi sections decide to participate in the process. Already, there are indications that large parts of the Iraqi Sunni community will boycott the elections in view of the human tragedy in areas such as Fallujah. Even if elections succeed, this will simply put a process in place requiring a consensus among all Iraqi groups so that a permanent constitution which provides for political and institutional arrangements can be issued. Bringing about such a consensus will be a Herculean task given the fact that all the groups are primarily trying to protect and promote their own interests. In such an environment, tensions appear unavoidable and could easily break out in the open if there are disagreements on issues considered vital for one group or another. The existence of militias and armed factions belonging to certain factions will undoubtedly exacerbate such situations.

There are other factors that affect the stability of a future Iraq including mounting economic and social problems, the slow pace of the reconstruction process, the widespread availability of arms, and the overall lack of transparency in the US occupation in terms of its aims and objectives. Economically, Iraq will take years to recover particularly because of the continued deterioration of the security situation, the almost complete devastation of the economic structure as well as the mounting problems of debt, compensation payments, unemployment and inflation. Added to this is the fact of the deteriorating standard of living and the difficulty in the rehabilitation of the oil sector so that it can assume a leading role in the reconstruction process. In short, Iraq's economy will not recover unless the political and security problems that have arisen in the post-Saddam Iraq environment are resolved.

4. The continuing tension between the US and Iran

Rising tension will also most probably characterize the US/Iran relationship in the coming years. With the re-election of President Bush having reaffirmed the administration in his policies and with the conservatives within the Iranian establishment having gained the upper hand over the past year, the likelihood of both sides working towards resolving their problems would appear impossible. This is in fact a gaping rift between the two sides that will become dangerous if the dispute over the Iranian nuclear program escalates into an open, possibly military, confrontation. In light of the possibility of a US military strike, with or without the support of Israel, Iran can be expected to retaliate in a number of ways to the detriment of both Washington and its allies in the region. In the meantime, a continued policy of excluding Iran from any future security arrangements in the region will certainly drive Iran to sabotage the process.

5. Continuation of American influence in the Gulf

With the US as the main international power in the Gulf, its role will remain strong in the foreseeable future. In light of strategic interests such as the continuation of the stable flow of Gulf oil, and the maintenance of its pre-emptive policy, Washington sees the Gulf region as an integral part of its overall foreign and security policy, also in relation to other world powers such as Russia, China, Japan and the EU. Due to the fact that no alternative has emerged in terms of a stable security structure that involves all the regional states including Iran, the GCC States will continue to depend on Washington for their security through security agreements and other arrangements.

Conclusion

Although the overthrow of Saddam Hussein will eventually benefit the Iraqi people, the failure of Washington to handle the post-invasion reconstruction process and its outright inflammation of the Iraqi people has brought about a political, economic, social and security situation that has completely deteriorated. As present, there is little indication that Iraq has become a safer place after Saddam as the American administration claims.

In that context, the Gulf region cannot be removed as an area of tension and conflict in the coming years. Iraq will not settle down for some time to come even if immediate steps were taken to put the country on the track of independence, development and democracy. The alternative of a disintegration of Iraq into three parts, with all the consequences thereof, remains a distinct possibility. Moreover, the continued tensions between the US and Iran will feed the instability in the region.

In such circumstances, the GCC countries will find themselves having to deal with complicated situations and awkward options in terms of having to balance an unstable Iraq, a volatile American/Iranian relationship, the absence of a Gulf security order, and the need for political, economic and social reform for their own societies. They will also need to be ready to deal with the internal consequences of their relations with Washington and the US policies towards certain Arab and Islamic issues. Given such circumstances, there would appear to be no alternative but to consolidate the internal cohesion between state and society as a means to build up legitimacy on the one hand and to enhance the coordination within the GCC in such a way that will enable them to better deal with the new challenges on the other hand. In addition, it is necessary to reformulate their relations with the outside world not least with certain big powers such as the EU, China, Japan and Russia in order to create a greater degree of independence at the international level.

Timelines

The Kingdom of Bahrain Timeline 2004

January

January 5
Five Members of Parliament submit a proposal calling for the review of all laws passed from 1975 until 2002.

January 9
The Desert Al Areen Resort project by Gulf Finance House gets underway in southern Bahrain.

January 17
The government announces a plan for a "Future Generation Reserve Bank Account."

January 18
Hardliners retain control over the leading opposition group, the Al Wefaq Islamic Society.

January 19
Qatar Steel Company signs a five-year contract worth $250 million for the purchase of direct reduction grade iron pellet from Bahrain-based Gulf Industrial Investment Co.

January 22
Parliament interrogates three ministers over alleged irregularities in the kingdom's two social security agencies (General Organization for Civil Service Retirement Fund and the General Organization for Social Security).

January 25
Under pressure from Parliament, the Cabinet approves a plan to restructure two social security funds.

January 26
The first round of negotiations for a Free Trade Agreement (FTA) between the US and Bahrain opens in Manama.

February

January 29
"Bahrain has been making serious efforts to bring freedom to the region," US President George W. Bush said in a message to His Majesty the King, Hamad bin Isa Al Khalifa.

February 15
The country marks the third anniversary of the referendum on the National Action Charter.

February 16
Four Bahraini political groups end a controversial conference with a call on the government to debate what they called the "constitutional crisis" in the kingdom.

February 18
Parliament suggests that only the king and MPs can make constitutional changes.

February

February 19

Kuwait bans four Shi'ite leaders of Bahraini opposition groups from entering the country.

February 24

Bahrain and Qatar finalize plans for a $2-billion causeway link and agree on a deal to supply Bahrain with Qatari natural gas.

February 28

Prime Minister Shaikh Khalifa bin Salman al-Khalifa rebuffs US plans to encourage democracy in the Middle East.

February 28

King Hamad bin Isa Al Khalifa arrives in Kuwait.

March   April

March 25

Hundreds of students and policemen clash near the headquarters of the US Embassy in Manama during a march to protest against the assassination of Palestinian and Hamas leader Shaikh Ahmad Yassin by Israeli forces.

April 13

US General Richard Meyers, Chairman of the Joint Chiefs of Staff, arrives in Manama.

April 16

The Parliament sets up a MP panel to prepare a list of proposed changes to the constitution.

April 21

Shura Council member Dr. Nada Abbas Haffadh is named as Bahrain's first woman minister to assume the health portfolio.

May

April 24

Four opposition groups gather signatures calling for political reforms.

April 27

Bahrain warns the opposition against demanding "illegal" constitutional amendments.

April 28

MPs agree not to question Minister of State Abdulnabi Al-Shoala over irregularities in one of the country's pension funds.

May 1

Authorities detain 16 people involved in collecting signatures for a petition on constitutional reforms.

May 15

Political societies call off their campaign to petition King Hamad for constitutional changes.

May 20

Twenty people, arrested for collecting signatures demanding constitutional changes, are released.

May 22

A protest against the US aggression on the holy shrines in Najaf and Karbala leads to clashes with police and injuries, forcing the removal of the interior minister on the grounds of high-handedness.

May 23

MPs clear two ministers over alleged mismanagement of two pension funds.

June

June 9
King Hamad bin Isa Al Khalifa participates in the G8 Summit held in the US.

June 21
The Cabinet agrees to a $66 million loan from Kuwait to finance the King Hamad Hospital in Muharraq.

June 24
Authorities release six men a day after they were detained on suspicion of supporting al-Qaeda and plotting terror attacks.

June 26
Parliament rejects a US warning that extremists are planning attacks on US interests in the country.

July

June 29
Bahrain announces plans for the $1-billion Amwaj Islands project that includes multi-storey buildings, hotels and commercial complexes.

June 29
Iraqi interim Prime Minister Iyad Allawi asks Bahrain, Oman and Morocco to send troops to supplant the coalition forces in Iraq.

July 1
The Telecommunications Regulatory Authority announces that the telecom market will be fully open for competition.

July 1
A Bahraini-Qatari summit is held in Manama to discuss the means of boosting bilateral cooperation.

July 3
Middle Eastern and North African countries agree to set up a regional body to combat money laundering and terror financing to be based in Bahrain.

July 4
Manama appoints Hassan Al-Ansari as Bahrain's new ambassador to Iraq. Al-Ansari was the charge d'affaires based in Baghdad.

July 5
The US Embassy in Manama abrogates Independence Day celebrations due to security fears.

July 6
The US evacuates families of its military staff from Bahrain amid reports of possible attacks against Americans.

August

July 14
Six Islamists are rearrested on suspicion of plotting a wave of attacks in the country.

July 19
A local firm announces the construction of a $500-million tourist project, Pearl Island.

July 25
Authorities release two detainees after they are cleared of any links to Al-Qaeda.

August 1
Bahrain signs a $500-million deal with the Belgian company Tractable and the Gulf Investment Corporation for its first private power plant to be built in the Hidd Industrial Area.

August

August 3
Bahrain pledges support for Iraq reconstruction during Iraqi Prime Minister Iyad Allawi's visit.

August 4
The Bank of Bahrain and Kuwait, through its representative office in Dubai, join a consortium to provide a $1.36-billion loan to Abu Dhabi-based Dolphin Energy Ltd.

August 8
Foreigners who have lived in other GCC countries for 15 years and have bank deposits of over $100,000 are allowed to make Bahrain their permanent home.

August 12
The US State Department lifts a cautionary warning it issued to its citizens to leave Bahrain and refrain from traveling to it.

August 14
Over 15,000 protesters call for an end to US attacks on the holy city of Najaf in Iraq.

August 23
A technical glitch at Al-Hid power station causes a major power cut-off to most regions across the country.

September

September 15
The US and Bahrain sign a free-trade agreement in a move aimed at boosting economic and trade ties

September 15
The UAE announces its consent to Bahrain's request to host the 25th session of the GCC summit in Manama due in December.

September 20
The first Bahraini-Iranian joint venture financial institution, Future Bank, is launched.

September 24
Human rights activist Abdulhadi Al-Khawajah, director of Bahrain Center for Human Rights, is arrested for taking part in a controversial seminar held at a cultural club and calling for the resignation of the prime minister.

September 29
The government dissolves the Bahrain Center for Human Rights, which was headed by Al-Khawajah.

October

October 1
Around two thousand Bahrainis take to the streets to demand the release of Al-Khawajah.

October 1
A group of labor activists disclose a project for the creation of a human rights monitoring association.

October 11
The Crown Prince is assigned to launch a national dialogue "to achieve political and economic development."

October 16
Al-Khawaja goes on trial.

October 19
Demonstrators call for the resignation of the prime minister and the release of "judicial" activist Abdul Hadi Al-Khawaja.

October

October 22
Al Oruba Club, which was closed for 45 days, after hosting two controversial meetings is reopened after an out-of-court deal with the government.

October 23
A $400-million commercial mall is announced in Manama.

October 28
Riots in the Al-Sanhajiya district erupt after a group of unidentified individuals set fire to old types.

October 28
Saudi Arabia suspends a donation of 50,000 barrels per day of oil to Bahrain pending talks on sharing the output of a joint offshore field in Saafa.

November

October 28
Bahrain-based Gulf Finance House announces plans for a $1-billion investment in a real estate project, Royal Metropolis, in Jordan.

October 29
Authorities detain 30 people for maintaining solidarity with human rights activist Khawaja.

October 31
The High Civil Appeals Court clears four people allegedly linked to Al-Qaeda.

November 12
An Iraqi group threatens to attack American interests in Bahrain.

November 12
Bahrain announces plans to have four new power substations in time to meet the expected peak demand of 1,840MW of electricity next summer.

November 17
Bahrain's associations issue a 'political association' draft law submitted by the Progressive Forum, the National Action and the National Action Charter associations as a substitute for the political associations law presented by the Bloc of Independents to the Parliament.

November 21
Bahrain's criminal court metes out a one-year sentence on to Al-Khawajah.

November 22
King Hamad pardons human rights activist Khawaja and orders his release from prison.

December

November 29
King Hamad becomes the first Arab leader to meet US President George W. Bush after his re-election.

December 5
Bahrain hosts the Gulf Dialogue Conference organized by the London-based International Institute for Strategic Studies. During the meeting Saudi Foreign Minister Saud al-Faisal launches a veiled attack on Bahrain regarding the latter's decision to sign a free trade agreement with the US.

December 10
Announcement of the creation of the Bahrain Center for Human Rights Monitoring.

December 13
A women's petition is sent to King Hamad calling for an end to the violations of women's labor rights.

December

December 17

Bahrain prepares a proposal to amend the GCC Charter to allow the establishment of a Gulf parliament.

December 21

Bahrain hosts the twenty-fifth GCC Summit, which Saudi Crown Prince Abdullah does not attend.

December 28

King Hamad and Saudi Crown Prince Abdullah hold talks in Dammam, Saudi Arabia reportedly to discuss the dimensions and implications related to Bahrain's trade deal with the US.

December 31

Bahrain's Association for the Defense of Expatriate Workers is announced.

Iran Timeline 2004

January

January 1
Relief efforts continue following the earthquake that hit the city of Bam on December 26, 2003.

January 3
US officials say Iran rejected an American proposal to dispatch relief teams to the city of Bam.

January 10
The Guardian Council's electoral oversight body announces that 3,600 out of 7,900 candidates had been disqualified from the race for seats in Iran's 290-seat Parliament.

January 11
The Guardian Council rejects the candidacy of some 877 reformists to stand at parliamentary elections. Signs of a political crisis loom large after 27 officials threaten to resign.

January 14
Iran's Supreme Leader Ayatollah Khameini orders the Guardian Council to revise their massive blacklisting of reformists.

January 23
Mohammed al-Baradei, Director-General of the International Atomic Energy Agency, says Iran must cooperate with the agency's efforts to monitor its nuclear program or it would face 'grave consequences'.

January 29
The Guardian Council lifts a ban on 1,160 candidates for next month's parliamentary elections.

February

February 2
More than 120 members of parliament resign in protest over the vote row.

February 10
A memorandum of understanding is signed in Teheran related to financial assistance to be provided by the GCC countries to reconstruct the city of Bam.

February 14
Iran's Foreign Minister Kamal Kharazi says Iran is capable of producing nuclear fuel and is ready to sell it on the international market.

February 20
Parliamentary elections are held throughout the country to choose 289 member of the Consultative Council.

February 25
The conservatives win a sweeping victory taking a total of 156 in the 290-seat assembly.

February | March

February 25

Iran signs a deal on Wednesday to form a Liquefied Natural Gas (LNG) production company with France's Total and Malaysia's Petronas.

March 5

John Bolton, US Deputy Secretary of State, reiterates the determination of Washington and her allies to pressure Iran into disclosing its nuclear weapons development program.

March 7

Conservative and reformist legislators scuffle in parliament after a reformist lawmaker called on a panel of clerics to examine the performance of Supreme Leader Ayatollah Ali Khamenei.

March 10

Iranian Foreign Minister Kamal Kharazi strongly criticizes the International Atomic Energy Agency.

March 12

The International Atomic Energy Agency reveals that Iran has taken a surprise decision to call off inspections by the Agency.

March 15

Hashemi Rafsanjani, former Iranian president, reiterates his country's determination to 'use nuclear energy for peaceful ends' and Mohamed El-Baradei announces Iran has agreed to let United Nations nuclear inspectors into the country.

March 17

President Mohammed Khatami acknowledges the failure of the pillars of his presidency, conceding his two key reform proposals that sought to check the powers of hardliners.

March 28

An Iranian official says Tehran has resumed work on enriching uranium.

April

April 1

The National Iranian Tanker Company (NITC) announces plans to acquire 51 new tankers to meet demand for energy transportation by 2010.

April 6

Mohamed El-Baradei says Iran and the International Atomic Energy Agency have agreed on a timetable for inspections.

April 15

A senior Iranian diplomat Khaleel Naeemi is gunned down in Iraq.

April 21

President Khatami warns US troops about attacking the Iraqi Shiite cities of Najaf and Karbala.

May

April 25

Iran closes a German government-funded language institute in Tehran as possible retaliation for a defamation campaign against Iran in Berlin.

April 25

Iran's parliament formally approves a minor reshuffle of President Khatami's cabinet, confirming the new appointees to the ministries of labor and finance.

May 7

A second round of voting takes place in constituencies that failed to return a winner in the February parliamentary elections.

May 10

Iranian Charge d'Affaires in Kuwait denies reports of a secret meeting between Iranian officials and a group of Kuwaiti Shiite delegates.

May

May 16
Several hundred Islamic students throw rocks at the British Embassy in Tehran.

May 22
Iran submits more than a 1,000-page report on its contested nuclear program to the UN Atomic Agency.

May 23
Gholam-Ali Haddad-Adel, an in-law of Iran's Supreme Leader, Ayatollah Ali Khamenei, is selected as the new speaker of the Majlis.

May 24
Iran's Foreign Ministry spokesman Hamid-Reza Asefi rejects a statement issued at the end of the Arab summit in Tunis on the three United Arab Emirates islands.

June

May 30
Foreign Ministry spokesman Hamid Reza Asefi rules out any cooperation with the US in its occupation of neighboring Iraq and demands that any new Iraqi government be given "full sovereignty."

June 1
Iran denies that Ahmad Chalabi informed Tehran that Washington has managed to decode the secret codes used by Iranian secret services.

June 6
UAE authorities confirm reports of seizing an Iranian fishing boat after it entered UAE territorial waters.

June 8
Yahya Safawi, Commander of the Revolutionary Guard, accuses the Iraqi interim government of 'treason' to the benefit of the US.

June 8
France, Britain and Germany submit a report to the International Atomic Energy Agency sharply criticizing Iran for lack of cooperation with the agency.

June 12
Iranian Foreign Minister Kamal Kharazi announces that Iran has forwarded 'interesting' intelligence to Saudi Arabia about a group of Al-Qaeda elements detained in Iran.

June 13
Iranian Foreign Minister Kamal Kharazi complains to Qatar's ambassador to Tehran after Qatari coast guards fired at an Iranian fishing boat in the Gulf Sea.

June 15
Iranian television announces that navy troops from the Revolutionary Guard have seized a UAE boat fishing near Iranian coats.

June 16
Two Iranian fishing boats are detained after they enter Qatari territorial waters without permission and using banned nets.

June 16
Iran threatens to resume its uranium enrichment operations in the event the International Atomic Energy Agency adopts a project to reprimand Iran for lack of sufficient cooperation.

June 19
Hussein Ruhani, Iran's senior nuclear negotiator, says Iran will review its decision to suspend uranium enrichment activities after a strongly worded criticism was issued by the UN.

June 21
Three British vessels are detained by Iranian navy after they entered Iran's territorial waters.

June

June 25
Iranian leader Ali Khamenei says his country does not seek to build a nuclear arsenal but will not abandon its right to acquire nuclear technology.

June 28
Iranian foreign minister says his country opposes any interference by NATO in Middle East issues.

June 29
Mohamed El-Baradei, head of the International Atomic Energy Agency, says in Moscow that the Bushir nuclear reactor is an issue related to Iran-Russia bilateral ties.

June 30
Iran's foreign ministry spokesman says Iran has released the crew of the UAE boats previously detained in Iran.

July

July 1
UAE foreign ministry says the UAE has released an Iranian boat and its crew it seized some time ago.

July 4
Former Iranian President Rafsanjani says former Iraqi president Saddam Hussein should be tried for crimes against Iran during the war between the two countries.

July 5
The head of Iran's judiciary directs the public prosecutor to open a case against Saddam Hussein in coordination with the foreign ministry.

July 9
Kuwait seizes three Iranian fishing boats after they strayed into its waters in the latest string of incidents involving Iran and its Gulf neighbors.

July 11
Iranian President Mohamed Khatami receives Abdulaziz al-Hakeem, President of the Higher Council of the Islamic Revolution in Iraq.

July 13
Iran's navy seizes two Qatari boats that strayed into its waters.

July 13
Khalid Al-Harbi, alias Abu Suleiman, surrenders to the Saudi Arabian Embassy in Tehran and is later deported to Riyadh.

July 15
Canada recalls its ambassador to Iran after Tehran abruptly ended the trial of an intelligence agent accused of killing a Canadian journalist.

August

July 20
Iraqi interior minister, Falah al-Naqeeb, lashes out at Iran accusing it of standing behind terrorist attacks in Iraq.

July 24
Iran's press agency says an Iranian court has handed out a 'non-guilty' verdict on an intelligence agent accused of killing the Canadian journalist Zahra Kazimi.

July 26
Iraqi Defense Minister Hazem al-Sha'alan accuses Tehran of sending spies into Iraq and supporting terrorist acts in the country, describing Iran as 'Iraq's number one enemy'.

August 1
Kamal Kharazi describes statements made by some Iraqi officials as further evidence that Iraq is still unstable.

August

August 7
The EU warns Tehran of escalated US pressure as a result of Iran's determination to acquire nuclear weapons.

August 8
US National Security Advisor Condoleezza Rice announces the US "will study all means possible' to put an end to Iran's nuclear program.

August 10
Kamal Kharazi announces that Tehran has sent a written invitation to Iraqi interim Prime Minister Iyad Allawi to visit Iran.

August 11
Iran claims to carry out a successful field test of the latest version of its Shahab-3 medium-range ballistic missile

August 16
Japanese minister of commerce says Tokyo will not change its program for developing Iranian oil fields despite US reticence.

August 19
Ali Shamkhani, the Iranian Defense Minister, warns the US and Israel that Iran is ready to launch pre-emptive strikes to stop them attacking its nuclear facilities.

August 20
Iranian President Mohamed Khatami calls on the Islamic Conference Organization to hold an emergency meeting to discuss developments in Iraq.

August 29
Iran and Iraq agree on forming joint committees to resolve sticking issues concerning the two countries.

September

August 31
Iran says it has arrested dozens of people for allegedly spying on the country's nuclear program.

September 1
The UN says Iran plans to convert a large amount of crude uranium into fluoride grade 6.

September 3
EU foreign ministers criticize Iran's nuclear program and hint at the possibility of taking Iran's nuclear file before the UN Security Council.

September 4
Iran announces it will begin extracting uranium from deep under its central desert in less than two years.

September 14
Iranian Foreign Ministry spokesman Hamidreza Asefi stresses that the three Gulf islands of Abu Musa as well as the Lesser and Greater Tunbs are integral parts of the Iranian territory.

September 17
Mohamed el-Baradei says the International Atomic Energy Agency did not find any evidence of nuclear activities at the Parchin site.

September 18
Iran, Iraq restore full ties 24 years after outbreak of war.

September 19
Hassan Rowhani says Iran rejected the decision taken by the International Atomic Energy Agency calling upon Tehran to freeze its uranium enrichment activities.

September

October

September 23

The Spanish oil group Repsol YPF and British-Dutch group Shell have signed a project framework agreement involving the Iranian oil company NIOC regarding liquefied natural gas in Iran.

September 25

President Mohammad Khatami postpones a visit to Turkey after the conservative-controlled parliament throws into doubt two major contracts signed with Turkish companies.

October 5

Hashemi Rafsanjani says Iran has the capability of launching 200-km-range missiles.

October 6

Oman's Sultan Qaboos bin Said and President Khatami hold talks in Muscat.

October 7

A Russian official confirms continued cooperation between Russia and Iran despite international pressures.

October 10

Iran and Russia announce that they are close to finalizing a long-delayed protocol on returning spent nuclear fuel to Russia.

October 12

Iranian Vice-President Mohammad Ali Abtahi, a close ally of President Khatami, resigns.

October 20

Iran announces it has tested an upgraded version of the 'Shihab 2' missile believed to be capable of reaching Israel.

November

October 27

Second Iran-EU round of negotiations kicks off in Vienna.

October 28

Iran's Foreign Minister Kamal Kharazi holds talks with Abu Dhabi's Crown Prince Shaikh Khalifa Bin Zayid Al Nahyan in Abu Dhabi.

October 30

Iran's parliament adopts a bill making it mandatory for the government to pursue the country's nuclear development program.

November 7

Iran's interior ministry fixes Friday May 13, 2005 as the date for the next presidential election.

December

November 14

Iran agrees to a full suspension of uranium enrichment in line with an agreement worked out with the European Union.

November 17

President Khatami says his country was ready to help the Americans get out of a "quagmire" in Iraq.

November 30

The Council of governors at the International Atomic Energy Agency issues a decision urging Iran to put an end to its sensitive nuclear activities in keeping with the EU agreement.

December 5

Iran reiterates its sovereignty over the three UAE islands in response to the latest declarations by the UAE President.

December

December 7

Iran, France and Malaysia sign an agreement on a liquefied natural gas (LNG) project which will have an annual production capability of 10 million cubic meters.

December 17

Hamid Asefi rejects statements made by Iraq's Defense Minister as unfounded.

December 19

Iran's foreign ministry says Iran sticks by its demand that Iraq should pay substantial reparations for the war between the two countries according to the Iranian Foreign Ministry.

December 23

Iran's Intelligence Minister confirms the arrest of a number of officials working for Iran's nuclear energy agency and three senior officials working at Busheir nuclear plant as part of investigations into leaked confidential information.

December 24

Former president Akbar Hashemi Rafsanjani lashes out at accusations of Iranian meddling in Iraq coming from the United States.

December 28

Iran threatens to boycott the Asian Games 2006 to be hosted by Doha in the event organizers use the term 'Arabian Gulf' instead of 'Persian Gulf'.

Iraq Timeline 2004

January

January 1
An explosion kills five at a restaurant in downtown Baghdad.

January 1
The UN transfers an outstanding US$2.6 billion, part of the "oil for food" program, to the coalition authorities.

January 1
A bloody demonstration in Kirkuk kills five Iraqis and wounds 24.

January 1
UK Defense Minister says British troops will stay in Iraq to provide support to the Iraqi transitional government.

January 5
An explosion kills six persons after Friday prayers at a Shiite mosque in downtown Baghdad.

January 6
The Iraqi Transitional Governing Council celebrates the anniversary of the foundation of the Iraqi army.

January 7
Two Iraqis are killed and four wounded in clashes between the Iraqi police and former members of the Iraqi army who were demonstrating in Basra city, demanding the increase of salaries which had not been paid for months.

January 8
The US Administrator of Iraq, Paul Bremer, and the Chairman for the Governing Council in Iraq, Adnan Pachachi, launch a program for releasing tens of thousands of detainees held by the occupation forces.

January 9
The US officially confers on former Iraqi president Saddam Hussein the title 'Prisoner of War'.

January 9
Nine Americans are killed in a helicopter crash in Fallujah.

January 10
An uprising for the unemployed in the construction sector leaves 6 British and Iraqi police forces killed.

January 11
The Shiite leader Ali Sistani reiterates his support for comprehensive and direct elections.

January

January 12

The Coalition Authority grants a contract for the development of the media sector in Iraq to US-based 'Harris Corp'.

January 14

Kuwait installs an iron barrier on its 217km borders with Iraq.

January 14

An American Apache plane is downed by the Iraqi resistance, the third incident of its kind within two weeks.

January 15

A huge exhibition opens in Kuwait under the slogan 'Reconstructing Iraq 2004'.

January 15

Tens of thousands of Iraqis demonstrate in Basra in support of the position held by the Shiite leader Ali Sistani regarding the need to hold general elections in Iraq.

January 19

A suicide bombing targets the headquarters of the occupation forces in downtown Baghdad killing 15 people, including two Americans.

January 20

Qatar and the UAE decide to write off most of Iraq's debts.

January 21

Kuwait announces its willingness to write off a substantial part of Iraqi debt if the decision is approved by the National Assembly.

January 22

Saudi Arabia announces its readiness to negotiate a substantial reduction of Iraqi debt.

January 23

David Kay resigns from his post as head of the US team in charge of searching for WMDs in Iraq.

January 23

Shiite leader Ali Sistani calls for an immediate cessation of all forms of demonstration calling for elections in Iraq.

January 24

Five US soldiers are killed and 13 wounded in a series of blasts, the most powerful of which occurred in Fallujah, Khaldiya and Samara.

January 25

750 Iraqi soldiers graduate from a US training camp, 120 of whom will join the Iraqi border guards.

January 25

A list of the names of political figures who received millions of barrels of oil from the former Iraqi president is made public.

January 26

Iraq's Interior Minister Nouri Badran announces that the Iraqi authorities have created an intelligence service to combat terrorism and crime.

January 26

The Iraqi Central Bank grants the Kuwaiti National Bank, the British Chartered Bank, and the British Bank licenses to open branches in the country.

February

February 2

Two suicide explosions rip through the headquarters of the two main Kurdish parties in Erbil.

February 2

The Iraqi Interim Governing Council bans al-Jazeera TV channel from entering its headquarters or attending its press conferences for one month.

February 2

Lebanon returns millions of frozen dollars to Iraq that was deposited by the former regime in Lebanese banks prior to the invasion.

February 3

Paul Wolfowitz, US Deputy Defense Secretary, states that a limited dose of federalism or federal regime in Iraq is inevitable.

February 11

An attack against a police center in Baghdad wounds 120 people and kills others.

February 11

A statement allegedly made by Al-Qaeda calls for attacks against the Shiite community in Iraq.

February 12

US General John Abu Zaid, head of US Central Command, survives a missile attack in Fallujah.

February 12

Iraq is granted Observer Status at the World Trade Organization (WTO).

February 12

An explosion at the headquarters for Iraqi army training kills 47.

February 13

A UN team headed by Lakhdar Brahimi recognizes the impossibility of holding general elections before a handover of power to the Iraqis next June.

February 15

The Foreign Minister of Iraq and the ministers of the neighboring states issue a statement condemning "terror" attacks and agree to bolster border security.

February 17

Iraqi nuclear professor Majeed Hussein, who taught at the College of Science at Baghdad University, is assassinated.

March

February 19

Some 11 Iraqis are killed and 23 others wounded including 8 coalition soldiers, as a result of an attack on a military base south of Baghdad.

February 19

Iraqi women demand 40% of the seats in the new legislative authority.

February 26

Fire breaks out at an oil pipeline south of Samara.

March 2

On the holiest day of the Shiite Muslim calendar, Ashura, simultaneous bomb attacks in Karbala and Baghdad kill more than 180 people and wound hundreds of others.

March

March 9

Iraq's Governing Council signs an interim constitution although the top Shiite cleric Ayatollah Ali Sistani refuses to endorse it.

March16

UN starts investigating claims on graft practices related to the 'oil for food' program.

March 16

Shiite cleric Ayatollah Ali Sistani calls on the UN to assume a role in Iraq's future.

March 21

Hundreds of thousands of anti-war protesters around the world march to denounce the US-led invasion and occupation of Iraq on the first anniversary of the war.

March 21

Iraq grants priority status to Gulf investments in Iraq's reconstruction program.

March 23

Iraq decides to undertake a special investigation to be conducted by world-renowned legal firms in order to uncover possible violations of the 'oil for food' program.

March 28

Iraq's Housing Minister declares that Jews have the right to recover their buildings and properties in Iraq.

March 29

Occupation forces in Iraq close al-Houzeh, a weekly newspaper supporting the Shiite leader Muqtada al-Sadr.

April

March 29

As part of a gradual handover of power, Paul Bremer, the US Administrator of Iraq, hands over the keys of the first ministry to Iraqis.

April 5- 8

At least 280 people are killed and more than 400 injured in the besieged Iraqi city of Fallujah as a result of clashes between US troops and Iraqi insurgents.

April 9

Numbers of foreign nationals are kidnapped in Iraq including three Japanese, eight Koreans, and one British citizen.

April 10

Four Italians and two Americans join the list of kidnapped foreigners in Iraq.

April 12

Armed men in central Iraq kidnap seven Chinese men while an US Apache helicopter is downed west of Baghdad.

April 13

Some 700 Iraqis are killed and 1,250 wounded in Fallujah in one week.

April 13

11 Russians are kidnapped; seven Chinese citizens are released.

April 14

The US occupation forces violate the cease fire in Fallujah and start an aerial attack on certain quarters of the city.

April

April 16
A senior Iranian diplomat is gunned down in Baghdad. Russia meanwhile announces that it is evacuating its citizens from Iraq.

April 19
Spanish forces withdraw from Iraq.

April 28
The International Committee of the Red Cross (ICRC) visits former President Saddam Hussein in his prison cell.

April 28
Saddam's wife assigns a Jordanian lawyer to defend her husband.

May

April 29
Figures issued by the US Defense Department says the number of US soldiers killed in Iraq in April has almost surpassed the number of US military men killed in the main battles between March 23 and the first of May 2003.

April 30
Iraq torture photos taken in 2003 showing American soldiers abusing Iraqis at Abu Ghuraib prison appear in the worldwide media.

May 7
Occupation forces kill 41 of Muqtada al-Sadr's supporters in battles in Najaf.

May 8
Al-Qaeda leader Osama bin Laden offers gold for killing top US and UN officials in Iraq.

May 10
An explosion in front of a Baghdad hotel results in several casualties, among them British and US citizens.

May 11
An explosion results in a large reduction in Iraqi oil exports from Basra.

May 12
Honduran forces withdraw from Iraq.

May 12-13
Parliamentary speakers from the eight countries neighboring Iraq end a two-day conference on Iraq by condemning the "flagrant violations" of US-led troops on Iraqi prisoners.

May 13
US Defense Secretary Rumsfeld makes a surprise visit to Iraq as the US struggles to quell criticism over the Abu Ghuraib prison scandal.

May 14
US forces intensify their war against Iraqi cleric Moqtada al-Sadr: for the first time sending tanks into Najaf's vast cemetery to blast guerrilla positions.

May 14
The chief editor of the British daily "Daily Mirror" submits his resignation after disclosing that the pictures published by the paper showing British soldiers mistreating Iraqi detainees are fake.

May 18
A suicide car bombing kills Governing Council Chairman Ezzedine Salim.

May

May 20

US troops kill 40 people at a wedding in an Iraqi desert town. The Pentagon says air strikes were conducted on a house used by foreign fighters near the Syrian border.

May 21

Iraqi police and US troops raid the house of Ahmad Chalabi, a leading member of the Iraqi Governing Council, and confiscate files and computers.

May 21

New Iraqi prison abuse images emerge.

May 22

In Lebanon, hundreds of thousands of Lebanese Shiite Muslims vow to help protect the holy sites in Iraq.

June

May 27

Shiite leader Moqtada Sadr and the council of Iraqi clerics agree on a truce to end fighting in the three cities of Najaf, Kufa and Karbala.

May 27

A female member of Iraq's interim Governing Council, Salama Al Khufaji, escapes an attack south of Baghdad.

May 28

Iyad Allawi, head of the 'National Reconciliation' party, is named as interim Prime Minister of Iraq.

June 1

The head of Iraqi Governing Council, Ghazi Al-Yawar, is nominated to serve as interim president of the state; Thamir Al-Ghadban is nominated oil minister in the new Iraqi government.

June 4

The government forms an electoral commission to organize elections planned for January 2005.

June 8

The US and Britain win unanimous UN Security Council approval for a new resolution on the future of Iraq (Resolution 1546).

June 11

The al-Mahdi army and the Iraqi police forces engage in the first confrontation between them since the announcement of a truce.

June 16

Explosions in oil pipelines in southern Iraq reduce oil exports to one-third of the state's export capacity.

June 16

Shiite cleric Moqtada al-Sadr calls on his supporters to withdraw from Najaf and Kufa in compliance with the truce.

June 20

Iyad Allawi announces a national security strategy based on mobilizing all security forces to confront attacks.

June 23

A South Korean hostage is beheaded in Iraq after Seoul refuses militants' demands to cancel a planned troop deployment to Iraq.

June 24

Prime Minister Allawi requests NATO's help in the form of training and other technical assistance. On June 27, NATO nations agree to train Iraq's new army.

June

July

June 28

Kuwait resumes diplomatic relations with Iraq.

June 28

The Iraqi Interim Government announces a limited general amnesty and a reenactment of the national law.

June 30

Saddam Hussein and eleven senior former Iraqi officials are officially turned over to Iraqi justice.

July 1

World TV stations screen shots of Saddam's trial video.

July 8

Interim Prime Minister Allawi signs defense and national safety laws that gives him the authority to impose emergency measures to safeguard the country's security.

July 15

The governor of Mosul is assassinated.

July 15

An assassination attempt against the Iraqi foreign minister fails.

July 17

Philippine and Thailand withdraw their forces from Iraq.

July 20

The governor of Basra is assassinated

July 21

Iraq's neighboring states - Jordan, Syria, Turkey, Iran, Saudi Arabia, Kuwait, and Egypt agree to hold a high-level security meeting and share intelligence about cross-border infiltration.

July 23

US President Bush lifts the American embargo on weapons sales to Iraq.

July 24

An Egyptian diplomat is kidnapped in Baghdad but released on July 27.

August

July 28

A suicide bomber kills 70 in an attack north of Baghdad.

July 29

Iraq and Saudi Arabia resume diplomatic relations and the kingdom allocates one billion dollars for the reconstruction of Iraq.

August 1

Car bombs explode outside five churches in Iraq in Baghdad and Mosul.

August 3

Kuwait and Iraq announce the recommencement of their complete diplomatic relations, severed 14 years earlier in the invasion of Iraqi forces of Kuwait.

August

August 6
US marines announce they killed 300 pro-Moqtada Al-Sadr fighters in violent clashes.

August 7
Iraq's Interim Government orders al-Jazeera to close its Baghdad office for one month.

August 9
The death penalty law is restored.

August 9
Shiite clergy Grand Ayatollah Ali Sistani travels to London for medical treatment.

August 10
Clashes in Najaf erupt before truce and oil production in Iraq's southern fields is interrupted.

August 10
The head of the Iraqi delegation to Athens's Olympic Games declares that the Iraqis are ready to play against Israelis if necessary.

August 12
Ahmad Chalabi returns back to Iraq despite the arrest warrant issued against him.

August 14
The truce collapses in Najaf and the Shiite cleric Muqtada al-Sadr calls for the resignation of the Iraqi government.

August 17
Muqtada al-Sadr agrees to receive a UN delegation led by the representative of the UN secretary general in Iraq, Ashraf Qadi, and a delegation of the Iraqi National Congress to discuss an end to clashes in Najaf.

August 22
Two French journalists are reported missing in Iraq.

August 24
Fighting continues in Najaf as US forces bombard parts of the city.

August 24
A Pentagon commission formed to investigate prisoners' abuse in Iraq's Abu Ghuraib prison lays the blame on the Pentagon's most senior civilian and military officials including Defense Secretary Rumsfeld.

September

August 25
Grand Ayatollah Ali Sistani returns to Iraq and urges Iraqis to march to save the "burning city" of Najaf.

August 27
Grand Ayatollah Ali Sistani negotiates with Moqtada al-Sadr in Najaf after 74 Iraqis are killed in Kufa.

August 29
Shiite cleric Moqtada Al-Sadr calls for an end of fighting.

September 1
Ahmad Chalabi, the former member of the Iraqi Governing Council survives an attempt on his life. A group called 'The Islamic Army' claims responsibility for the attack.

September

September 5
Iraq's interim parliament appoints four vice-presidents instead of two.

September 5
Iraqi police breaks into the al-Jazeera TV office after extending its closure.

September 6
A demonstration takes place in Baghdad in protest against terrorism and interference by Iraq's neighboring countries

September 15
Two oil pipelines are blown up in Iraq.

September 15
More than one hundred detainees are released from Abu Ghraib jail.

September 20
The Iraqi ambassador in Tehran submits his credentials for the first time since the start of the Iraqi-Iranian war in 1980.

September 21
The Al-Zarqawi group beheads American hostage Eugene Armstrong.

September 24
New Zealand withdraws its forces from Iraq.

October

October 1
35 children are killed in blasts in separate areas of Baghdad.

October 9
The killing of British hostage Kenneth Bigley is confirmed.

October 14
Iraq receives back its voting rights at the UN.

October 23
British Prime Minister refuses to abide by the demands of the kidnappers of the British hostage Margaret Hassan.

October 25
An unknown armed group kills 49 army recruits in one of the bloodiest attacks in Iraq.

October 26
The International Atomic Energy Agency (IAEA) stresses that hundreds of tons of traditional explosives are missing from Iraqi military arsenals.

October 30
Iraqi interim president Ghazi Al-Yawar pays a historic visit to Kuwait, the first such visit by an Iraqi official since Iraq's invasion of Kuwait in 1990.

October 30
An unknown group called 'Kataeb 1920' claims responsibility for the attack against the offices of Al-Arabiya channel in Baghdad, killing seven people.

November

November 8

26 Saudi scholars call on the Iraqi people to unite and resist occupation. Riyadh severely criticizes the statement.

November 8

The Iraqi government declares a 60-day state of emergency throughout most parts of the country, paving the way for an all-out assault on the city of Fallujah.

November 12

18 US soldiers are killed in Fallujah and 178 wounded in action since the start of the assault on the city.

November 16

Hungary decides to withdraw its forces from Iraq.

November 21

The Paris Club decides to reduce Iraqi debt by 80 percent.

November 22

Iraq sets January 30, 2005 as Election Day.

November 23

The final communiqué of the Sharm el-Sheikh international conference on Iraq asserts Iraq's sovereignty, independence and territorial integrity as well as the leading role played by the UN as an adviser to the electoral process in the country.

November 23

A second member of the Council of Religious Scholars is killed.

December

November 24

US diplomat, Jim Molen, is killed in Baghdad.

November 26

Iraqi police forces foil an attempt to smuggle 325kg of hashish into Iraq.

December 4

Attacks in several Iraqi cities leave 43 Iraqis and two US soldiers killed.

December 5

Twin attacks against the holy Iraqi Shiite cities of Najaf and Karbala kill 66 people and wound over 200.

December 21

A suicide attack targeting a US base in the city of Mosul kills 22 including 19 Americans in the deadliest strike on a US military base in Iraq. More than 60 people are wounded in the attack.

December 27

A suicide car bomber kills 13 people outside the offices of a major Iraqi Shiite political party, but SCIRI leader Abdel Aziz al-Hakim survives the attack.

December 28

At least 43 people are killed as insurgents launched a series of attacks on the Iraqi security forces.

December 29

Pitched battles between US troops and Iraqi insurgents in Mosul leave 25 dead. Another 30 people are killed when a Baghdad house rigged with explosives blew up during a police raid.

December

December 29

The Higher Commission announces that 7471 candidates will compete in the upcoming elections in Iraq.

State of Kuwait Timeline 2004

January

January 2
The Parliamentary Interior and Defense Committee approve a draft proposal on amending the electoral constituencies' law.

January 5
Kuwait identifies 61 of its prisoners in Iraq among remains found in mass graves in that country.

January 6
Kuwait announces it has completed 178 major indictments against Saddam Hussein and his top aides for war crimes committed during Iraq's 1990-1991 occupation of the country.

January 13
Parliament approves a draft law to open the banking sector to foreign banks for the first time in the history of the country.

February

January 16
US designates Kuwait a major non-NATO ally.

February 1
Deputy Prime Minister and Minister of Defense Sheikh Jaber Al Mubarak talks about Kuwait's vision for the future Iraqi army.

February 7
Kuwait and the US sign a Trade and Investment Framework Agreement (TIFA).

February 17
Parliament unanimously approves the formation of a committee to investigate corruption charges in deals providing the American army in Iraq with fuel.

March

February 18
Four prominent Bahraini politicians are banned from entering Kuwait.

February 28
The Emir of Kuwait, Sheikh Jaber Al Sabah, meets King of Bahrain Hamad bin Issa Al Khalifa in Kuwait.

March 2
The Islamic Constitutional Movement (ICM) announces a new political platform to cope with changes and developments at the local and regional levels.

March 6
Tax on foreign investors, a major obstacle for foreign oil companies, is reduced by the National Assembly's Finance and Economic Committee.

March

March 8

The Minister of Finance survives the no-confidence vote motioned by members of Parliament.

March 9

Prime Minister Sheikh Sabah Al Ahmad rejects the so-called US-sponsored Greater Middle East Initiative.

March 17

In reference to the US initiative to spread democracy in the Middle East, Prime Minister Sheikh Sabah Al Ahmad Al Sabah says: "We believe there should be reforms, but they should emerge from the people and the regimes and not be imposed from outside."

March 17

Kuwait calls for the execution of Saddam Hussein over crimes he committed against Kuwait.

April

March 25

A bomb is hurled at the Egyptian consulate in Kuwait.

March 29

Kuwait lifts a 13-year ban on the recruitment of Iraqi manpower.

April 5

The cabinet accepts in principle a parliamentary proposal to amend the election law.

April 6

Prime Minister Sheikh Sabah warns of "elements" trying to fuel sectarian tension between Sunni and Shiite Muslims in the emirate.

April 11

Prime Minister Sheikh Sabah states that violence in Iraq may lead to its break-up and could stir trouble in neighboring states.

April 17

Fighting in Iraq and clashes with Islamic militants in Saudi Arabia causes the government to boost security along its borders.

April 25

Kuwaiti opposition MPs accuse the government of failing to resolve the "humanitarian" ordeal of tens of thousands of stateless Arabs, known as Bidoons, living in the emirate for decades.

April 29

Interior Minister Nawah Al Ahmad Al Sabah confirms reports of terrorist threats against foreign and local targets.

May

May 10

The Foreign Ministry summons the Iranian Charge d'Affaires over a reported meeting in the Iranian Embassy between Kuwaiti Shiite Muslims and an Iranian government envoy.

May 10

The government announces tough security measures in Kuwaiti ports following warnings of possible attacks.

May 16

The Cabinet approves a draft law permitting women the right to vote and to stand as candidates in parliamentary elections.

May 18

Foreign Minister Sheikh Mohammad Al Sabah visits Syria for talks with President Bashar al-Assad on regional developments ahead of Arab summit.

June

June 2
Jordan's King Abdullah II arrives in Kuwait on a two-day official visit for talks on bilateral relations and the renewal of an oil grant.

June 4
Energy Minister Sheikh Fahd Al Ahmad Al Sabah said in comments that political parties and "rotation of power" will be allowed in the country at "one stage."

June 6
A criminal court convicts seven Kuwaiti Islamic extremists of involvement in the 2002 shooting attack on US Marines.

June 7
Syrian President Bashar al-Assad arrives in Kuwait for talks on improving economic cooperation between the two countries.

June 19
A criminal court convicts a prominent Islamist scholar, Hamid Al Ali, of insulting Kuwait's ruler and questioning his rights to make decisions related to the war in Iraq; he was handed a suspended sentence.

June 23
Kuwaiti liberal and Islamic opposition political groups accuse the government of "foiling" political reforms in the country.

June 27
A Kuwaiti soldier who killed a US serviceman in a drive-by shooting is sentenced by a criminal court.

June 28
Prime Minister Sheikh Sabah reiterates Kuwait's willingness to provide all needed support to establish security and stability in Iraq.

July

July 3
Newspaper reports indicate that the US government has warned Kuwait that it suspects nine Kuwaiti nationals of having links with Al-Qaeda.

July 5
Foreign Minister Sheikh Mohammad Al Sabah holds talks with his Chinese counterpart Li Zhaoxing.

July 7
Former Oil Minister Sheikh Saud Nasser Al Sabah expresses concern that the United States may coerce the emirate into making territorial concessions to Iraq.

July 9
Kuwait seizes three Iranian fishing boats after they strayed into its territorial waters.

August

July 23
Kuwaiti authorities arrest several people on suspicion of involvement in recruiting youths to fight US forces in Iraq following the extradition of four suspects from Syria.

July 28
The US warns Americans in Kuwait to be vigilant after the government detained several individuals for suspected activities against the US military.

July 31
Iraqi interim Prime Minister Iyad Allawi starts a visit to Kuwait.

August 2
Iraq and Kuwait announce the restoration of diplomatic relations after a 14 year hiatus.

August

August 16

A report suggests that Kuwait plans to buy 10 additional F/A-18 fighter jets from the US in addition to 40 bought in 1992.

August 18

Kuwait launches a campaign to rehabilitate youths coming back from Iraq.

August 25

Ten years after its formation, the Kuwait Human Rights Society receives official governmental authorization to operate.

August 26

Kuwait and Pakistan sign three bilateral agreements slated to boost investment, security and cultural cooperation between the two countries.

September | October

August 28

Seven truck drivers for the Kuwaiti Transportation Company KGL are held hostage in Iraq. The firm decides to halt operations in the country to secure their release.

September 3

The Kuwaiti Fund for Arab Economic Development offers Iraq $60 million to develop services and infrastructure in the country.

October 1

Kuwait's Foreign Minister announces that although the country recognizes Yasser Arafat as the legitimate leader of the Palestinian people, it does not deal with him.

October 9

The government considers scrapping the "sponsor" system for foreigners living and working in the country.

October 26

Foreign Minister Sheikh Mohammad Al Sabah describes talks with the visiting Iranian Foreign Minister Kamal Kharrazi as "very positive."

October 26

Kuwait's Emir Sheikh Jaber Al Ahmad Al Sabah opens the new legislative term of parliament by urging MPs to pass a bill granting women full political rights.

October 29

Islamist members of parliament agree to extent the right to vote to women although not the right to stand as candidates in elections.

October 30

Iraqi President Ghazi al-Yawar arrives in Kuwait on the first ever official visit by an Iraqi head of state.

November | December

November 3

Lawmakers in parliament make a rare call on the long-ailing Crown Prince Sheikh Saad al Abdullah Al Sabah to retire from political life.

November 25

The government announces that it will ask parliament to approve an 80 percent reduction in Iraq's estimated 16-billion-dollar debt.

December 10

The United Nation's panel overseeing compensation for victims of Iraq's 1990 invasion of Kuwait approves awards worth $2.9 billion for environmental damage.

December 11

Minister of State for Cabinet Affairs Mohammad Al-Sharrar survives a parliamentary interrogation without a vote of no-confidence over allegations of squandering funds.

December

December 12

PLO chairman Mahmoud Abbas apologizes to Kuwait for the organization's stand during the 1990 Iraq invasion, as he arrives on a landmark visit to the emirate aimed at healing a 14-year rift.

December 17

Seventeen Kuwaiti activists form a new political grouping called the Justice and Development Movement to "defend democratic achievements."

December 24

The US State Department issues a warning stating that it has information that terrorist groups are developing plans for possible attacks in Kuwait in the near future.

December 26

The country's criminal court sentences Fuad Khalid Jaffar and Fahad Al Sabah, a member of the ruling family, to 30 years and 15 years, respectively, for embezzling public funds.

December 30

The Kuwait Ministry of Information tells all hotels to cancel New Year's Eve celebrations in an apparent move to cater to criticism from Islamist groups.

The Sultanate of Oman Timeline 2004

January

January 3
Muscat announces a new civil law which will upgrade ID cards to multipurpose cards.

January 4
Oman announces its 2004 budget, with spending at 3.425 billion Omani Riyals ($8.9bn).

January 6
Sultan Qaboos and the Emir of Qatar, Sheikh Hamad bin Khalifa Al Thani, hold talks in Muscat.

January 24
Dolphin Energy Limited announces that the company's first supplies of natural gas from Oman were safely received by pipeline at its control station in Al Ain.

February

January 28
The US State Department warns its citizens in Oman against possible terrorist attacks.

February 8
Sultan Qaboos issues a number of royal decrees announcing a cabinet reshuffle.

February 16
Egyptian President Hosni Mubarak and Sultan Qaboos hold talks on ways to boost bilateral cooperation.

February 17
According to an officially published royal decree, citizens in the Gulf Cooperation Council (GCC) can begin to own property in Oman.

March   ## April

February 24
Oman launches the Seeb Seafront Resort Development Project, an $805 million resort project set to stretch along 7.3km of beachfront.

March 2
The ninth meeting of the Omani-Qatari Joint Committee begins in Muscat.

March 9
Dr. Raweyah Bin Masoud Bin Ahmad Al-Bouseidi is appointed Minister of Higher Education, becoming the first woman to become a member of the Cabinet.

April 10
Yemeni President Ali Abdullah Saleh signs into law a maritime border agreement between the Sultanate and the Republic of Yemen.

April

April 11
Five women are among some 30 newly appointed public prosecutors.

April 25
Sultan Qaboos and Kuwaiti premier Sheikh Sabah Al Ahmed Al Jaber Al Sabah hold talks in Muscat.

April 28
The 13th session of the Political Joint Committee between the Sultanate and Iran concludes in Muscat.

May

May 9
Sultan Qaboos reshuffles the Omani government for the second time in the year.

June

June 9
Rajiha bint Abdul Amir bin Ali is appointed as the country's second female Cabinet member as the Minister of Tourism.

June 14
Dr. Mohammed Redha Aarif, first Vice-President of the Islamic Republic of Iran, arrives in the Sultanate.

June 22
Oman and Germany review relations during a visit of German Foreign Minister, Joschka Fischer.

June 22
Oman and China sign a memorandum of strategic understanding in Shanghai.

July

July 24
Oman signs a contract to buy 20 military helicopters from the French NHA company.

July 25
Oman's Minister for Foreign Affairs Yusuf bin Alawi bin Abdullah states that Oman's armed forces will not work outside the scope of the GCC security cooperation.

August

August 3
Oman and Bahrain hold bilateral talks in the Omani province of Dhofar.

August 26
Oman issues a decree nationalizing jobs of drivers.

September

September 11
Chinese Foreign Minister Li Zhaoxing visits Muscat to review the status of relations between Oman and China.

September 22
Oman's first Human Development Report is released.

October

October 6
Iranian President Sayyed Mohammed Khatami begins a two-day official visit to the Sultanate.

October 12
Sultan Qaboos calls for an end to the daily suffering endured by the Palestinian people.

October

November

October 21

Sultan Qaboos issues a decree forming the Ministry of Sports and appoints a third woman as a member of the Cabinet.

October 30

Oman's Supreme Court rejects the appeal of a young German woman sentenced to life imprisonment after being convicted of killing her father with the help of four Omanis.

November 22

For the first time, the government approves the establishment of a journalist association. The body is to be registered as a non-governmental organization at the Ministry of Social Development.

November 29

Oman and Croatia sign a memorandum of understanding on political consultation which would give a new thrust to bilateral ties.

December

November 30

Deputy President of the Majlis Al-Shura, Ishaq bin Salim Al Siyabi, heads the Omani delegation to the fifth general assembly of the Association of Asian Parliaments for Peace in Islamabad.

December 4

Foreign Minister Yusuf Bin Alawi calls for a new Gulf economic grouping, uniting the six states of the Gulf Cooperation Council with Yemen, Iraq, Iran and Pakistan.

December 19

Palestine Liberation Organization chairman Mahmoud Abbas briefs Oman's Sultan Qaboos on preparations for next month's elections for a successor to Yasser Arafat.

December 25

Oman extends its support for India's permanent membership of the Security Council.

December 30

The Omani-Egyptian Joint Committee's 10th session, chaired by Foreign Minister Yusuf bin Alawi and his Egyptian counterpart Ahmed Abu Al-Ghait, ends.

State of Qatar Timeline 2004

January

January 1
In an unprecedented move, Qatar elects Dr. Hala Al-Issa to assume the management of the department of 'Technology and Science' at the Secretariat-General of the GCC Council in Riyadh.

January 6
Qatari Emir Sheikh Hamad bin Khalifa Al Thani and Oman's Sultan Qaboos hold talks during a short visit to Muscat.

January 10
The Second Conference of the US-Islamic Dialogue kicks off in Doha.

January 12
Dolphin Energy Limited (DEL) announces that Japanese engineering giant JGC Corporation has won a contract for a gas processing and compression plant in Qatar.

January 15
Qatargas and Gas Natural SDG, SA, of Spain sign an agreement to supply Spain with LNG.

January 20
Qatar pledges to waive most of Iraq's debt.

January 24
Qatar signs a contract with the US construction giant Bechtel to develop the new Doha International Airport.

January 30
India receives the first cargo of liquefied natural gas (LNG) from Qatar.

February

February 9
Al-Jazeera TV channel denies charges by Saudi Arabia that it is "inciting terror."

February 12
Former Chechen President Zelimkhan Yandarbiyev is killed in a car bomb in Doha.

February 16
Qatar promulgates its first anti-terrorism law stipulating the death penalty for all acts of terror.

February 20
Qatar announces that it is holding two suspects in the assassination of Yandarbiyev.

February

March

February 22

Crown Prince Sheikh Tamim visits Bahrain.

February 24

The US State Department's human rights report notes "significant steps" taken by Qatar toward democratic governance.

February 27

Moscow demands the release of the two Russian suspects charged with the murder of Yandarbiyev.

March 2

The ninth meeting of the Omani-Qatari Joint Committee begins in Muscat.

March 4

Qatar criticizes Arab states for rejecting the controversial US Greater Middle East Initiative.

March 11

Qatari Emir Sheikh Hamad arrives in Amman.

March 21

Qatari Emir Sheikh Hamad leaves Damascus following discussions with Syrian President Bashar al-Assad.

March 23

Qatari Emir Sheikh Hamad appoints Sultan Dossari as the new Minister of Municipal Affairs and Agriculture in a minor Cabinet reshuffle.

April

March 23

Russia frees two Qataris detained the previous month in Moscow.

March 24

Polish President Aleksander Kwasniewski announces the establishment of a joint Qatari-Polish committee.

April 5

The Emir of Qatar states during the opening session of Qatar's Conference on Democracy and Free Trade that the Arab states should study US proposals for democratic reform.

April 11

Trial of the two Russian secret agents accused of assassinating Yandarbiyev opens in Doha.

April 12

Diplomatic tensions between Qatar and Moscow rise when two Russian journalists are detained for working without proper accreditation.

April 14

The Emir of Qatar Sheikh Hamad bin Khalifa Al Thani receives Yemeni President Ali Abdullah Saleh. The two leaders review developments in the region.

April 18

French Minister of Defense Michele Alliot-Marie begins talks in Doha with the Qatari Emir and the Crown Prince on regional issues, specifically Iraq.

April 18

Russia tells Qatar it wants a "friendly verdict" in the trial of its two Russian agents.

April

April 19

A conference on "NATO transformation and Gulf security" is hosted in Doha by Qatar's Foreign Ministry in cooperation with the US-based Rand Corporation.

April 23

Qatar's Foreign Minister announces that Qatar is preparing for the first parliamentary elections in the history of the country in line with the new constitution.

April 28

US Secretary of State Colin Powell accuses al-Jazeera of harming otherwise strong ties between the US and Qatar.

April 28

The Emir of Qatar and King of Bahrain Hamad bin Isa Al-Khalifa hold talks on ways to boost bilateral cooperation between the two countries and review developments in the region and the world.

May

June

May 1

Sheikh Hamad bin Jassim announces the foundation of the Qatari-American Diplomatic Friendship League.

May 6

The Emir of Qatar issues a decree establishing a military intelligence department.

May 21

Qatari Emir Sheikh Hamad issues new labor legislation giving Qatari nationals the right to form associations.

June 8

Sheikh Hamad promulgates the country's first written constitution.

June 10

Sheikh Hamad and Riyadh Governor Prince Salman bin Abdul Aziz hold talks on a yacht off Monte Carlo in a meeting organized by the Kuwaiti Prime Minister.

June 13

Iran's Foreign Ministry summons Qatar's ambassador to Tehran to protest over an alleged fatal attack on an Iranian boat by a Qatari naval vessel in the Gulf.

June 16

Qatari coast guards seize two Iranian fishing boats that violated Qatar's territorial waters and used banned fishing nets.

June 30

Qatari court sentences Anatoly Belashkov and Vassily Bogachev to life imprisonment for killing a Chechen rebel leader in the Gulf state and accuses the Russian leadership of being behind the assassination.

July

June 30

UN Secretary-General Kofi Annan arrives in Qatar.

June 30

Al-Jazeera television is ordered to suspend its coverage of events in Algeria.

July 4

Qatar Petroleum (QP) and Royal Dutch/Shell seal a deal to build the world's biggest plant to convert natural gas into liquid fuels.

July 7

Qatar and the Republic of Bolivia sign a protocol establishing diplomatic relations.

July

July 10

Qatar calls on the world community and the UN to pressure Israel to abide by international law.

July 13

Iran's Ministry of the Interior declares that Iran has seized two Qatari steam-powered boats that strayed their way and entered Iran's territorial waters.

August

August 5

Iraq's interim government orders Qatar-based al-Jazeera satellite television network to close its Baghdad office for one month.

September

September 4

The Iraqi government extends the ban on al-Jazeera television and seals the Baghdad office of the Arab news channel.

September 17

Qatar's Foreign Minister reveals details at a press conference held in France of his meeting with former Iraqi president Saddam Hussein before the war broke out in March 2003.

September 19

Foreign Minister Sheikh Hamad bin Jassim meets French President Jacques Chirac in Paris.

September 19

The Emir of Qatar visits Washington.

September 21

Malaysia opens its diplomatic mission in Doha.

October

September 21

Qatari Emir Sheikh Hamad addresses the 59th session of the UN General Assembly.

September 26

The UAE and Qatar governments sign an International Pipeline Agreement (IPA).

October 10

Qatari Emir Sheikh Hamad holds talks with Egypt's President Hosni Mubarak in Cairo.

October 11

Qatari Emir Sheikh Hamad ends his visit to Syria during which he discussed with Syrian President Bashar Al-Assad the means of formulating an Arab unified stance towards the dangerous developments unfolding in the region.

October 14

Qatar's deposed Emir Sheikh Khalifa bin Hamad al-Thani returns to Doha to attend his wife's funeral.

October 17

Mashael Ad-Dirham is appointed secretary-general of the municipal council.

October 29

US warns its citizens in Qatar of a possible terrorist attack directed at hotels in Doha that are frequented by Americans.

October 29

Qatari Emir Sheikh Hamad issues a decree reconstituting the Advisory Council by inducting 14 new members and extending the terms of office of 21 existing members.

November

November 1

Qatar tightens security measures at hotels in the capital city of Doha after a US warning of possible terrorist attacks.

November 5

The US revokes the security alert.

November 25

Qatar formally approves proposal to set up a regional center for training and documentation in the field of human rights.

November 25

Al-Jazeera announces launch of English-language satellite channel by late 2005.

December

November 29

Qatar's conference on the family kicks off in Doha.

December 1

The Emir of Qatar issues a decree on confirming Qatar's accession to membership in the 1980 convention on the protection of nuclear material.

December 2

A major power failure hits Doha.

December 11

The Emir of Qatar and Libyan leader Muammar Qaddafi review major fields of cooperation between the two countries and a number of other issues of mutual interest.

December 16

NATO Deputy Secretary-General Alessandro Minuto Rizzo tells Al-Sharq al-Awsat newspaper that NATO received a "positive response" from Qatar for its Istanbul Cooperation Initiative.

December 22

Emir of Qatar Sheikh Hamad holds talks with President Sheikh Khalifa bin Zayed Al Nahyan in Doha to discuss the latest regional and international developments, including the construction of a bridge linking Qatar and the UAE.

December 23

Qatar says it will hand two Russians intelligence agents serving prison sentences for killing Chechen leader Yandarbiyev over to Moscow at Russia's request.

The Kingdom of Saudi Arabia Timeline 2004

January

January 1
Some 150 Saudis, including judges and university professors, sign a document warning against changing the Islam-based school curricula.

January 5
Saudi security forces defuse a bomb planted in a power meter at a building located in the Sultaniya district in Riyadh.

January 6
Saudi Arabia's Foreign Minister Saud al-Faisal announces the possibility of a joint European-Arab move to activate implementing the Roadmap to settle the Palestinian-Israeli conflict.

January 15
In an address to the nation, Crown Prince Abdullah reaffirms the kingdom's commitment to the course of gradual and well-studied reform but makes it clear that Saudi Arabia would not follow the path of "reckless adventure."

February

January 17-19
The Jeddah Economic Forum opens with a keynote speech from Lubna Al Olayan, Senior Chief Executive Officer of Olayan Financing. The forum, featuring unveiled women and conference halls where women mixed with men, inspires a denouncement from the Grand Mufti Sheikh Abdulaziz Al Sheikh.

January 22
Saudi Arabia and the US announce a joint initiative against the Al-Haramain charity association as part of the so-called campaign against terror funding.

January 28
Five security men are killed in a shootout with suspected militants in Riyadh's eastern district of Nassim.

February 6
Al-Jazeera television channel broadcasts a video tape of armed men preparing to carry out the suicide attack against the al-Muhayya complex in Riyadh in November 2003. The newly appointed assistant to the director of intelligence, Prince Abdul Aziz Bin Bandar later describes the airing as "an act to incite terrorism."

February 10
Saudi and Yemeni authorities hold talks in a bid to defuse tension over a so-called "security screen" being erected by the kingdom along its border with Yemen. The Yeminis later announce on February 18 that Saudi Arabia agreed to halt the construction in exchange for greater border security cooperation.

February 17
Saudi Arabia's Foreign Minister Saud al-Faisal accuses the international community of using double standards regarding weapons programs in the Middle East region stating during a visit to Switzerland:" We know that Israel possesses nuclear weapons but nobody talks about them."

February 17
An official from the Saudi Ministry of Defense denies Reuters reports on any nuclear cooperation with Pakistan or the purchase of Chinese missiles.

February 18
Discussions to boost Saudi-European relations between Foreign Minister Saud al-Faisal and Javier Solana in Brussels.

February

February 19

The European Union (EU) opens its diplomatic mission in Riyadh.

February 22

Hundreds of Saudi academics and professionals send a petition to Crown Prince Abdullah urging him to speed up political reforms and implement the recommendations from the National Dialogue meetings.

February 24

Saudi Arabia and Egypt reaffirm their rejection of any reform initiative imposed by external forces on Arab and Muslim countries.

February 29

A decree approved by King Fahd establishes the Saudi Civil Council for Relief and Charity Work Overseas.

March

March 3

The National Human Rights Organization (NHRO), the first non-governmental and independent group in charge of defending human rights, is established in the kingdom.

March 7

Saudi Arabia signs landmark gas exploration contracts with Lukoil of Russia, Sinopec of China, Italian ENI and Spanish Repsol.

March 15

Security forces announce the death of two wanted terrorists.

March 16

Seven prominent liberals and moderate Islamists are arrested on charges that their actions "do not serve national unity and threaten social fabric built on the rules of Islam." Some of them had called for the transition in the kingdom to a constitutional monarchy. Most of the detainees are released within two weeks but three remain in custody and are put on trial beginning in August.

March 17

Security forces announce the killing of Khaled Ali Haj, a Yemeni, the suspected leader of the al-Qaida network in the Gulf region.

March 19

A source at the Saudi Foreign Ministry expresses disappointment with the US critical statement on the arrest of some Saudi citizens advocating political reform.

March 21

Saudi's foreign minister lashes out at the US initiatives to reform the countries in the region.

March 22

The Saudi government decides to break up the Ministry of Labor and Social Affairs into two separate ministries: the Ministry of Labor and the Ministry of Social Affairs.

April

April 4

Saudi Arabia signs a bilateral agreement with China in another step toward accession to the World Trade Organization (WTO).

April 14

A cabinet reshuffle includes the Ministry of Labor, the Ministry of Social Affairs and the Ministry of Water and Electricity.

April 15

Washington decides to recall junior diplomats based in Saudi Arabia for security reasons.

April 17

Saudi authorities arrest the reformist Saeed bin Za'eer.

April

April 21
A car bomb destroys the building of the Traffic Department and Security Services in Riyadh killing 6 people and wounding over 100.

April 22-23
In a gun battle in the port city of Jeddah, security services kill 5 and arrest one wanted terrorist.

April 29
Oil Minister Ali Al-Naimi states that the kingdom is committed to the $22-28 p/b of oil but that Saudi Arabia has little control over the actual price policy.

April 29
In an annual report on international terrorism, the US State Department lauds the role of Saudi Arabia.

May

May 2
Five Western engineers and a local man are killed by gunmen in the Red Sea port of Yanbu.

May 5
GCC interior ministers sign a landmark counterterrorism pact calling for concerted efforts to combat terrorists.

May 9
Crown Prince Abdullah vows to hunt down militants for "decades" if necessary and warns Saudis not to sympathize with the attackers who are bent on toppling the ruling family. "Anyone who remains silent ... becomes an accomplice."

May 14
Al-Harmain Kataeb, a group with links to al-Qaeda, claims responsibility for the attack which left ten people killed in Yanbu.

May 20
A statement by the Saudi Ministry of Interior says four hard-line suspects and a policeman were killed in a fire exchange in Buraida.

May 27
Abdulaziz Al-Muqrin, the leading al-Qaeda suspect inside the kingdom, issues a battle plan for urban guerilla warfare for future operations in the country.

May 29
In a string of attacks in the city of Khobar, militants attack three housing compounds killing 22 people including 19 foreigners before taking hostages and fleeing.

May 30
The US Embassy in Riyadh calls on US citizens to leave the kingdom after the Khobar attacks.

June

May 31
The Saudi Ministerial Council agrees on a number of measures slated to create job opportunities for women.

June 2
Saudi Arabia announces the near dissolution of the Al-Haramain charity organization and the creation of a special committee to supervise charity work overseas in order to cut off funds that go to terrorist groups.

June 2
Al-Qaeda claims responsibility for a shoot-out targeting US servicemen in the kingdom. One US soldier was wounded.

June 7
Two female Saudi journalists gain membership to the first board of directors of the Saudi Journalists Association.

June

June 8
Unidentified gunmen kill a US citizen in Riyadh in the second such attack against foreigners in one week.

June 10
The Emir of Qatar Shaikh Hamad bin Khalifa Al-Thani and Riyadh Governor Prince Salman bin Abdul Aziz hold talks in a meeting arranged by the Kuwaiti prime minister.

June 11
Informed sources reveal details of terrorist plans to assassinate Saudi Crown Prince Abdullah bin Abdulaziz with suggestion of Libyan leader Muammar Qaddafi's involvement in the conspiracy.

June 12
Iranian Foreign Minister Kamal Kharazi states that Iran passed valuable information to Saudi authorities on a number of al-Qaeda elements under detention in Iran.

June 13
Al-Qaeda announces the killing of a US citizen and the kidnapping of Paul Johnson, an aviation engineer working for Advanced Electronics Co.

June 19
Saudi security forces kill Abdulaziz al-Muqrin and a number of fellow militants in Riyadh shortly after his group Al-Qaeda in the Arabian Peninsula had carried out the beheading of the American hostage Paul Johnson.

June 20
Al-Qaeda announces that Salih al-Oufi would lead the group in Saudi Arabia after the death of al-Muqrin.

June 21
The Saudi Ministerial Council endorses the establishment of a Higher Council for Education.

July

June 23
The Saudi government announces a one-month amnesty for "misguided" extremists who surrender to the authorities.

June 23
A US State Department spokesman confirms that the report submitted by the September 11 Committee did not find any evidence whatsoever regarding official or governmental Saudi funding of al-Qaeda.

July 12
Saudi Arabia starts the first phase of handing over border sites to Yemen in line with the 2000 Jeddah Agreement.

July 12
Saudi Arabia announces the completion of procedural measures to carry out the first municipal elections in the country.

July 14
Saudi authorities admit the possible involvement of Saudi citizens in the insurgency in Iraq.

July 15
The US House of Representatives in a largely symbolic vote stripped financial assistance for Saudi Arabia from a foreign aid bill because of criticism that the country has not been sufficiently cooperative in the US war on terror.

July 18
A video recording on the Internet shows pictures of Paul Johnson, the American hostage who was beheaded in the previous month.

July 21
Issa Al-Awashan, one of al-Qaeda's theorists, is killed.

July

July 23

The offer for amnesty ends with the disappointing results of only 6 militants surrendering and a key suspect Salih al-Oufi remaining at large.

July 29

Iraq and Saudi Arabia agree to resume diplomatic relations following a 13-year hiatus.

August

August 3

An Irish citizen living in Saudi Arabia is killed at his office in Riyadh.

August 5

The Municipal Affairs Ministry announces that elections for the municipal council will start in November.

August 9

Three Saudi reformists arrested in March go on trial in Riyadh on charges of calling for a constitutional monarchy.

August 9

The electoral list of candidates for the municipal elections is issued.

August 11

A wanted terrorist is killed in Makkah after he hurled a bomb at security forces who tried to negotiate with him.

August 16

Crown Prince Abdullah announces that the major battles against terrorist elements are over and that there only a few remnants remaining. Since May 2003, 90 people had been killed and hundreds injured in terrorist attacks throughout the country.

September

August 17

About one hundred Saudis, including twelve women, sent a petition to Crown Prince Abdullah bin Abdulaziz, calling for the release of three reformists accused of calling for a constitutional monarchy.

August 28

According to the Saudi Monetary Agency, the budget for 2004 is projected to reach a record surplus of $34.6 billion.

August 30

Interior Minister Prince Nayef announces that security forces had foiled a large number of attacks: "I can confidently say that what has taken place (among the terrorist attacks) does not exceed five or six percent of what was prevented."

September 3

Abdullah bin Abdulaziz bin Ahmad Al-Muqrin, one of the masterminds of al-Khobar attack in May, surrenders to Saudi authorities.

September 8

During a visit of the Chinese Foreign Minister Li Zhaoxing, Saudi Arabia and China agree to hold regular political consultations.

September 12

The first round of landmark municipal elections is delayed until February 10, 2005.

September 14

The government warns civil servants that they will face disciplinary measures including loss of employment if they engage in criticism with the media inside or outside the country, directly or indirectly, of state policies and any government program.

September 19

The General Committee for Municipal Elections announces that women would not be allowed to run in the upcoming municipal elections.

September

September 19

Saudi academic Saed Bin Zaer is sentenced to a five-year imprisonment for "provoking sedition".

September 25

Saudi Arabia announces it is ready to write off part, and not all, of Iraq's debt.

October

October 2

Authorities announce the launch of a forum under the title 'Ihssa National Islamic Meeting' east of the kingdom.

October 10

Prince Nayef says women's participation in elections is not on the cards.

October 12

Three gunmen are killed and seven security officers are wounded in a clash with a group of wanted terrorists in Riyadh.

October 13

A spokesman for the Saudi Ministry of Interior announces the death of Abdulmajeed Al-Manee', a prominent figure on the most wanted list.

October 18

The Ministry of al-Awqaf and Islamic Affairs orders the closure of the Al-Haramain charity foundation.

October 19

The Iraqi government and Washington reject a Saudi plan to send an Islamic force to Iraq.

October 20

The Saudi cabinet approves amendments to the nationality law.

October 25

The Iranian foreign minister reiterates Iran's desire to boost cooperation with Saudi Arabia.

October 30

The Saudi Ambassador to London, Prince Turki bin Faisal, comments that Iraq has become a magnet for terrorists, that there are insufficient security forces on the ground and that the fragmentation of Iraq would be a threat to Saudi Arabia and the region.

October 30

Three suspects in Riyadh are arrested in a police crackdown operation. Security forces find a cache of explosives, weapons and ammunition.

November

November 1

The Saudi branch of al-Qaeda acknowledges the death of Salih Al-Oufi and announces the appointment of Saud Al-Otaib.

November 7

Three policemen are killed and seven suspects are arrested south of Buraida.

November 7

Three Saudi reformers on trial send a letter to Crown Prince Abdullah complaining that the trial is not fair and propose to hold it in an open forum.

November 7

26 religious scholars release a statement declaring their support for the militants fighting in Iraq, stating that "jihad against the occupiers is a duty for all who are able." The government criticizes the statement noting that the signatories do not represent the great majority of the Saudi people.

November

November 8
Saudi Arabia and China sign a Memorandum of Understanding.

November 11
A booby-trapped car explodes near the Saudi American Bank in Jeddah wounding one person.

November 15
The US State Department announces that Saudi Arabia figures on the US-designated list of countries 'violating religious freedom'.

November 15
A British citizen is killed in Riyadh.

November 21
Al-Qaeda in Saudi Arabia claims responsibility for the death of a British citizen in Riyadh.

November 23
Registration begins for Saudi citizens who will vote in the municipal elections in February 2005.

November 25
Preliminary demographic census results show the size of Saudi population to have reached 22,673,538 with Saudi citizens accounting for 73 percent.

November 28
Saudi security forces kill Essam Siddiq Qassem Mubaraki, one of the plotters of the al-Muhayya compound attack, in Jeddah.

December

November 29
Saudi Arabia announces its support for efforts to make the Middle East region free of weapons of mass destruction.

December 2
Saudi Arabia presents a paper at the meeting of the GCC ministers of information held in Riyadh calling for a ban on material published or/and broadcast by the media that might help terrorist activities.

December 6
Five gunmen hurl bombs at the gates of the US consulate in Jeddah.

December 6
Saudi Foreign Minister Saud al-Faisal criticizes what he described as "GCC neighbors that forge separate economic agreements with foreign powers."

December 7
The fourth national dialogue meeting is held in the eastern province under the title 'Youth Issues: Current Conditions and Future Prospects.'

December 9
A spokeswoman for the US Embassy in Riyadh states that a special US marine team has arrived in the kingdom to reinforce security at the US consulate in Jeddah.

December 12
Saudi Arabia and Yemen sign a series of historic accords to strengthen their political and economic cooperation.

December 13
Shaikh Khalifa bin Zayid, President of the UAE, visits Saudi Arabia to hold discussions on ways to boost bilateral relations in the various fields.

December

December 17

A call by the London-based Movement for Islamic Reform for peaceful protests inside the kingdom fails to materialize with only a few supporters turning up. 14 people are arrested in Jeddah and Riyadh.

December 19

Saudi media report that Crown Prince Abdullah will not attend the annual GCC meeting hosted by Bahrain.

December 22

The kingdom summons its ambassador from Libya over what it called an "atrocious" Libyan plot to assassinate Crown Prince Abdullah.

December 23

The UN Security Council imposes sanctions on British-based Saudi dissident Saad al-Faqih, head of the Movement for Islamic Reform.

December 26

The registration of candidates to the municipal elections starts in Riyadh.

December 26

The Saudi Minister of Justice declares that his ministry will grant a greater role for women in order to better serve women judicially and follow on women's legislative demands.

December 27

Saudi authorities ban the Administration of Mosques and Charity Projects from providing help inside Saudi Arabia and put an end to its activities overseas.

December 29

A booby-trapped car explodes in the capital Riyadh causing extensive damage to the Ministry of Interior. Another bomb explodes outside the headquarters of the Special Forces Unit.

December 29

Following the twin car bomb attack, security forces raid a villa in the Al-Tawuun District in the north of the capital, killing seven suspected militants, including two from the 26 most wanted list.

United Arab Emirates Timeline 2004

January

January 7
Shaikh Khalifa Bin Zayid Al Nahyan, Abu Dhabi Crown Prince and Chairman of the Abu Dhabi Executive Council, issues a decree nominating General Shaikh Mohammad Bin Zayid Al Nahyan as Deputy Chairman of the Abu Dhabi Executive Council.

January 10
Shaikh Dr. Sultan bin Mohammad Al Qasimi, Ruler of Sharjah, issues a decree appointing 40 new members to the Sharjah Consultative Council, including seven women.

January 12
UAE Minister of Information and Culture, Abdullah bin Zayid Al Nahyan, states during a forum on challenges facing the Gulf region that Yemen is not qualified to join the Gulf Cooperation Council (GCC) in the short-term.

January 18
Dolphin Energy Limited (DEL) appoints Emirates General Petroleum Corp. (Emarat) as responsible for the operation and maintenance of its new Al Ain-Fujairah gas pipeline.

January 21
The UAE announces it is prepared to write off most of Iraq's debts estimated at more than 14 billion AED ($3.8 billion).

January 24
Dolphin Energy Ltd. announces that the company's first supplies of natural gas from Oman were received by pipeline at its control station in Al Ain - the first ever cross-border gas transmission in the history of the GCC.

February

February 16
The UAE announces that it would start receiving US-built F-16 jet fighters before the end of 2004 after a long delay due to technical and logistic reasons.

February 17
Egyptian President Hosni Mubarak and Shaikh Zayid bin Sultan Al Nahyan hold discussions centered on the latest developments in Iraq and Palestine.

March

March 8
Shaikh Hamdan bin Zayid Al Nahyan, UAE Deputy Prime Minister and Minister of State for Foreign Affairs, states in a meeting with Zafrullah Khan Jamali, Pakistan's Prime Minister, that tension-free relations between India and Pakistan are very important for the security and economic progress of the region.

March 17
Shaikh Khalifa bin Zayid Al Nahyan, Abu Dhabi Crown Prince, discusses with the British Foreign Secretary bilateral cooperation and various other issues of mutual interest.

March 21
The UAE and the US voice their resolve to further bolster cooperation and friendship under a bilateral strategic partnership.

March 24
The US Embassy and Consulate in the United Arab Emirates close after a "specific threat" and fears of a bomb attack.

March

April

March 27

The US Embassy in Abu Dhabi re-opens after the person involved in the threats that led to closing the Embassy was arrested.

March 31

Shaikh Zayid bin Sultan, President of the UAE, issues a federal law regulating the establishment of financial free trade zones.

April 3

The Governor of the UAE Central Bank, Sultan Nasser Al-Suwaidi reiterates that the UAE abides by all the UN measures and regulations related to money laundering.

April 5

Government authorities shut down a Dubai-based computer firm that allegedly helped Libya and Iran develop their nuclear programs.

April 14

During a visit to Japan, UAE Deputy Prime Minister Shaikh Hamdan bin Zayid Al Nahyan meets Japanese Prime Minister Junichiro Koizumi.

April 21

Abu Dhabi Crown Prince Shaikh Khalifa bin Zayid Al Nahyan says that the UAE is backing efforts for stability and development in Iraq.

April 25

French Defense Minister Michele Alliot-Marie affirms the strong ties between the UAE and France.

April 28

Germany and the UAE sign a treaty to turn their cooperation into a "strategic partnership" on a range of areas from economic and trade links to security.

May

April 29

The UAE issues an appeal to the UN to establish an international body to research ways for effective and serious implementation of the 1995 nuclear non-proliferation review conference resolution on the Middle East which calls for a nuclear-free Middle East.

May 2

A government report stipulates that the private sector in the country employs only two per cent of the UAE nationals.

May 11

Shaikh Mohammad bin Zayid Al Nahyan, Abu Dhabi Deputy Crown Prince and Chief of Staff of the UAE Armed Forces, meets US Secretary of State Colin Powell and US National Security Advisor Condoleezza Rice.

May 16

Shaikh Mohammed bin Rashid Al Maktoum, Crown Prince of Dubai, says that administrative and political reforms are vital to tackle the economic woes of the Arab world.

June

May 18

The Federal National Council criticizes the government for ignoring rural areas of the country where there is a lack of decent amenities and infrastructure.

May 23

President Shaikh Zayid bin Sultan Al Nahyan assigns the UAE Red Crescent Authority (RCA) to reconstruct more than 400 houses in Gaza City and Rafah that were destroyed by Israeli forces.

May 29

UAE Minister of State for Foreign Affairs, Shaikh Hamdan bin Zayid Al Nahyan, pledges solidarity with the Kingdom of Saudi Arabia in its war against terrorism.

June 6

The UAE confirms the detention of an Iranian fishing boat and its crew after the vessel had entered UAE territorial waters (On July 2, it is announced that the crew had been released).

June

June 15
Iranian television announces that the navy had seized a UAE vessel near Iran's coasts.

June 20
The Higher Ministerial Legislative Committee concludes a meeting devoted to the discussion of a bill on a federal anti-terrorism law.

June 22
Shaikh Khalifa bin Zayid Al Nahyan, Abu Dhabi Crown Prince and Joschka Fischer, German Foreign Minister, hold talks reviewing bilateral relations and issues.

June 24
Shaikh Mohammad bin Rashid Al Maktoum, Crown Prince of Dubai, makes it clear that "the UAE has neither an intention nor a plan to normalize ties with the Jewish entity."

July

July 1
The UAE foreign ministry announces that the authorities have released a detained Iranian boat and its crew.

July 19
A number of prominent UAE nationals including lawyers, academics, and journalists submit an application with the Ministry of Labor and Social Affairs for the establishment of the first-ever association for human rights in the country.

July 28
President Shaikh Zayid bin Sultan Al Nahyan issues a decree denouncing terrorism.

July 29
Shaikh Hamdan bin Zayid Al Nahyan, UAE Minister for Foreign Affairs, holds discussions with the Iraqi interim Prime Minister Iyad Allawi.

August

August 4
The UAE and Germany agree to fund the training of new Iraqi military personnel as part of strategic ties between the UAE and Germany.

August 4
The UAE expresses its readiness to support Iraq in order to build a new Iraqi army.

August 8
Pakistani Information Minister Shaikh Rashid confirms that Qari Saifullah Akhtar, a senior operative in Osama bin Laden's terror network, was captured in the UAE and turned over to Pakistan.

August 10
Shaikh Khalifa bin Zayid Al Nahyan, Abu Dhabi Crown Prince, receives US General Richard Meyers, Chairman of the Joint Chiefs of Staff.

August 10
Immigration officials say that a new amnesty to illegal residents will not be offered and warned they should turn themselves in or face severe punishment.

August 20
UAE Minister of Interior, Dr. Mohamed Al Badi, issues a ministerial decree approving a UAE domestic security strategy.

August 30
UAE and Libyan officials hold talks to determine ways to enhance economic, trade and investment cooperation.

August 31
The UAE confirms that conditions in Iraq entail further regional and international support for the war-battered country.

August

August 31

Harald Kujat, Chairman of NATO Military Committee, lauds the military cooperation between the UAE and Germany as evident in providing training to Iraqi troops.

September

September 7

The US Middle East Partnership Initiative, a program launched to promote US democracy initiatives in the Middle East, opens a regional office in the US Embassy in Abu Dhabi.

September 17

US Ambassador-at-large J. Cofer Black, coordinator of the fight against terrorism at the US State Department, says the UAE is a secure country.

September 23

Addressing the UN General Assembly, the UAE Foreign Minister Rashid Abdullah Al Nuaimi calls on the international community to urge Iran to engage in bilateral negotiations over the three occupied islands.

October

September 29

NATO Deputy Secretary-General Alessandro Minuto Rizzo visits the UAE.

October 7

UAE urges the international community to take adequate and effective measures to press Israel to join the Non-Proliferation Treaty (NPT).

October 11

UAE reiterates its call for the allocation of a permanent seat for Arabs in the United Nations Security Council, adding that it should be represented by rotation.

October 11

A federal law legalizing trade unions in the UAE will be issued soon according to a senior official in the Ministry of Labor and Social Affairs.

November

October 27

Iran's Foreign Minister Kamal Kharazi holds talks with Abu Dhabi's Crown Prince Shaikh Khalifa bin Zayid Al Nahyan in Al-Ain.

October 29

The UAE announces its adoption of two Arab draft resolutions urging the establishment of a nuclear-weapon free zone in the Middle East.

November 2

A presidential decree announces a major cabinet reshuffle.

November 2

President His Highness Shaikh Zayid bin Sultan Al Nahyan dies at the age of 86.

November 4

Shaikh Khalifa bin Zayid Al Nahyan, Ruler of the Emirate of Abu Dhabi, is elected unanimously by the UAE Supreme Council as the new president of the UAE.

November 8

The UAE calls on the UN to protect the Palestinian people against Israeli aggressive policies.

November 15

The UAE announces its consent to Bahrain's request to host the 25th GCC summit in Manama.

November 17

The US Defense Department announces plans to sell to the UAE 1,000 Javelin anti-tank missiles.

November

November 21

The newly-appointed cabinet ministers take their oath before President His Highness Shaikh Khalifa bin Zayid Al Nahyan.

November 26

President Shaikh Khalifa bin Zayid Al Nahyan and Kuwaiti Prime Minister Shaikh Sabah Al Ahmad Al Sabah hold talks on regional and international issues.

November 27

The UAE announces it will allow the creation of human rights organizations.

November 28

US General John Abizaid, Commander of the US Central Command hails the bilateral cooperation between the UAE and the US.

December

December 2

UAE president calls for a peaceful solution for the Islands question with Iran.

December 5

Shaikh Mohammad bin Zayid Al Nahyan, Abu Dhabi Crown Prince, receives Abdulaziz Al-Hakeem, President of the Higher Council of the Islamic Revolution in Iraq.

December 9

President Shaikh Khalifa bin Zayid Al Nahyan forms a new Executive Council in a major reshuffle of the Abu Dhabi government.

December 10

Abu Dhabi Crown Prince, General Shaikh Mohammad bin Zayid Al Nahyan, welcomes German Defense Minister, Peter Struck, and holds talks regarding military and defense affairs.

December 13

President Shaikh Khalifa bin Zayid Al Nahyan visits Saudi Arabia; the first visit he conducts as President of the UAE.

December 13

Shaikh Mohammad bin Rashid Al Maktoum, Dubai Crown Prince, calls on Arab leaders at the Arab Strategic Forum to enact required changes for the sake of development and progress.

December 15

Shaikh Hamdan bin Zayid Al Nahyan, UAE Deputy Prime Minister and Minister of State for Foreign Affairs, assures the Iraqi foreign minister of his country's readiness to contribute to the international efforts to stabilize Iraq.

December 18

The UAE ratifies the GCC Anti-terrorism Agreement adopted in May 2004.

December 19

President Shaikh Khalifa bin Zayid Al Nahyan receives Mahmoud Abbas (alias Abu Mazen) the Chairman of the Palestinian Liberation Organization and the accompanying delegation. The two sides discussed the prevailing conditions in the Palestinian territories.

December 20

President Shaikh Khalifa bin Zayid Al Nahyan leads the UAE's delegation to the 25th summit of GCC leaders in Bahrain.

December 22

President Shaikh Khalifa bin Zayid Al Nahyan and Shaikh Hamad bin Khalifa Al Thani, Emir of Qatar, hold talks on the latest regional and international developments and ways of enhancing bilateral cooperation.

December 22

The UAE and Qatar reach an agreement to set up a joint company to supervise the construction of a bridge linking Qatar and the UAE.

December

December 27

The UAE reiterates its support for India's candidacy to win a permanent seat at an expanded UN Security Council.

December 28

Shaikh Mohammad bin Rashid Al Maktoum, Crown Prince of Dubai and Indian Foreign Minister Natwar Singh hold talks about bilateral cooperation in all fields.

December 30

Shaikh Khalifa bin Zayid Al Nahyan issues a federal decree forming the board of the Emirates National Identity Authority under the chairmanship of General Shaikh Mohammad bin Zayid Al Nahyan, Crown Prince of Abu Dhabi.

Yemen Timeline 2004

January

January 12

UAE Minister of Information and Culture, Abdullah Bin Zayid Al Nahyan, states during a forum on challenges facing the Gulf region that Yemen is not qualified to join the Gulf Cooperation Council (GCC) States in the short-term.

February

February 2

Yemen notifies Saudi Arabia of its objection to build a separation wall along its borders.

February 6

A Yemeni newspaper reports that talks are under way between Yemen, Bahrain, and Oman to prepare the groundwork for a security deal including cooperation in training, exchange of intelligence and expertise, and the extradition of suspected criminals.

February 7

Egyptian President Mubarak and Yemeni President Ali Abdullah Saleh hold a summit meeting in Cairo to discuss regional developments.

February 11

President Ali Abdullah Saleh announces in Cairo his country's readiness to abandon a project to establish an Arab federation that will be an alternative for the Arab League.

February 11

Saudi Arabia and Yemen begin talks in Jeddah over a barrier that the kingdom is building on the border between the two countries.

February 18

Saudi Arabia and Yemen announce the end of their differences over the cement wall being built by Riyadh on the Yemeni border.

February 19

Saudi Arabia and Yemen agree to bolster their border security cooperation at the conclusion of a two-day visit to Riyadh by Yemeni President Ali Abdullah Saleh.

February 22

President Ali Abdullah Saleh calls on Yemen's Gulf Arab neighbors to help Yemen join the Gulf Cooperation Council.

March

March 2

The French Embassy in Sana'a raises its security protection level for itself and all other French interests in Yemen due to rising security fears.

March 2

The Emir of Qatar, Sheikh Hamad Al-Thani and Yemen's President discuss bilateral relations during a meeting in Sana'a.

March 6

Yemen hands over six Egyptians suspected extremists, including the former leader of al-Islam group, Sayed Imam al-Sharif.

March

March 9
Yemeni security forces announce the arrest of 18 suspected members of Al-Qaeda and Islamic Jihad.

March 19
The Interior Ministry announces the capture by Yemeni security forces of two of the main suspects in the bombing of the USS Cole in Aden port. The suspects are Jamal al-Badawi and Fahd al-Qasaa.

March 19
Yemen's President orders the formation of a higher national committee for eliminating acts of revenge.

March 20
Saudi Arabia and Yemen exchange 18 suspected terrorists including five wanted Saudis.

April

March 21
General John Abizaid, Commander of US Central Command, discusses military and security cooperation with Yemen's President Ali Abdullah Saleh during a short visit.

March 25
Yemeni President Ali Abdullah Saleh appoints his eldest son as commander of the Republican Guard.

April 2
Yemeni authorities announce that they will try 11 al-Qaeda suspects linked to the attacks on the USS Cole and the French tanker Limburg.

April 10
President Ali Abdullah Saleh signs into law a maritime border agreement between the Sultanate of Oman and the Republic of Yemen.

April 14
A court in Sana'a sentences a ban on the correspondent of the Quds press news agency and secretary of the Journalists Union in Yemen from practicing journalism for 6 months.

April 19
Omani Minister of Interior Sayyid Saud bin Ibrahim Al Busaidi visits Yemen.

April 20
Yemeni authorities announce having frozen the bank accounts of some 62 individuals and 16 non-governmental originations as part of the war on terror.

April 26
Pakistan and Yemen sign a Memorandum of Understandings (MoU) to establish a political consultation mechanism between the two countries.

May

April 26
President Saleh calls for an immediate withdrawal of US soldiers from Iraq.

April 30
Some 275 Muslim scholars and preachers in Yemen appeal to President Ali Abdullah Saleh to refute US terror charges leveled at top Islamist Abdul Majid al-Zendani.

May 10
Riyadh hands over 14 Yemeni citizens detained for security violations in exchange for one Saudi citizen detained in Yemen.

May 29
The Saudi-Yemeni border demarcation operations are finalized.

May

May 29

Fourteen Yemenis go on trial charged with terrorist acts, including the October 2002 attack on a French super-tanker Limburg.

May 30

President Saleh orders his government to abolish prison terms for journalists violating press guidelines.

June

June 13

Yemen's President Ali Abdullah Saleh expresses his satisfaction with the outcome of his visit to the US and his participation in the G8 summit.

June 22

Hundreds of security forces begin a siege of the village in Sa'adah governorate to force militant preacher Sheikh Hussein Bader al-Houthi to surrender himself.

June 26

Yemen says 46 followers of Sheikh Hussein al-Houthi had been killed and 35 wounded in clashes with security forces.

June 27

Yemeni mediators try to persuade Sheikh Hussein al-Houthi to surrender following nearly a week of deadly clashes between his supporters and the army.

July

July 4

Oman and Yemen give a final push to their demarcation of sea borders.

July 10

Yemeni forces kill 25 more supporters of an anti-US rebel religious leader and offer a $ 54,000 reward for his capture.

July 11

Saudi Arabia hands over to Yemen a military airport and two border guard centers on the kingdom's southeastern border.

July 13

Yemen begins recovering vast tracts of desert land the size of Switzerland from Saudi Arabia under an agreement signed four years ago which ended a decades-long border dispute.

July 22

President Ali Abdullah Saleh orders government forces to suspend attack on strongholds of Hussein Bader Al-Houthi to give a "last chance" for the besieged man and his followers to surrender.

August

August 22

Soldiers storm the home of Sheikh Hussein al-Houthi in northern Yemen and detain 200 of his followers in the surrounding area, but al-Houthi remains elusive.

August 26

Yemen beefs up security at seaports following tips that a foreign terrorist group is planning to stage attacks on its ports.

August 22

A Yemeni court hands down sentences to 15 militants convicted of a series of terror attacks.

September

September 1

The United States lifts a ten-year embargo on arms sales to Yemen to reward efforts by Arab states in fighting terrorism.

September 9

Iraqi Foreign Minister Zebari starts an official visit to Yemen, the first for an Iraqi official since the collapse of the regime of former President Saddam Hussein.

September

October

September 10

Yemeni forces kill Sheikh al-Houthi and tens of his supporters.

September 21

Yemen says that Abdullah al-Razami surrendered himself, together with another two, to the authorities yesterday.

September 29

Yemen's special court sentences two Yemeni Al-Qaeda militants to death for the 2000 bombing of the US destroyer Cole which killed 17 sailors.

October 3

A Yemeni court sentences a judge who supported Al-Houthi to 10 years in jail.

November

October 28

President Ali Abdullah Saleh vows to release repentant Al-Qaeda suspects and other religious extremists during Ramadan.

November 1

Yemeni President Ali Abdullah Saleh discusses with the Emir of Qatar, Sheikh Hamad bin Khalifa, ways of boosting bilateral cooperation between their two countries and review developments in the region.

November 5

Yemeni Foreign Minister Dr. Abu-Baker Al-Qirbi states that his country would eventually earn full membership of the Gulf Cooperation Council (GCC).

November 22

Yemen's President Ali Abdullah Saleh discusses with German officials means of fostering cooperation between Germany and Yemen.

December

November 25

Yemeni authorities release 113 militants belonging to the Al-Qaeda network including at least five once accused of involvement in the deadly bombing of the USS Cole after they recanted their extremist views.

November 27

A group of Yemeni clerics endorse the call by 26 Saudi clerics to support the insurgency in Iraq.

December 3

At least 29 people are killed and 20 wounded in two days of clashes between rival tribesmen in northeastern Yemen.

December 6

The Yemeni foreign minister announces that Sana'a will be the permanent headquarter of the Democratic Dialogue Center with the task of boosting democracy in the Middle East and North African countries.

December 12

Yemeni-Saudi Council for Coordination concludes with signing 11 bilateral agreements and a Memorandum of Understanding slated to boost bilateral cooperation between Sana'a and Riyadh.

December 20

Yemen calls on the GCC leaders to consider its membership in the bloc during the annual meeting of GCC leaders in Manama, Bahrain.

December 27

The President of Yemen calls on Djibouti, Eritrea and Somalia to join the Sana'a Grouping of Red Sea and Horn of Africa nations to promote reconciliation and peace in the region.

Notes on Contributors

Dr. Ahmad Youssif Ahmad is a Professor of Political Science at Cairo University and the Director of the Institute of Arab Research and Studies at the Arab League. Dr. Ahmad has published several books and studies, notably: *Introduction to International Relations, The Egyptian Role in Yemen in the Period between 1962 and 1967, The Impact of Oil Wealth on Arab Political Relations,* and *Intra-Arab Conflicts in the Period between 1945 and 1981: A Survey Study*. Dr. Ahmad also supervised the editing of a great number of publications, mainly: *Egypt's Policies in a Changing World; Water Problems in the Arab World* and; *Peace Settlement of the Arab-Israeli Conflict and its Impact on the Arab World*. He is an expert on international relations and Arab politics.

Prof. Hussein Abdullah Al-Amri is a Professor of Contemporary Yemeni History at Sana'a University, Yemen. He is also a member of the GRC Editorial Board and the editor of the Series of Yemen Studies. He received his Ph.D. in History from the University of Cambridge in 1976 and has since published numerous books including *One Hundred Years of Yemen's Modern History, Yemen's Modern and Contemporary History, Al-Manar and Yemen, Chronicles of Modern Yemeni History-Four Volumes* and *Enslaved Princes and Mameluks in Yemen*. Professor al-Amri also edited many books and historical manuscripts. He is an expert on the ancient and modern history of Yemen.

Dr. Dhafer Al-Ani is the Research Manager of the GCC-Iraq Relations program at the Gulf Research Center. He earned his Ph.D., MA, and BA from Baghdad University in Political Science and has published several articles and papers on issues related to Iraq, Iran and the GCC States. He is an expert on Gulf affairs with particular emphasis on Iraq.

Dr. Mustafa Alani is a Senior Consultant and Director of Security and Terrorism Studies at the Gulf Research Center. He was born in Baghdad, Iraq, and was educated in the Department of Politics at the University of Baghdad. He went on to complete his studies at Keele University's Department of International Relations and Exeter University's Department of Politics. Since 1988, he has been a consultant and advisor to official institutions and major commercial organizations on political and security developments in the Middle East. His special focus is on the politics and security of the Gulf States, including Iraq and Iran, and he has studied Islamist fundamentalist groups and Islamist terrorist organizations for many years. He has published three policy papers: *The Probable Attitude of the GCC States towards the Scenario of Military Action Against Iran's Nuclear Facilities* (Dubai, Gulf Research Center, 2004) *Deciding the Fate of Former Iraqi President Saddam Hussein and the Blunders of Intelligence Speculations* (Dubai, Gulf Research Center, 2004) and *Terrorist Groups and the Phenomenon of Political Kidnapping* (Dubai, Gulf Research Center, 2004.) His other publications include *Operation Vantage: British Military Intervention in Kuwait* (London: LAAM, 1990), "Saudi Arabia: the Threat from Within" in Jane's Intelligence Review no. 12, "Saudi Arabia" in Jane's Sentinel (1996), and *The Future of Iraqi Oil* (co-author; Robertson Research International, 1998).

Dr. Ibrahim Mubarak Al-Dossari is the Advisor for Educational Affairs to the Secretary-General of the Gulf Cooperation Council. He received his Ph.D. in Educational Psychology from the University of Wisconsin with a dissertation on "Quantitative Measures and Methods." He is the author of *Referential Framework for Educational Assessment*, which was written for the Arab Bureau of Education for the Gulf States. He is an expert on educational assessment, measurement and examinations.

Muhammad Yousif Al-Ju'aili is an Affiliated Researcher at the Gulf Research Center. He holds a BA in political science from the University of Khartoum, Sudan, 1974, a post-graduate diploma in African and Asian Studies from the University of Khartoum, 1976, and a DEA, the first part of the Third Cycle Doctorate in African Studies from the University of Bordeaux, France, 1981. He is the author of *Arab-African Relations: Mechanisms and Prospects*, Paris, 1981 and is an expert on the security of the Red Sea and on GCC-African Relations.

Dr. Ebtisam Al-Kitbi is an Assistant Professor of Political Science at UAE University. She received her PhD in economics and political science from Cairo University in Egypt. Dr. Al-Kitbi authored *Political Elite in UAE*, in Political Elite in the Arab World, Cairo University, 1997; *Legislative of the UAE*, in Legislative of the Arab World, Cairo University, 1998; *Indian-Emirates Relations*, New Delhi, 1998; *Judiciary in the UAE*, in Judiciary in the Arab World, Cairo University, 1999; *Democratic Transformations in GCC Countries*, Al-Mustaqbal Alarabi, July, 2000; *Visions of India and Pakistan for Security During 1990s*, ECSSR, Abu Dhabi, 2001; *Succession and State in GCC Countries*, Middle East Policy, Summer, 2002; *The Dilemma of Democracy and Violence in the GCC States*, Bahrain, 2003 ;*Women in GCC Countries between Obstacles and Empowerment*, Abu Dhabi, 2003; *Political role for women in GCC States* , Gulf in

2003, Gulf Research Center, Dubai,2004. *Political violence in GCC states*, Doha, May 2004; *The nature of reform in the Arab Region*, Conference on What Role for outsiders? The Mediterranean and the middle East: A New Agenda, Institute for Strategic and International Studies, Lisbon, May 2004; *Women's Political Status in the GCC States*, Arab Reform Bulletin 2, Issue 7, July 2004; *The global community and the war on terrorism: threat or opportunity?*, The Mediterranean, the Middle East and Eastern Europe: The EU and Nato's wider new neighbourhood, XXII Lisbon International Conference, Institute for Strategic and International Studies, Lisbon Dec. 2004. Her research interests include political systems, civil society, democratic transformations and socio-political developments in the GCC countries.

Muhammad Salem Al-Mazroo'i is the Secretary-General of the Federal National Council of the UAE. He received his MA from Port Saeed University, Egypt, and is a Ph.D. candidate at the same institution. He is the author of *Political Developments in the GCC States: the Role of the Legislative Institution from a Comparative Perspective* and is an expert on legislative studies and women's issues in the Gulf.

Dr. Baqer Al-Najjar is Professor of Sociology at the University of Bahrain. He is a member of the Gulf Research Center Editorial Board and a member of the Council of Trustees for the GRC Prize for Social Sciences and Humanities. He received his Ph.D. in Sociology from the University of Durham in 1983. His latest works include: *Society and Education in the Arabian Gulf* (London: al-Saqi Bookshop, 2003), *Dream to Migrate to Wealth: Foreign Labour in the Gulf* (Beirut: Centre for Arab Unity Studies, 2001) and *Women and Modernity in the Gulf* (Beirut: Arab Cultural Centre, 2000). He is an expert on civil society organizations and social developments in the Gulf region.

Prof. Ghanim Al-Najjar is a Professor of Political Science at Kuwait University, a member of the Gulf Research Center Editorial Board and Editor of the Journal of Gulf Studies, published by the GRC. He received his Ph.D. from the University of Exeter and is an expert on political systems, democracy, civil society, and human rights in the Gulf and Iraq. He authored "Human Rights in a Crisis: the Case of Kuwait After Occupation" in *Human Rights Quarterly* (2001), *The Universal Declaration of Human Rights: a Western Invention?* (2003), and "Challenges Facing Kuwaiti Democracy," in *Middle East Journal* (2002).

Dr. Muhammed Abdullah Al-Roken is an Associate Professor of Public Law at the UAE University's Faculty of Shari'ah and Law and a member of the GRC Editorial Board. He received his Ph.D. in Constitutional Law from the University of Warwick, UK, in 1992. He has published several research papers and books and is an expert on federalism, human rights, and legislative assemblies.

Dr. Fatima Al-Shamsi is an Assistant Professor of Economics at the UAE University. She received her Ph.D. in Economic and Industrial Development from the University of Exeter, 1990, her MSc. in Economics from the University of Maryland - Baltimore in 1985 and her BA in Economics from Cairo University in 1978. Dr. Al Shamsi is the author of 'The Economy of the UAE: General Aspects & Determinates of Growth' in Joseph Kechichian (ed), *A century in 30 Years: Sheikh Zayed and the UAE*, (Washington, DC: Middle East Policy Council, 2000); "Capital Labor Substitutability in a Labor Importing Country: The Case of the United Arab Emirates," in *Middle East Business And Economic*

Review 13 no.1 (July _2001); and "Industrial Development in Abu Dhabi" in Abdul-Razak Al-Fares (ed.), *The Economy of Abu Dhabi* (Abu Dhabi: Crown Prince Office Publications, 2001). Her research focuses on GCC industrial economies and human resources development.

Prof. Bulent Aras is an Associate Professor of International Relations at Fatih University, Turkey. He received his BA in Political Science and International Relations from Bosphorous University and his Ph.D. in International Relations from the same university. He was visiting scholar at Indiana University's Center for Eurasian Studies in 1998 and Oxford University's St. Anthony's College in 2003. Dr. Aras is the author of *Palestinian-Israeli Peace Process and Turkey* (Novascience, 1998), *New Geopolitics of Eurasia and Turkey's Position*, (Frankcass, 2002), *Turkey and the Greater Middle East,* (TASAM, 2004), editor of *War in the Gardens of Babylon*, (TASAM, 2004), co-editor of *Oil and Geopolitics in the Caspian Sea Region*, (Praeger, 1999), and *September 11 and World Politics,* (FUP, 2004) His articles have appeared in *Middle East Policy, the Journal of Third World Studies, the Journal of South Asian and Middle Eastern Studies, Futures, the Journal of Southern Europe and Balkans, Mediterranean Quarterly, Nationalism and Ethnic Policy* and *Central Asia/Caucasus*. His expertise is on Turkish Foreign Policy, Middle Eastern Politics, Central Asia and Caucasus, Nationalism, Religion and Politics. Dr. Aras has done consulting work with such organizations as Oxford Analytica, Microsoft, Turkish Asain Center for Strategic Studies, Human Rights Watch, Eurasian Center for Strategic Studies and the Canadian Government.

Prof. Anoush Ehteshami is the Head of the School of Government and International Affairs in the University of Durham, UK. He is also a member of the GRC Editorial Board and the editor of the Series of Iran Studies. He holds a Ph.D. in international relations from the University of Exeter. His most recent publications include *The Middle East's Relations with Asia and Russia,* co-editor (Curzon: Routledge, 2004); *The Foreign Policies of Middle East States,* co-editor, (Lynne Rienner, 2002); *Iran's Security Policy in the Post-Revolutionary Era,* co-author, (RAND, 2001); *Iran and Eurasia*, co-editor (Ithaca Press, 2000); and *The Changing Balance of Power in Asia* (ECSSR, 1998). He is an expert on the Asian balance of power in the post-Cold War era, the international politics of the Red Sea sub-region, foreign policies of Middle Eastern states since the end of the Cold War, and the impact of globalization on the Middle East.

Prof. F. Gregory Gause, III is an Associate Professor of Political Science at the University of Vermont and director of the university's Middle East Studies program. He is the author of *Relations between the Gulf Cooperation Council States and the United States* (Dubai: Gulf Research Center, 2004), *Oil Monarchies: Domestic and Security Challenges in the Arab Gulf States* (New York: Council of Foreign Relations Press, 1994), *Saudi-Yemeni Relations: Domestic Structures and Foreign Influence* (New York: Columbia University Press, 1990) as well as numerous articles in academic journals and edited volumes. Prof. Gause received his Ph.D. from Harvard University in 1987. He studied Arabic at the American University of Cairo and Middlebury College.

Li Guofu is the Director of the Department of South Asian, Middle Eastern and African Studies at the China Institute of International Studies and is also Senior Research Fellow at the China Institute of International Studies. He is an expert on China-GCC relations and researches cooperation between

China and the Arab world in general and the Gulf region in particular.

Yoshiki Mickey Hatanaka is the Director of the Middle East and Energy Program at the International Development Centre, Tokyo, Japan. He is a graduate of the faculty of economics, University of Keio, Japan, 1974. He has written *Oil Geopolitics: The Middle East and USA* (2003); *The Issues for Japan*, co-writer, (2003); *Iraq War: Verification and Prospects* (2003) and *The Middle East Development*, co-author, (1998). Mr. Hatanaka is an expert on the economics of energy in Japan, the Middle East and the Gulf region in particular.

Dr. N. Janardhan is the Editor of Gulf in the Media at the Gulf Research Center, Dubai, UAE. He was formerly with the *The Asian Age*, an English daily in India; night editor and columnist at *The Gulf Today*, an English daily published in Sharjah, UAE; and the Gulf correspondent for the Inter Press Service, a Bangkok-based news agency that provides analytical articles to organizations in over 100 countries. He has more than 300 opinion articles published in newspapers in India and the Middle East. His academic publications include *The Al-Sabahs and the Kuwaiti National Assembly - The Legitimacy Factor* (Jawaharlal Nehru University, New Delhi: 2001). His research areas include political and social developments in the Middle East, media and democracy in the Gulf region, and Gulf-India relations.

Dr. Christian Koch is Program Director for GCC-EU Relations at the Gulf Research Center. Prior to his appointment, he worked as Head of the Strategic Studies Section at the Emirates Center for Strategic Studies and Research, Abu Dhabi. Dr. Koch received his Ph.D. from the University of Erlangen-Nürnberg, Germany. He also studied at the American University in Washington, D.C. and the University of South Carolina. Dr. Koch has published on various issues related to Middle Eastern political development and Gulf strategic issues. He is the editor of Unfulfilled Potential: *Exploring the GCC-EU Relationship* (Dubai: Gulf Research Center, 2005), the co-editor of *Gulf Security in the Twenty-First Century* (Abu Dhabi, ECSSR, 1997), and a contributor to *Elections in Asia: a Data Handbook* (Oxford: Oxford University Press, 2001) and *Der Irak: Ein Land zwischen Krieg und Frieden* (Heidelburg: Palmyra, 2003). Dr. Koch has also contributed to Jane's Sentinel Publications on Gulf issues. His particular research interests are political liberalization in the Gulf States as well as Europe's role in the Gulf.

Prof. Bahgat Korany is a Professor of Political Science at the American University of Cairo and a member of the GRC Editorial Board. He received a BA (honors) in 1961 from the University of Cairo, an MA in International Relations from the University of Sussex, England in 1966, a Diploma in Development Studies (Economics and Sociology) from the Institute of Development Studies in Geneva in 1968, and a Ph.D. in Political Science from the University of Geneva in 1974. Prof. Korany has authored more than 95 conference papers, was guest-editor of three special issues of international journals (*International Political Science Review, Etudes Internationales, Third World Quarterly*), has published 3 monographs, 8 books, contributed chapters to about 24 other books and about 40 articles in such periodicals as *International Social Science Journal, Journal of the Social Sciences, Annals of International Studies, Etudes Internationales, Revue Francaise de Science Politique, Peace Research Society Papers* (Canada), *International Journal of Middle East Studies, Third World Quarterly, Journal of Asian and African Studies, Third World Affairs Yearbook,* and *World*

Politics. His book *Social Change, Charisma and International Behavior* was awarded the 1976 Hauchman Prize. Since 1994, Bahgat Korany has been included in the annual Canadian *Who's Who*.

Prof. Giacomo Luciani is Professor of Political Economy and Co-Director of the Mediterranean Program of the Robert Schuman Centre for Advanced Studies, European University Institute, Florence, Italy. His career has been marked by repeated crossings between academia, industry and government. Prof. Luciani came to the Mediterranean Programme after 10 years with ENI, the Italian Oil Company, where his last position was Group Vice-President for International New Ventures Promotion & Studies. Before joining EM, he worked for the Bank of Italy and for the Italian Institute of International Affairs. He has taught at UCLA and at the Institut d'Etudes Politiques in Paris, and has consulted for various international organizations and Gulf governments. Luciani is a recognized international expert on strategic energy matters, with special expertise in issues linking energy and international politics. He is the author of several books and articles, including *The Mediterranean Region* (Croom Helm, 1984), *The Oil Companies and the Arab World* (Croom Helm, 1984), *The Rentier State* (Routledge, 1987), *The Politics of Arab Integration* (Routledge, 1988) and *The Arab State* (Routledge and California. 1990). Luciani was educated at the University of Rome, Yale University and Harvard University.

Amb. Dr. Jameel Mirdad is Associate Professor of International Relations at the Institute of Diplomatic Studies, Ministry of Foreign Affairs, Saudi Arabia and an Ambassador in the Ministry. He holds a Ph.D. in political science and international relations from the University of North Texas. Dr. Mirdad has extensively published on issues of foreign policy and globalization, including "Saudi Arabia's Stand and Role in Fighting Terrorism," a paper submitted during the session for the habilitation of the Foreign Ministry's functionaries based overseas and *Peace and Peaceful Settlement of Conflicts in King Fahad Ibn Abdulaziz's Political Thought* (Riyadh: Al-Jazeera Press for Printing and Publishing, 2002).

Musa Qallab is the Research Manager for the Defense Program at the Gulf Research Center. His military expertise stems from his experience in military training and management courses from 1970 until 1992. He also received a diploma in Journalism from London in 1976. He has published in various military magazines and daily newspapers on strategic issues and is an expert on defense issues and military affairs.

Sameh Rashed is a freelance writer. He holds a BA in economics and political science from Cairo University and is currently working on his MA in international relations at the Arab Center for Research and Studies in the Arab League. He has contributed to many publications, such as the *Arab Strategic Report, World Politics, Middle Eastern Affairs* and numerous other Arabic newspapers. His expertise is in GCC and Arab affairs.

Emilie Rutledge is an economics researcher at the Gulf Research Center. She is currently a PhD candidate at the University of Durham, where she is writing her dissertation on the GCC currency union. She received her MSc in Economics from Birkbeck College, University of London and her BA Hons in Arabic and Economics from the School of Oriental and African Studies, University of London. She is the author of "Establishing a Successful GCC Currency Union - Preparations and Future Policy Choices" (Dubai, Gulf Research Center, 2004) as well as "The success of Bahrain's economic diversification, 1991-

2001" for the Bahrain-British Foundation and is the co-author of the paper "Oil and gas markets in the UK: evidence for asymmetric and non-linear adjustment from a cointegrating approach," (2004). She also contributed to the Roberts' Review report entitled "Set for success: The supply of people with science, technology engineering and mathematical skills" for HM Treasury, UK in April 2002. Her research interests include currency unions, regional economic integration, international macroeconomics and the political economy of the Middle East.

Dr. Mahmood Sariolghalam is an Associate Professor of International Relations and the Research Director of the Center for Scientific Research and Middle East Strategic Studies at the National (Shahid Beheshti) University, Iran. He is also a member of the GRC Editorial Board. He received a Post-Doctoral degree in international relations from Ohio State University his Ph.D. and MA in the same subject from the University of Southern California. He has published numerous titles including *Foreign Policy of the Islamic Republic of Iran: Theoretical Renewal and the Paradigm for Coalition* (Tehran: Center for Strategic Research, 2001); *Research Methodology in Political Science and International Relations* (Farsi) (Farzan Publications, 2001, second edition 2002); *Rationality and the Future of Iran's Development* (Center for Scientific Research and Middle East Strategic Studies, 2nd ed., 2004); *Iran and Globalization: Forces of Convergence and Divergence* (Tehran: Center for Strategic Research, 2003).

John Sfakianakis is a Chief Regional Economist at the Saudi-American Bank (SAMBA Financial Group), Riyadh, Kingdom of Saudi Arabia. Dr. Sfakianakis received his Ph.D. from the School of Oriental and African Studies (SOAS), University of London, 2003; his MA in Near and Middle Eastern

Studies, SOAS, 1993 and BSc (Econ. Honors) form the London School of Economics and Political Science in 1992. He is a regular contributor to *Al Ahram Weekly* and *Oxford Analytica*. He contributed to "In Search of Bureaucrats and Entrepreneurs: The Political Economy of the Export Agribusiness Sector in Egypt," in Ray Bush (ed.), *Egyptian Agriculture in the Twenty-first Century* (London: Zed Press, 2002); "The President, the Son, and the Military: Succession in Egypt," in *Arab Studies Journal*, (with Robert Springborg - both under pseudonyms), IX, No. 2, Spring 2002 and; "Civil Military Relations in Egypt," in *Journal of Arabic, Islamic Middle Eastern Studies* 5 (with Robert Springborg), No.2 (1999): 39-54. His research interests involve the political economy of and public policy in the Middle East.

Dr. Alexander Shumilin is the Director of the Center for Middle East Conflict Analysis at the Institute for USA and Canada Studies and the Editor of http://www.mideast.ru. He has published numerous articles and papers in journals, magazines, and newspapers in which he analyzing the broader implications of conflicts in the greater Middle East.

Prof. Hasanain Tawfiq is a Professor of Political Science at Cairo University where he also received his Ph.D. Prof. Tawfiq has published several books, including *Political Violence in the Arab Political Systems* (1992), *The New Global System: Issues and Complications* (1992), *The Political System and the Muslim Brotherhood in Egypt* (1998), *Political Economy for Economic Reform in the Arab World* (1999), *The State and Development in Egypt* (2000), *Future of the State and Political System in Iraq* (2001), *Contemporary Directions in Studying Arab Political Systems* (2002). His research interests include Arab political systems and democratization in the Middle East.

Vahan Zanoyan is the President and CEO of PFC Energy an international energy consulting firm specializing in the financial, strategic, commercial, political aspects of the international oil, gas and power industry. He holds graduate degrees in Economics from the University of Pennsylvania and the American University in Beirut. He received his B.A. in Political Science from AUB. More recently, he has focused on business development strategies in the Middle East and North Africa, in addition to the challenges that national companies face in their relationships with host governments and international oil companies.

About the Gulf Research Center

The *Gulf Research Center* (GRC) is an independent research institute located in Dubai, United Arab Emirates (UAE). The GRC was founded in July 2000 by Mr. Abdulaziz Sager, a Saudi businessman, who realized, in a world of rapid political, social and economic change, the importance of pursuing politically neutral and academically sound research about the Gulf region and disseminating the knowledge obtained as widely as possible. The Center is a non-partisan think-tank, education service provider and consultancy specializing in the Gulf region. The GRC seeks to provide a better understanding of the challenges and prospects of the Gulf region.

GRC Publications

Books Published by GRC

Gulf in a Year 2003	Gulf Research Center	ISBN 9948-400-26-7
Unfulfilled Potential: Exploring the GCC-EU Relationship	Edited by Christian Koch	ISBN 9948-424-30-1

Policy Analysis

Reforms in Saudi Arabia	Abdulaziz Sager	ISBN 9948-400-24-0
Arab Peace Forces	Abdulaziz Sager	ISBN 9948-424-19-0
Political Kidnapping	Mustafa Alani	ISBN 9948-424-03-4
Saddam's Fate	Mustafa Alani	ISBN 9948-424-02-6
Military Action against Iran's Nuclear	Mustafa Alani	ISBN 9948-400-99-2
Establishing a Successful GCC Currency Union	Emilie Rutledge	ISBN 9948-424-22-0
A WMD Free Zone within a Broader Gulf and Middle East Security Architecture	Peter Jones	ISBN 9948-424-40-9

Journal of Gulf Studies
A peer-reviewed bilingual periodical that includes academic studies and research on the GCC political, economic, social, defense and security affairs.

Gulf Studies
A peer-reviewed bilingual series that includes academic studies and research on GCC states' political, economic, social defense and security affairs.

Iran Studies
A peer-reviewed bilingual series that includes academic studies and research on Iranian political, economic, social defense and security affairs.

Iraq Studies
A peer-reviewed bilingual series that includes academic studies and research on Iraqi political, economic, social, defense and security affairs.

Yemen Studies

A peer-reviewed bilingual series that includes academic studies and research on Yemeni political, economic, social, defense and security affairs.

The Yemeni Parliamentary Elections	Ahmed Abdul Kareem Saif	ISBN 9948-400-77-1

Gulf Papers

Present the findings of a series of workshops conducted by the Gulf Research Center within the framework of the 'Gulf Studies Program' individually or in cooperation with leading peer research centers. Bringing together area specialists, each series of workshops tackles a specific issue with the aim of reaching a common understanding on a specific issue in the region and presenting a set of recommendations.

UN Security Role in the Gulf Region: A Comparative Perspective	Youssif M. Benkhalil	ISBN 9948-400-75-5
Back to the Developmental Future: (Re)Empowering the Gulf's City-System	Bruce Stanley	ISBN 9948-400-60-7
Dubai Emirate and Australian Relationships	Patricia Berwick	ISBN 9948-400-84-4
Obstacles facing the Industrial Establishments In Sohar Industrial Estate, Oman	Adil Hassan Bakheet	ISBN 9948-400-85-2
The Role of Gold in the unified GCC currency	Eckart Woertz	ISBN 9948-424-28-X

GRC Lectures

A growing collection of lectures by leading scholars and experts. The lectures cover a variety of issues related to the Gulf and provide valuable insight into ongoing political and academic debates inside or outside the Gulf region. It is published in both Arabic and English.

Research Papers

Peer-reviewed bilingual research papers and studies written by specialists in Gulf issues. The research papers are comprehensive in character and meant to open the door for more specialized Gulf studies.

GCC- EU Military and Economic Relations	Elizabeth Stevens	ISBN 9948-400-30-5
Judicial Systems in the GCC States	Ahmed Abdul Kareem Saif	ISBN 9948-400-32-1
Constitutionalism in the Arab Gulf States	Ahmed Abdulkareem Saif (Edited)	ISBN 9948-400-35-6
GCC- US Relations	Gregory Gause	ISBN 9948-400-36-4

| GCC-EU Relations: Past Record and Promises for the Future | Giacomo Luciani & Tobias Schumacher | ISBN 9948-400-37-2 |
| Israel's New Friendship Arch: India, Russia and Turkey | P. R. Kumaraswamy | ISBN 9948-424-46-8 |

Event Papers

Presents the proceedings of conferences, workshops and seminars conducted by the GRC within the framework of the 'Gulf Studies Program', individually or in cooperation with leading peer research centers. Each event brings together area specialists and tackles a specific issue with the aim of reaching a common understanding of the issue and a set of recommendations.

| Arab Perspectives and Formulations on Humanitarian Intervention in Application to the Arab Countries | Mohamed Kadry Said (Edited) | ISBN 9948-424-26-3 |